Mediterranean Capitalism Revisited

The final volume in the series

Cornell Studies in Political Economy
Edited by Peter J. Katzenstein

A full list of titles in this series is available at www.cornellpress.cornell.edu and at the end of the book.

Mediterranean Capitalism Revisited

One Model, Different Trajectories

Edited by Luigi Burroni, Emmanuele Pavolini, and Marino Regini

Cornell University Press
Ithaca and London

First published 2021 by Cornell University Press

Library of Congress Cataloging-in-Publication Data

Names: Burroni, Luigi, editor. | Pavolini, Emmanuele, editor. | Regini, Marino, 1943– editor.
Title: Mediterranean capitalism revisited : one model, different trajectories / edited by Luigi
   Burroni, Emmanuele Pavolini, and Marino Regini.
Description: Ithaca [New York] : Cornell University Press, 2021. | Series: Cornell studies in
   political economy | Includes bibliographical references and index.
Identifiers: LCCN 2021009271 (print) | LCCN 2021009272 (ebook) | ISBN 9781501761072
   (hardcover) | ISBN 9781501761263 (paperback) | ISBN 9781501761089 (ebook) |
   ISBN 9781501761096 (pdf)
Subjects: LCSH: Economic development—Europe, Southern. | Economic development—
   Mediterranean Region. | Capitalism—Europe, Southern. | Capitalism—Mediterranean Region. |
   Europe, Southern—Economic conditions. | Mediterranean Region—Economic conditions.
Classification: LCC HC244.5 .M38 2021 (print) | LCC HC244.5 (ebook) | DDC 338.9182/2—dc23
LC record available at https://lccn.loc.gov/2021009271
LC ebook record available at https://lccn.loc.gov/2021009272

Contents

Part II. Policies and Processes of Change

Preface

The last months of writing this volume were marked by very dramatic events linked to the COVID-19 pandemic, which in addition to its health-related impact will have important socioeconomic repercussions for at least part of the current decade. The medium-term impact of the pandemic crisis, as was the case with the 2007–2009 economic crisis, could once again be asymmetrical, with some economies suffering more and longer than others. In this perspective, the outlook for the countries considered in this volume is not encouraging: the *European Economic Forecast* produced in November 2020 by the European Commission estimates that Southern Europe will be the European region most severely hit by the economic crisis in the near future. Spain, Italy, Portugal, and Greece (in decreasing order), together with France and Croatia, were expected to face the largest fall in real gross domestic product among the twenty-seven European Union (EU) countries in 2020. Also, Spain, Greece, and Italy will suffer from the highest unemployment rate in the EU in 2022, signaling a greater difficulty to recover than the rest of Europe. Thus, as already happened in the recent past, the impact of the economic crisis, this time triggered by the COVID-19 pandemic, is likely to be greater and longer in the Mediterranean countries than in other advanced economies.

From this point of view, it remains to be seen how the Southern European countries will be able to react to two major crises in the span of just twelve years. Analyses of the vicissitudes of these political economies in recent decades could help in understanding what might take place in upcoming years. Therefore, this book risks being dramatically timely as it investigates the institutional foundations that make Mediterranean countries more sensitive to crises in comparison to other European regions.

This volume is the outcome of almost five years of research and discussion among a large group of scholars who are experts of the Southern European political economies. Our study of the contextual dynamics in the fields of growth models, state performances, sociocultural modernization, and supranational regulation as well as our comparative analysis of such key institutional arenas as labor markets, industrial relations, welfare, corporate governance, education, and innovation offers important insights as to why and how a recurrent issue in Mediterranean capitalism is its difficulty in recovering from external shocks.

However, one should not overlook a major difference from the 2007–2009 economic crisis. It was not until 2012 that the European Central Bank, with the famous "Whatever It Takes" speech by Mario Draghi, firmly stated its willingness to save the euro during the Great Recession, providing direct support to Southern Europe too. This time, the European Central Bank immediately and more consensually announced strong monetary policies, backing the European economies severely hit by the pandemic. Even more importantly, while the EU answer to the economic crisis was austerity policies surveilled by the Troika and the request for "structural reforms," the current answer is more inspired by a neo-Keynesian approach and at least a partial willingness toward the mutualization of public debt. The initiative taken in this direction by Germany and France and the ensuing NextGenerationEU plan can represent a potentially fundamental turning point for Southern European political economies and the EU as a whole.

In the short run, the four Southern European countries risk being the most severely hit by the economic consequences of the COVID-19 pandemic. The structural weaknesses described in this book provide enough evidence about the reasons why these forecasts might be correct. In the medium long run, however, a robust neo-Keynesian approach, such as the one inspiring both the European Central Bank and the European Commission "Recovery and Resilience Facility," could be very helpful not just to contain the negative socioeconomic consequences of the pandemic but also to give impulse to a modernization agenda in many policy fields. In other words, for all its atrocity, the pandemic could turn out to be a window of opportunity to improve Mediterranean capitalism.

The ways in which the institutional arenas studied in this book will react to the new challenges and the potential support from EU institutions as well as the role that national actors will play in exercising their agency will be crucial in this respect. Forward-looking political actors and efficient public bureaucracy will be required to exploit this opportunity. In order to be "saved by Europe," the Mediterranean political economies will need to be prepared and do their homework.

Acknowledgments

As we have written in the preface, this book is the outcome of almost five years of research and discussion among a large group of scholars who are experts of the Southern European political economies. Inevitably, during these years we have presented our work in progress in several conferences and to a varying audience, and we have benefited enormously from comments and questions raised in those contexts. So, the persons—mostly colleagues and friends—we want especially to thank are the discussants and the organizers of these events. Without their many acute observations and deep interest in discussing our findings, the analyses presented in this volume would be far less developed.

The first opportunity we were given to think of Mediterranean capitalism as an understudied topics, worth far deeper research and more sophisticated analyses, was the conference of the AIS-ELO, the Italian labor sociologists' association, held in Cagliari in October 2015. One of us (Marino Regini) was asked to introduce and chair the inaugural session titled "Mediterranean Capitalism during the Crisis" that featured papers by Lucio Baccaro, Manos Matsaganis, Fausto Miguelez, and Hermes Augusto Costa. While the two former participants have ended up being among the contributors to this volume, the two latter ones have not, but their contribution to better define the topics has been equally precious. Hence, we want to thank them together with two conference organizers, Gianfranco Bottazzi and Clementina Casula, who took care of the inaugural session. It was in that setting that we started planning further research on Mediterranean capitalism.

The next opportunity we had to present early findings and to enlarge the group of scholars interested in this topics was the SASE (Society for the Advancement of Socio-Economics) conference held in Lyon in June 2017. Within that conference, the three of us organized two sessions titled "Mediterranean Capitalism: What's Next?" in which several contributors to this volume presented papers or acted as discussants. Other participants were Sergio González

Begega, Alberto Gherardini, Chrysafis Iordanoglou, and Amilcar Moreira. Our warm thanks for contributing to a very lively discussion go to all of them.

Several informal meetings followed that helped develop a common theoretical framework for understanding the trajectories of Southern European political economies, not just between the three of us but with a wider network of scholars. This convinced us to outline the structure of a collective volume on Mediterranean capitalism that could count on contributions by the best specialists on a variety of topics but at the same time on quite homogeneous lines of interpretation. In late 2018 we addressed the editor of the Cornell Studies in Political Economy series, Peter Katzenstein, with a rather articulated volume proposal. Peter immediately and quite strongly backed our proposal, giving us invaluable advice on how to improve it. He is the one person we are most grateful to. Without his continued and friendly support, this book would have never seen the light of day.

Other colleagues deserve our heartfelt thanks for reading, listening to, and commenting on draft versions of our introduction and conclusion as well as the chapters included in this volume during several meetings. Dorothee Bohle, Giovanna Fullin, Anton Hemerjick, Andrea Lippi, and Carlo Trigilia served as discussants to these draft versions at the conference we organized at the University of Florence in September 2019, providing very useful comments.

Giovanna and Anton, together with Guglielmo Meardi, played the same role, providing equally useful suggestions in the annual *Stato e Mercato* seminar "Institutions, Politics and Models of Capitalism" held in November 2019 in Bologna. Other contributors to that seminar were David Soskice and Bruno Palier, whom we also thank for their acute observations.

Finally, a session titled "Paths of Development and Mediterranean Capitalism" was held in January 2020 at the conference of the SISEC, the Italian economic sociologists' association, in Turin. Our warm thanks to Paola De Vivo and Francesco Ramella who acted as discussants.

Last but not least, our sincere gratitude goes to the anonymous reviewer who read the whole volume and carefully commented on all the chapters. That extremely detailed and useful review bears witness to what rigorous scholarship and a sense of belonging to the academic community can do. In our case to the extent that we have been able to incorporate the reviewer's comments, they certainly contributed to improving this book.

The very long process of editing this volume and writing several chapters has required more than acute scholarly observations and useful comments by many colleagues. A precondition has been working in supportive environments. This is why we wish to end by thanking our families for their patience and continuing encouragement.

Luigi Burroni, Emmanuele Pavolini, and Marino Regini

Mediterranean Capitalism Revisited

Introduction

Which Road to Development? The Mediterranean Model Revisited

Luigi Burroni, Emmanuele Pavolini, and Marino Regini

1. Three Good Reasons to Study Southern European Political Economies

Mediterranean Capitalism Revisited focuses on Southern Europe (SE), in particular Italy, Spain, Portugal, and Greece. Overall, in comparative political economy (CPE) studies these countries have not received as much attention as the continental, Anglo-Saxon, or Nordic countries. The typologies most often adopted for Western capitalist systems usually make it difficult to pinpoint the cluster to which these countries belong. For instance, in the original varieties of capitalism (VoC) literature SE was hardly included. Hall and Soskice (2001) underlined that these countries display a distinctive variety of capitalism. Further research then highlighted a relationship between the specificities of SE political economies and the legacy of high levels of state intervention in the economy (i.e., Hall and Gingerich 2009; Schmidt 2002). More insights are found in specific branches of CPE, such as industrial relations, labor market regulation, and welfare state studies. However, in these fields too there is still lively debate as to how specific SE is as a whole. Although interesting studies have been produced in the first two decades of the twenty-first century (e.g., Molina and Rhodes 2007; Amable 2003), an in-depth debate on Mediterranean capitalism has never taken off. Nevertheless, there are several good reasons why SE should be studied more carefully.

First, this European region's relatively extensive contribution to European wealth should not be overlooked. Italy and Spain are the third- and fourth-largest European Union (EU) economies in terms of gross domestic product (GDP), respectively (they were fourth and fifth before Brexit; see table I.1). Despite losing ground during the previous ten years, in 2018 SE produced slightly more than one-fifth of total GDP in the EU-28 (again including the United Kingdom). Counting almost 130 million inhabitants, around a quarter

Table I.1 The role of different European regions in the EU-28 economy and demography (year 2018)

EU regions	Share of total GDP produced in the EU-28 (%)	Share of total population in the EU-28 (%)
Nordic countries	5.0%	4.2%
Anglo-Saxon countries	15.4%	13.9%
	(13.6% UK)	(13.0% UK)
Continental countries	42.7%	36.7%
	(19.7% Germany; 13.6% France)	(16.2% Germany; 13.1% France)
Southern European countries	21.2%	25.3%
	(11.3% Italy; 8.3% Spain)	(11.8% Italy; 9.1% Spain)
CEE countries	14.2%	20.0%
	(5.3% Poland)	(7.4% Poland)

Source: Eurostat (indicators: nama_10_gdp; demo_pjan).

of EU citizens live in SE. SE societies and economies are one of the main pillars sustaining the EU (not to forget the euro as a currency). A possible worsening of conditions in this region would have severe consequences for the rest of the EU and its member states.

Second, it is important to improve the more analytical knowledge and understanding that CPE scholars have of those capitalist models that are not usually studied (i.e., models outside the United States, Germany, etc.). In this respect, there is a burgeoning amount of interesting literature on Central and Eastern European (CEE) countries (Bohle 2017; Ban 2019; Bohle and Greskovits 2012) and other regions outside Europe (Vasileva-Dienes and Schmidt 2019). SE has been somewhat left out of the picture so far, and it is no longer satisfactory to frame SE economies simply in terms of mixed-market economies.

Third, as also recently underlined by Hall (2018), the euro crisis that started in 2010 has brought to the attention of scholars and policymakers that SE was not just the most severely hit EU region during the crisis but also the one that experienced the most difficulty in recovering. All of the SE countries were hit harder than most other European countries by the Great Recession, and although at different paces (Spain and Portugal fared better, Italy and Greece worse), altogether they found it more difficult to come out of the economic crisis. The situation of SE countries is even more striking if CEE countries are brought into the picture: whereas the former have kept on losing ground to continental and northern EU countries in terms of economic growth, since 2000 the latter have managed to continue to converge toward continental and Northern Europe. Overall, what data seem to show is that the specificity of Mediterranean capitalism is not its inability to grow but rather the unstable growth (with peaks and troughs) and the fragile bases of this growth in the medium term.

In particular, the four Mediterranean economies, especially Italy, appear incapable of finding their own institutional competitive advantage vis-à-vis other types of capitalism in order to provide viable and stable answers over time to the new challenges of postindustrial economies. This inability is especially striking if one compares SE economies not just to the core continental economies but also to the Nordic and CEE economies.

The Nordic political economies consistently tried to respond to globalization and the crises of the 1990s and 2007–2009 by following an export-based model entailing high wages, high skills, high worker cooperation, and high product quality, which generally ensured high growth and social cohesion (Dølvik and Martin 2015). CEE countries, on the other hand, where such supply-side institutions as the welfare state and wage-setting institutions were extremely weak when they started the transition to capitalism, until recently also strove to seek export-led growth but based on low wages and low worker involvement.

The Mediterranean countries have had difficulties in following any of the above roads in a consistent manner. Their political economies are too heavily regulated to compete with CEE countries and even more so with developing economies on price or flexibility of the labor market. At the same time, so far they have not managed to adopt a type of growth based on highly skilled human capital, innovation, and high social cohesion like in the Nordic model.

Table I.2 compares GDP per capita levels and how this indicator has evolved since the early 1990s in Europe by looking at the four SE countries and comparing them with a set of countries considered in the literature as representative of different models of capitalist growth. Over a period of almost thirty years (1991–2018), Italy and Greece grew the least among all the countries considered in the table, whereas the pace of growth in Spain and partly in Portugal was stronger and in line with, if not above, the rate seen in the other European countries outside SE. Only the Visegràd countries (+4.1%) performed better than Spain and Greece in the same time span, and the Portuguese performance was in line with the Western European average. Portugal and Spain came to an abrupt halt with the Great Recession, but in 2015 they started recovering the growth rates of the previous decades. Greece grew strongly in the decades before the Great Recession but was hit especially hard by the crisis. Italy seems to have severe long-standing growth problems: already in the period between 1991 and 2007 its average yearly growth rate was around +1.5%, while in Spain and Greece it was +3.1% and in Portugal +2.1%.

The reason why the CEE and SE countries (apart from Italy) might have had higher growth rates in recent decades (or at least until the 2007–2009 economic crisis) could be that at the beginning of the 1990s they had lower levels of economic development than continental and Northern Europe. The data on GDP growth could mix a strong capacity to grow with the fact that it can be easier to improve a country's economic performance if it starts from relatively low levels. Therefore, it is also important to compare GDP per capita

Table 1.2 GDP per capita and GDP growth over time in Europe (1991–2018)

	Average yearly GDP growth rate (%)				GDP per capita at purchasing power parity (PPP) (EU11=100)*		
	1991–2018	1991–2007	2007–2018	2015–2018	1991	2007	2018
Italy	+0.7	+1.5	−0.4	+1.2	103.9	93.6	81.1
Spain	+2.1	+3.1	+0.5	+2.9	80.2	85.0	80.8
Portugal	+1.3	+2.1	+0.2	+2.3	71.9	69.7	67.5
Greece	+0.9	+3.1	−2.4	+1.1	70.0	79.3	57.8
Germany	+1.4	+1.5	+1.3	+1.9	107.7	100.5	104.6
France	+1.6	+2.1	+0.9	+1.7	98.2	92.7	90.1
United Kingdom	+2.1	+2.8	+1.1	+1.7	88.2	95.8	93.0
Nordic countries	+2.1	+2.8	+1.1	+2.3	101.0	108.7	104.7
Visegrad countries	+3.6	+4.1	+2.8	+4.0	39.5	54.0	67.0
EU-15	+1.6	+2.2	+0.8	+2.0	96.8	95.4	92.9

* Measured in terms of distance from the weighted average GDP per capita in the EU-15, having excluded the four Southern European countries (EU-11=100).

Source: OECD.Stat.

levels and how they have changed over time. The right part of table I.2 shows that in the early 1990s compared to the GDP per capita level in Central and Northern Europe, defined as EU-11, among the SE countries only Italy had a similar, if not higher, level of economic development. The crisis was a great downward equalizer for SE: from 2007 to 2018 all four SE countries dramatically lost ground to the EU-11 countries, and in 2018 the GDP per capita in the Visegràd countries was equal to if not above that of Greece and Portugal. It must be added that between 2015 and 2018 Spain and Portugal started to cut down the distance from Central andNorthern Europe again, whereas Italy and Greece were not able to do so. In sum, the CEE area was able to grow in the last decades and reach some of the SE countries, having also reduced the distance from Central and Northern Europe by half.

Overall, these reasons make Mediterranean capitalism a very important subject to explore.

2. How to Study SE Political Economies Using Old and New Analytical Tools

The VoC strand of research can be considered the leading approach in CPE studies in Europe and North America in recent decades. Either its original version or later developments and integrations have been at the core of the discussion on the transformation of (mature) capitalist systems. As is well known, the first version of VoC identified two ideal types: liberal market economies (LMEs) and coordinated market economies (CMEs) (Hall and Soskice 2001).

Since its introduction, VoC has proven to be a powerful tool for studying capitalism in its various forms; many European countries fit one or the other ideal type relatively well. However, SE countries are anomalous in this respect in that they cannot be easily included in either of them. As stated in the previous section, Hall and Soskice (2001) emphasized that these countries display a distinctive variety of capitalism that cannot easily fit into the LME versus CME dichotomy.

In the discussion that followed, SE started to receive more analytical and empirical attention. Amable (2003) treated the Mediterranean countries as a model of capitalism in themselves, and Molina and Rhodes (2007) introduced the category "mixed-market economies," which included the Mediterranean countries and France. Since then, the contributions looking at these countries from a comparative analysis point of view have multiplied, and the category of Mediterranean capitalism has begun to spread (Regini 2014). At the same time, SE countries have also been considered a distinct cluster by other strands of research such as comparative industrial relations (Gumbrell-McCormick and Hyman 2013), welfare state studies (Ferrera 1996; Castles et al. 2010), and research on skill formation and education systems (Busemeyer and Trampusch 2012; Busemeyer 2015).

However, the definition of this type of capitalism remains problematic. As various contributions in this volume show, a distinct SE cluster appears to be more coherent in some policy areas and economic phenomena and less coherent in others. Indeed, industrial relations studies often include the French case in the SE cluster, while welfare studies as well as some comparative studies, such as that of Amable (2003), define France as part of the continental model.

In the majority of the above-mentioned contributions, Mediterranean capitalism is often defined as being characterized by two facets: the absence of complementarity in the functioning of its institutions and the core regulatory role played by the family and the state.

In the VoC approach, the strength of both LMEs and CMEs depends not just on the regulation and functioning of individual supply-side institutions (vocational training, corporate governance, etc.) but also on complementarities among these institutions: in order to be supportive to firms, these institutions have to offer a coherent set of incentives, rules, and potentially "virtuous constraints." In this respect, the definition of Mediterranean capitalism as "mixed" can take two meanings. It can refer either to the fact that its main institutions cannot be framed as clearly belonging to an LME or a CME model and are often halfway between the two or to their lack of complementarity, meaning that certain institutions are designed and function according to an LME approach while others follow a CME approach. Not all scholars who have applied the "mixed-market economy" label to Mediterranean capitalism assign both meanings to the concept of "mixed." Some use the concept in a more neutral way, referring to a different SE approach to regulate the economy compared to the main ideal types. However, others use it with a more evaluative meaning, implying that the lack of complementarity is the main source of these countries' unstable growth capacity.

The other characteristic that is often used to describe Mediterranean capitalism in a comparative perspective is the pivotal role played by two regulatory agencies: the family and the state. Indeed, the family plays a double role in SE political economies. On the one hand, the family acts as a social safety net in support of its members who are in conditions of economic and employment uncertainty. On the other hand, the family is also an important source of financial resources to start private economic activities, directly supporting entrepreneurship and hence leading to the development of a large number of small businesses in all four countries.

As regards the state's role, the state was very active in SE until the 1990s, playing a more pivotal role than in most CMEs and LMEs in owning and directly running large sectors of the economy (from manufacturing to energy production, banking, and communication), regulating the labor market, and providing social protection.

The present volume adopts the approach described above in its analytical framework but integrates it in several ways, thanks to more recent findings in the CPE literature. In a recent article, Hall (2018) set the agenda on how to extend and improve the explanatory capacity of VoC theory in a way that is especially useful when addressing the specificities of SE. First, he argued that it is important to reevaluate the relationship between VoC and regimes of macroeconomic policy while paying attention to the emerging literature on growth models (Baccaro and Pontusson 2016) and integrating the functioning and regulation of the demand side of the economy into theories primarily oriented to its supply side. Second, it is essential to draw attention to the international dimension, especially by looking at the important role of supranational regulation in influencing economies. This second innovation is important when studying countries belonging to the Eurozone, such as the SE ones, and how they have tried to adjust to problems generated by shocks exogenous to the domestic political economy. In this case, the attention is on the ways in which the monetary union itself has contributed to the divergence in terms of economic performance between Europe's northern and southern countries.

One topic that has received less attention in the literature quoted so far is the new role now played by the state in SE economies. A wave of privatization and managerialization started in the 1990s that attempted to transform the role of the state in the economy and the ways in which public administrations work in many countries. This wave of change, inspired to some extent by the New Public Management (NPM) approach (Pollitt and Bouckaert 2011), is of particular importance for SE countries, given the traditional pivotal role played by the state in these economies and the not brilliant performance of their public administration. In this respect, in recent decades the role of the state in the field of economic growth, compared to the fields of welfare and the labor market, has changed. SE states have started to intervene less than in other European countries to support growth and innovation, hindering the shift toward a competitive strategy based on quality, productivity, and innovation. Conversely, in the fields of welfare and the labor market, the state has kept a central role, with a long season of reforms to increase financial sustainability. Moreover, the capacity of state bureaucracies to efficiently implement their decisions—which is an important topic in CPE—has been at the center of attempts at managerialization in SE too.

One last topic that has received scarce attention in most recent analyses, including the VoC approach, is the role played by sociocultural and structural factors, such as social values and the functioning of core social networks (starting from families), in explaining economic growth. Despite being a traditional issue in socioeconomic studies (from Max Weber to Talcott Parson's modernization theory) and still often being used when studying other types of capitalism (especially Asian political economies), these factors have practically disappeared from the analyses applied to Europe.

Overall, this volume adopts a complex analytical toolkit, embracing a perspective that focuses on the functioning and influence of a plurality of institutions and factors. While stemming from the study of the original VoC supply-side institutions (labor market regulation, social protection, corporate governance, industrial relations, and skills formation), this perspective is nevertheless integrated with an emphasis on demand-side factors and growth regimes, the role of the international dimension (in particular the supranational regulation of the Eurozone in influencing the SE economies), the institutional capacity of the public administrations, and the role of culture and social networks. What is more, a particular focus is devoted to the role and type of economic innovation in SE.

All of the chapters tend to share the same methodology, based on policy analysis, some quantitative analysis of secondary data, and comparative historical analysis focused on tracing policy processes, analyzing their impact, and underlining various actors' logic of action.

3. The Book's Goals and Research Questions

Mediterranean Capitalism Revisited has two goals. On one hand, it aims to provide a good in-depth description and reconstruction of the SE political economies since the 1990s, given the continuing gap in the literature. In this respect, this volume brings together different streams of research and investigation on several specific issues. On the other hand, it intends to answer two specific questions.

The first question is *why, for all their differences, do SE economies share difficulties in being competitive and finding a stable growth pattern in the global economy?* As already underlined in the first section, what seems to characterize Mediterranean capitalism is its unstable growth (with peaks and troughs) and the fragile bases of this growth in the medium term, especially in the eastern part of SE (Greece and Italy), as shown in table I.2. The World Economic Forum Global Competitiveness Index for 2019 ranks the four SE countries between twenty-third (Spain) and fifty-ninth place (Greece), while Italy is thirtieth and Portugal is thirty-fourth, all well below other Western European countries. In this respect, some CEE countries seem in a relatively similar position to most of the SE countries (the Czech Republic is in thirty-second place, and Poland is thirty-eighth).

A good indicator of the low level of competitiveness is labor productivity in the SE countries compared to other European countries (table I.3). SE countries—especially Portugal and Greece—show far lower labor productivity than Germany and Sweden in the overall economy and in each economic sector. This means that labor productivity in Mediterranean capitalism is low not just because the low-productivity sectors are more developed but also because there are relatively few activities with a medium-high intensity of research and development (R&D). Such low productivity is the outcome of quite different trajectories in the four SE countries. In Greece, Portugal, and Spain,

Table I.3 Hourly labor productivity (current purchasing power parity $)

	Medium-high R&D intensity activities	Manufacturing	Construction, trade, tourism	Total productivity
Italy	42.8	34.4	24.5	47.5
Spain	44.4	37.1	24.5	47.2
Portugal	24.4	16.5	15.5	32.4
Greece	20.7	21	12.2	30.9
Germany	83.3	53.9	29.5	59.9
United Kingdom	64.5	35	25.1	47.9
Sweden	80.8	52.7	36.2	56.4
Poland	11.9	10.5	11.2	29.1

Source: OECD STAN Database.

productivity has grown slowly over time but not to the point of reaching the level of other European countries. On the other hand, in the early 1990s Italy had very high productivity, just below Germany but above Sweden. However, Italy showed no growth after this period.

The second question is *how likely it is that the four countries will follow different paths in the future and increasingly diverge?* In recent decades, at least until the onset of the 2007–2009 economic crisis, SE countries pursued rather different solutions in order to foster socioeconomic growth. Of course, internal diversity is not specific to the Mediterranean model. Indeed, Bohle and Greskovits (2012) identify three types of capitalist development within the CEE model. As for the Nordic model, several authors (e.g., Mjøset 2011; Dølvik, Andersen, and Vartiainen 2015) show how Denmark, Sweden, Norway, and Finland followed somewhat different paths of evolution. However, in SE wider and deeper processes of differentiation were and still are at work. What is more, their paths of recovery have been markedly different. As regards economic and employment growth, Spain and Portugal have displayed more encouraging improvements, whereas Greece has been laboriously trying to recover from a series of very tough reforms, while Italy has shown a slow and uncertain recovery if not outright stagnation. If we turn to welfare and social cohesion, the four countries apparently share common features, but on taking a closer look, important differences appear: for example, Italy and Greece are so-called pension welfare states much more than Portugal and Spain, while the latter two countries have invested more in the coverage of new social risks. Important differences can also be found in the field of politics, with a populist and anti-European reaction that has been decidedly stronger in Italy and Greece and much less marked in Spain and Portugal. The roots of this process of diversification predate the 2007–2009 crisis: as many chapters of this volume will illustrate, Mediterranean capitalism was already showing large internal differences at the beginning of the 1990s, and these diversities were simply magnified by the economic crisis.

4. In Search of Answers: A Set of Explanations and Hypotheses in Order to Understand Mediterranean Capitalism

This volume adopts the analytical toolkit introduced in section 2 to answer the two questions just raised. While all of the analytical tools have been used in order to describe the SE political economies, to answer the two questions posed in the previous section they have been used in different ways. In particular, for the first question a set of hypotheses has been formulated, and the hypotheses are tested throughout the volume. For the second question, an exploratory approach is adopted, first of all looking at a set of institutions and factors and then providing some answers and forecasts in the concluding chapter.

This section sets out the debate on the first question, namely why SE economies share difficulties in being competitive and finding a stable growth pattern in the global economy. With the progression of globalization and the severe impact of the Great Recession, SE economies have found it difficult to pinpoint their possible competitive advantages vis-à-vis the other advanced economies. The obvious question among both scholars and policymakers has been how to explain this phenomenon. Basically, there are two main explanations for the poor performance of Mediterranean capitalism, assumed to be common to all SE economies: the features of the Mediterranean social model (i.e., the type of welfare regime, labor market regulation, and industrial relations system that characterizes SE countries), which in one way or another is thought to hinder the competitiveness of these economies, and the peripheral position of these economies in the Eurozone, with all the consequences that such a position entails. There is also a third explanation that so far has received less attention in the debate: the low degree of investment in R&D and highly skilled human capital in SE political economies, which impedes their ability to innovate and follow a high road to competitiveness.

We will first briefly illustrate these three explanations and then develop hypotheses on how they can help us understand SE specificities.

4.1. Three Lines of Explanation

4.1.1. The Supply-Side Structural Limits of the Mediterranean Social Model

Neoliberal economists have tended to blame the poor economic performance of some countries on the institutions that affect the ability of their businesses to compete. The emphasis has been on the supply-side institutions that have historically contributed to the development of a European social model, namely the unique combination of a generous welfare regime, strict labor market regulation, and a highly institutionalized industrial relations system that characterizes Western Europe.

The CPE literature has also emphasized how institutions (welfare regimes, industrial relations, vocational training, corporate governance) affect economic performance but early on developed typologies that account for the different ways such institutions may work. This is the case of the well-known typology of three welfare regimes proposed by Esping-Andersen (1990) in which all continental European countries were grouped under the same ideal type. Just a few years later, Ferrera (1996) proposed adding a fourth type called the "Mediterranean welfare regime." Its distinctive features were a strong role of the family in welfare provision, less universalistic coverage, and labor market regulation that makes it rigid and unfavorable to outsiders. Later on in a less convincing way, a "Mediterranean model of industrial relations" was proposed (Ebbinghaus 2003). This was based on trade unions divided along political-ideological lines yet capable of exerting some influence on the political and economic systems, frequent recourse to short-lived social pacts, etc.

Therefore, the similarity of these political and social institutions in the SE countries has been increasingly taken for granted by economists as well. The literature on the European social model(s) has been built on this assumed similarity and has therefore consistently contrasted a Mediterranean social model with the continental, Nordic, and Anglo-Saxon ones, often to show the former's worse performance in terms of both efficiency and equity (Sapir 2005).

The scholars who have adopted this explanation have usually focused on two specific institutions: (1) wage setting and labor market regulation and (2) social protection. In particular, the argument is that employers, trade unions, and the state in SE are less able to control wage increases. The excessively fragmented wage setting in sheltered sectors (public and private) results in a general increase of inflation with a consequent loss of competitiveness in the export sector (Hancké 2013; Johnston, Hancké, and Pant 2014). Those who study the welfare state have argued that SE social protection systems are not efficient or effective at protecting from many social risks because they only concentrate on some old social risks (i.e., pensions) and on labor market insiders (those who work in the core economic sectors and enjoy a high degree of social and labor market protection).

4.1.2. The Peripheral Position of the SE Economies

The second explanation focuses on the role played by exogenous factors related to the peripheral position of the SE economies in the Eurozone. In a nutshell, the argument is that since Italy, Spain, Portugal, and Greece are peripheral economies in the Eurozone, they cannot strongly influence the EU's macroeconomic policies or the Eurozone architecture in ways that favor their national interests as the core economies led by Germany can do. This makes the peripheral economies less competitive than the core economies even though their production systems are not necessarily less efficient (for instance, several sectors of the French production system are less competitive on international markets than their Italian counterparts). Rather, as peripheral economies, they bear the burden of the structural imbalances deriving from the euro, which is meant to foster the competitiveness of core countries. Austerity has ended up increasing the structural divergence between the Eurozone economies. Their differential growth reflects the great heterogeneity in the production regimes and their ability to generate income and employment.

4.1.3. The Lack of Investment in R&D and Human Capital

A third explanation for the poor performance of Mediterranean capitalism is linked to its low degree of investment in highly skilled human capital and R&D, which hinders its ability to innovate (especially radical innovation) and to follow a high road to competitiveness. Productivity depends increasingly on the development of scientific and technological knowledge available to a production system. In this respect, SE countries have not been able to follow this path due to very low investment in R&D and human capital, which has instead been the driving force behind the competitiveness of the Nordic model (Dølvik and Martin 2015) and later of the continental economies as well. The data provided by the annual European Innovation Scoreboard (European Commission 2016a) vividly show the weakness of SE's National Innovation Systems: all the SE countries are included in the "Moderate Innovators" group, with performances below the EU average.

According to Donatiello and Ramella (2017), these countries score low on at least three fronts: investments in qualified human capital and ongoing training, financial resources allocated to R&D activities, and interorganizational partnerships that foster innovation through cooperative learning processes that promote the circulation and exchange of knowledge. The comparison they propose between three Mediterranean countries (Italy, Spain, and Portugal) and the four EU countries that are "innovation leaders" (Germany, Sweden, Denmark, and Finland) on a number of innovation indicators shows this vividly.

4.2. The Three Explanations: How Strong and Convincing Are They?

The three explanations above enjoy a decreasing order of popularity in both scholarly and public debates. However, our main hypothesis is that their explanatory power is inversely proportional to their popularity.

4.2.1. The Great Limits of Adopting the Mediterranean Social Model as an Explanation

The available explanations, especially but not only from mainstream economists, for SE's poor economic performance overwhelmingly tend to focus on the role of the supply-side institutions that characterize their social model. *Mediterranean Capitalism Revisited* challenges this view, and our hypothesis is that—as many critics have pointed out—an exclusive focus on the supply side ignores the fact that this social model has evolved rather differently in the four SE countries but is still assumed to produce the same effects in all of them. Moreover, by adopting an approach that is also based on growth models, we show that a strategy based solely on asking for reforms on the supply side, not on the structure of the demand, will most likely result in future failures (and partially explain the current ones).

In particular, recent studies show that all of the SE political economies followed rather divergent paths in the period before and during the Great Recession. For instance, Pavolini et al. (2015) have shown that SE welfare states followed different trajectories before the 2007–2009 economic crisis, and it was only after this crisis and the ensuing austerity measures that they started to partially converge. As for industrial relations, Regalia and Regini (2018) maintain that the Italian case cannot be compared to the other Mediterranean countries because trade unions and collective bargaining were far stronger and more deeply entrenched in Italy's economy during the Great Recession and remain so (see also Bulfone and Afonso 2020).

Beyond in-depth qualitative studies, the most commonly used quantitative indicators of the dimensions of a social model also clearly show the different paths followed by SE economies, especially as regards Spain (see Supplementary Table I.A at https://hdl.handle.net/1813/103525). The analyses by Guillén (2010), Pérez (2014), and Pavolini et al. (2015) of the divergent Spanish trajectory in the decade before the Great Recession not only appear to be confirmed with relation to the welfare regime but can also be extended to the other social model dimensions. Indeed, while the percentage of social expenditure on GDP grew substantially in the other three SE countries in the decade before the 2007–2009 crisis, it rose only slightly in Spain, so much so that Spain moved from second position (after Italy) in terms of social expenditure in 1995 to the last position among the SE countries. The same trend applies to the other quantitative indicators of the social model: in 2008 Spain had the lowest level of employment protection against dismissals for regular contracts as well as the lowest trade union density and bargaining coverage rate (the latter having substantially decreased since 1995). To summarize, before the Great Recession, the Spanish social model had already evolved in a different direction. Yet the austerity doctrine pointed to the need for further structural reforms of this model. As for Italy, quantitative data appears to largely confirm the analysis by Regalia and Regini (2018). In 2013, all of the indicators in this country showed a greater resilience when compared to 2008 than was the case for the other SE countries.

Several studies have shown that all European social models, especially the Mediterranean one, have been through an incremental process of erosion as a consequence of major reforms and minor adjustments (Pérez and Rhodes 2015; Regini 2018). Although the extent of this erosion may have been over-emphasized, it would be difficult to see these social models today as the powerful factors of rigidity and inefficiency they were considered to be twenty years ago. However, although the features of the Mediterranean social model play a weak role in determining economic performance, their irrelevance should not be exaggerated. In spite of the harsh austerity policies that have contributed to a partial dismantling of their welfare regimes, labor market regulation, and industrial relations systems, the SE economies continue to be far more densely regulated than either the Anglo-Saxon or CEE ones. Although the SE social model is by no means the main cause of the poor economic and social performance of SE countries, as neoliberal economists have long maintained, what is left of it prevents Mediterranean capitalism from trying to compete solely on price through further internal devaluation. The SE economies continue to have a level of social expenditure and bargaining coverage that is not too dissimilar from the continental and Nordic ones, while this level is far above that of CEE and Anglophone economies as well as other advanced economies. Roughly the same pattern also applies to the level of employment protection, although here CEE countries are close to the Organization for Economic Co-operation and Development (OECD) countries' average. In addition, in spite of welfare cuts, during the recession the level of social expenditure in SE increased far more than the average level of the OECD countries.

Hence, competing on costs with more deregulated economies, not to speak of the emerging economies, is simply impossible for countries whose social model has developed to a point where further generalized compression would give rise to widespread social protests.

4.2.2. What about the Peripheral Position of the SE Economies?

The negative consequences of being peripheral economies in the Eurozone have become a popular explanation too. Unlike the previous explanation, our hypothesis is that it is difficult not to partially agree with this explanation but that it overlooks the fact that some of these negative situations were already at work before the monetary union or probably would have occurred even without it.

Moreover, the distinction between (Northern European) save-and-invest economies on the one hand and (SE) borrow-and-spend economies on the other is too stylized. Italy does not fit this picture well, as for a long time it had a partly export-led growth model and an extremely high level of private savings.

Yet this distinction grasps important elements of the peripheral position of SE economies in the Eurozone and the consequences on their competitiveness.

To be sure, there may be somewhat different views on the causes and consequences of the conflict of interests between Southern and Northern European economies. Streeck (2015, 1), for instance, focuses on the consequences of the different growth models. "A unified monetary regime for (North-European) save-and-invest economies on the one side and (South-European) borrow-and-spend economies on the other cannot serve both equally well. If one wants a common currency, one of the two political economies has to 'reform' its social system of production, and the social peace treaty founded on it, in the image of the other. Right now, the treaties place the onus on Mediterranean countries, obliging them to change so that they become 'competitive,' with Germany as their hard-currency task master." Pérez (2014, 41), on the other hand, maintains that "it is widely understood by financial market actors that the Eurozone is deeply flawed in its macro-institutional architecture. . . . Given the protracted failure to reach agreement on macro-institutional reform of the Eurozone, the burden of adjustment has been placed—often with perverse consequences—on the transformation of debtor country social models by way of 'structural reform' (the prevailing euphemism for labor market liberalization and social spending cuts)." Moreover, we need to adopt a more nuanced approach to the interplay between the financial systems of the different countries in the Eurozone by looking at their banking systems and the interaction among these systems.

At the same time, an explanation of the poor performance of SE economies based on their position in a badly designed Eurozone is only partially convincing. Indeed, some aspects of their poor performance (e.g., slow productivity growth and high public debt in Italy and Greece, high rates of unemployment in Spain, etc.) were present even before they joined the Eurozone, while others (e.g., the real estate bubble and the bank crisis in Spain) were likely to happen anyway, though at different times and to different degrees.

4.2.3. The Lack of Investment in R&D and Human Capital: Where to Point the Finger

Far greater explanatory power should be given to a third factor, namely the low degree of innovation in SE economies stemming from a set of reasons among which the low level of investment in R&D and highly skilled human capital is especially important.

We observe a huge gap in Gross Domestic Expenditure on R&D (GERD) between SE and all the other advanced economies. All SE economies fall far below both the OECD average and the EU-28 average, and their expenditure on R&D as a percentage of GDP is less than half that of Germany. Spain and Portugal even decreased this type of expenditure during the Great Recession—a trend they share with only a few other advanced economies that, however, spend from two to four times as much as the SE countries. The only other group of advanced economies whose level of expenditure on R&D is roughly similar is CEE; here, however, unlike SE the response to the Great Recession was a countercyclical increase in this type of expenditure. This very low private investment in R&D is matched by an extremely low percentage of researchers among employees, at least in Italy and Spain.

As we will see in chapter 8, this gap between the SE economies and other advanced economies depends primarily on their production systems, whose competitiveness is not primarily based on innovation, highly skilled human capital, or the technological content of their products. These countries are all underspecialized in high-tech sectors and have a large endowment of small and medium-size enterprises. But the only explanation for the widening of this gap is that a vicious circle is at work. A production system that is not based on innovation apparently makes even a low level of investment in higher education and R&D redundant, as university graduates experience difficulties in finding jobs consistent with the time spent in education, and research outcomes are not easily transferred into product or process innovation. This in turn encourages the production system as a whole to keep relying on low-skill, low-quality products that are very price sensitive and easily fall prey to globalization or on sheltered and therefore less competitive sectors such as construction, tourism, etc.

5. The Structure of the Book

As previously underlined, most studies on SE political economies have focused on supply-side institutions, two in particular: (a) the labor market and wage-setting institutions and (b) the welfare state. In the present volume, we expand our view by looking more carefully at other supply-side institutions as well as other actors and factors.

The volume is divided into two parts. Part one adopts a broad view on factors usually less studied in traditional VoC approaches: growth models, the role of the state and public bureaucracies, the functioning and effects of the Eurozone, and the sociocultural roots and characteristics of SE societies. Part two makes a detailed reconstruction of the evolution and characteristics of core supply-side institutions and policies in SE: the welfare state, labor market and wage-setting institutions, corporate governance, and human capital formation, R&D, and innovation. Each topic is developed in a specific chapter of the book, although certain issues are so complex that they are discussed from different perspectives in several parts of the volume.

The concluding chapter provides a general interpretation of the findings of the volume in terms of the development of SE political economies since the 1990s and answers the questions raised in this introduction, opening up future fields of research on Mediterranean capitalism.

PART I

Economic Features and Institutional Context of Southern European Countries

Chapter 1

Is There a "Mediterranean" Growth Model?

Lucio Baccaro

This chapter seeks to determine whether the Mediterranean countries—Greece, Italy, Portugal, and Spain—have a common "growth model" and if so what its features are. A growth model can be identified by examining the components of aggregate demand—household consumption, investment, government expenditure, and exports—that account for the greatest contribution to growth in a particular country over the business cycle. Generally, a growth model is based on one or more key sectors and within sectors by producer group coalitions whose interests are of paramount importance for the national political economy and are more likely to be taken into account in the formulation of public policy (Baccaro and Pontusson 2016, 2018; Iversen and Soskice 2019).

Previous research on growth models has identified four distinct constellations (Baccaro and Pontusson 2016; Stockhammer 2015a). First, there is the debt- and consumption-led growth model, typical of the United Kingdom before the crisis and of the United States, in which the main demand contributor to growth is household consumption. This in turn is fueled by the expansion of household debt. A specular alternative is the export-led growth model, epitomized by Germany, in which the main contributor to growth is exports (i.e., foreign demand). A third model is the "balanced" growth model, epitomized by Sweden before the crisis, in which there is not a clear demand driver of growth but rather a combination of different drivers, which may predominate in different phases of the cycle. Consumption and exports are both drivers or alternate: exports may pull the economy out of a recession, then consumption may drive the expansion. A key characteristic of the balanced growth model is the absence of a significant trade-off between consumption and exports, that is, exports do not suffer much when consumption increases, and this is due, according to the argument developed by Baccaro and Pontusson (2016), to the limited price sensitivity of exports, which in turn is a function of sectoral specialization. The fourth "model," or rather lack thereof (epitomized by Italy), is characterized by stagnation due to the absence of a sufficiently powerful driver of growth.

In what follows, I extend the analysis in Baccaro and Pontusson (2016, 2021) to the Mediterranean countries: Greece, Italy, Portugal, and Spain. These countries are examined before and after the Great Recession of 2007–2009 and are compared to Germany and France. The discussion begins with a brief summary of the growth model perspective, emphasizing the differences with previous approaches in comparative political economy. Following this discussion is an analysis of the demand regimes of the Mediterranean countries, aimed to identify their growth drivers. Then the export and consumption drivers are examined separately, looking at the composition and technical sophistication of exports on the one hand and at the trajectory of wages, productivity, household debt, and housing prices as drivers of consumption on the other.

The analysis leads to the conclusion that the Mediterranean countries share a common growth model, which is a variant of the debt- and consumption-led growth model but an unstable variant. This can be called a *peripheral consumption-led model* (see Ban and Helgadóttir 2019). The main problem with it is the absence of viable mechanisms for durably relaxing the current account constraint that consumption-led growth is generally faced with, that is, the tendency to accumulate foreign debt through sustained current account deficits.

In the first decade of the euro, the implicit guarantee of mutualization of debt (which led to de facto annihilation of country risk and convergence of interest rates) provided such institutional mechanism, allowing for hefty growth particularly in Spain and Greece. However, the implicit promise of joint liability in case of insolvency evaporated with the sovereign debt crisis. After the crisis, the policy response dictated by the European institutions and implemented by national governments pushed the Mediterranean economies in the direction of the export-led growth model. The analysis suggests that this transition is unlikely to be successful for various reasons. In the southern countries the export sector is too small to be able to assume the role of growth driver. Furthermore, exports are of limited technological sophistication, and this condemns these countries (for the time being) to producing intermediate goods for global supply chains (such as the German car industry) or low value-added services for rich northern customers (such as tourism and old age care services). Finally, there is a fallacy of composition problem: if all economies try to become export-led simultaneously, none of them will be able to. For export-led growth to be possible at all, someone else must be consumption-led.

The analysis confirms that Italy is a sui generis case (Baccaro and Pontusson 2016). Italy's economy is neither consumption-led nor export-led. The export sector is too small and price-sensitive and is held down by an uncompetitive real exchange rate. Consumption remains a more important driver than export, but neither of the possible stimulants of consumption—real wage growth or debt—has expanded sufficiently to sustain growth in the past several years. Not surprisingly, this economy has been stagnating for the past twenty-five years.

1.1. The Growth Model Perspective

The growth model perspective makes a shift from comparative political economy analyses primarily focused on the supply side to a primary focus on the demand side. Rather than concentrating on cross-country differences in institutional sets and associated complementarities (Hall and Soskice 2001), the perspective directs attention to the main sources of aggregate demand (Baccaro and Pontusson 2016).

The new perspective builds on two intellectual traditions: the French Regulation School (Boyer and Saillard 2002) and post-Kaleckian economics (Lavoie 2009; Lavoie and Stockhammer 2013). From the Regulation School the perspective draws a vision of capitalism as an intrinsically unstable system that may go through extended phases of stability but even in these phases remains internally conflictual, with actors working at the margin to alter the terms of the status quo to their advantage. Ultimately, any appearance of stability is undone by endogenous forces and external change, which may usher in a new period of surface stability. From post-Kaleckian economics the perspective borrows the emphasis on effective demand as the main determinant of output and employment (as opposed to supply-side forces) and on the importance of the functional distribution of income between labor (characterized by a higher propensity to consume) and capital (characterized by the opposite) as a determinant of aggregate demand. These intellectual elements are combined to produce a stylized account of the evolution of capitalism's growth models (Baccaro and Howell 2017, chap. 9).

Until the beginning of the globalization era—around the late 1980s—large Western European economies were wage-led growth models (Onaran and Galanis 2014). An increase in the wage share (which may be caused by greater trade union assertiveness and labor market regulation) had a tendency to stimulate growth because it led to higher demand, higher investment, and higher productivity through the force of "beneficial constraints" (Streeck 1997).

This model of wage-led growth no longer exists in its original form. It has been undermined by both endogenous dynamics, such as the tendency to produce inflation spouts, and international economic changes, such as free capital mobility, which has increased the remuneration requested for capital investment, and trade liberalization, which has amplified the importance of wage moderation for trade competitiveness. Most importantly, the wage-led growth model has been destabilized by sociopolitical change, which has reduced the institutional power of workers to capture productivity gains and by so doing fuel demand and investment (Baccaro and Howell 2018; Glyn 2006). The result has been an excess of savings, leading to "secular stagnation" tendencies (Storm 2017; Summers 2014).

The crisis of wage-led growth model has led to the emergence of alternative (post-Fordist) growth models, all seeking to replace the wage driver of growth with alternative drivers. These alternatives are essentially debt and exports (Stockhammer 2015b). Other solutions, such as investment-led growth and public consumption-led growth, are theoretically possible but not empirically realized. Export-led growth relies on foreign demand, which it seeks to stimulate through internal demand compression and real exchange rate devaluation (in the presence of fixed exchange rates). Debt-led growth stimulates domestic consumption by facilitating household access to debt.

Export-led growth and consumption-led growth come in two variants: core and periphery (Ban and Helgadóttir 2019). The core export-led model has national firms at the top of global supply chains; the periphery variant has instead national firms as suppliers of intermediate goods or as suppliers of low value-added, labor-intensive final services. The core debt- and consumption-led model does not face a binding current account constraint. This allows its citizens to consume beyond their means because the rest of the world is willing to lend to them by purchasing their financial assets. The peripheral variant can escape the current account constraint only for some time, if at all. Sooner or later, however, the current account constraint returns to be binding, and the countries are exposed to the risk of sudden stops and associated crashing recessions (Frenkel and Rapetti 2009; Copelovitch, Frieden, and Walter 2016). This is what happened to the Mediterranean countries with the sovereign debt crisis (Cesaratto 2015; Iversen, Soskice, and Hope 2016; De Grauwe 2013).

1.2. Demand Drivers of Growth

The growth performance of Mediterranean countries is very different in the pre- and postcrisis periods. In the precrisis period (1994–2008), Spain and Greece in particular but also (to a more limited extent) Portugal grew faster than France and Germany, while Italy's growth performance was disappointing. After the crisis all four countries experienced negative growth rates, with Greece shrinking by almost 6% on average between 2009 and 2013. In 2014–2018, Spain and Portugal returned to growth rates higher than those for Germany and France, while Greece and Italy continued to stagnate.

Italy's growth trajectory was the most dismal of the lot. While Spain and Greece experienced a boom in the run-up to the crisis, nothing of the sort happened in Italy. Although there was no precrisis boom, Italy was hit by the crisis almost to the same extent as the other three countries (table 1.1). To understand which demand drivers pulled growth along, table 1.2 presents a decomposition

Table 1.1 Average annual growth rates (%)

Period	Greece	Italy	Portugal	Spain	France	Germany
1994–1998	3.79	1.94	0.96	3.16	2.38	1.78
1999–2003	4.19	1.51	3.89	3.97	2.27	1.23
2004–2008	2.82	0.98	1.81	3.19	1.90	1.93
2009–2013	−5.89	−1.55	−2.98	−1.84	0.45	0.68
2014–2015	0.68	0.94	0.89	2.75	1.40	1.95

Source: OECD Economic Outlook.

exercise in which the average growth rate is divided into the contribution attributable to domestic demand (consumption, investment, and government expenditure) and the contribution attributable to exports, using Organization for Economic Cooperation and Development (OECD) data from input-output tables available between 1995 and 2015. The peculiarity of this decomposition exercise is that the value added of imports is subtracted not entirely from the value added of exports, as is usually done in growth decomposition exercises (based on net exports) but also from consumption, investments, government expenditures, and exports according to their shares of utilization of imports (Kranendonk and Verbruggen 2008). Economically, this type of decomposition makes more sense than the usual one. While a portion of imports is incorporated as input in the production of exports, a greater portion of imports is either directly consumed by households, purchased as investment goods, or consumed by government. Unlike the traditional method of growth decomposition—which subtracts the value added of imports entirely from the value added of exports and thus overestimates the contribution of domestic demand and underestimates the contribution of exports—this method provides a more realistic assessment of the importance of exports for growth.

The import-corrected decomposition of demand drivers suggests the following (see table 1.2):

1. Germany is very clearly an export-led growth model. The growth contribution of exports is always greater than the contribution of domestic demand, including in the postcrisis period. Furthermore, there is no visible sign of fundamental rebalancing of the German economy in the postcrisis period.
2. France's growth is mostly pulled by domestic demand, although the contribution of exports was slightly more important than domestic demand in 1994–1998 and predominant in 2014–2015, when French (import-corrected) exports accounted for almost the entirety of the paltry 1% growth rate.
3. Greece was very clearly domestic demand-oriented until 2008. The crisis then led to a dramatic collapse of gross domestic product (GDP), almost entirely accounted for by the fall of domestic demand. In 2014–2015 domestic demand

Table 1.2 Import-adjusted contributions to growth of exports and domestic demand

	Period	Export	Domestic	Total
Greece	1994–1998	0.68%	2.68%	3.36%
	1999–2003	0.98%	3.19%	4.17%
	2004–2008	0.97%	1.88%	2.85%
	2009–2013	−0.43%	−5.46%	−5.89%
	2014–2015	1.25%	−1.10%	0.15%
Italy	1994–1998	0.91%	0.94%	1.86%
	1999–2003	0.07%	1.42%	1.49%
	2004–2008	0.42%	0.57%	0.99%
	2009–2013	0.03%	−1.58%	−1.55%
	2014–2015	0.70%	−0.18%	0.52%
Portugal	1994–1998	1.19%	2.60%	3.79%
	1999–2003	0.23%	1.66%	1.89%
	2004–2008	0.62%	0.74%	1.36%
	2009–2013	0.60%	−2.22%	−1.61%
	2014–2015	1.01%	0.35%	1.36%
Spain	1994–1998	1.63%	1.71%	3.34%
	1999–2003	0.57%	3.40%	3.97%
	2004–2008	0.39%	2.80%	3.19%
	2009–2013	0.62%	−2.46%	−1.84%
	2014–2015	1.11%	1.40%	2.51%
France	1994–1998	1.21%	1.15%	2.36%
	1999–2003	0.38%	1.88%	2.26%
	2004–2008	0.52%	1.41%	1.92%
	2009–2013	0.24%	0.19%	0.43%
	2014–2015	0.92%	0.11%	1.03%
Germany	1994–1998	1.31%	0.28%	1.60%
	1999–2003	1.12%	0.06%	1.19%
	2004–2008	1.85%	0.14%	1.98%
	2009–2013	0.45%	0.17%	0.62%
	2014–2015	1.59%	0.37%	1.96%

Source: Own elaborations on AMECO and OECD data.

continued to fall, but exports gave a small contribution to the overall growth rate.

4. Spain's growth was also mostly driven by domestic demand, especially between 1999 and 2008. After the crisis period (when domestic demand fell), the return to growth was again mostly pulled by domestic demand, even though the contribution of exports was nonnegligible.

5. Portugal's trajectory is similar to Spain's (i.e., domestic demand-led), but the contribution of exports was more remarkable in the postcrisis period.

6. The little growth that Italy managed to produce in the precrisis period was largely attributable to domestic demand, while the contribution of exports was negligible except in 2014–2015, when all of the paltry growth came from exports.

Table 1.3 Current account balances (% of GDP)

Period	Greece	Italy	Portugal	Spain	France	Germany
1991–1993						−1.21
1994–1998		2.68	−6.08	−1.02		−0.93
1999–2003	−7.64	0.17	−9.15	−3.94	1.62	−0.05
2004–2008	−11.67	−1.39	−10.15	−8.19	0.02	5.51
2009–2013	−7.92	−1.53	−5.35	−2.02	−0.70	6.30
2014–2015	−1.76	2.17	0.13	1.45	−0.63	7.93

Source: OECD Main Economic Indicators.

Two elements stand out from the above analysis. First, all Mediterranean growth models are domestic demand-driven. Second, all of them have been shifting toward export-led growth in the postcrisis period (2014–2015). This also applies to France. The data above do not allow distinguishing within domestic demand between consumption, investment, and government expenditures. However, considering the high share of household consumption in GDP, the general stagnation of investments, and the limits on government expenditures imposed by European fiscal rules, it is highly likely that the most important growth impulse within domestic demand is from household consumption. As a matter of accounting identity, if consumption goes up (keeping total income fixed), savings go down, and if savings decline more than investments, a current account deficit emerges. Unsurprisingly, the other face of domestic demand-led growth in the Mediterranean countries was the accumulation of sizable current account deficits, which reached more than 10% of GDP in Greece and Portugal in the 2000s and came close to 10% in Spain (table 1.3). The current account deficit was smaller in Italy.

A current account deficit implies borrowing from abroad. In other words, the rest of the world finances the excessive consumption (i.e., insufficient savings) of a country in external deficit. This situation is sustainable until there are willing lenders. However, as is now well known, with the sovereign debt crisis the Mediterranean countries—first Greece, then Ireland, Portugal, and the Spanish banking sector—ran into a sudden stop whereby they could no longer find foreign lenders, and even domestic capital flew out of the country (Cesaratto 2015). The consequence was that all these countries had to drastically reduce their foreign borrowing by shrinking the economy. This explains why they all moved into a current account surplus (except Greece).

Table 1.4 Share of exports in GDP

Period	Greece	Italy	Portugal	Spain	France	Germany
1991–1993	14.38	18.41	23.94	16.55	21.15	22.06
1994–1998	15.14	23.70	26.47	23.39	23.80	23.55
1999–2003	20.88	24.44	27.31	26.99	27.32	31.01
2004–2008	21.82	25.80	29.51	25.45	27.48	40.47
2009–2013	25.13	26.27	33.84	28.59	27.72	43.49
2014–2019	33.44	30.42	41.87	34.39	30.69	46.71

Source: AMECO.

1.3. Size and Composition of the Export Sector

Data on demand drivers of growth suggest that exports have played a greater role in the postcrisis period. However, for exports to be a viable growth driver, the export sector has to be large enough to be able to take the whole economy onto its shoulders (Bowles and Boyer 1995). Table 1.4 displays export shares of GDP, a proxy for the size of the export sector. In 1991 (i.e., soon after German reunification) all six economies were in the same ballpark, with export shares between 15% of GDP (Greece) and 25% of GDP (Portugal). However, in the subsequent precrisis period, the export sector grew much faster in Germany than in the other countries, getting close to 50% of GDP, a figure comparable to a small open economy. After the crisis, the export sector grew more rapidly in all Mediterranean countries as part of a general turn toward export-led growth, but the growth was especially strong in Portugal. It seems fair to say that in Greece, Spain, and Italy the export sector is still too small to play the role of growth driver. Portugal may be a different story, with some provisos related to the composition of Portuguese exports, which are discussed below.

In addition to size, another obstacle that the export sector faces in Mediterranean countries is the real exchange rate. It is well known that in the first few years of the euro, the Mediterranean countries experienced an appreciation of the real exchange rate. This was the consequence of a faster increase of domestic prices than in trade partners (especially in Germany) combined with a monetary regime, the euro, which prevents adjustment of the nominal exchange rate. Germany experienced the opposite trend of depreciation of the real exchange rate for the opposite reason, that is, lower growth of domestic wages and prices (Flassbeck and Lapavitsas 2015; Johnston, Hancké, and Pant 2014; Scharpf 2011). The asymmetric trajectory of real exchange rates is reported in figure 1.1, which also suggests that despite years of austerity, the gap in competitiveness with Germany is far from having been closed by the Mediterranean countries, especially Italy.

An uncompetitive real exchange rate is likely to hinder exports more if they are highly price-sensitive. In this case, demand will be significantly affected

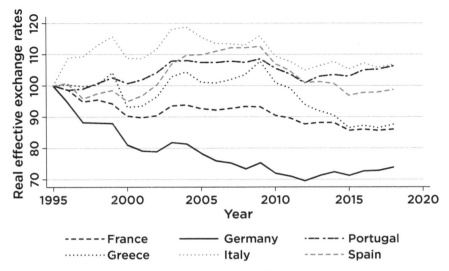

Figure 1.1. Real exchange rates. Source: OECD Employment Outlook.

by a loss of price competitiveness. In turn, price competitiveness is a function of the technological sophistication of exports: The more high-tech the exports, the lower their price sensitivity (Wierts, Van Kerkhoff, and De Haan 2014). Thus, by examining the technological complexity of the Mediterranean countries' exports, we can have an idea of the extent to which they are affected by the loss of price competitiveness brought about by the first decade of membership in the Eurozone.

Table 1.5, which uses the OECD classification of technological sophistication by sector, suggests that while Italian and Spanish exports are not too different in composition from the German ones—there is a predominance of medium-high exports even though medium-low exports have a greater share than in Germany—the exports of Greece and Portugal are largely dominated by medium-low goods, which implies lower value-added markets and probably a subordinate position in global supply chains.

In addition to exports of goods, exports of services are also important for the Mediterranean countries. In Greece, service exports accounted for up to 60% of total exports in the mid-2000s and now account for about 45%. Service exports account for about 30% of total exports in Spain and Portugal, while the Italian share of service exports is lower and comparable to Germany (18% and 17%, respectively).

Even though the OECD does not provide a classification of service exports by skill levels or technological intensity, the breakdown by sector can be used as a proxy (table 1.6), since it is likely that exports based on finance, telecommunication, the transfer of intellectual property rights, or the provision of business services (e.g., consulting, legal, architectural services, etc.) are more

Table 1.5 Export goods by technological complexity (share of total)

	Period	High	Medium high	Medium	Medium low	Low
Germany	1990–1993	12.83	51.49	11.86	18.79	1.76
	1994–1998	12.83	51.49	11.86	18.79	1.76
	1999–2003	14.38	51.65	10.98	17.02	1.71
	2004–2008	17.49	50.31	10.29	15.87	1.51
	2009–2013	16.62	49.30	11.13	16.19	1.94
	2014–2018	16.54	49.54	11.40	16.79	2.22
France	1990–1993	15.60	38.19	12.46	24.58	7.13
	1994–1998	15.60	38.19	12.46	24.58	7.13
	1999–2003	19.13	37.88	11.36	22.73	5.57
	2004–2008	21.47	40.15	11.17	21.07	4.70
	2009–2013	20.96	39.15	11.65	22.14	4.95
	2014–2018	24.36	35.53	10.98	22.45	5.51
Greece	1990–1993	1.96	8.14	15.28	58.00	14.72
	1994–1998	1.96	8.14	15.28	58.00	14.72
	1999–2003	4.33	11.56	15.16	53.45	13.41
	2004–2008	9.12	13.91	16.21	46.62	11.34
	2009–2013	9.77	15.41	17.25	44.18	10.03
	2014–2018	7.25	11.29	14.07	55.20	9.52
Italy	1990–1993	8.68	37.25	15.63	34.62	1.97
	1994–1998	8.68	37.25	15.63	34.62	1.97
	1999–2003	8.47	39.21	15.55	33.35	1.71
	2004–2008	9.70	38.78	15.00	32.65	1.58
	2009–2013	8.27	40.27	16.22	31.56	1.69
	2014–2018	9.05	39.09	16.40	31.76	1.98
Portugal	1990–1993	5.72	19.73	8.48	64.26	1.48
	1994–1998	5.72	19.73	8.48	64.26	1.48
	1999–2003	7.30	28.84	8.47	53.54	1.57
	2004–2008	10.40	29.59	10.06	47.47	2.20
	2009–2013	9.41	27.94	13.19	44.46	2.98
	2014–2018	6.26	28.42	13.89	47.40	3.62
Spain	1990–1993	7.92	41.72	15.52	25.54	7.88
	1994–1998	7.92	41.72	15.52	25.54	7.88
	1999–2003	7.89	43.17	14.19	25.21	7.17
	2004–2008	9.00	43.15	13.07	25.56	6.69
	2009–2013	9.22	41.00	14.90	26.36	6.29
	2014–2018	8.55	37.79	13.43	29.47	6.64

Source: OECD STAN Database.

skill- and technology-intensive than travel, which is mostly tourism. In the Mediterranean countries the most important source of service exports is tourism, which accounts for 50% of total service exports in Spain and Portugal, 45% in Greece, and 40% in Italy. France's tourism sector is thriving and yet accounts only for slightly more than 20% of French service exports, while the most

Table 1.6 Breakdown of exports of services by sector

	Year	Transportation	Travel	Financial	Intellectual property	Telecom	Other business services
France	2010–2014	19.57	22.56	4.34	5.83	6.75	29.32
	2015–2017	16.10	21.93	4.58	5.97	6.69	32.26
Germany	2010–2014	22.77	15.11	9.63	4.43	9.68	28.50
	2015–2017	19.89	13.12	8.21	6.16	11.55	28.81
Greece	2010–2014	47.81	39.23	0.44	0.20	2.55	4.36
	2015–2017	42.79	44.14	0.44	0.20	2.86	5.33
Italy	2010–2014	13.91	38.87	4.47	3.45	7.87	23.70
	2015–2017	13.95	39.99	4.74	3.46	8.41	22.31
Portugal	2010–2014	25.34	43.09	1.71	0.22	4.50	15.93
	2015–2017	21.95	47.68	1.22	0.36	4.85	16.63
Spain	2010–2014	13.22	48.33	3.35	1.04	9.44	16.52
	2015–2017	12.84	48.24	2.79	1.53	9.17	18.00

Source: OECD International Trade in Services Statistics.

important contribution to French service exports comes from business service provision, which is also the dominant export service sector in Germany.

Overall, the analysis in this section suggests that the Mediterranean countries do not have particularly propitious conditions for export-led growth: The export sector is relatively small and saddled by an uncompetitive real exchange rate. Furthermore, the composition of exports does not favor export-led growth. Greece and Portugal export primarily medium-low products, which are likely to be price-sensitive, and their main export service is tourism. Italy and Spain export more technologically sophisticated goods, even though the share of low- and medium-tech goods is greater than in Germany. For them too, tourism is the main source of service exports. The only Mediterranean country that seems close to realizing the conditions for export-led growth at the moment is Portugal. However, its growth is heavily reliant on the "travel" (tourism broadly defined) sector, not on high value-added goods or services.

1.4. Drivers of Consumption-Led Growth

Having examined the export driver of growth, we now shift attention to consumption. There are two main ways for households to finance consumption: through real wage increases (which in turn depend on productivity increases and on the distribution of productivity increases between labor and profit income) and through higher household debt. This section examines both channels in turn, moving then to the role of fiscal policy.

1.4.1. Real Wages and Productivity

Looking at wages in the Mediterranean countries as compared to core countries such as France and Germany, one is struck by the variation in levels. The latest data provided by the OECD (for 2016) suggest that German real wages (deflated with the Consumer Price Index) are around 31 euros per hour in manufacturing, 23 in construction, 24 in business services as a whole, and 26 euros overall. The corresponding figures for France are 24, 26, 25, and 24. By comparison, the Greek and Portuguese wages are considerably lower: 5, 10, 8, and 8 (Greece) and 7, 8, 9, and 9 (Portugal). Italy and Spain are in intermediate position with 14, 18, 17, and 17 (Italy) and 13, 17, 15, and 15 (Spain) (see table 1.7).

Another noteworthy trend is the widening wage gap between manufacturing and the rest of the economy in Germany, which contrasts starkly with more stable intersectoral wage differentials in the other countries, especially France.

Between 1995 and 2008, real wages increased by 34% in Greece, 10% in Italy, 17% in Portugal, 3% in Spain, 17% in France, and 1% in Germany. If one considers that these increases are spread over an interval of thirteen years, none of them seems particularly high with the possible exception of Greece.

Table 1.7 Evolution of hourly real wages, deflated with CPI (in euros)

	Period	Total	Construction	Industry	Business services
Germany	1991–1993	20.54	19.40	22.91	19.45
	1994–1998	21.72	20.33	24.76	20.77
	1999–2003	22.74	20.38	26.58	21.60
	2004–2008	23.31	21.02	27.83	22.14
	2009–2013	23.28	20.94	29.02	21.86
	2014–2016	24.47	21.88	30.11	23.15
France	1991–1993	18.69	17.60	18.91	20.57
	1994–1998	18.80	19.05	19.63	19.93
	1999–2003	19.86	19.47	21.28	20.95
	2004–2008	21.75	21.83	22.93	22.39
	2009–2013	22.89	22.82	24.76	23.91
	2014–2016	23.46	23.67	25.57	24.47
Greece	1991–1993				
	1994–1998				
	1999–2003	8.78	5.94	10.01	8.07
	2004–2008	10.50	7.02	11.51	9.48
	2009–2013	10.90	6.19	11.71	9.80
	2014–2017	8.58	5.75	9.78	7.87
Italy	1991–1993	15.57	13.02	13.65	16.24
	1994–1998	15.27	12.12	14.22	16.07
	1999–2003	15.48	12.26	14.76	16.18
	2004–2008	16.21	12.95	15.34	16.34
	2009–2013	16.82	13.25	16.60	16.62
	2014–2016	16.48	13.77	17.33	16.38
Portugal	1991–1993				
	1994–1998				
	1999–2003	8.69	5.82	7.08	9.05
	2004–2008	8.92	6.40	7.43	8.84
	2009–2013	9.27	7.05	7.93	9.07
	2014–2016	8.45	6.95	7.69	8.40
Spain	1991–1993				
	1994–1998				
	1999–2003	14.78	12.12	15.03	15.32
	2004–2008	14.60	12.19	15.03	14.53
	2009–2013	16.30	14.78	17.17	15.46
	2014–2017	15.22	13.43	17.00	14.77

Source: OECD STAN Database.

In the same period, labor productivity growth was 14% in Greece, 1% in Italy, 13% in Portugal, −6% in Spain, 16% in France, and 27% in Germany. There was massive redistribution in favor of profits in Germany, where virtually none of the productivity increases went into real wages. In the other countries, real wages increased faster than productivity: by 20% in Greece, 9% in Italy, 4% in Portugal, 9% in Spain, and 1% in France (table 1.8).

Table 1.8 Growth of labor productivity and real wages (CPI deflator)

		Labor productivity		Real wages	
		1995–2016	1995–2008	1995–2016	1995–2008
France	Total	23.73%	15.71%	25.52%	16.93%
	Construction	−11.79%	−4.89%	25.82%	17.17%
	Industry	83.03%	53.18%	31.46%	19.80%
	Business services	17.87%	11.26%	23.90%	15.44%
Germany	Total	31.54%	27.02%	15.63%	1.43%
	Construction	24.33%	16.10%	12.26%	−2.75%
	Industry	61.84%	42.62%	23.12%	9.82%
	Business services	22.91%	22.32%	15.91%	0.97%
Greece	Total	7.67%	14.39%	9.76%	34.24%
	Construction	34.85%	−15.13%	1.50%	26.07%
	Industry	33.90%	24.48%	2.01%	17.11%
	Business services	2.29%	21.13%	7.32%	33.26%
Italy	Total	1.35%	1.54%	11.40%	10.19%
	Construction	−12.02%	−12.07%	19.35%	9.13%
	Industry	18.89%	11.07%	25.18%	13.82%
	Business services	−11.35%	−7.66%	5.01%	2.86%
Portugal	Total	17.16%	13.15%	12.18%	16.83%
	Construction	−17.04%	−17.82%	41.30%	38.29%
	Industry	68.92%	53.18%	24.48%	22.77%
	Business services	8.04%	6.99%	6.23%	10.11%
Spain	Total	5.02%	−5.98%	3.68%	3.08%
	Construction	−10.28%	−34.66%	−0.11%	2.43%
	Industry	41.67%	18.55%	7.44%	3.64%
	Business services	−11.89%	−19.95%	0.37%	−3.11%

Source: OECD STAN Database, own elaborations.

Considering the entire period between 1995 and 2016 (i.e., including the postcrisis period), labor productivity increased by 8% in Greece, 1% in Italy, 17% in Portugal, 5% in Spain, 24% in France, and 32% in Germany (see table 1.8). This implies that labor productivity declined in Greece in the postcrisis period and remained flat in Italy while increasing moderately (by 4%) in Portugal and more robustly (by 11%) in Spain (see table 1.8). The reversal in Spain is likely a compositional phenomenon connected to the shrinking of the low-productivity construction sector.

Between 1995 and 2016, real wages per hour worked (deflated with the Consumer Price Index) increased by 10% in Greece, 11% in Italy, 12% in Portugal, 4% in Spain, 26% in France, and 16% in Germany. In the postcrisis period (2009–2016), real wages declined strongly in Greece and moderately in Portugal while remaining essentially flat in Italy and Spain. In France, real wages grew more or less continuously throughout the period. In Germany, they picked up after the stagnation of the precrisis period. In Greece, the cuts in real wages were partially counterbalanced by declining labor productivity.

Overall, with the possible exception of Greece before the crisis, real wage growth was probably not sufficiently strong to fuel consumption-oriented growth in the Mediterranean countries. However, the gap between wage and productivity growth contributed to competitiveness losses vis-à-vis Germany.

1.4.2. Household Debt and Housing Prices

In post-Fordist consumption-led growth models, the greatest stimulus to domestic demand usually does not come from wage growth—wage growth, far from operating exogenously as demand stimulus, is induced by demand expansion (see Baccaro and Pontusson 2016)—but instead comes from easier access to credit, which causes a rise of household indebtedness. This story has been told many times and goes approximately as follows (Mian and Sufi 2011; Rajan 2010). As part of a general shift in the business model of commercial banks from lending to firms to lending to households, standards for obtaining credit were relaxed, and customers could more easily take out loans. This shift was associated with and perhaps made possible by financial innovation (such as securitization), which gave the impression—but, as it turned out, only the impression—that risk had been reduced and not simply shifted from one actor (corporates) to another (customers). Access to debt allowed working families to increase their consumption levels (Behringer and van Treeck 2019), thus providing a functional substitute to lagging real wage growth.

Growing household debt interacted with rising housing prices as both cause and effect in the sense that the greater availability of credit stimulated demand for housing, thus leading to higher prices, and rising prices in turn stimulated further investment in housing, leading to higher levels of debt (Kohl 2018). Growing debt and rising housing prices encouraged consumption through essentially two channels: (1) part of the additional debt could be used to finance additional purchases, and (2) with the appreciation of asset prices, households experienced a wealth effect that made them more willing to spend. Furthermore, they could use their more valuable properties as collateral for larger loans. Rapid growth of household debt tends to go together with rising housing prices and the stimulation of household consumption.

In our sample, the country that comes closest to the above scenario of private debt-driven growth (heavily reliant on construction) is Spain. In Spain, household debt increased from 80% of disposable household income in 1999 to 155% in 2007 (figure 1.2), and housing prices increased by 349% between 1991 and 2007 (figure 1.3). Furthermore, the Spanish construction sector was for many years considerably larger than in other countries, accounting for 11–12% of value added and employment before the crisis. After the crisis, the construction sector shrank to 6% of value added and 5.5% of employment (based on OECD STAN data not shown here).

Similar developments can also be observed in Greece, where household debt passed from a negligible 17% in the mid-1990s to a peak of 120% of household income in 2012. Interestingly, in Greece household debt continued to rise even after the beginning of the sovereign debt crisis—a sign that households initially responded to austerity by increasing their level of indebtedness. Housing prices increased by 160% between 1997 and 2008. However, the Greek housing sector was always smaller than the Spanish one: it grew from 7% to 8% of employment (5–7% of value added) in the fifteen years before the crisis and then contracted to 5% (3% of value added). In Portugal the trajectory of household debt was somewhat decoupled from housing prices: while the former rose from 55% in 1995 to 155% in 2012, the latter increased "only" by 73% between 1991 and 2007. In Italy household debt increased from 39% to 91% between 1995 and 2012, and housing prices increased by 97% between 1991 and 2008. The trends in Mediterranean countries contrast sharply with those of export-led Germany, where household debt remained stable before the crisis (from 97% in 1995 to 99% in 2009), and housing prices slightly declined between 1994 and 2008. Between 2009 and 2018, however, German housing prices increased by 47% on a national basis and by much more in large cities.

Overall, the Mediterranean countries display the features of a consumption-led growth model in different proportions: in Greece, both real wages and household debt increased; in Spain, there was a spectacular increase of household debt but a less remarkable increase for wages; in Portugal and especially in Italy, both wages and debt rose but probably not sufficiently to significantly stimulate growth.

1.4.3. Fiscal Policy

Which role did public expenditures and fiscal policy play in the growth process of Mediterranean countries? This question is especially relevant in light of early assessments of the European sovereign debt crisis as having been caused by the fiscal profligacy of the southern countries plus Ireland (Buti and Carnot 2012).

Table 1.9 reports various measures of public deficit (in total, excluding investment expenditures and interest expenditures) and public debt as a share of GDP. The table shows that in the precrisis period, Italy's fiscal stance was much more restrictive than the Greek and Portuguese stances. For example, the primary balance (excluding interest payments) was in surplus for 2.4% on average between 2000 and 2004 in Italy, while it was in deficit for 0.76% in Greece and

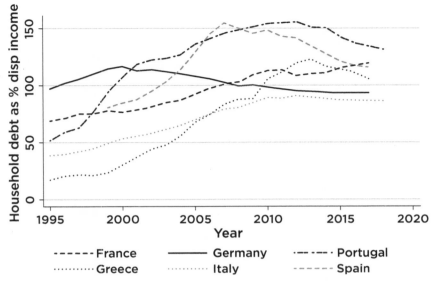

Figure 1.2. Household debt as % of disposable income.
Source: OECD National Accounts Statistics.

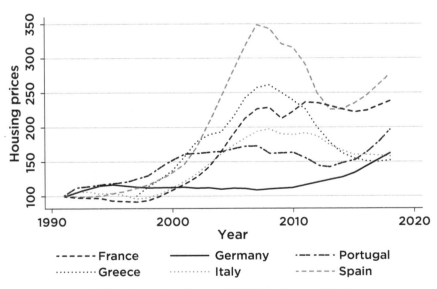

Figure 1.3. Housing prices. Source: OECD Main Economic Indicators.

Table 1.9 Fiscal policy stance

Public deficit as % of GDP

Period	Greece	Italy	Portugal	Spain	France	Germany
1991–1994	—	—	—	—	−4.81	−2.85
1995–1999	−7.20	−4.31	−4.21	−4.07	−3.33	−4.05
2000–2004	−6.44	−3.04	−4.64	−0.48	−2.69	−3.10
2005–2009	−8.83	−3.34	−5.36	−2.12	−3.77	−1.60
2010–2014	−9.41	−3.32	−7.54	−8.59	−5.00	−0.93
2015–2019	−0.42	−2.35	−1.97	−3.48	−3.11	1.29

Public deficit excluding fixed capital formation as % of GDP

Period	Greece	Italy	Portugal	Spain	France	Germany
1991–1994	—	—	—	—.	−0.18	0.25
1995–1999	−2.71	−1.58	0.77	−0.15	0.61	−1.60
2000–2004	−0.94	−0.11	−0.02	3.47	1.19	−0.94
2005–2009	−3.57	−0.07	−1.66	2.50	0.24	0.49
2010–2014	−6.25	−0.62	−4.46	−5.47	−1.03	1.31
2015–2019	3.21	−0.11	−0.09	−1.33	0.30	3.58

Public deficit excluding interest payment as % of GDP

Period	Greece	Italy	Portugal	Spain	France	Germany
1991–1994	—	—	—	—	−1.73	0.21
1995–1999	1.71	4.79	−0.15	0.32	0.06	−0.68
2000–2004	−0.76	2.40	−1.82	2.13	0.22	−0.12
2005–2009	−4.14	1.26	−2.47	−0.47	−1.09	1.09
2010–2014	−4.03	1.38	−3.17	−5.73	−2.54	1.22
2015–2019	2.79	1.43	1.83	−0.88	−1.35	2.38

Public debt as % of GDP

Period	Greece	Italy	Portugal	Spain	France	Germany
1991–1994	88.35	105.98	53.58	50.13	43.17	43.03
1995–1999	99.22	113.18	55.19	62.86	59.87	58.25
2000–2004	104.24	106.97	60.52	51.24	61.57	61.00
2005–2009	110.05	107.98	76.42	42.05	69.67	67.31
2010–2014	166.84	126.63	121.60	82.63	90.40	79.54
2015–2019	177.39	135.04	126.08	98.27	97.86	65.53

Source: AMECO.

1.82% in Portugal. In the postcrisis period, the primary balance remained in surplus in Italy (1.38% between 2010 and 2014) despite the long and deep recession, while the primary balance became negative, often considerably so, in Greece (−4.03%), Spain (−5.73%), and Portugal (−3.17%). In the period 2015–2019, all southern European countries were pushed by austerity policies into primary surpluses with the exception of Spain, which maintained a small primary deficit (−0.88%). Italy's fiscal position was more conservative than France's and Germany's as well as the other Mediterranean countries' throughout the period. The reason is the very high level of public debt with which Italy entered the crisis: 104% of GDP in 2007 versus 42% in Spain and 76% in Portugal (but 110% in Greece).

Overall, it cannot be excluded that fiscal profligacy contributed to Greece's remarkable growth record in the precrisis period and the consistent fiscal conservatism contributed to Italy's growth stagnation. In the postcrisis period, Spain's and also Portugal's more rapid growth appears to have been helped by a less restrictive fiscal policy stance than Italy's. With a high and growing debt to GDP ratio, stagnating growth, and interest rate risk premia relative to other Eurozone countries, Italy seems to be caught in a vicious cycle of stagnation leading to a tendency for the public deficit to increase, causing the need for continuous fiscal adjustments.

1.5. A Peripheral Consumption-Led Growth Model

The Mediterranean countries are all members of the Eurozone, and their economies are heavily conditioned by its rules. Before the crisis the Eurozone allowed for two types of growth models: an export-led growth model based on external competitiveness, epitomized by Germany, and a debt-financed consumption-led model, epitomized by Spain.

The export-led growth model is based on a large price-sensitive export sector, the ability to contain price growth below the rate of increase of competitors, and a fixed exchange rate (the euro), which leads to a competitiveness advantage vis-à-vis other members of the currency union (which are no longer able to engage in compensatory devaluations) and a lower real exchange rate than would be allowed by a national currency vis-à-vis other countries (Höpner 2018). The export-led growth model hinges on export-oriented manufacturing as a key sector. The consumption-led growth model is instead based on the ability to stimulate consumption through easier access to private debt. The combination of mortgage finance and construction is key for this second growth model (Baccaro and Pontusson 2019).

Both growth models are unstable as well as complementary: in order for a country to have an export surplus, other countries have to import, and in order for a country to have an import surplus, foreign lenders have to be willing to finance the resulting external deficit. The export-led growth model can only exist as an exception. If all countries try to pursue export-led growth, the result is a fallacy of composition that makes everyone's attempts futile. Furthermore, an export-led growth presupposes an open economy and that trade partners do not retaliate by limiting access to their markets for the country in endemic surplus.

The debt-led growth model has several instabilities of its own. Its growth relies on asset bubbles and growing levels of private debt, the accumulation of current account deficits, and the willingness of foreign lenders to compensate for insufficient domestic savings through cross-border capital outflows. The model's sustainability may be relatively unproblematic, as a country benefits from the "exorbitant privilege" of being able to easily sell financial assets denominated in its own currency to foreigners (Gourinchas, Rey, and Truempler 2012).

In regard to their structural characteristics and recent record, the Mediterranean economies appear to be variants of the consumption-led growth model, with consumption being financed by different mixes of real wages and household debt. In the Spanish, Greek, and Portuguese cases consumption led to a severe deterioration of current account balances, less so in the Italian case. How constraining current account deficits are for a country's growth depends on whether the consumption-led model is of the core or periphery type.

For core countries such as the United States and the United Kingdom, current account deficits are not a big problem. There is no risk of sudden stop for them (Frenkel and Rapetti 2009; Copelovitch, Frieden, and Walter 2016), since countries in the rest of the world are willing to purchase assets denominated in their currency and by so doing finance their external debt even for an extended period. However, the Mediterranean countries do not enjoy this privilege, or rather, after enjoying it for some time in the first decade of the euro they no longer enjoy it. Until the outbreak of the sovereign debt crisis, northern banks were happy to recycle their surplus reserves by lending to southern banks, thus providing the capital needed to finance the southern countries' current account deficit. After the sovereign debt crisis, however, northern banks came to see lending to southern banks as excessively risky, and thus the cross-banking flows stopped. For some time, the Target 2 payment system replaced northern banks in the role of funding agency for banks, leading to growing Target 2 liabilities of southern countries vis-à-vis the European Central Bank (Schelkle 2017). Nonetheless, the crisis forced Mediterranean countries to reduce foreign debt by shrinking imports through direct conditionality or indirectly (Sacchi 2015). The Target 2 balances continued to deteriorate, but this was no longer due to the financing of current accounts and instead was due to capital flight from the periphery toward the center (table 1.10). Clearly, the Mediterranean consumption-led growth model no longer has a viable mechanism for relaxing the current account constraint as consumption expands and is therefore more precarious than core consumption-led growth models.

Despite its limitations, the Mediterranean growth model worked rather well in the precrisis period for some countries. Spain and Greece experienced small booms, less so Portugal. In contrast, Italy had a lackluster growth performance both before and after the crisis. Although a full treatment is beyond the scope of this chapter, a few remarks about the Italian case are in order (based on Baccaro and D'Antoni 2020).

The Italian economy performed well in comparative perspective as a highly conflictual wage-led growth model until the 1970s. However, Italian society

Table 1.10 Target 2 balances (yearly averages, in billion euros)

Year	Germany	France	Greece	Italy	Portugal	Spain
2008	96.06	−81.89	−21.41	40.00	−15.60	−21.88
2009	157.39	−73.10	−39.56	66.33	−18.51	−36.18
2010	256.39	−34.17	−79.53	35.86	−50.05	−60.34
2011	376.95	−45.01	−94.16	−43.73	−61.70	−75.93
2012	666.36	−38.98	−105.00	−257.66	−68.79	−339.11
2013	577.28	−37.46	−61.97	−229.61	−64.15	−275.89
2014	471.77	−21.23	−40.61	−179.06	−57.18	−214.17
2015	545.70	−49.17	−98.15	−199.78	−56.22	−220.96
2016	669.46	−36.20	−84.01	−303.13	−66.58	−294.45
2017	850.01	−8.69	−69.13	−412.45	−77.16	−370.30
2018	930.95	−48.86	−39.22	−467.32	−80.55	−395.80
2019	897.17	−4.84	−24.57	−455.69	−80.97	−396.62
2020	816.50	−32.62	−25.79	−383.98	−74.09	−384.15

Source: ECB.

remained deeply divided. The clearest sign of internal tension was the inflation rate, which was consistently higher than in other advanced countries.

In the 1980s Italian growth remained good in comparative perspective, but a series of problems began to materialize. Loose fiscal policy combined with a marked increase in real interest rates led to the doubling of the stock of public debt as a percentage of GDP (from 60% to 120%). Although the inflation rate was reduced, inflation remained a lingering problem, especially when combined with Italy's membership into the semifixed Exchange Rate Mechanism (ERM) since 1979. The combination of higher inflation than for trade partners and semifixed exchange rates produced competitiveness loss. Italian large firms entered into a crisis, although Italian manufacturing remained strong thanks to the flexibility and innovativeness of industrial districts in the center north (De Cecco 2007).

These vulnerabilities became more visible in the 1990s. First, in 1990 Italy decided to narrow the fluctuation band within the ERM, thus accentuating the competitiveness problem. Ultimately, the unsustainability of the fixed exchange rate parity led to the exchange rate crisis of 1992 and Italy's exit from the ERM. The recession that followed was deep but also V-shaped thanks to a massive real exchange devaluation (produced by the combined effect of nominal exchange devaluation and wage moderation). In the mid-1990s, Italy had a short spout of export-led growth but soon decided to reenter the ERM as a prologue to joining Economic and Monetary Union in 1999. In order to qualify for membership in the union, the Italian policymakers engineered an exchange rate appreciation and a large fiscal consolidation followed by large primary surpluses until the early 2000s. In this period, growth and labor productivity began to slow down.

In the 2000s, Italy's growth model went through a series of unfavorable developments. The capacity to export was impaired by an overvalued real exchange rate, which resulted from the combination of competitiveness loss and an inability to devalue as a member of the Eurozone. Fiscal policy was heavily constrained by the attempt to reduce the stock of debt and by European fiscal rules. The primary fiscal balance remained in surplus. Simultaneously, Italian small-firm districts suffered due to competition from Chinese firms, while large firms continued their crisis. The least that can be said about the large privatization wave of state-owned firms in the 1990s and 2000s is that it did not help to rejuvenate Italian large firms.

Labor productivity stagnated, and this was likely due to the combination of stagnant aggregate demand (through the Kaldor-Verdoorn effect, which links aggregate demand to labor productivity) and the relaxation of labor rigidities, which reduced incentives for the introduction of labor-saving technical innovation (Storm and Naastepad 2012). With stagnating labor productivity, it became much more difficult to ensure the sustainability of Italian public debt, thus requiring constant fiscal adjustment to respect the budget rules of the Eurozone.

As the data presented above have shown, in these years Italy saw some elements of debt-financed consumption-led growth, such as the growth of household debt and of housing prices. However, these impulses were not sufficient to stimulate growth. When the sovereign debt crisis hit, Italy was forced into austerity like other Mediterranean countries, thus depressing growth even further.

It should be emphasized that the explanation of the Italian decline sketched above—based on unfavorable changes on the demand side, membership in the euro and misplaced labor market liberalization reforms that contributed to the decline of labor productivity—is different from traditional explanations of the Italian decline. These see Italy as being blighted by long-term "scourges" (small firms, familistic management, clientelism and corruption, and so on). When the economy was still relatively protected and technical change less tumultuous, so the argument goes, Italy's economic performance was still acceptable. When the economy became fully exposed to competition from low-cost countries, however, and when information technology became a more important competitive factor, the scourges led to stagnation (Capussela 2018; Toniolo 2013). Adaptation to the changed environmental conditions would have required, according to this line of argument, a more aggressive liberalization effort by policymakers and a more sustained reduction of the role of the state in the economy.

The main problem with this explanation is that it underplays the large number of liberalizing reforms introduced in Italy since the early 1990s, ranging from corporate governance reforms aimed at making corporate control more contestable to privatization of the main state-owned banks and enterprises as well as reforms enhancing labor market flexibility and increasing product-market competition (Simoni 2020). Contrary to received wisdom, the Italian economy was extensively liberalized. However, these reforms did nothing to rekindle growth and may even have contributed to economic stagnation.

1.6. Concluding Remarks

This chapter has sought to determine whether there is a Mediterranean growth model and if so what its features might be. For this purpose, the chapter has examined data on growth contribution of aggregate demand components, wages, productivity, household debt, and housing prices. The conclusion is that the Mediterranean growth model is of the consumption-led variety. In the pre-crisis period, it was driven by the accumulation of debt: private debt in the Spanish case, private and public debt in the Greek case. However, the absence of institutions and mechanisms for relaxing the current account constraint has made the debt-led growth process vulnerable to current stops in cross-border financial flows. The sovereign debt crisis has been one of those sudden stops.

If in the precrisis period the euro allowed for two complementary growth models—export-led in Germany and debt- and consumption-led in (parts of) the south (Johnston and Regan 2016)—in the postcrisis period it only allowed for one model: export-led growth. In response to the crisis, the Mediterranean countries have been subject to austerity and associated structural reforms, aimed to turn them into export-led growth models. Yet the Mediterranean countries are not export-led economies (for a similar assessment of the Spanish economy, see Álvarez, Uxó, and Febrero 2018). The export sector is for the time being too small and backward in these countries and exports are too price sensitive to make German-style export-led growth a realistic scenario. Only in Portugal has the size of the export sector grown significantly after the crisis and has the contribution of exports been meaningful in terms of growth. Even in Portugal, however, exports are of low value-added manufactures and services (primarily tourism). Furthermore, the strategy of promoting export-led growth becomes self-defeating if it is adopted by more than a limited number of (preferably small) countries.

At best, the Mediterranean economies can turn themselves into peripheral export-led models. They can maintain a manufacturing presence by becoming suppliers to German multinational corporations, or they can become suppliers of recreational and care services for the rich countries' visitors and pensioners. Overall, the future does not look very bright for the European periphery.

Chapter 2

States' Performance, Reforms, and Policy Capacity in Southern European Countries

GILIBERTO CAPANO AND ANDREA LIPPI

2.1. Introduction

Southern European countries have always been a problem in the varieties of capitalism framework. In particular, the Old Southern Fours (OSFs), together with France and Turkey, have been characterized by a hybrid type of capitalism. According to Hall and Soskice (2001, 21), "they may constitute another type of capitalism, sometimes described as 'Mediterranean,' marked by a large agrarian sector and recent histories of extensive state intervention that have left them with specific kinds of capacities for nonmarket coordination in the sphere of corporate finance but more liberal arrangements in the sphere of labor relations." Thus, these four countries appear to be different from liberal market economies, in which there is arm's-length interaction among market actors and the state behaves as a distant regulator, and coordinated market economies, in which the state matters greatly since it plays the role of active promoter. In the four Mediterranean countries, the state is considered to play an active interventionist role to compensate for the weaknesses of institutional arrangements/complementarities. As a result, the state is a significant driver of the development of capitalism.

Thus, economies embodying this third type of capitalism have been variously called mixed-market economies (Molina and Rhodes 2007; Featherstone 2008; Hopkin and Blyth 2012; Paraskevopoulos 2017) or state-influenced market economies (Schmidt 2007). This hybrid type of capitalism is characterized by a high level of statism in the political economy due to the weaknesses of institutional conditions. At the same time, the high grade of statism does not guarantee effective policies that compensate for institutional weaknesses. From this point of view, statism has not been capable of guaranteeing some form of coordination to ensure the needed institutional complementarities. The state has been particularly weak in guaranteeing three pivotal drivers when the quality of government is assessed: government effectiveness. bureaucratic efficiency, and regulatory quality (Rothstein 2012; Rothstein and Teorell 2008). It could be said, then, that the hybrid type of capitalism is characterized by a paradox: the need for active statism in the presence of a weak state is clearly represented by the inefficient and often ineffective performance of the related public administration. Thus, exactly where there is the need for dense and deep intervention by the state, the state has been weak, ineffective, inefficient, and often characterized by particularistic rather than universalistic actions. As is well known, a full Weberian state did not develop before the beginning of the democratization process, and this has been the cause of porosity and a lack of resistance with respect to the invasion of new democratic political elites (Morlino 1998). Thus, as described by some seminal studies (Sotiropoulos 2004a; Kickert 2007, 2011; Ongaro 2010a), in Southern Europe the state has been characterized by recurrent evidence of centralism; political control over bureaucracy; lack of reputable administrative elites; party patronage and clientelism in personnel recruitment (including a conservative role played by public-sector unions); legalism rooted in the Napoleonic tradition, complemented by informal shadow governance structures; uneven distribution of resources; institutional fragmentation; and insufficient mechanisms for policy coordination (Barzelay and Gallego 2010). These common characteristics had driven us to emphasize the trajectories and the results of the common efforts toward pursuing administrative reforms as very similar. However, as we will see, not necessarily similar conditions of departure lead to common results.

It is not a case, for example, that even if they are very similar with respect to the role of the state and the characteristics of public administration (as well other social, cultural, and economic aspects), the OSFs also experienced relevant differences in the timing of democratization and in their political systems and decentralization. Thus, we could expect that some differences should have developed over time in the role and characteristics of the state and its contribution to expediting the modernization and development of these countries.

Furthermore, inefficient state action is a common problem that has often appeared in the policy and political agendas of these countries. The idea that the state, its bureaucracy, and the features of policymaking should be reformed has always been very high on the agendas of all four countries. Thus, these countries' public administrations have been targets of repeated attempts at reform. For instance, since 2010 all four countries have shared the commonality of external pressures promoting state reforms in light of fiscal crises (Ongaro 2010a). While in regard to Greece this fact has been documented by a steep path of provisions enacted by the central government to adjust the public sector to financial needs (Featherstone 2015, 301), similar evidence is not available for all remaining three. However, in general the prevalent and diffused poor performing that induced the fiscal crisis is well displayed by financial indicators and the subsequent recommendations provided by the European Union (EU) and the World Bank. As a result, reforms have been adopted in light of different contingencies and with different intensities but are uniformly associated with financial indicators (e.g., the spread).

These attempts at reform have obviously tried to remove the obstacles to a more strongly performing role for the state in the related socioeconomic systems and thus render it more coherent and congruent with respect to the need for systemic coordination. Overall, the comparative literature has substantially agreed on the OSFs not only having a common Napoleonic tradition but also being modernized in very similar ways with very similar results (Sotiropoulos 2004a; Ongaro 2010b; Kickert 2011). Thus, the contribution of public administrations to the socioeconomic development of these countries and to the transformation of the forms of national capitalism has been very poor or negative. But is this statement completely true? Have these countries developed similar administrative reforms with similar timing and similar targets? Have these four states changed in very similar ways in terms of centralization/ decentralization and roles in public policies? Are the national bureaucracies so politicized that they impede the effective neutrality/proactivity of state intervention? Finally, are the results of the diachronic evolution of the four states truly as similar as argued by the literature?

As we show in this chapter, the response to these questions will confirm, unlike the literature that has underlined and emphasized the similarities among the OSFs, that they underwent different trajectories of administrative reform that have produced different outcomes in terms of improvement of the state policy capacities. Portugal emerges to have developed a very deliberate and effective trajectory that has allowed the country to significantly improve its state policy capacity. Spain has reached some improvement despite institutional resilience and conflictual intergovernmental relations, while Italy has not been capable of improving its weak policy capacity due to the schizophrenic oscillation of the reforms. Finally, Greece has not been capable at all of improving its original very weak state policy capacity due to a substantial lack of real attempts to improve administration performance.

2.2. The Starting Point: States' Performance and Policy Capacity across Southern Europe

Our comparison of the evolution of administrative reforms in the OSFs starts by struggling with empirical evidence regarding their state capacity measured by performance.

In figures 2.1 and 2.2, we present data from the Worldwide Governance Indicators to show the diachronic evolution of the four countries with respect to two relevant indicators, quality of governance and governance effectiveness, that can be considered good proxies for assessing state capacities.

What is impressive here is that according to World Bank indicators— confirmed by other sources (OECD 2019a; Bertelsmann Stiftung 2018; see

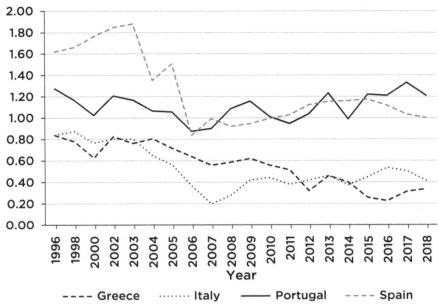

Figure 2.1. Government effectiveness in Greece, Italy, Portugal, and Spain (1996–2018). Our elaboration on World Bank data.

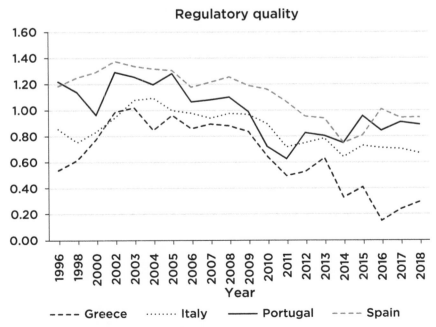

Figure 2.2. Quality of regulation in Greece, Italy, Portugal, and Spain (1996–2018). Our elaboration on World Bank data.

also Lampropoulou 2018)—Portugal and Spain state actions have performed better than those of Italy and Greece; overall, Portugal performs best.

It is also interesting to observe that Portugal and Spain have always outperformed the other two countries when governance effectiveness is under scrutiny. This preeminence is quite notable, as is the persistent gap over time between the two pairs of countries. Regarding the quality of regulation the difference is less marked, and for a few years around the 2007–2009 Great Recession, Italy improved more than Portugal. At the end of the analyzed time range Italy was still performing worse, while Portugal and Spain appeared to be improving.

These differences are relevant and very challenging from the theoretical point of view. It is possible that the potential contribution of the state and its administration has been significantly different in the four countries, although they are considered to belong to the same family of countries regarding the type of state and ways in which public administration works.

In fact, the above-described evidence shows how OSFs perform in different ways starting from presumedly similar conditions. In the following sections, three different dynamics are isolated and described separately for each country: the evolutionary arrangement of the state, including the transition to democratic regimes; the modernization of the administrative system through different waves of reforms; and the steering role of the public hand and its policy capacity in steering economic development. Thanks to this reconstruction, we are able to extract four causal drivers that contribute to explaining the similarities and differences among the OSFs in terms of state changes and capacities.

2.3. Greece

2.3.1. Evolutionary Frame of the State

Since the end of World War II, the Greek administrative system has maintained Napoleonic tradition grounded in high centralism, hierarchical relations, legal formalism, and a heavy set of rules (Lampropoulou and Oikomomou 2018, 110). This arrangement was preserved across decades and was only partially accentuated in terms of the authoritative approach and centralism during the military junta from 1967 to 1974. Apart from this fact, the overall arrangement was never significantly revised. Democratization instead induced some relevant aspects that were added to the consolidated arrangement. The public sector gradually assimilated a wide range of social, economic, and productive activities, reflecting broader expansionary and protectionist economic policy (Pagoulatos 2003). Public organizations became large-scale bureaucracies that functioned on the basis of formal rules and procedures and were subjected to the direct control of the political system. This fact engendered an increase in public employment, public expenditures, public debt, and fiscal imbalances (Spanou 2012). More relevantly, some recurrent problems of the Greek public sector increased at the time and were never diachronically overcome until the external conditionality imposed by the EU in May 2010 severely impacted public administration. These problems include the political manipulation of bureaucracy, including corruption, party patronage and clientelism, poor performance, limited institutional capacity, legalism, formalism, fragmented and inconsistent procedures, lack of coordination, ad hoc arrangements, and frequent changes at the top administrative levels (Spanou 2001; Sotiropoulos 2004a; Spanou 2008; Ladi 2014).

2.3.2. Reforms' Trajectories

Despite this path-dependent landscape, the Greek public administration system was repeatedly subjected to reforms aimed at solving the aforementioned persistent deficiencies. Assuming this perspective, three broad phases can be detected based on the different types of reforms enacted to manage the fragmented and highly patronage-dependent system (Spanou 2001).

The first phase (1950–1980) was characterized by the consolidation of the Weberian arrangement and Napoleonic centralism and gradually moved toward a public service approach, with support from the democratic transition. These changes did not affect the listed problems but in some way fueled the persistent poor performance and the high party dependence. In contrast, the other two phases were characterized by attempts to address embedded deficiencies through relevant modifications, such as decentralization and managerialization (Spanou and Sotiropoulos 2011; Spanou 2012).

The second phase started in the mid-1990s and lasted until the fiscal crisis (2008). The general aims of this reform were related to Europeanization and modernization. Significant decentralization was promoted by reorganizing subnational authorities and empowering local governments. The EU conditionally pushed for innovations, such as e-government, government regulatory agencies, and independent authorities. This turning point was supported by programs such as Politeia in 2001 and the subsequent Administrative Reform Program in 2007. Both encouraged a modernization version of the New Public Management (NPM) (Pollitt and Bouckaert 2011) through a more European, more efficient, and more accountable state.

The third phase partially reshaped the contents and goals of the former phase and reinforced the efficiency aims under the Memorandum of Understanding and the fiscal conditionalities imposed by the Troika. The idea of external empowerment was a driving force (Spanou 2014; Featherstone 2015, 303–7). There was an enormous increase in measures enacted after the EU intervention, and a European task force was created that simultaneously managed four critical areas for intervention: finance, personnel, organization, and audit and performance.

On paper, this program was extremely disruptive, calling for five ambitious aims: increased operational efficiency, the enfranchisement of the public sector politically, the consolidation of human resource management, the deep review of state provision according to input-outcome results, and finally, the opening up to external review and expert advice. As shown by Featherstone (2015, 309–10), this incentive model worked only to a point. Resistance and delegitimization strongly affected this "alien agenda," although a number of specific provisions related to the aforementioned areas were adopted by the central government until 2017 (Ladi 2014).

The overall effect was twofold. On the one hand, an extraordinary effort to mobilize a significant strategy was outstanding and, to a limited extent, successful. On the other hand, the match between the exogenous inputs and the endogenous capacity was aborted, and the most relevant finding remains the permanent climate of "non implementation" that marked the previous reforms (Tsekos 2013, 460).

More precisely, Sotiropoulos (2012) listed a number of specific permanent failures of the Greek trajectory of reform in coping with "insurmountable obstacles at the stage of implementation": the withdrawal of programs when submitted to deliberation in representative bodies, the voting down of bills encapsulated in the reform, the inability to implement the deliberated measures, quick policy reversal in the face of a lack of outcomes or resistance in the form of public opinion, and no real change after compliant implementation. Additionally, a further element has been displayed from other scholars (Papacostantinou, Tsagkanos, and Siriopulos 2013) that argue how the degree of corruption in the Greek bureaucracy severely affected any trial of change regarding the implementation of challenging provisions, such as the dismissal of public workers. Again, the matter of "not implementation" argued by Tsekos (2013) has been the mainstream for any attempt.

2.3.3. State Policy Capacity in Steering Economic Development

This trajectory confirmed the consolidated perception of the Greek policy style and its (in)ability to steer economic development through a systematic and coherent design. This fact is clear when examining three different aspects: the triangle of economic development, the role of society, and the relevance of intergovernmental relations.

As noted by Lampropoulou and Oikonomou (2018, 110), the state-society-economy relationship corresponded "to a corporatist-like scheme that in practice allowed selective access to the resources of public administration by rent-seeking groups." Recent attempts to implement an economic intervention by shocks, namely by external strategies aimed at rendering the public sector proactive and efficient, went against traditional resistance to consolidated relations. The economic and financial restoration of Greece in the previous decade and the subsequent crisis in relation to the EU strictly intertwined economic policy with administrative reform and performance (Spanou 2015). Most if not all of the adopted measures (particularly tax policy and revenue, financial management, privatizations, procurement, pension and health care systems, labor market, business environment, regulated professions and professional qualifications, network industries, and the impact of EU structural and cohesion funds) included administrative components of provisions. The failure of the administrative reform did not allow for real and substantial improvement of the administrative system and, more relevantly, severely undermined the success of the economic strategy and contributed to preserving corporatist localism and fragmentation (Liddle 2009).

The public sector has little room remaining for the involvement of societal actors in the administrative process, apart from clientelistic and privileged relations between the government and some limited interests with specific access to decisional bodies (Ongaro 2010a). The weakness of civil society in Greece is complementary to a strong but uncoordinated and inefficient state. Public administration is involved in many economic activities. As argued by Tsakalotos (1998, 129), this involvement "has had important consequences for the nature of the private sector, which has concentrated its activities on expanding the degree of protection or level of subsidy rather than relying on its own dynamism to improve its competitiveness or restructure its production." Some limited attempts (by the center-left cabinet in the 1990s) to introduce a coordinated design of development policy were described as unsuccessful and were considered inviable with respect to the policy capacity of the Greek public sector and the needed process adapting external and innovative programs to difficulties and the slow learning of the administrative system (see also Pagoulatos and Triantopoulos 2009).

Analogously, policies and institutions were eroded by self-interest pressures. Society seemed absent and passive with regard to administrative goals and performance. In other words, the policy capacity of the Greek administrative system is depicted as fragmented and discontinuous in the long run, as strongly dependent on specific contingencies, and as lacking an overall scheme of intervention: microprovisions and clientelistic exchange between groups and some branches of the public sector have nurtured uncoordinated and sporadic policies (Ladi 2014; Spanou 2015).

Finally, intergovernmental relations were ambiguous and contradictory, characterized by a pendulum between decentralization and recentralization. In the first wave, local governments were invested with new power and became a barycenter for the management and delivery of public services according to the transformation of the Napoleonic pattern (Kuhlmann and Wollmann 2014) of local government (e.g., Spain and Italy). Thus, the so-called most centralized state in Europe promoted the idea of empowerment of local politics and municipal experience (Hlepas 2003, 2010). Economic development was implicitly assigned to the quality of public service and to the logic of closeness: the empowerment of intergovernmental relations was intended as a specific aspect of Europeanization and modernization. Nevertheless, as is known, this attempt was subsequently considered ambitious and unrealistic and was reversed by a strong U-turn promoting the drastic downsizing of the number of municipalities by the Kapodistrias reform of 1998. In light of the fiscal maneuver, the subsequent depression at the municipal level pushed the pendulum back to the center (Hlepas 2012; Hlepas and Tsekos 2018).

The overall picture of the Greek state and its role in promoting economic development still seems affected by the same pathologies as before the reform waves, that is, by fragmentation, politicization, clientelism, and inertia.

These aspects have recently been interpreted by scholars (Lampropoulou and Oikonomou 2018) as a specific deviation of the Greek public administration with respect to the other southern Napoleonic countries. This difference indicates that Greece still faces Napoleonic problems and limits, in addition to specific problems that pertain only to the Greek case: a specificity that severely undermines its policy capacity and hope for improvement in terms of performance and coordination.

2.4. Italy

2.4.1. Evolutionary Frame of the State

Italy was the first among the four Mediterranean countries to undertake the process of democratization after an authoritarian regime; thus, there has been a longer period during which public administration has been the object of modernization and efforts for reform. In the first decades after World War II, these attempts to reform Italian public administration were characterized by significant failures. Furthermore, we must underscore the persistence of parallel administrations and agencies created by the fascist regime (and this track of the public system was in charge of the more interventionist activities in the economic system of the Italian state).

The Italian state has changed considerably in recent decades: it has become more decentralized, and its public administration has been the object of various attempts at modernization according to the NPM recipe. These two discontinuities in the administrative legacy have been paired with two relevant continuities, which have weakened the implementation and thus the impacts of reforms. The first continuity is the persistence of the historically rooted style in the design of administrative reforms, indicating a focus on the law as the central tool of the reform without any attention to its implementation. The second is the substantial absence of political parties as real promoters and supporters of administrative reforms (Di Giulio and Vecchi 2019). Furthermore, it must be emphasized that the decentralized system and the lack of a real political interest in effectively reforming public administration have been factors of impermeability with respect to the many administrative innovations arising at the local level (Vecchi 2020).

However, to better understand the dynamics and the evolution of Italian public administration, it is necessary to consider the regional arrangement of the state and to note that over the last twenty-five years there has been a formal shift of power toward municipalities and also, thanks to the constitutional reform approved in 2001, toward regions.

2.4.2. Reforms' Trajectory

During all of the years of the so-called First Republic, the various reforms adopted were incapable of truly changing the bureaucratic, formalistic, and legalistic characteristics of public administration (Capano 1992; Sepe 1995; Melis 1996).

From this point of view, it could be said that the real attempts to drastically reform the structure and characteristics of the Italian state started in 1992 due to a deep financial crisis and were followed and pushed forward by the change in the working arrangement of the Italian political system. In fact, at the beginning of the 1990s when the entire Italian political system was undergoing a period of severe crisis, the administrative reform failures of previous years were replaced by a permanent cycle of reform introduced by the governments led by prime ministers Giuliano Amato (1992–93) and Carlo Azeglio Ciampi (1994) and by the center-left coalitions (1996–2001). This decade, particularly the latter half, was a triumphant period for supporters of administrative reform in Italy. Not one single sector of public intervention, not one central, peripheral or local organizational structure, and not one decisional process or procedure managed to escape this tidal wave of change sweeping over the formal rules employed. From the structure of the central government to the character of public office, from accounting procedures to the educational system, and from universities to political and administrative decentralization, not a single area of the public sphere remained unaffected by change, at least in theory (Rebora 1999; Capano 2003). With regard to the most relevant structural administrative dimensions, the most important interventions during this golden reform decade were the privatization of public employment, the establishment of the National Agency for the Collective Bargaining of Public Employment, the introduction of managerial accounting in local governments, the redesignation by the government of the duties and powers of regional and local governments, the reform of the public-sector bargaining system, the reform of the macrostructure of government, and the introduction of the annual law on de-legislation and simplification.

Hundreds of regulations changed rules regarding the personnel system, the bargaining system, and control and evaluation systems in administrative procedures, including the introduction of a new control and evaluation system (to be implemented independently by all public administrations and organizations), the reform of the duties of the administrative courts, the unification of all rules governing the administrative process, and the unification of all rules governing public employment.

None of the other three countries underwent such a massive, radical process of redesign of the basic rules of public administration. After the golden decade, the reform of public administration slowed. During the first decade of the third millennium, the most relevant interventions were adopted by the center-right governments. These interventions included the introduction of the spoils system to the appointment of the top bureaucrats in the ministry and the 2009 reform by which a new system of evaluating administrative performance was introduced, as was a system of evaluation of public employers through which only a part of the system could obtain additional salary based on individual performance. In 2015 the center-left government introduced a new reform of public employment, revitalizing the role of unions in industrial relations, and this reform redesigned the procedure for selecting top bureaucrats (through centralization of recruitment, which was rejected by the Constitutional Court for its attempt not to consider the role and autonomy of regional and local governments).

Furthermore, since 2010 relevant interventions have addressed the prevention of corruption, the improvement in transparency, the rules of tendering procedures for public contracts, and the introduction of various forms of e-government (Di Mascio and Natalini 2014, 2016; Bolgherini and Dallara 2016).

Thus, what has happened is that the relevant changes the Italian state has undergone over the last decade more resemble a process of adaptation to new times—by, for example, straight reforms as well as oblique provisions (Bolgherini and Lippi 2021), administrative solutions, and political demand—than a real process of radical reform capable of introducing definitive discontinuity to its organization and above all its policy and governance capacities (Capano 2003; Di Mascio et al. 2017). The final result is a very fragmented bureaucracy characterized by loss of a sense of identity and, at the same time, by an increased historical tendency to interpret its role very legalistically (Cassese 2019).

2.4.3. State Policy Capacity in Steering Economic Development

The role of the Italian state in steering economic development has undergone a well-known trend, from being the pivotal actor until the end of 1990s to the age of privatization (1990s) and the subsequent decades, with a lack of industrial policies and troubles in resolving some relevant constraints of a stagnating economy. It should be underscored that the process of privatization has been very large (involving not only public enterprises but also banks and public utilities) but conducted in a way that has been characterized by low transparency (Goldstein 2003). Furthermore, some structural problems depending on the ways in which public administration works have not been solved at all, notwithstanding the many reforms emphasized above such as resolving insolvencies, paying taxes, and dealing with permits for economic activities. The weak bureaucratic performance in supporting administrative activities has been accompanied by the poor efficiency of the civil justice system. Furthermore, the decentralization process, through the strengthening of the powers of regions, has had relevant effects in terms of different administrative performances between the north and the south. This geopolitical administrative divide is well represented by the low effectiveness of the impact of EU structural funds in southern Italy (Milio 2007; Ufficio di Valutazione del Senato della Repubblica Italiana 2018), which can be explained by not only the different socioeconomic contexts (and social capital) but also the very low administrative capacity of the southern regions. Thus, from this point of view, the process of decentralization in its asymmetric implementation can be considered to have created the conditions for a significant segmentation of the overall policy capacity of the Italian state. Finally, it should be borne in mind that the characteristics of the Italian economic system (based on small to medium-size companies) represent a structural constraint on the state to design an effective economic development policy.

2.5. Portugal

2.5.1. Evolutionary Frame of the State

The evolution of the state in Portugal was characterized by the Carnation Revolution in 1974. The first stage of the process of democratization was devoted to reshaping the characteristics of the state. Here, there are different positions in the scholarship. On the one hand, some scholars have emphasized that only after the end of Salazarism did the Portuguese state reach the status of a full Weberian state (Ongaro 2010b; Magone 2011), while others have underscored how the administrative reforms introduced during the fifty years of the authoritarian regime (and especially the reforms of 1926 and 1935) could be considered pillars for concrete and definitive redesign of the Portuguese administration in Weberian terms (Carapeto and Fonseca 2005). Overall, what matters here is that the juridical order of the public administration was ready for the next step (to become a Weberian state in a democratic system).

However, to connect these two dimensions, it was necessary to dismantle all of the ideological characteristics of the authoritarian regime impacting the administration as well as some rules that were unacceptable (such as the absence of taxation for civil servants' wages).

2.5.2. Reforms' Trajectory

This first phase of the reorganization of the state has been defined as a "capacity building strategy" (Corte-Real 2008). In this phase there was no breakup of the previous administrative order, and as in the process of democratization in other Southern European countries, the "purification" of the top levels of administration deeply tied to the authoritarian regime was minimal (Opello 1983). This partial continuity does not seem to have influenced the democratization process of the administration, while in a certain way it was a factor favoring one of the characteristics of the rising new Portuguese administration: the intrusive role of political parties and their constant aim to control administration and every aspect of policymaking (Araújo 2002). This intrusion was originally due to the program of the new ruling leftist government, which was clearly oriented toward an interventionist policy style. This policy strategy, which meant significantly increasing both the welfare state and the economic role of the state, was not interested in real change in the inherited legalistic characteristics of the national public administration. Thus, during the first decade of its existence as a democratic system, the Portuguese public administration maintained its inherited characteristics and was considered a tool directly in the hands of decision makers. However, it must be emphasized that the traditional public administration was coupled with new nationalized enterprises during the first months after the revolution (when insurance, banking, power production, transport, chemistry, and shipbuilding were completely nationalized).

Things started changing in 1986 with EU accession and with Cavaco Silva leadership. Thanks to Portugal's inclusion in the EU and its policies and to the political program of the new social-democratic government, the Portuguese public administration achieved its first attempt at deep reforms. First, between 1989 and 2000 the privatization policy launched by the government was enormous, and if assessed according to the percentage of gross domestic product, Portugal can be considered a major privatizer during this period (Schneider 2003), which is remarkable. Furthermore, at the end of the 1980s public administration underwent relevant reforms focusing on de-bureaucratization, improving transparency and relationships with citizens, decreasing costs for enterprises, and increasing the skills of public servants (Corte-Real 2008). With the new socialist government in 1995, a second wave of administrative reforms focused on improving the quality of services provided to citizens and private economic actors. Between 2002 and 2005 under the right-wing government, NPM reforms were introduced for financial motivation.

This process was conducive to further centralization of the administration and an increase in the politicization of bureaucratic appointments. The subsequent socialist government should be noted because it reshaped the central administration through various mergers (50% of public employees changed their original administration) (Rocha Oliveira and Esteves de Araujo 2007). Following the financial crisis of 2008, Portugal chose to focus on similar administrative reforms in its Memorandum of Understanding with the EU and prioritized efficiency and cost-effectiveness actions, along with the goal of rationalizing its administrative apparatus. It should be noted that in this "emergency" Portugal did not decide, as other countries did, to cut salaries, although working hours were increased (Lampropoulou 2017). The recent years under the leftist government (since 2015) have not been characterized by relevant intervention in the field of public administration except for the decrease in weekly work hours to thirty-five hours for public servants and the blockage of the privatization of local transport. As is well known, the brilliant success of this government, from the macroeconomic point of view, is due especially to its fiscal policy and liberalization initiatives.

What can be said of this process of reform is that it has not been particularly different from that of other countries in Southern Europe. In fact, many observers have underscored that the process of modernization of public administration has not changed the original characteristics of the Portuguese public administration, which is considered to have maintained its patrimonialistic characteristics (Magone 2011). Portugal's implementation capacity has not been difficult to interpret, and there is different empirical evidence on it (Lampropoulou 2017; Hardiman et al. 2019).

2.5.3. State Policy Capacity in Steering Economic Development

The Portuguese state policy capacity seems to have been relatively good. Regarding this characteristic, it should be emphasized that Portugal has not changed its centralized public administration, notwithstanding EU pressures for decentralization (Rodrigues and Madureira 2010), and on the same contingencies has strengthened it. Furthermore, it should be noted that some relevant reforms have been adopted by following a process characterized by the adoption of an evidence-based approach; that is, reforms have been initiated by the Resolution of the Council of Ministries, prepared by committees of experts providing the content of and implementing subsequent legislation (Rocha Oliveira and Esteves de Araujo 2007).

The relevant state capacity is attested to, for example, in the way that privatization during the 1990s was managed as well as by the implementation of the Memorandum of Understanding with the Troika after the 2008 crisis. In both cases, the final performance can be considered quite high and shows a strong, capable commitment to steering the main drivers of economic development. Here, however, it should also be borne in mind that there are some characteristics of the Portuguese economic system that could have helped the state's capacity in driving economic development (and in fighting crises such as that in 2008), such as the connection with other Portuguese-speaking countries (which have undergone relevant economic development since the early 1990s) as well as with the former colonies, the small percentage of the economy based in construction compared with the three other countries, and the low exposition of Portuguese banks to the subprime market (Corkill 2014).

2.6. Spain

2.6.1. Evolutionary Frame of the State

The Spanish public administration was shaped by a historical legacy dating back to the Napoleonic invasion at the beginning of the nineteenth century. This fact allowed for hybridization between the incoming and innovative bureaucratic arrangements and the old feudal administration grounded in aristocracy (Crespo Gonzales and Albaladejo 2002). This initial shape is a crucial driver that has been protracted until now. The Spanish state gradually and incrementally adapted to different historical contexts and political climates over two centuries (Alba 2001).

This original imprinting shaped the change in the Spanish public administration before and after the authoritarian regime of Francisco Franco from the 1930s to the 1970s and the subsequent democratic transition. Scholars have delineated phases to demonstrate the different historical seasons of the administrative system; however, with the exception of specific periods, there is a common legacy underlying the changes and readjustments that sheds light on the slow and situational adaptation to contingencies (Alba and Navarro 2011).

2.6.2. Reforms' Trajectory

As a result, the overall picture is that of a moderate change in continuity. The Napoleonic arrangement gradually adjusted to the different political inputs according to the new needs and aims but did not lose its original bureaucratic approach (Nieto García 2014). In any case, different stages have influenced the evolutionary path of this conservative apparatus. Parrado (2008) classified three different modernizations that occurred in the agenda: the modernization importing the Planning, Programming, and Budgeting System from the United States before the democratic transition (until 1974,) the democratic modernization after the democratic transition at the end of the 1980s, and the José Luis Zapatero cabinet's modernization (2004–2011) oriented toward the dynamism fostering the productivity of the economy, the territorial devolution, and the NPM.

Other scholars, such as Arenilla Sáez (2017), have adopted a more in-depth scheme showing the detailed and fragmented agenda of reforms. He identified five incremental—and not totally coherent—phases after the democratic transition: from 1977 to 1985, from 1986 to 1995, from 1996 to 2003, from 2004 to 2011, and from 2012 to the present. This piecemeal and gradual process is strongly influenced by domestic politics and the national political climate, which influenced reforms according to contingencies. While the first step was only a preliminary attempt to reform the Spanish state according to the democratic transition, the second and third steps represented significant efforts toward modernization. In particular, three outstanding reports from 1990 to

1993 framed the political agenda. The reports included a diagnosis of the state of the art of Spanish public administration and identified the need for incisive modernization (the Plan de Modernisaciò of 1992) through a soft orientation toward efficiency and decentralization.

The third step is considered the real focus of administrative change in Spain. In 1997, the parliament enacted Ley de Organizaciòn y Funcionamento de la Administracion General del Estado (Law of Organization and Functioning of the General State Administration, LOFAGE) and the subsequent Ley de Gobierno (Government Law). Both provisions pushed for managerialization and updating of the old apparatus to align with the political climate of the incoming new millennium. LOFAGE can be interpreted as the main effort by the central government to promote a significant change away from incrementalism and the conservative attitudes that characterized the legacy of the public sector. The law modified the features of senior ministerial roles and restructured administrative roles in the central government's network of field-based ministerial service organizations (Barzelay and Gallego 2010). LOFAGE also addressed the courageous plan that aimed at moving the public administration away from bureaucracy and legalism. Intense lawmaking followed this reform and ruled on other specific provisions regarding public service, top managers, digital change, evaluation, procedural simplification, agencification, and public-private partnerships.

The fourth step reinforced the provisions adopted in the previous step oriented toward devolution to the seventeen regions—called *Comunidades autonomas* (particularly in favor of Catalunya)—and efficiency, simplification, and an orientation toward citizens. Until the economic crisis of 2008, the central government issued an intense and fragmented wave of microprovinces that promoted reforms in the field of autonomy in favor of local authorities, privatization, externalization, quality, and the role of human resources.

Finally, the fifth step addressed the fiscal crisis and provided measures under the umbrella of the austerity wave favoring retrenchment and downsizing of functions and funds and disfavoring local authorities and regions toward recentralization and budget cuts. Many provisions supported the rationalization of the public sector envisaged by the specific commission for public administration reform, which advised specific sets of measures to achieve efficiency in public expenditures and simplification.

This long sequence of reforms demonstrated the incremental path along which the Spanish public administration performed some isolated but politically relevant acts that opened limited seasons of reform in light of the contingent political climate and step-by-step innovation. Analogously, the evolutionary change included partial implementation and/or misfit implementation as well as partial outcomes and failures.

As documented by Torres and Pina (2004), the most significant NPM wave at the end of the 1990s showed how the Napoleonic and conservative Spanish public administration was not ready for exogenous shocks and only gradually internalized exogenous innovations. In other words, the innovative inputs toward modernization repeatedly clashed with the context and administrative culture of the state. Nevertheless, change was occasionally adopted by the central government and favored moderate modernization thanks to specific waves of innovation. The piecemeal legislation and overall orientation toward continuity shed light on the relevance of the original pattern and its capacity to survive across different historical trends.

2.6.3. State Policy Capacity in Steering Economic Development

Overall, the Spanish public sector preserves the main Napoleonic feature related to innovations: it is still centralistic despite strong devolution in favor of regions, it is still uniform despite its flexibility, and it is still bureaucratic despite the managerialization that affected public administration in recent decades. This fact means that neocentralism and decentralization, legalism and management, and innovation and inertia coexist and overlap. The overall result is partially contradictory, since public managers obtained power and partially replaced old bureaucrats, but at the same time they did not disappear. The creation of the regions did not push for innovative management approaches or renew human resources, since the organizational pattern was inherited from the ministries, while a relevant percentage of civil servants at the central level moved to the regions. As shown by Gallego and Barzelay (2010), the main attempt at innovation (e.g., the LOFAGE reform and the following waves of innovations) also faced contingent pressures from politics: the decisional agenda and implementation were both undermined by the fragmentation of the process, the influence of politics, and the resistance of bureaucrats. In fact, the central administration was duplicated. Additionally, Europeanization and quangoism were subjected to similar dynamics.

As argued by Alba and Navarro (2011, 798), path dependency in reforming public administration in Spain can be assumed to understand adaptation and innovation trends. They called for recurrent evidence about lack of outcomes (the reform machinery did not produce significant impacts), adaptation to new developments according to historical trends and the relevance of external conditions in promoting change (especially by the Europeanization of NPM agencies), decentralization as a source of change, target priorities as drivers of change (fiscal austerity, budget cutting, fighting corruption) in light of an emergency, and the relevance of promoting coalitions within the cabinets thanks to opinion leaders or experts.

The special corps continued to enjoy strategic positions within the politico-administrative machinery despite periods of change and strong pressure, indicating that the public administration changed only gradually in adjusting to the environment; it preserved some limits, such as the blurred divide between politics and managers, clientelism, legalism, and cultural resistance to innovation but also preserved its points of strength.

The subsequent policy capacity was partially influenced by slow and incremental adjustments to external pressure in light of strong path dependence and the historical self-esteem of the public sector in the country. This allowed the country to implement its economic development provisions while considering some territorial contractions that threatened overall performance. Some scholars have interpreted this as showing the resilience of the Spanish administration and particularly of local authorities who continued to do their jobs in hard times while adjusting to environmental pressures (Navarro and Pano 2018).

Finally, the policy capacity of the Spanish economy was generally restrained by the public sector in terms of power and influence on politics and the heavy resistance to economic innovation by a conservative culture (Barzelay and Gallego 2010). The welfare state was not pivotal in economic development, but as shown by Del Pino (2017), it was able to bring together fragmentation and performance in a sustainable way.

2.7. Driving Factors and Performance of Administrative Reforms in the Old Southern Fours: A Comparison

Southern European countries have been described as being under a common umbrella: they are post-Napoleonic states grounded in a fragmented arrangement and a legalistic culture that disfavors the development of economic and societal innovation through poor performance, weak policy capacity, and a policy style oriented more toward political control over the bureaucracy than sound proactive intervention. Scholars who have published on Southern European public administrations (Sotiropoulos 2004a, 2006; Kickert, 2007, 2011; Verney 2009; Barzelay and Gallego 2010; Ongaro 2010a, 2010b; Lampropoulou 2018) basically agree with this evidence and the discontinuity with regard to the other European bureaucracies.

More specifically, the debate has recently moved from the study of the structural and institutional conditions that affected this area of Europe toward the reciprocal influences between the state and society and between the state and the economy during so-called times of austerity. Here, we make some remarks about the change in the public administration–induced impact of fiscal consolidation programs on southern bureaucracies and the push for administrative reforms toward financial efficiency.

In other words, the fiscal crisis triggered the reactivation of administrative reform in these countries in light of austerity, and some studies have specifically examined the relationships between the state and the economy and between the state and society in terms of efficiency and effectiveness. Lampropoulou (2018, 17) in particular showed how fiscal measures triggered a readjustment of the Napoleonic pattern without an explicit and conscious change in the public sector and consequently how the Napoleonic arrangement has been a "critical mediating variable in the interplay between the external reform pressure and the endogenous administrative dynamics."

None of the four countries seriously considered a deep revision of the state organizational path and its capacity but continued incremental reform. Other scholars (Lippi and Tsekos 2018) have integrated this perspective by describing the different types of policy transfers of austerity measures among southern countries with regard to the different degrees of acceptance, refusal, assemblage, or passive penetration. These elements shed light on the recent trends of the public sectors in Southern Europe and on the relevance of reforms' trajectories and their capacity to modify the status quo.

Examining these aspects, two points are acknowledged. On the one hand, as argued by Lampropoulou (2018), the dynamics respond more to external pressure than to conscious involvement. These countries moved the public administration somewhere far from the original point but without a plan, and their approach was still mediated by the Napoleonic arrangement: new wine in old bottles. On the other hand, the trajectories differed considerably. Hence, we know that all four public administrations share a similar path dependence: bureaucratic legacy matters greatly and incisively influence the policy style and policy capacity of each state to shape and steer its economic development. However, apart from this commonality, the trajectories show different potentialities.

First, the countries experienced reform seasons in different ways despite being incisively determined by contingencies, prominently due to exogenous conditionality and not by endogenous domestic plans. In particular, the Italian case should be isolated from the others. While in Greece, Spain, and Portugal the modernization of the public administration managed a transition to democracy from an authoritarian regime, in Italy it arose from the crisis of the democratic system and the quest for a rescue of the state. Indeed, the Greek, Spanish, and Portuguese reforms started well before the Italian reform. They were more coherent and had different aims: initially they were oriented toward democratization and relegitimization of the public sector, and in the second stage they encapsulated issues related to a more explicit orientation toward efficiency and performance, Europeanization, and decentralization.

Portugal was the first mover, while the Greek case was more inertial. In contrast, the Italian process was more ambiguous, uninterrupted, and blended: decentralization, NPM, and Europeanization were included in piecemeal and incremental legislation that lasted almost thirty years, overlapping straight and oblique changes (Bolgherini and Lippi 2021). In other words, when reforms distinctively arose as separate attempts to change the public sector according to specific and discrete plans, they also seemed to be more effective.

As a result, the hybridization of the Napoleonic bureaucracy toward a neo-Weberian state seemed more performative. Portugal is a case in point, while the Spanish case was more fragmented and rhapsodic. Thus, some reforms were more uncertain and ambiguous and consequently weakened attempts to change policy in a way that was not necessarily similar to Central European approaches. While the Italian case was specifically incremental and related to political contingencies, the Portuguese and Spanish cases were more planned in advance and based on better polling and design. Finally, the Greek case was explicitly influenced by a contingency (i.e., austerity) and was oriented toward a restoration of capacity and performance, but it was an unconvincing and latecomer attempt to modernize the state.

Furthermore, all four countries claimed to bring an end to centralism by reforms, but these attempts failed or took a U-turn toward softer and more ambiguous arrangements. This change was particularly obvious in Italy, where decentralization remained at an ambiguous and contradictory middle point, while Greek decentralization was ephemeral and provisional (Hlepas 2010, 2012). In contrast, Spain experienced an intentional and conscious decentralization that provoked conflicts and ambiguities in intergovernmental relationships, especially because, according to the post-Napoleonic pattern of local government (Kuhlmann and Wollmann 2014), public service management and delivery are grounded at the local level. Nevertheless, as displayed by Navarro and Pano (2018), a specific reaction in terms of resilience and pride typified Spanish administrative performance in light of a consolidated tradition.

Portuguese centralism seemed more committed, but recentralization after austerity was similar to that in the other cases. In other words, in Portugal the swinging pendulum between decentralization and recentralization seemed less affected by contingencies and the political climate and the subsequent window of opportunities than in other countries, where changes demonstrably occurred opportunistically and were influenced by other factors, such as party politics, the fiscal crisis, and international pressures. This moved the center of gravity to the local authorities by downscaling responsibilities, partly a result of delivery without central coordination and a specific design. This change added a burden to local authorities and weakened their potential to steer and coordinate development policies apart from fragmented and local intervention.

In fact, in all four countries but more so where policymaking was shared among levels, policy capacity was undermined. The U-turn toward recentralization did not represent a distinct and significant driver when intergovernmental relations were nevertheless ambiguous or conflictual but did accentuate detrimental effects when relations were poor. In other words, recentralization per se did not enhance performance but did play a role in reinforcing path dependence, in which task allocation and administrative tradition were more consolidated.

As a third point, structural conditions must be considered. The case in point is provided by the widespread inequalities across the OSFs and the different economic development that has affected them. Disparities in economic structure and heterogeneity in administrative performance have sharply affected Italy and Spain. Greece equally suffered from irregular geography, while in Portugal this aspect seemed slightly milder. This structural path dependence has heavily undermined the policy capacity to reform the public administration and the policy capacity in each country. It is particularly visible and evident in Italy.

Examining the aforementioned aspects, we can gather some provisional comparative reasoning by examining the collected evidence of the administrative reforms in the OSFs, which are summarized in table 2.1.

Regarding Greece, it seems that this country has never been capable of definitively improving its state capacity. Obviously, the historical characteristics of its state that we have underscored above—fragmentation, politicization, and inertia—can easily explain this persistence. It was a very weak state and has remained so, incapable of addressing contemporary challenges.

Regarding Italy, the persistent divide between the north and south and the incremental and piecemeal stream of reforms nurtured fragmentation, overlapping, and conflicts in the allocation of tasks and responsibilities. State policy capacity steered the economy, but the new decentralized powers to regions and municipalities have been a factor of further administrative decline in southern Italy (Milio 2007).

Regarding Portugal, notwithstanding the persistence of the administrative legacy and of some patrimonialistic characteristics and the strong patronage system in the relationship between politicians and bureaucrats, something has happened. Obviously, better performance in terms of the quality of governance and regulation could be attributed to Portugal starting behind the others, but this assumption is disconfirmed by its good performance that has lasted since the mid-1990s. There could be factors endogenous to the country that are not necessarily linked to the public administration or the characteristics of the state. However, it appears that the combination of bureaucratic centralization and the capacity to design reforms coherent with the characteristics of the country and its administration could be seriously considered.

Regarding Spain, the state's performance decreased significantly during the first years of the new millennium but remained higher than in Italy and Greece. This fact is interpreted as being due to two inherited legacies: the role of the "special corps" of the bureaucracy and the attitude of the state to behave in a centralistic way notwithstanding the deep regionalized institutional arrangements. The fragmented and alternate recourse to administration in Spain did not undermine the stability of the Napoleonic state, indicating that Spain's performance is likely related more to the resilience of its institutions than to the schizophrenic oscillation of reforms.

2.8. Concluding Remarks: Similar Path Dependence, Similar Reforms, but Different Policy Capacities

It is true that different neo-Weberian states shared a common post-Napoleonic pattern and similar pathologies and experienced similar paths of reforms to improve their capacity to achieve different results. As shown, the impacts are

Table 2.1 Drivers of reforms and performance in the Old Southern Fours

Driving factors	Greece	Italy	Portugal	Spain
Most relevant structural conditions	High path dependence due to inequalities, clientelism, and underdevelopment	Strong geographical and economic divide in social capital, high political fragmentation, and prevalence of small to medium-size companies	Absence of significant divides among territories and institutions	Institutional and socioeconomic divides, gradual modernization induced by external pressure
Domestic agenda for administrative reforms	New legitimacy in the democratization process	Modernization	New legitimacy in the democratization process	New legitimacy in the democratization process
Reforms' trajectory	Hesitant, uncoordinated, and delayed sequence of provisions	Overlapping, layered, and uninterrupted sequence of oblique and straight changes	Distinct sequence of separate and deliberate innovations	Partially distinct and partially rhapsodic sequence of innovations
State's policy capacity	Weak, still affected by fragmentation, politicization, and inertia	Some improvement but jeopardized by persisting territorial divide, incrementalism, and intergovernmental conflicts	Significantly improved, enhanced by persisting and effective centralization	Very weak, with enhanced resilience favored by a legacy and limited incrementalism

differentiated, and the subsequent policy capacity was either empowered or weakened. In light of the available literature, some interpretations can be offered.

The first concern regards the strength of legacy. Path dependence is likely related to the strength of the bureaucratic pattern. Hence, the Portuguese and Spanish bureaucracies were influenced by outstanding legacies. The identity and self-esteem of both Napoleonic states allowed them to face challenges gradually and sometimes incoherently, but the core of the states' identity was jeopardized only superficially. This is not only a consequence of centralism, since Spain experienced a strong devolution, but also pertains to the path dependence of special corps, which did not allow for revolutionary improvement but safeguarded them from regression and confusion. This aspect perhaps allowed Spain and Portugal—especially the latter, since Spain must cope with threatening territorial contradictions—to limit the crisis of the state and the economy and to be supported by tradition.

In contrast, slow and gradual abandonment of the Napoleonic pattern could be interpreted as less detrimental than rapid abandonment (Greece) or incremental and schizophrenic oscillation (Italy). In both cases, the post-Napoleonic bureaucratic tradition was fragmented and weaker (and supported by very low self-esteem), and it receded lightheartedly and without a conscious design, influenced by contingencies. While Greece triggered an unforeseen and dubious pendulum between decentralization and centralization and toward NPM or austerity efficiency measures without serious commitment, Italy repeatedly triggered a similar confusing and layered pendulum by overlapping Europeanization, NPM, austerity measures, and decentralization. In other words, the uncertain, ambiguous, and overlapping commitment to reforms by Italy and Greece, especially the latter, impeded any learning and undermined performance by dismantling something without replacing it with something else.

The second concern regards the overall governance supporting policy capacity. Although all of the OSFs have shared task allocation among levels of government and conflictual intergovernmental relations, the resulting governance has varied substantially. On the one hand, Portugal and Spain in some way enacted coordinated governance to promote economic development, which is more visible in Portugal, where centralistic governance without strong territorial economic divides was still distinctive. On the other hand, Italy and Greece triggered an uncoordinated strategy swinging around the barycenter of decisions and producing confusion and overlap. Additionally, Spain contributed to the overlapping functions, and this approach seemed less influential and detrimental at the same time.

Some interpretive remarks can be deduced from this reasoning about governing effectiveness and regulatory quality. Portugal was less weighed down by territorial tensions and pendulums, allowing it to achieve coordinated governance and steer economic development more coherently with the resulting outcomes. Spain has had a similar impact, more effectively due to the aforementioned, not fatal contradictions. More contradictory and confused than Spain, Italy frantically assembled reforms and measures by overlapping them. Territorial governance was only partially coordinated, and policy capacity was subsequently undermined. Finally, Greece is the worst performer, since its commitment to reforms was fake and provisional, governance coordination was entirely driven by societal and political factors, and the state was not capable of enacting a credible strategy for supporting economic development.

Overall, the OSFs still share a common background that has severely weakened their policy capacity and distinguished them from the rest of Europe. Therefore, Mediterranean capitalism suffered from interventionist and uncoordinated state performance due to similar structural divides and the same pathologies. From this perspective, the OSFs still continue to perform differently with regard to the other varieties of capitalism. Structural and institutional path dependencies, together with exogenous and only partially committed reforms, have incisively undermined the overall policy capacity in coordinating economic development.

However, by examining this preliminary evidence and focusing more on our sample, significant variability can be detected in assessing regulatory quality and government effectiveness in favor of Iberian states. This administrative gap could represent a signal of the bifurcation of the dynamics of the Mediterranean family of capitalist countries and could provide an incentive to scholars to pay more attention to the differences inside this family rather than focusing on the differences between this family and other families.

The investigated variability calls for a deep analysis of the differences among the OSFs to grasp the extent to which the documented trend toward differentiation can be assumed to be definitive, with the Mediterranean pattern subjected toward a shift or, better, toward a significant divide. In this case, we can move to two interpretive hypotheses for further steps away from the collected (and limited) evidence.

On the one hand, we have two states (Portugal and Spain) that, in light of path dependence (perhaps to have been large colonialist states matters), gradually adjust to exogenous change and preserve some ability to respond to economic and societal pressures. On the other hand, we have two states (Greece and Italy) that lost their Napoleonic identity and increasingly shifted toward path-dependent intensification while sliding toward bad performance and a loss of capacity.

This observation is a matter of not only legacies but also political commitment and the capacity of reforms. Although all four countries missed an endogenous and voluntary reform strategy, some trajectories seemed more coherent and consequently more promising. Hence, we leave room for further analysis, since the four countries differentiated greatly: one case with a stated and effective trajectory (Portugal), one case with a less coherent and conflictual trajectory between the center and periphery (Spain), one case with an oscillating and never-ending trajectory (Italy), and one without any trajectory (Greece).

It is obviously difficult to generalize from these four national trajectories. They look very idiosyncratic and linked to national characteristics. However, there is the impression that the four trajectories can show how the historical characteristics of the bureaucracies, together with the way through which countries have dealt with their democratization processes, could make the difference and thus justify the variations in performance, in terms of state capacity improvements, between Portugal and Spain with respect to Italy and Greece. However, this is a potential explanatory hypothesis that would need further research.

Overall, the analysis of the differences in the paths followed helps us delimit the differences in the commonalities and push the reasoning a step forward toward deeper analysis of the destiny of the four states as well as their dividing in terms of varieties of capitalism.

Chapter 3

Which Level of Analysis?

Internal versus External Explanations of Eurozone Divergence

Sofia A. Pérez

Two decades after joining the Eurozone and on the eve of the COVID-19 crisis, the economies of Southern Europe all still bore the heavy mark of the debt crisis that engulfed the region following the world financial crisis of 2007–2009. Having experienced deeper and longer recessions than the countries of the Eurozone's northern core, they continued to suffer from higher public debt burdens than they had when the crisis began, and their labor market performance remained weak. Though most had returned to growth, their economic contractions (from 2010 on) were far larger and longer lasting than those experienced in the Eurozone's northern states. Unemployment rates remained high, in particular among the young, with large numbers of skilled young professionals emigrating and talk of a lost generation. Not surprisingly, almost all the countries of Southern Europe had also suffered crises of political legitimacy and rising polarization, often displaced onto other typically identitarian dimensions such as regional separatism and the rise of anti-immigrant parties. In this last regard, Southern Europe has not proven particularly different from the rest of Europe. Yet the economic scene in the Eurozone on the eve of the COVID-19 crisis remained that of a community divided between northern creditor states that had long recovered from the Great Recession and southern debtor states that remain financially vulnerable when not distressed.

Those who seek to explain this schism most often emphasize differences in domestic factors thought to set the southern states apart from their northern neighbors in the Eurozone. To really gauge the importance of such domestic factors, however, it is critical that we understand the ways in which monetary union itself contributed to the divergence. This chapter argues that we cannot understand the different economic performance of the two halves of the Eurozone by focusing solely on national differences. Instead, we must recognize that the economic performances of different areas of a currency union cannot be considered to be independent of each other. Once countries adopted a common currency, their economic performance became intimately related to each other. The most important source of this interdependence, I argue, involves the workings of cross-border financial markets, in particular that of interbank markets.

More specifically, this chapter argues that monetary union created a very particular set of incentives for banks in the Eurozone core to channel credit to the countries of the Eurozone periphery (those countries that prior to monetary union had faced higher external financing costs due to currency risk). The economies of Southern Europe were deeply affected by these financial flows and by their sudden reversal once the global financial crisis hit. The sudden stops that Southern Europe experience, however, were aggravated by the Eurozone's governance model, in particular the long delay before the European Central Bank (ECB) committed to intervening in sovereign debt markets and by the manner in which financial assistance was conditioned on fiscal austerity. These two decisions fed bond market panic and aggravated recessions in Southern Europe. At critical times, they also helped recoveries in the core countries in particular Germany, which became a safe haven for those who wanted to hold euro-denominated assets. In addition, the decisions resulted in a deep fragmentation of Eurozone credit and debt markets that lasted at least until the ECB initiated its own version of quantitative easing in 2015.

These financial market dynamics had important effects on the evolution of the "real" economies of Southern Europe. Yet they cannot be appreciated unless we shift the level of analysis from the national level to that of the Eurozone as a whole. Other chapters in this volume explore important differences between the countries of Southern Europe, challenging the notion that these countries share a distinct model of capitalism. Earlier attempts to integrate the experiences of Southern Europe (Ferrera 1996; Amable 2003) have sometimes resulted in a reification of the similarities observed at one point in time in what were different attempts at catch-up economic modernization in Southern Europe. Important differences in domestic institutions and sociopolitical trajectories were often left out (see Pérez and Rhodes 2015; Petmesidou and Guillén 2014; Guillén and Pavolini 2015), while similarities with the recent trajectories of other capitalist economies have sometimes been underappreciated (Regini 2014). Nevertheless, it is also important to recognize that with monetary union, the economies of Southern Europe jointly experienced a similar set of shocks, starting with the sharp rise in foreign demand for financial assets issued by their sovereigns and banks followed by two consecutive sudden stops in financial inflows. Any look at their labor market performance also suggests that they have had greater difficulty in recovering from the Great Recession than their richer neighbors to the north. As several analyses point out, they have also lost ground at a time when other states in the European Union (EU), notably the Visegràd countries, experienced substantial convergence in their living standards toward the EU average (Demertzis, Sapir, and Wolff 2019; Tokarski 2019).

Among those domestic factors that have received most attention as explanations for the divergent financial positions of southern and northern Eurozone states are labor market institutions, especially patterns of wage bargaining. Because such institutions shape the evolution of wages across different sectors, they are thought to represent a key aspect of the supply-side conditions under which firms operate. Recent scholarship has emphasized the role of economic demand in explaining both distributive outcomes and economic growth across countries, in particular whether growth has historically been based principally on internal or external demand. This growth-model literature typically identifies the economies of Southern Europe (as well as France) as countries in which growth is best achieved through domestic demand (Hall 2018; Baccaro and Pontusson 2019). Others have argued that the Eurozone's governance model, focused on fiscal constraints, placed countries whose institutions fit the export-led strategy at a distinct advantage over those whose institutions were geared toward domestic demand-led growth (Matthijs 2016).

My argument in this chapter is different. Rather than differences in domestic institutions, the principal factor that placed the economies of Southern Europe in such a weak position coming out of the Great Recession involved the way in which they were affected by cross-border market dynamics, specifically interbank markets, in the period leading up to 2008 and by the rapid unravelling of those flows twice, first in the immediate aftermath of the US financial crisis and a second time after the imposition of austerity measures across Europe in 2010. These financial flows were the result of the push factors (the strategies of foreign banks and institutional investors) rather than pull factors (such as the characteristics of wage bargaining or banking regulation in the south). The rush of cross-border lending to Southern Europe following monetary union had different macroeconomic consequences depending on whether countries joined the Eurozone with higher (Italy) or mounting (Portugal) public debt or with lower levels than the Eurozone benchmark of 60% of gross domestic product (GDP) (Ireland or Spain). In the first group, Eurozone rules required fiscal authorities to put on the fiscal breaks, often in quite procyclical fashion, even prior to 2008 when the economy stalled. In the latter group, monetary union set off a self-reinforcing and apparently virtuous circle of rising private credit and investment, fast GDP growth, falling public debt ratios, and rising growth expectations that further accelerated capital inflows. In all cases, however, the strong foreign demand for financial assets (loans or securities) issued in the periphery states biased credit flows toward those activities that could more readily be collateralized, typically construction and real estate.

Independently of whether periphery states experienced rapid growth or relative stagnation in the period up to 2008, financial inflows tended to produce lower aggregate productivity growth because they shifted credit supply to lower productivity sectors. After 2008, cross-border financial market dynamics had very similar effects all across the southern states. The sudden stop in debt markets left governments and private banks in dire straits, as foreign institutions pulled their lending to the private sector and, especially from 2010 on, dropped their holdings in peripheral Eurozone sovereign debt. Domestic banks across Southern Europe became the principal holders of their own government's sovereign debt, a situation that remained a source of financial fragility for banks on the eve of the COVID-19 crisis.

In the following sections I first offer a global view of how the four main southern states in the Eurozone fared following monetary union. I then juxtapose two types of explanations for the divergence between north and south: the first centering on labor costs and specifically wages, and the second involving financial flows. I show why the first is contradicted by much economic evidence and why financial flows offer a better explanation of Southern Europe's fate in the Eurozone. I explain why key metrics (such as nominal unit labor costs) are often a misleading indicator and why the common experience of rising external debt (such as all of Southern Europe saw during the run-up to 2008) cannot be attributed to current account deficits. Instead, this is better explained by incentives that monetary union created in cross-border financial markets. I then look at the particular experience of Italy. Finally, I explain why the financial dynamics described in this chapter are unlikely to have been the consequence of poor banking regulation and oversight in the states of Southern Europe.

3.1. Southern Europe under Monetary Union: Growing Apart and Falling Behind

One of the principal justifications for the introduction of the euro and for the participation of a broad spectrum of countries was the notion that monetary union would powerfully boost integration of financial markets and thereby drive convergence among participating countries (Blanchard and Giavazzi 2002). By the end of the currency's second decade, however, a number of institutional research centers were pointing out a worrisome development. The countries of Southern Europe appeared to be falling behind in their living standards rather than catching up with growth in the Eurozone's northern half. Divergence rather than convergence appeared to be taking place (see Demertzis et al. 2019; Tokarski 2019; Franks et al. 2018). This was particularly troublesome, as Southern European government had instituted important domestic reforms (in both labor and product markets) in accord with the recommendation of European institutions over the previous decade. The divergence in incomes between the northern and southern halves of the Eurozone that took place after 2010, moreover, contrasts with the experiences of the former Visegràd countries, which since the start of the twenty-first century have seen considerable convergence

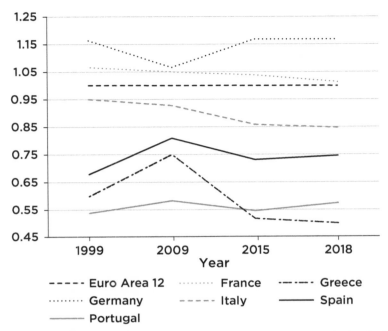

Figure 3.1. Real GDP per capita relative to euro area 12 average. Source: Author's calculations based on OECD, GDP per capita in US dollars. The euro area 12 average is set at 1.

toward the EU income average. The Central and Eastern European countries even outperformed European Commission growth forecasts for the period 2003–2017 (Demertzis et al. 2019). While this convergence of the Central and Eastern European countries had been expected (given their relatively recent economic transformations and their accession to the single market), the record of Southern Europe under the euro marks a departure from the not too distant past when these countries experienced rapid catch-up growth.

Figure 3.1 shows the evolution of GDP per capita in Southern Europe in relation to the average of the initial twelve Eurozone countries (the average is represented by the value 1). The figure shows that while France had converged toward the EU average, as required by convergence, and Germany's growth performance widened the gap in the Eurozone from 2010, the southern economies performed poorly. Italy's real GDP per capita declined almost continuously in relation to the average (itself rising in the period up to 2009), while Spain and Greece had experienced rapid growth followed by steep divergence. Spain, which performed best within the group, had converged only marginally by 2018 from where it stood in 1999. Greece's GDP per capita had fallen substantially relative to the original euro states, and Portugal, the poorer of the countries at the start, saw a virtual stagnation in its convergence process.

Table 3.1 Economic performance following monetary union

	Change in GDP				Public debt
	1999–2008	*2008–2010*	*2010–2013*	*2008–2019*	*1999*
Eurozone12	*0.19*	*–0.02*	*0*	*9*	
Netherlands	22	–2	0	11	58.60
Belgium	22	1	3	15	116.40
France	19	–1	3	11	60.50
Austria	23	–2	4	12	66.70
Germany	14	–2	5	14	60.10
Italy	11	–4	–4	–3	113.30
Greece	37(26)**	–10	–19	–23	104.9***
Spain	35	–4	–5	7	60.80
Portugal	13	–1	–7	5	55.40

Source: Eurostat. GDP is based on chain-linked figures at current prices with the year 2010 as the base. Employment Rate in Full Time Equivalents: Eurostat.

Figure 3.1 also shows that the divergence of the southern states away from the average, with the exception of Italy, is due to their economic evolution since 2009. In the period up to 2008, the growth performance of the southern states differed widely. While Spain and Greece (and of course Ireland, not shown) experienced strong growth in this period, Italy experienced a very short boom followed by bust in 2001 and thereafter relative stagnation. Portugal's record was similar to Italy's. Of course, France and Germany also experienced slow growth up to 2005, and their governments, as in the case of the Italian and Portuguese, remained in almost continuous breach of the Stability and Growth Pact's 3% deficit rule. But what Greece and Spain gained in the period up to the crisis they lost in the postcrisis period.

Table 3.1 summarizes some other important metrics, including overall economic growth in the period from 1999 to 2008 and in the period thereafter, the evolution of the public debt in the two periods, total employment (measured in full-time equivalents), and the evolution of the anchored poverty rate (using 60% of the median income in 2008 as the poverty threshold).[1]

The general pattern over the period does not mean that the countries of Southern Europe had a uniform experience after joining the Eurozone. Spain experienced strong growth and an important decline in its public debt (already one of the lowest in the Eurozone at the start) up to 2008 and then a very large rise in public debt from 2010 on. Italy's public debt continued to decline for a

as % GDP		Change in anchored poverty (2008–2018)	Employment rate in full-time equivalents	
2007	2019		2008	2018
50.50	62.50	−0.4	76.9	79.2
94.60	118*	−0.5	73.8	76.2
75.90	124.00	−0.6	69.9	71.3
69.00	88.90	−0.5	68	69.7
66.20	68.20	−3.1	74	79.9
110.20	154.60	3.9	62.9	63
112.80	200.20	26	66.3	59.5
42.30	117.30	5.8	68.5	67
80.50	136.30	−1.7	73.1	75.4

*The figure for Belgium is for 2018. ** The figure in parenthesis reflects growth from 2001 to 2008.
***The figure is for 2001, the year Greece joined the Eurozone.

number of years following monetary union but by 2008 stood at virtually the same level as it had in 1999. Portugal experienced a moderate rise in its public debt up to 2008 and thereafter a much more important rise. There were also important differences in employment growth up to the world financial crisis, with Spain experiencing spectacular growth in employment up to 2007 and a very large loss of jobs thereafter and with Greece and Portugal experiencing more modest employment gains up to 2008, followed by a large net loss thereafter. It is also important to point out that Greece's overall contraction in the period after the world financial crisis was more extreme than that of any other country. However, the very large net destruction of jobs in Spain since the crisis is also striking. Another contrast is that while the depth of the recession in 2010–2015 was far worse in Greece, Spain, and Portugal (in that order) than in Italy, the recession in Italy lasted much longer. Still, Italy also did not experience the overall level of net employment destruction in the post-2008 period that the other countries did. An earlier return to growth in Spain than in Italy came at the price of a much larger fall in employment (when measured in full time equivalents).

Looking beyond these differences, the most striking fact is that all of the southern states ultimately found themselves in a similar position when international credit markets seized up in late 2007. It would not be until the decisive change in the ECB's stance in 2012 that capital outflows were brought under control, and it would be at least another three years (up until the ECB's adoption of its own version of Quantitative Easing in 2015) that credit conditions in Southern Europe could improve and employment could begin to recover. As late as 2018, none of the southern states had recovered the level of GDP they had reached at the start of the crisis. And independently of whether they had started the crisis with low or high levels of public debt, all of the southern states had much higher public debt (in relation to GDP) than they had in 2010; this in spite of the states having carried out enormous fiscal consolidation measures (Pérez and Matsaganis 2018, 2019). As periodic spikes in Italian and Spanish bond spreads suggest, the southern states also remained vulnerable in world financial markets. The consequences of the euro crisis remained strongly palpable across Southern Europe.

The most common view of why all the southern member states of the Eurozone faced problems in bond markets after 2008 is that they had delayed domestic adjustment to a world of more competitive international trade markets and had used the reduction in interest rates to borrow heavily externally. The reason for this borrowing would have been the desire of domestic actors (governments and private borrowers) to maintain or raise domestic levels of consumption as well as excessive growth in wages. Both would have made firms in the periphery less competitive in international markets, producing the rise in the current account deficits that southern Eurozone states saw in the period up to 2008. In these accounts, the direction of causation runs from domestic excesses to the rise in current account deficits and foreign debt.

By definition, current account deficits have to be equaled by (net) capital inflows recorded in balance of payments statistics. Yet, as much scholarship on the behavior of financial markets points out, capital flows, in particular those in the form of cross-border lending and financial securities (bond) purchases by banks, tend to be driven by factors that are far more volatile than trade. Capital flows can hence drive current account developments rather than vice versa. In the following section I juxtapose the evidence on two different views, first focusing on the trade-, or "competitiveness-," centered view that attributes the rising external debt and current account deficits of southern euro states to the evolution of supply-side conditions in the debtor states. These include wage dynamics said to have undermined export competitiveness. A second domestic factor that has been emphasized by some scholars involves the characteristics of domestic financial systems and the way they were regulated across the Eurozone. Following this, I turn to an alternative explanation according to which divergence in current account deficits and in the external debt of both governments and private banks in Southern Europe was driven by the incentives that monetary union created for banks operating in cross-border markets and how these markets responded to macroeconomic decisions by European institutions and governments after 2010.

3.2. Labor Costs and Competitiveness: The Trade-Centric View of Divergence between Creditor and Debtor States

In the early days of the Eurozone debt crisis, it was common for international observers to identify fiscal excess in the debtor states as the primary problem behind the crisis (for instance, Buiter 2008; Schäuble 2011; Zahariadis 2013; Boltho and Carlin 2013, 389–91). The fact that the crisis began with the revelation of the hole in Greek government finance may help account for this. But the "fiscal incontinence" view could not be sustained once it became clear that some of the states among those with the lowest public debt ratios (Ireland and Spain) also faced trouble in world financial markets. The common denominator identified thereafter as the principal culprit was the deterioration in relative "competitiveness" (measured by the evolution of relative nominal unit costs) of the southern states vis-á-vis Germany and some of the other northern creditor states. The southern states, it was argued, had used external borrowing to maintain domestic demand, and this had resulted in excessive wage increases. Wage dynamics, in turn, had produced higher inflation rates in the debtor states. The loss of trade competitiveness this all implied for firms in the debtor states had remained hidden until the financial crisis, which had become the moment of reckoning for these excesses. This "competitiveness" argument was advanced not just by German economists (Zemanek, Belke, and Schnabl 2009; Belke and Dreger 2011; Sinn 2014) but also by the leadership of the ECB (Trichet 2011; Draghi 2014).

While "competitiveness" is commonly interpreted to describe the ability of firms to compete in international markets for goods and services, it is in practice measured in a very specific way by institutions such as the ECB, the EU Commission, and the International Monetary Fund (IMF). The most common measure is called the nominal unit labor cost (NULC), a ratio that is calculated based on aggregate macroeconomic statistics on GDP, inflation, and total employee compensation in an economy. A country's NULC is the ratio of the nominal labor compensation in the economy per persons employed (at current prices) to GDP per employed person in constant terms. This measure, NULC, appears as a key measure in the European Commission's scoreboard indicators for the macroeconomic imbalances procedure. And it diverged significantly over the first eight years following monetary union, with the NULC ratio of all Eurozone countries rising faster than those of Germany and the southern Eurozone economies plus Ireland, seeing the largest divergence.

Comparative political economists have also focused on this measure to explain the euro crisis and its aftermath. Some have sought to build on insights from the literature on corporatism and wage-setting institutions in Europe to explain the current account deficits and rising external debt of northern and southern member states. Wage-setting institutions in the southern countries have often been thought to produce higher wage growth and inflation because of lower levels of wage coordination or a lack of export-sector leadership

(Scharpf 2011, 2012; Hall 2012, 2014; Hancké 2013; Johnston, Hancké, and Pantf 2014; Höpner and Lutter 2018). Like the analyses of the ECB, this literature follows the assumption that the financial fragility of periphery states during the euro crisis was driven by developments in their "real" economy, in particular wage and trade dynamics.

Yet there are reasons to doubt this trade-centric account. It is important to understand that the NULC ratio emphasized by the ECB and the European Commission is only loosely related to the actual wage developments that are experienced by firms. The measure is particularly influenced by uneven growth across economic sectors, including uneven employment growth (or destruction). As Knibbe (2019) points out, an increase in the production of natural gas in the Netherlands automatically lowers Dutch unit labor costs, while an increase in construction employment raises them. Indeed, it is not unusual for the NULC ratio to rise or fall while actual wages are moving in the opposite direction. The evolution of GDP per worker is also influenced by sectoral growth patterns, with faster growth in lower-productivity sectors (usually services) producing a rise in NULC independent of any wage developments. Both GDP growth and inflation are also influenced by changing demand, which can be strongly influences by capital flows in particular in a currency zone (Blanchard 2007; Lane and Benetrix 2013; Reis 2013; Benigno and Fornaro 2014; Benigno, Converse, and Fornaro 2015).

The principal problem with the wage- and trade-centered interpretation of Southern Europe's problems is that it clashes with a great deal of evidence on actual wage and current account developments in the period leading up to the Eurozone debt crisis. There is much research that shows that the divergence of NULC in the Eurozone prior to 2010 had fairly little to do with real wage growth in the debtor states (as measured in labor cost surveys of firms). The principal factors were the large upward shift in productivity growth in German manufacturing tied to the reorganization of global value chains of that sector in the early 2000s, alongside a rather dramatic downward shift in wage growth (specifically in services and the public sector) in that period in addition to a divergence in inflation rates (Felipe and Kumar 2014; Gaulier and Vicard 2013; Pérez 2019). Real wage growth in Spain, Italy, and Portugal was in line with that in France, the Netherlands, Belgium, and Austria (Pérez 2021). Felipe and Kumar (2014) also show that "average" unit labor costs, which are more likely to reflect wage developments than nominal labor costs per unit of GDP, grew below productivity growth in all the southern states except for Greece. Gaulier and Vicard (2013), on the other hand, decompose the contribution of wages and prices (inflation) in different sectors, showing that wage growth in the debtor states was not the driver of different inflation rates. Taking a different approach, Gabrisch and Staehr (2014) test for causality in the evolution of relative NULC and current account positions in the Eurozone, showing that the latter drove the former rather than vice versa. And Chen, Milesi-Ferretti, and Tressel (2013) show that the principal contribution to the changing current account deficits of the Southern European states came not from labor costs or inflation but rather the evolution of the euro's nominal appreciation vis-á-vis other world currencies.

The idea that the financial fragility of the Southern European countries was a reflection of problems with trade competitiveness also clashes with other findings. Chen et al. (2013) show that monetary union coincided with three exogenous developments that disproportionally advantaged German exports and disadvantaged the export sectors of the Eurozone's southern states: the rise in oil prices, which hit Southern Europe manufacturers harder; the already noted integration of the Visegràd countries into European but particularly German production chains; and the rise in Chinese demand for German luxury goods (see also Kollman et al. 2015; Gros 2012). In spite of this, various authors point out that the export performance of the southern states compared to that of Eurozone creditor states was not worse. Gaulier and Vicard (2013) use input-output data to calculate the contribution of energy costs, the sectoral composition of exports, and demand in established exports markets for each Eurozone country in the period 1999–2007. They find that once the sectoral and geographic characteristics of exports are taken into account, the export performance of the four main southern Eurozone states was better than that of creditor states as a group. Indeed, Italy's export performance, given these factors, was not much different from Germany's and considerably better than that of the Netherlands. Spain's was better than Germany's, and Spain even managed to increase its share of world merchandise exports at a time when most almost all advanced economies lost ground to emerging market economies (OECD 2015; Eppinger et al. 2018). Gros (2012) also observes that the southern euro states did not reduce their share of exports within the EU.

All of these findings run counter to the widespread view that attributes the problems that Southern European states faced from 2009 in external financial markets to a matter of wage and trade dynamics.

3.3. The Financial Drivers of the Eurozone's Debt Imbalances and the Eurozone Debt Crisis

Accounts that emphasize labor costs generally view a country's trade account as the primary driver of external debt and liabilities. Labor costs rise because of either inflationary wage bargaining dynamics or fiscal policy, undermining exports and increasing consumption of imports. Capital flows adjust to "finance" trade deficits. This view, however, dismisses the possibility that financial markets have their own dynamics and that financial inflows, including cross-border loans and the purchase of financial securities by foreign residents (the two main types of flows that make up external debt), may happen for reasons that are quite independent of trade flows. It is a view of the world that takes an accounting identity (produced by the double-entry system whereby balance of payments statistics are obtained) and gives it a causal interpretation, one in which current account balances drive financial flows and in which financial institutions are simply barter institutions whose activity is limited by some predetermined quantity of "loanable funds."

Yet modern debt markets do not operate in this way (at the domestic level or the cross-border level), and cross-border lending and borrowing can respond to quite different incentives. Banks make money on financial transactions (for instance, originating loans that then create deposits at other banks). When banks face incentives to make money by lending to banks in other countries or to increase their purchases of financial assets (such as government debt or collateralized debt securities) issued in those countries, banks in those other countries have incentives to increase the type of lending that foreign banks seek as collateral. This in turn means that credit will flow to those sectors in which loans are considered relatively secure (foremost among these is real estate). In turn, credit feeds domestic demand. Such a process appears to have been powerfully at play in the Eurozone following monetary union.

Economists began to notice early on that monetary union set off a sharp rise in cross-border interbank flows to the Eurozone's periphery. Noting that both Greece and Portugal soon developed current account deficits after joining the Eurozone, Olivier Blanchard and Francesco Giavazzi, writing in 2001, explained that this was exactly what "can and should happen when countries become more closely linked in goods and financial markets" (2002, 148). Poorer countries in the Eurozone should run larger current account deficits, they explained, and richer countries should run larger current account surpluses so as to further convergence. The elimination of currency risk had simply removed an obstacle that had previously limited the benefits of financial integration and a larger financial market in Europe. Greece and Portugal thus were now simply open to "a much more liquid [interbank] market than the small domestic market in which [their banks] previously had to operate if they did not want to face currency risk" (173).

In the years that followed monetary union, capital flows to the Eurozone's south (as well as Ireland) did in fact balloon. And these capital flows principally occurred through interbank lending and securities purchases, including securitized debt issued by banks in the southern states (Lane and Milesi-Ferretti 2005; Milesi-Ferretti and Tille 2011; Hobza and Zeugner 2014). Interbank markets also became the primary way in which sovereign debt was allocated and traded following monetary union (Hale and Obstfeld 2016). Bank-led capital flows meant that the growth of cross-border debt assets and liabilities grew far more rapidly than direct foreign investment. This made those countries that were the ultimate target of the new foreign demand for financial assets much more than susceptible to a sudden reversal of capital flows, as debt markets are far more volatile than direct investment.

In the period leading up to the world financial crisis (between 2001 and 2007), cross-border claims between banks in the Eurozone tripled, reaching

Table 3.2 External debt liabilities as percentage of GDP

	1998	2002	2007	2012	2015	2018
Germany	76	117	136	147	124	115
France	67	109	172	186	156	193
Netherlands	124	207	290	377	361	339
Belgium	158	213	311	210	181	167
Austria	92	153	203	187	156	132
Spain	56	93	145	151	146	137
Italy	69	90	114	111	114	109
Portugal	91	160	203	223	191	167
Greece	50	99	144	239	239	230

Source: Lane 2013 (through 2007) and IMF International Investment Position Statistics based on the IMF's *Balance of Payments and International Investment Position Manual*, 6th ed. (2009), for the years after 2008. External debt liabilities include debt securities held by foreign residents and other debt liabilities for all domestic sectors.

500% of the area's GDP, a scale that far surpassed that of banks in the United States and Japan (Lane 2013, 7–8; Emter, Schmitz, and Tirpak 2018). The intensity of interbank flows also surpassed that of flows to emerging markets during the decade (Spiegel 2009). As table 3.2 shows, between 1998 and 2007 the foreign liabilities of all Eurozone countries rose dramatically (by either twofold or threefold in most cases). This was true of both core Eurozone states (often referred to as creditors) and Southern European debtor states. The rise in liabilities took principally the form of debt (bank loans and foreign purchases of financial securities, or bonds). The gross foreign liabilities of some creditor states (in particular Germany and Belgium) in fact saw larger increases than most of the states in Southern Europe in relation to their GDP. However, Lane (2013) shows that interbank claims within the Eurozone were dominated by claims of banks in the Eurozone core on banks in the euro periphery. The sectors to which these funds flowed in the latter (the ultimate borrower) varied among countries. In Italy and Greece, about half went into foreign holdings of public-sector debt (reflecting a large rise in interbank purchases of Italian and Greek sovereign debt by foreign banks), while the other half funded credit to the private sector (Lane 2013, 42). In the case of Ireland, it was overwhelmingly households that were the end borrowers, while in Spain most flowed to nonfinancial corporations.

Other authors have pointed out that this explosion of interbank lending and borrowing in the Eurozone appears to have had little to do with trade flows. Hobza and Zeugner (2014) show that the correlation between trade flows and financial flows unraveled following monetary union. And other findings also suggest that increased interbank loans to the Eurozone periphery were not a response to developments in the "real" sectors of economies but instead were driven by their own dynamics. Hale and Obstfeld (2016) show that banks in the Eurozone core economies became heavily engaged in a form of carry trade in the period up to the financial crisis. They borrowed in international wholesale markets at almost a one-to-one ratio in order to increase their lending to the Eurozone's periphery as the financial crisis neared to the point that it became a central piece of their business model.

It is important to understand that this type of carry trade was incentivized by monetary union itself. Monetary union forced the convergence of interest rates (one of the Maastricht convergence criteria) from 1995 on and eliminated currency risk altogether (Kalemli-Ozcan, Papaioannou, and Peydró 2010), thereby lowering the cost of finance in relation to the return on investments in the poorer countries without doing so in the core states. From a regulatory standpoint, interbank markets were already integrated in Europe, yet this was boosted by further financial services directives instituted by the EU in 2000–2003 intended precisely to boost the wholesale market in interbank funding. Monetary union also put core Eurozone banks in a position to profit from channeling funds from world financial centers to the Eurozone periphery because it lowered their transaction costs in lending to the periphery by a larger margin than it did for banks outside the Eurozone (Coeurdacier and Martin 2009; Spiegel 2009). The amount of lending directed to Southern Europe during the run-up to 2008 thus was not a simple function of a savings surplus in Germany, France, or Belgium.

The size of the cross-border flows from the Eurozone core to the periphery was bound to have important consequences. Lane and McQuade (2013) show that interbank flows explain the degree of credit growth in Eurozone countries. And as Blanchard et al. (2015) eventually noted, in a monetary union in which there is no direct exchange rate appreciation as a result of large capital inflows, such inflows were bound to have macroeconomic and structural effects. Contrary to the orthodox view that financial integration always improves the allocation of capital across economies, there was evidence that large bank-led flows tend to reduce productivity growth in the receiving economy because such flows are directed toward sheltered sectors such as real estate: the sector that offers the best collateral (mortgages, land, and real estate) and thus was also considered safer by regulators. Yet, because the real estate and construction sectors are characterized by lower absolute levels of labor productivity than manufacturing, faster employment growth in these sectors also implies lower productivity growth in the aggregate. This in turn shows up as a rise in NULCs, an effect that had already been observed in emerging markets prior to the euro crisis (Benigno and Fornaro 2014; Kalantzis 2015).

Cross-border debt markets also proved critical in dictating events during the Eurozone crisis. Banks in the Eurozone's core (and the United Kingdom) were exposed to the U.S. market in securitized debt and could no longer raise funding in those markets during the financial crisis. Thus, they had to pull back their lending to the Eurozone periphery. Following the Eurozone debt crisis much attention was paid to the fact that sudden stops are not driven by the size of a country's net financial assets or liabilities (the difference between assets and liabilities of all national residents, including the government), bound to equal the current account deficit in balance of payments statistics. Instead, what sets off a crisis is usually a slowing of new lending to refinance debt that comes due, and what determines whether the slowdown becomes self-accelerating is the size of gross financial flows (the sum of outflows by nonresidents and inflows by residents) (Milesi-Ferretti and Tille 2011; Borio and Disyatat 2015; Brunnermeier et al. 2012; Broner et al. 2013).[2] The financial assets and liabilities that domestic banks, households, and nonfinancial corporations hold at home and abroad all have different maturities and accrue to different entities within those sectors. Thus, even if domestic actors can in theory repatriate funds from abroad as foreign banks stop extending credit, financial institutions and businesses face serious liquidity problems when gross financial flows rise. Gross capital flows are far more volatile than net flows and spiked at numerous times between 2007 and the first quarter of 2015 for many countries in Southern Europe, reaching several times the size of their current account deficits not just in 2008 but also in the period 2010–2013 and at other points thereafter (Claeys et al. 2017).

Gross capital flows are also particularly sensitive to fiscal and monetary policy signals (see Schmidt and Zwick 2015), and this helps explain the evolution of the Eurozone crisis. Although Southern Europe saw a first sudden stop in 2008, the far more serious sudden stop, turning to outright capital flight, began in 2010 following the turn to fiscal austerity across Europe at the time of the decisions on the first Greek bailout. In between those two points in time, the retreat of lending to Southern Europe had been stabilized by the action of the Federal Reserve and the G20, which reached an agreement in 2009 to engage in some coordinated fiscal stimulus.

As Schelkle (2017) has pointed out, the type of self-accelerating retreat of lending that Europe experienced from 2010 on is a phenomenon that had in the past been associated with emerging market economies and in countries whose currencies lack sufficient standing among investors to allow monetary authorities to prevent a collapse of the currency in which foreign debt is denominated. In the case of the Eurozone, the first thing that proved critical was the stance taken by the ECB, which did not clarify that it would step in as a lender of last resort until mid-2012. Bondholders were taken by surprise by this stance because it stood in sharp contrast to the responses of other monetary authorities including the US Federal Reserve, the Bank of Japan, and even the Bank of England, all of which were engaging in some form of quantitative easing by 2009, and were also accompanied by assertive fiscal stimulus. The second factor was the turn to austerity in 2010 that led to bond market contagion from Greece to Ireland and on to Portugal in 2010 and from there to Spain and Italy, the two countries considered to be too large to bail. Milder forms of such fiscal stimulus were also attempted by Eurozone countries, such as Spain. In each case, the package imposed on one country led to bond market speculation about the situation of the next.[3]

Constancio (2012) has shown that the rise in the interest rate spreads of the sovereign debt of Italy and Spain during this period (2010–2012) went far beyond what would have been expected from the economic fundamentals and credit ratings of banks and sovereigns at the time when the crisis spread to these countries. The threat that the bond market contagion would go too far in the case of the two larger economies was in fact what prompted the ECB to change its stance, first in 2011 with the extension of its long-term refinancing operations to banks at the end of that year and subsequently in July 2012 with Mario Draghi's announcement that the central bank stood ready to engage in outright monetary transactions. This was effective in calming bond markets. But it left credit and sovereign debt markets in the Eurozone highly fragmented, with banks across the southern states becoming saddled with disproportionate holdings of their sovereigns (a phenomenon that came to be known as the "diabolic loop," as it threatened the creditworthiness of both banks and sovereigns). The problems that this created for the transmission of monetary policy ultimately led the ECB to start its own version of quantitative easing in 2015. By then, however, the Great Recession had dragged on across Southern Europe, with a steep cost in employment destruction and poverty creation from which none of the states of Southern Europe had fully recovered on the eve of the COVID-19 crisis.

3.4. Were Differences in Financial Regulation to Blame for the Fate of Southern Europe?

So far this chapter has argued that the financial dynamics set off by monetary union and the macroeconomic response of European authorities in the face of the Eurozone debt crisis offer a more convincing explanation for Southern Europe's financial fragility after 2008 than do labor costs and current account deficits. There remains, however, another alternative explanation, or other factors, that has been emphasized by some scholars. This involves the governance of financial institutions and failures in regulatory oversight (Quaglia and Royo 2015; Howarth and Quaglia 2015).

The world financial crisis certainly exposed an absence of oversight of the cross-border activity of large European banks. The realization of the extent of exposure for banks in the Eurozone core economies to the US subprime market and the systemic risks this created in the Eurozone led the ECB to prompt the creation of the European Systemic Risk Board in 2010 (Quaglia 2013; McPhilemy 2014).[4] The lack of cooperation among national regulators who sought to shift the losses of distressed banks with cross-border exposures from one national jurisdiction to another became the prime motivation for creation of the single supervisory mechanism at the end of 2015, under which all Eurozone banks are now either directly or indirectly supervised by the ECB. But were there differences in the quality of banking regulation between Southern and Northern Europe that can explain why the banking crises in Southern Europe were ultimately so much costlier?

The flows of funds from banks in the Eurozone core to the euro periphery in the run-up to 2008 was clearly central to Southern Europe's financial vulnerability. It was the halt in those flows in 2008 and more seriously so from 2010 onward that put the southern states in such a vulnerable position. But could those financial flows and the lending patterns to which they contributed also have been due to laxer financial supervision and prudential regulation in Southern Europe?

Table 3.3 summarizes the dimensions of banking crises in the Eurozone in terms of the state aid that governments had to use to rescue their banking sectors and offers several insights. First, with the exception of Ireland, the countries in which banks were hit hardest at first were the major creditor states of the Eurozone, not the debtor states. The crisis in the creditor states was concentrated in from 2008 to 2010, whereas it was only after the Greek crisis broke out in 2009 that major banking losses began to be experienced in Southern Europe. Second, in some of the southern states the overall cost of the banking crises through 2014 was not larger (as a proportion of GDP) than in the creditor states. Ireland and Greece were the exceptions. The Belgian banking crisis required state aid that was higher in terms of GDP than was the case for Italy, Spain, or Portugal, and the share of GDP expended in Spain was not substantially larger than it was in the Netherlands. Italy's banking crisis was one of the smallest in relation to GDP (at least prior to 2015). The fact that losses in the south were concentrated in the period from 2010 on also suggests that the evolution of banking losses in those countries was closely related to the turn to fiscal austerity and its effect in deepening the crisis in the debtor states.

Given that the banking crises of Southern Europe were so intimately linked to macroeconomic variables, it is also important to find measures of the quality of banking oversight that were taken independently of the eventual outcome of the crisis. Any banking crisis in hindsight can be interpreted as a failure of banking oversight. Yet doing so is potentially misleading, as we know that banking crises are often the result of unpredictable economic shocks (Demirgüç-Kunt and Detragiache 1998). In the case of the Eurozone, bank regulators in the southern states could not have known the extent to which banks in the Eurozone's core had leveraged their lending to the periphery in international financial markets and how exposed they had become to those markets. Yet, both factors clearly influenced how quickly those core banks had to unravel their lending to Southern Europe in 2008.

Data on the characteristics of bank regulation and oversight can be divided into two types: information about formal banking regulations (such as reporting

Table 3.3 Dimension of banking crises in Eurozone countries (2008–2014)

Member state	Used state aid totals in euros (billions)							Total, 2008–2014	Total 2008–14 as ratio to 2014 GDP
	2008	2009	2010	2011	2012	2013	2014		
Belgium	23.359	58.014	32.780	26.418	57.917	41.570	37.590	89.447	0.223
Denmark	146.086	16.462	24.956	23.240	1.162	1.083	0.157	158.066	0.596
Germany	52.040	192.750	188.426	38.365	11.374	3.041	2.000	283.923	0.097
Ireland	180.250	295.250	234.122	127.085	84.211	38.070	10.641	350.537	1.815
Greece	0.473	9.528	33.583	65.525	95.989	53.660	62.200	110.047	0.618
Spain	2.331	56.744	87.145	83.743	141.395	60.430	11.069	186.042	0.179
France	21.865	103.181	91.528	71.759	55.948	46.900	36.137	118.976	0.056
Italy	0.000	4.050	0.000	10.900	87.679	83.579	21.995	93.629	0.058
Cyprus	0.000	0.557	2.817	2.826	4.050	1.000	2.500	6.126	0.349
Luxembourg	2.944	1.882	1.563	1.271	1.979	3.810	0.657	6.503	0.132
Hungary	0.000	2.676	0.001	0.006	0.000	0.000	0.000	2.681	0.026
Netherlands	28.107	71.400	53.625	36.924	23.112	20.310	4.650	99.317	0.150
Austria	3.325	21.743	19.916	17.121	13.893	4.128	4.750	31.679	0.096
Portugal	2.242	8.970	11.896	11.021	23.525	15.513	8.399	36.258	0.209
Slovenia	0.000	1.000	2.150	1.804	0.683	2.547	2.448	5.988	0.160
Sweden	0.538	14.790	19.921	14.020	4.447	1.326	0.098	20.701	0.048
United Kingdom	82.985	215.213	203.809	151.660	54.598	39.090	38.048	332.074	0.147

Source: European Commission Competition Directorate, State Aid Scoreboard 2014, Aid in the Context of the Financial and Economic Crisis; table as it appears in Pérez (2017).

and public disclosure requirements and the independence and powers of bank supervisors) and independent assessments of how rules were implemented.

The most comprehensive source on de jure rules are the surveys carried out, coordinated with the World Bank, by Barth, Caprio, and Levine (2013). For information on actual supervisory practices, the best comparative source are the IMF's Financial Stability Assessment Reports (FSAPs). A coding of these reports, together with an index of the quality of supervisory governance calculated by Masciandaro, Verga Pansini, and Quintyn (2013), is summarized in table 3.A (see supplementary table 3.A at https://hdl.handle.net/1813 /103526). The table shows a count of the times each country was found to have failed to comply with Basel II standards by the IMF in the last FSAP prior to 2008 as well as the grades received on two core principles considered particularly important in shaping the behavior of banks in the period up to 2008: the disclosure of supervisors and the public and the quality of host-home monitoring between supervisors covering cross-border banks.

Finally, the table includes the overall governance scores calculated by Masciandaro et al. (2013), as some have suggested that there was a serious problem of regulatory capture in both the United States and the Eurozone (Buiter 2008; Claessens and Kodres 2014; Monnet, Pagliari, and Vallée 2014).

These metrics allow us to make several observations. First, there were significant differences in the extent to which countries complied with the Basel II principles in the period leading up to the 2008 crisis. Among the countries with banking losses concentrated in the first two years of the crisis, Germany and Austria were falling particularly short, failing compliance on seven principles.[5] By contrast, the countries of the Eurozone's periphery (Ireland, Portugal, Spain, and Italy) were all highly compliant. Italy failed on one single principle (legal protection for supervisors) and received the highest rating of "Compliant" on all others. The principal contrast among Eurozone countries appears to have involved the supervision of "connected lending" (lending to institutions connected by cross-ownership) and investment and lending risk assessment procedures in these two countries. Germany also scored badly on principle 24 (coordination with other supervisors whose institutions operated in Germany), and on the quality of supervisory governance calculated by Masciandaro et al. (2013) Germany attained the lowest rating on this index, followed by France. All others scored were considerably higher. Finally, Germany also stands out on the measures produced by Barth et al. (2013) for 2007. It had the second-lowest rating on the index of supervisory powers, with only Italy having a lower rating on this index. Belgium and the Netherlands, on the other hand, had the lowest rating on rules that restrict banks' activities. All in all, the countries of the Eurozone's periphery had scores that either equaled or bettered those of the creditor states.

The absence of a clear relationship between the dimensions of banking crises across the Eurozone and any of the measures of the quality of supervision is striking. But it is also telling. As a group, the countries of the Eurozone periphery were deemed to be highly compliant with Basel principles almost without exception. Eurozone's periphery banks had also not become significantly exposed to the US subprime market (although Irish banks relied heavily on the sale of their own bonds to UK and US banks and where hit hard when the transatlantic interbank market seized up in 2008). By contrast, Eurozone core country banks—in particular German banks, followed by French—were significantly invested in US mortgage derivatives. It is possible that Germany's lack of full compliance with numerous core principles contributed to this outcome and that Germany's and France's scores on the Masciandaro et al. (2013) index also captured this. The data on the quality of bank regulation and oversight, in any case, would not have led us to expect the size of the losses that banks in Southern European would ultimately take.

This counterintuitive finding, can, however, be explained when we consider the direction of cross-border financial flows within the Eurozone prior to the crisis coupled with the reversal of those flows when countries in the core of the Eurozone pulled back. The finding is also consistent with others that show that financial outflows from the United States reversed with the adoption of the fiscal stimulus package in that country (accommodated, of course, by the Federal Reserve) and that the crisis of many banks in Southern Europe occurred as a result of the sudden turn to fiscal austerity in mid-2010 (Lane 2013).

3.5. The Italian Experience in Context

The foregoing sections have argued that the dynamics of cross-border financial markets, in particular bank-led flows, were the principal common factor that explains why all countries of Southern Europe faced financial distress following the world financial crisis. The reversal of capital flows, coupled with highly procyclical austerity measures that accentuated problems in the banking sector, in turn explain why the economic recessions in Southern Europe were so much deeper and longer than in the Eurozone's core states. The divergence that we see in the Eurozone by 2018 is thus the result of a sequence of events that in both cases was driven principally by cross-national financial flows. Even in countries that managed to return to growth in the period since 2015, the economic contraction had been so large that they had barely recovered the GDP per capita levels prior to the crisis.

Nevertheless, it can be argued that the experience of Italy appears distinct from that of other southern states in that the country experienced lower overall growth even during the heyday of credit flows to Southern Europe. Italy's recovery from the recession was also particularly slow in coming. This contrast deserves to be addressed. How can it be that Italy's growth performance was so weak at a time when core Eurozone banks were buying large amounts of

Italian debt securities? And why do we not see improvement in Italy's productivity growth?

No analysis of the evolution of an economy as large and complex as that of Italy can, of course, be reduced to a single factor. Nonetheless, it is worth focusing on those factors that have impinged on domestic demand levels in Italy since 1990. One aspect that has received particular attention in this regard is the evolution of private investment in Italy. Recent European Commission reports (European Commission 2017a; Briguglio et al. 2019) that limited fiscal space, lack of access to finance by smaller Italian firms, and low growth expectations were the principal obstacle to a revival of private investment. While the reports note other factors that impinge on private investment, this represents an implicit acknowledgment that Italy's economy has been caught in a vicious circle. Recent research shows that weak demand has been a major driver of this productivity slowdown because companies react to it by reducing investment. Low demand has also been linked to lower technology adoption and productivity growth within firms, a relationship for which there is increasing cross-national evidence (Anzoategui et al. 2016; Remes, Mischke, and Krishnan 2018).

A key cause of low domestic demand in Italy and hence low incentives for productivity-enhancing investment (outside of the export-oriented manufacturing sector) has surely been the long stretch of time in which Italian governments have been unable to engage in countercyclical demand management during economic. This points to the role of the Eurozone's governance rules, which have dictated fiscal retrenchment during fiscal downturns as soon as slower GDP growth is reflected in the GDP to debt ratio. The clear contrast here is to Spain, which joined the Eurozone with a low public debt (achieved through earlier fiscal adjustment programs that came at a heavy cost in prior decades) so that the Stability and Growth Pact constraint never kicked in during the run-up to 2008.

One objection to the argument that there is a relationship between Eurozone rules and the performance of Italy's economy is that the productivity slowdown in Italy can be traced back to the mid-1990s. Yet indeed, the restrictive turn in fiscal policy in Italy (as well as other Eurozone states) can be traced precisely to this period. The efforts of Italian governments to reduce the high public debt (accumulated principally during the years just prior to the 1992 political and economic crisis) began with the technocratic Giuliano Amato and Carlo Azeglio Ciampi governments (following the 1992 Exchange Rate Mechanism crisis). Fiscal consolidation, often during downturns, has thus been a virtually permanent feature of Italian policy for almost three decades.

However, it is also important to note that while fiscal policy put downward pressure on domestic demand (counteracting the effects of bank flows on overall growth), the Italian economy was not immune to the effects that these flows had on sectoral patterns of bank lending. In the period between 1999 and 2007 but in particular after 2004, banks in Italy expanded their credit considerably, particularly to households. Italy also experienced a substantial rise in real estate prices over this period, with the principal indicator (the residential property prices index) rising by almost 40% between 1999 and mid-2007. This was less than half the percentage rise in the same index for (by 96%) over the same period. Yet the fall in housing prices in Italy starting in 2007 was commensurate with the sudden stop in credit flows, and in mid-2019 the index remained just below the level it had stood at in early 1999. As in other states in Southern Europe, the rise in interbank lending to Italy prior to 2008 thus appears to have affected patterns of lending in Italy, with more flowing to households and invested in real estate development.

It is also notable that, while EU Commission reports on Italy consistently refer to a misallocation of credit by banks following monetary union to explain low productivity growth and, more recently, to a lack of access to credit by small firms as a reason for low levels of investment (Briguglio et al. 2019), they do so without referring to the Eurozone-wide dynamics described above. On the other hand, Manaresi and Pierri (2018) estimate that the credit contraction in Italy from 2007 to 2009 may have accounted for a quarter of the contraction in total factor productivity growth in that period because of its negative impact on productivity enhancing investments. By the same token, labor market reforms that put downward pressure on wages, and with it domestic demand, can also have negative consequences on productivity growth by limiting the growth prospects of firms (Antenucci, Deleidi, and Paternesi Meloni 2019; Girardi and Pariboni 2020).

3.6. Conclusion

This chapter has argued that the divergence between the Eurozone's north and south cannot be understood in terms of domestic factors alone. Divergence has also been driven by the combination of monetary union and the functioning of cross-border financial markets, both in the period leading up to the Great Recession and in the period thereafter. Monetary union resulted in an enormous rise in lending and securities purchases by banks in the Eurozone's core of financial assets issued in the Eurozone's periphery up to 2008. From 2008 on, Eurozone governance—in particular the failure of the ECB to clarify its stance as lender of last resort coupled with the adoption of procyclical austerity measures—subjected Southern Europe to repeated sudden stops in lending and the fragmentation of interbank markets. This left governments in Southern Europe having to address the consequences for their domestic financial institutions and these in turn having to take on greater holdings of sovereign debt.

It is these financial dynamics, I suggest, that best explain the long and acute character of recessions in Southern Europe and, ultimately, the divergence between the southern and northern states from 2010 on. Europe's response to the crisis largely ignored the central role of interbank markets in the rise of Southern Europe's gross external debt up to 2009 and the asymmetric ways in which capital flows affected southern states and core states from 2010 on. The initial delay in the ECB's response, and the reaction of sovereign debt markets to austerity in 2010 spread and expanded the financial crisis and raised its social and economic costs across Southern Europe. In some cases, it also vastly expanded public debt levels, further complicating Eurozone reform.

This is not to say that there were no differences among the southern states. Indeed, in the period up to 2008, the macroeconomic effects of capital flows were significantly mediated by the level of public debt with which states had joined the Eurozone. In countries that had joined with a high level (Italy) or a rising level (Portugal) of public debt, fiscal policy was constrained by the Stability and Growth Pact. These governments were hence compelled to take procyclical fiscal measures even prior to the Eurozone crisis. Countries that had joined the Eurozone with a particularly low level of public debt (such as Spain or Ireland) faced no such constraint prior to 2008. Instead, they experienced a seemingly virtuous cycle of falling public debt and rapid growth. However, in all the southern states, bank-led financial inflows skewed credit flows toward sectors characterized by lower labor productivity levels such as real estate. Once the cross-Atlantic financial crisis broke out in 2008, the pattern of capital flows unraveled. Banks in the Eurozone core first stopped their lending to the southern Eurozone as credit markets seized up. Yet, even after the U.S. Federal Reserve came to the rescue, the ECB's slow response contributed to the flight to safety to the creditor states (in particular Germany). This reversal of financial flows was heavily aggravated by the turn to fiscal austerity in 2010, which produced a second, far more serious sudden stop in capital flows to Southern Europe and contagion in sovereign debt markets.

On the eve of the COVID-19 crisis, many of these tensions remained unresolved. While there had been big advances in the regulation of cross-border risk-exposure and supervision of banks by the ECB, the effort to create a true banking union remained incomplete. Risk-sharing mechanisms such as joint deposit insurance and, more critically, agreement on the issuance of some form of jointly backed financial instrument that could serve as a safe-asset on banks' balance sheets had yet to be reached. Despite its heavy costs, the COVID-19 crisis has allowed for some important breakthroughs by bringing a clearer sense of interdependence. It remains to be seen, however, how far the experience of the new crisis will go in shedding light on the recent past.

Notes

1. Because with a large economic contraction median income also falls, the anchored poverty rate offers a better measure of social dislocation than poverty based on a moving threshold. For further discussion, see Pérez and Matsaganis (2018).

2. Both nonresidents and residents are mostly banks.

3. Bond market volatility increased when the ECB raised its key interest rates two months later (July 13, 2011) at a time when both the United States and the Japanese monetary authorities had moved aggressively to quantitative easing.

4. The European Systemic Risk Board was created to gauge systemic risks and make recommendations for macroprudential regulation.

5. These included measures of the supervisors' independence, legal protections, guidelines on assessing investment risk, market risk, and connected lending. Other core Eurozone states did better, with France and Belgium failing only on three principles and the Netherlands failing only on two. The measure is not available for the Netherlands because the only precrisis report (2005) did not include explicit ratings, and the country was working on a major overhaul of banking regulation during that time.

Chapter 4

Following Different Paths of Modernization

The Changing Sociocultural Basis of Southern Europe

Emmanuele Pavolini and Gemma Scalise

4.1. The Sociocultural Roots of Mediterranean Capitalism: Toward a Process of Internal Divergence?

Comparative political economy provides an insightful framework for understanding the mutual influence among economic, social, and political arenas and their regulation in different institutional contexts. In particular, the debate on the varieties of capitalism (VoC) that has been ongoing since the 1980s has focused on the different institutional forms of advanced economies and has highlighted the existence of various models used to regulate economic activities. In an effort to explain these differences, research has mostly focused on the institutional and political structures that have historically arisen in different countries (Albert 1991; Hall and Soskice 2001; Amable 2003; Bohle and Greskovitz 2012). Most of these analyses aim to explain the interplay between several institutions, the labor market, and economic development and usually focus on sociopolitical institutions used to regulate the economy, with sociocultural institutions receiving much less attention. However, the role of sociocultural variables in explaining differences among political economies is critical, as these variables determine how values and social networks influence the path of economic growth and institutional change.

As Bruff (2008) argues, in the VoC literature culture tends to be conflated with institutional norms and conventions. However, culture is much more than a set of shared understandings (Hall and Soskice 2001); indeed, culture shapes capitalism. Capitalist development is deeply interwoven with how people organize even the most personal aspects of their social lives (Streeck 2012). Value orientations and collective beliefs shape behaviors, identities, and attitudes, all of which influence and legitimize political actions and economic organization.

This work complements other chapters in the present volume on economic outcomes and institutions by focusing on how sociocultural attitudes and values ultimately affect institutions. We find support for insights gained by previous approaches to developmental and comparative political economic studies by examining the role played by sociocultural and structural elements—such as social values and core social networks (beginning with families)—and assess whether Southern European countries show relative homogeneity in this respect or are (increasingly compared to the past) different among each other.

As the chapter demonstrates, the sociocultural setting influences both the supply of and demand for policies in key institutional arenas in the VoC approach, and the evolution of social attitudes and cultural values has led to an internal differentiation within the Mediterranean model. A cluster analysis based on data selected from several databases reveals the connection between traditional attitudes on gender roles and the feminization and structure of the labor market; how family values and organization influence the configuration of the welfare system and the development of social policies; the impact of social capital on labor relations, entrepreneurship, and cooperation between and within companies and the mechanisms through which innovation is produced; and how values influence the structure and development of education systems.

4.2. The Relevance of Sociocultural Factors

In economic sociology and political science, at least four important strands of studies have examined the role of sociocultural variables since the end of World War II. The first is the so-called theory of modernization, which was developed in the 1950s and maintains a typical functionalist approach with the goal of explaining differences in economic growth while also recognizing the role played by sociocultural values. Talcott Parsons (1964) can be considered the pivotal scholar of this approach whose core idea is that traditional societies need to change in their sociocultural features in order to become modern and be able to exploit technological change and economic opportunities. A shift from particularistic values and ascribed status to more individualistic and universalistic values based on individuals' capacity and performance allows societies to become better equipped to exploit innovation and thrive economically. According to this perspective, a process of functional differentiation renders the economic sphere increasingly independent from the cultural and religious spheres (Smelser 1959; Eisenstadt 1966). Traditional religious beliefs and cultural traits thereby become less important as modernization takes hold. An increasingly educated population, scientific rationalism, and technical knowledge are all keys to transforming traditional societies into modern ones.

Since the 1960s another strand of research, which stems from the sociology of organization, has highlighted the importance of sociocultural elements in explaining economic innovation and change. On the one hand, the so-called ecological approach to organizations (beginning with Stinchcombe in 1965) introduced the idea that a relationship exists between the sociocultural characteristics of a given environment and the creation of innovative organizations. The liability of newness concept explains why new and innovative organizations have greater chances of failing than do other types of organizations. This approach emphasizes the extent to which a society is open to innovation (in this respect Stinchcombe follows a similar argument to that found in the theory of modernization, namely that modern societies have greater chances of accepting new ways of organizing economic activities than do traditional societies) and the degree to which members of an organization are able to cooperate with and trust one another (this concept was successively developed by the so-called social capital approach). On the other hand, the neoinstitutionalist approach to organizations, which began in the 1970s, highlights the importance of normative (cultural) institutions as well as cognitive institutions in shaping the emergence and diffusion of certain types of organizations (Di Maggio and Powell 1983).

A third strand of research emerged in the late 1980s as a new and innovative elaboration of the theory of modernization of the 1950s. In fact, the theory of modernization was subject to major critiques in the 1970s and 1980s as it conceived a unidirectional, universal trajectory of development in which traditional values decline. In the late 1980s, however, a new wave of research on the relationship between culture and economy acknowledged both the potential importance of this relationship and the limits of the earlier theories. If the theory of modernization of the 1950s and 1960s considered Western values to be the values that societies needed to incorporate in order to become modern and economically successful, the new approaches from the late 1980s—especially those that became labeled the "new comparative political economy" (Evans and Stephens 1988)—adopted a Weberian perspective on the influence of some original traits from different cultures and civilizations that help societies successfully address similar socioeconomic issues in different ways, as shown by studies on Asian capitalisms (Dore 1987; Hamilton and Biggart 1988; Hamilton 1994). Among other factors, these studies highlight the role of social networks (at least those based on communities and family ties) in influencing the creation of successful economic networks among enterprises and the role of religious heritages (e.g., Confucianism) in providing obstacles to as well as resources for capitalist economic development. In this respect, Dore stressed the necessity of examining the extent to which sociocultural values favor the legitimization of authority, interpersonal trust, work ethics, and elites' orientation toward supporting technological innovation.

In parallel to the new comparative approach to political economy, the 1990s and the following decades bore witness to a fourth strand of research, which is based on the concept of social capital and its relationship with economic development. This strand of research stems from the works of Bourdieu (1986), Coleman (1990), and Putnam (1993) and has continued to expand. Concepts such as institutional and interpersonal trust, networks and associations, public involvement, and the respect of norms of civicness have been used increasingly often to explain differences in economic growth. In Putnam's work, for instance, the endowment of social capital at the local/national level plays an important—direct and indirect—role in terms of fostering economic development: directly because it promotes collaboration among economic actors and reduces transaction costs among them and indirectly because it fosters a better and more efficient public administration.

Since these groundbreaking works, Émile Durkheim's concepts of primary social ties, community trust and support, informal obligations, and reciprocity have gained again a central role in theories explaining economic development. At the same time, since the 2000s cognitive theories have been increasingly used in debates in relation to how political economies change. Ideational forces—that is, enduring modes of thought and discourse that are informed by culture and values—are today considered key factors in explaining the production and legitimization of changes in economic policies and practices (Blyth 2002; Schmidt 2008; Rodrik 2014; Ban 2016). Ideas are defined as historically constructed beliefs, values, and perceptions, and they shape human behavior and policy decisions (Béland 2016). Campbell (2004) conceives of them as public sentiments—that is, widely shared assumptions regarding embedded national cultures and understandings in the economy.

These most recent approaches to the study of different political economies bring the role played by sociocultural factors back into the debate on VoC. Following Max Weber's insights, we assume that normative patterns as well as changes in cultural symbols, rules of behavior, social organizations, and value systems influence economic and political institutions. This assumption has remained largely unexplored in the VoC literature. However, as highlighted in the following sections, a full understanding of the growth trajectories of contemporary capitalisms requires a focus on not only the interplay between political and economic institutions but also the sociocultural factors that frame and shape these institutions and serve to conceptualize interests.

4.3. How Sociocultural Values and Social Capital Influence VoC Models

The VoC approach postulates that several institutions shape the chances of economic innovation and socioeconomic growth. These institutions can play both a direct and indirect role in socioeconomic growth.

If we examine the direct role, we can begin our analysis with macroeconomics theory, which postulates that medium- and long-term economic growth stems from several factors: capital accumulation, technology, and the size of the labor market in the medium term; education, the capacity/attitude toward saving economic resources, and the quality of the bureaucracy/government; and the capacity to innovate in the long term (Blanchard 2012). These factors also play a significant role in economic sociology and in VoC analysis, both of which examine the institutional roots of such factors and hence also of economic growth. In the present chapter we focus on sociocultural institutional roots, in particular their roles in relation to the size of the labor market and their capacity to foster innovation.

Moreover, the sociological and VoC literatures have highlighted the important role of families within different VoC not only as a potential source of support or limitation for direct economic action (Granovetter 1985) but also as welfare producers for their own members. As indicated in the introduction to the present volume, one of the core and distinguishing traditional characteristics of Southern European countries is supposedly the very strong role played by the family in welfare provision, which reaches a level that can be defined as familialism (Saraceno and Keck 2010). We next examine in detail how sociocultural values can shape or interact with these factors and dimensions.

4.3.1. The Size of the Labor Market

If economic growth can stem from an increasing size of the labor market, this size can increase in two main ways in European countries. Given that male activity rates are relatively high (they reach almost 80% for individuals between twenty and sixty-four years of age), a further growth in size can come either through female labor market participation or through migration. Both of these phenomena are strictly connected to sociocultural elements and involve the ideas a society has regarding women's roles as well as its openness to "outsiders." In this respect, attitudes toward women and their participation in the labor market—as well as attitudes toward migrants—can partially shape the size of the labor market. Indeed, these attitudes can affect women's and migrants' chances in the labor market and the positions they hold in it. These dimensions are intertwined with family structures, gender roles, and attitudes toward (gendered) entrepreneurship, which can inhibit or enhance the development of the female labor force and women's contribution to the economy.

Additionally, social capital and education have an impact on the size of the labor market, as they are both tools for boosting job opportunities. On the one hand, networks of friends, family ties, and wider social connections are important when it comes to creating job opportunities and job-related contacts (Granovetter 1978). Both strong and weak ties can facilitate job searching by yielding information, providing personal recommendations, or even influencing the hiring process. On the other, education increases employment chances, which is particularly true in advanced postindustrial societies.

4.3.2. Human Capital Accumulation

In the VoC literature, the focus on the role of innovation in firms as a method of supporting economic growth (Hall and Soskice 2001) has paved the way toward a more nuanced approach to the role of education. In this respect, education provides a more skilled labor force that can exploit more innovation opportunities. The educational level reached by the population is a good indicator in this sense as are attitudes toward gender equality and roles within family, given that women are an important source of human capital accumulation. In many countries, women's educational level can be similar—if not superior—to that of their male peers.

Moreover, social capital within both the family and the community can play a role in creating human capital, since interpersonal family networks can be a resource in children's education just as both family financial capital and human capital are (Coleman 1990; Bourdieu 1986).

4.3.3. The Capacity to Innovate

From a sociocultural perspective, innovation can be sustained through different mechanisms. If we examine modernization theories as well as the socio-organizational approaches à la Stinchcombe, the problem of the "liability of newness" for new and innovative organizations can be found to be negatively correlated with how traditional and closed to diversity a society is. Therefore, indicators that measure attitudes toward traditional values and diversity as well as those related to gender equality and migrants all capture the same underlying concept of how open or closed a society is to new and innovative ways of organizing (economic) activities. Attitudes toward entrepreneurship and creativity exist along similar lines. In addition, education increases the chances that innovations—especially radical ones—will take place. Social capital has been studied as a source of economic collaboration and innovation.

4.4. Methodology and Data

The analysis presented in this chapter aims at discovering the extent to which Southern European countries can be grouped together when framed within a European perspective. For the analysis we constructed a database with results from surveys on attitudes and behaviors for which information on all European Union (EU) countries was available, which thereby enabled us to highlight sociocultural variation among VoC and across time. Given that our interest also lies in a diachronic analysis, we chose databases that contain data over time. The most used databases were the European Social Survey (ESS) and the European Value Survey (EVS), which have been ongoing since the 1990s on a regular basis; the Eurobarometer, which runs surveys on several (often rotating) topics every year; Eurofound, which has run three Pan-European surveys since the 2000s; and Organization for Economic Cooperation and Development statistical data collections. Given that these databases do not always cover all EU countries over time, we decided to exclude from the analysis Luxemburg, Romania, Lithuania, and Latvia—countries for which data were often missing.

The items selected from each database were mainly related to gender equality, tolerance toward diversity, social capital, family values and traditions, and entrepreneurship (see supplementary table 4.A at https://hdl.handle.net/1813/103527). The single items were synthetized through a principal component analysis (PCA), and we clustered the countries based on PCA results. Four items were usually used to measure each dimension, and Cronbach's alpha as well as the Kaiser-Meyer-Olkin value reveal that items are quite linked to one another in each dimension. We tested the validity of our findings by also using other items that measure single dimensions. We kept all items that had data available on all four Southern European countries for the PCA.

4.5. Sociocultural Values and Behaviors: Southern Europe in a European Context

The single dimensions strongly correlate with one another, especially attitudes toward gender equality, tolerance toward diversity, family values, and social capital (see supplementary table 4.B at https://hdl.handle.net/1813/103528). If countries score low on intolerance, they also score high on gender equality, have good stocks of social capital, and adopt nontraditional family values. It is also important to highlight the fact that attitudes toward entrepreneurship have a strong correlation with the other dimensions, although this correlation is not as strong as the one that exists among the other dimensions.

We used the five above-mentioned indicators to run a cluster analysis, the results of which are presented in figure 4.1. The main findings of the analysis are presented below (see also supplementary table 4.C at https://hdl.handle.net/1813/103542).

First, two main country clusters exist in Europe in terms of sociocultural factors. Central and Eastern European (CEE) countries and some Southern European countries (those in the central-eastern Mediterranean area: Italy, Greece, and Cyprus) belong to the first cluster. Western European countries (including those on the Iberian Peninsula (i.e., Spain and Portugal), Estonia, and Slovenia belong to the second group.

Second, whereas the first cluster is relatively homogeneous, the second cluster contains two subclusters. Nordic countries together with the Netherlands show partially different characteristics than the rest of Western Europe.

Third, the different clusters display a relatively homogenous overall profile in relation to sociocultural values and attitudes. CEE and central-eastern Mediterranean countries score relatively low on gender equality, tolerance toward diversity, social capital, and attitudes toward entrepreneurship, but they score high on traditional family values. On the other hand, Nordic countries and the Netherlands score high on four dimensions and low on traditional family values, whereas the rest of Western Europe shows medium to high levels on all dimensions except for traditional family values.

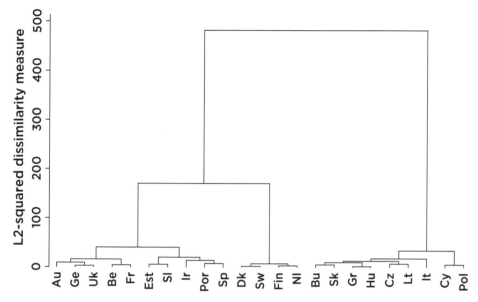

Figure 4.1. Sociocultural values and attitudes in Europe: the main country clusters.
Source: Authors.

Fourth, with very few exceptions, a deep divide exists between Western Europe and CEE countries: Slovenia and Estonia belong with Western Europe, whereas Italy, Greece, and Cyprus belong with Eastern Europe. This finding is highly interesting for the overall implications of this chapter and for the entire book. Southern Europe is not homogenous in terms of sociocultural values, and its four countries belong to two different clusters: Spain and Portugal group together, as do Italy and Greece. In the following subsections, we provide details regarding the differences and similarities among countries along each of the five dimensions.

4.5.1. Attitudes toward Gender Equality and Female Labor Market Participation

Overall, Southern Europe does not seem to cluster together on gender equality or female labor market participation, as a clear divide exists between Iberian countries and central-eastern Mediterranean countries. Table 4.1 reports values for Southern Europe and the three main clusters introduced above for the four variables used to measure this dimension. A very small percentage of people in Northern Europe and the Netherlands agree that men should have more rights to a job when jobs are scarce, and relatively few agree with this statement in the rest of Western Europe with the exception of Italy (22.5%) and (to a greater extent) Greece (46.7%). In this respect, these two countries

Table 4.1 Views on gender roles, tolerance, and social capital

Percentage of individuals who agree	Cluster 1	Cluster 2.1	Cluster 2.2	Spain	Portugal	Italy	Greece*
Gender equality and female labor market participation							
Men have more rights to a job than women when jobs are scarce (ESS 2016)	30.4	3.7	9.2	7.1	12.9	22.5	46.7
The most important role of a woman is to take care of her home and family (Eurobar 2017)	71.0	20.0	42.5	29	47	51	69
Strong approval for men taking parental leave to take care of their children (Eurobar 2017)	35.1	80.2	55.2	66	57	36	48
Strong approval for men doing an equal share of household activities (Eurobar 2017)	34.8	75.5	52.2	72	55	35	39
Tolerance							
Allow few/no immigrants from different ethnic/race groups than majority (ESS pooled data 2014–2016)	67.4	24.2	39.5	39.2	36.6	58.2	85.5
National culture is undermined by immigrants (ESS pooled data 2014–2016)	38.0	12.9	20.6	14.8	15.9	38.3	58.2
Would feel uncomfortable with an immigrant as a friend, colleague, doctor, family member, manager, or neighbor (at least one of social relations above (Eurobar 2018b)	56.1	25.7	28.0	11	16	48	60
Gays/lesbians are free to live as they like (ESS pooled data 2014–2016)	54.8	90.2	81.4	89.5	80.5	66.2	51.5

(continued)

Table 4.1 (continued)

Percentage of individuals who agree	Cluster 1	Cluster 2.1	Cluster 2.2	Spain	Portugal	Italy	Greece*
Social capital							
Most people can be trusted (% agreement)	32.3	70.3	43.0	40.8	21.5	36.5	25.5
Percentage of individuals interested in politics	34.3	61.2	45.4	40.9	42.1	26.8	30.0
Percentage of individuals who trust parliament	18.2	57.5	29.6	25.7	22.1	20.5	7.7
Percentage of individuals who trust the legal system	33.5	74.7	47.8	28.8	27.6	39.2	21.4
Percentage of individuals involved in work for voluntary or charitable organizations at least once a month in the last twelve months	5.1	18.2	15.7	18.5	5.3	14.1	5.0
Items not included in the PCA							
Most people try to be fair (% agreement)	35.8	77.6	54.8	48.2	43.4	38.9	21.3
Share of wallets reported in the money condition (2019)	N/A	79.5	62.8	59.0	46.0	48.0	52.0

* ESS data for Greece refer to 2010.

Source: ESS, various years; Cohn et al. (2019).

share views typically held in CEE (cluster 1). Similar patterns apply in relation to the other three items considered: CEE residents as well as Italians and (to an even greater extent) Greeks typically share the view that taking care of the home and family is the most important role for women, and men are not expected to take parental leave in order to take care of their children or perform an equal share of household activities. These views are shared by a minority in Northern Europe but by a larger minority in the rest of Western Europe. Even if we consider other items that we could not include in the PCA due to missing data (in this case the EVS of 2017, from which data for Portugal and Greece are not available), the pattern does not change. A majority of individuals in CEE (36.8%) and Italy (40.1%) believe that children suffer if their mother works full-time, and a large minority agree that men should be responsible for earning an income and that women should take care of household duties (46.5% in CEE, 34% in Italy). The opposite view is found in Western Europe including Spain (12.8%), which often is more similar in these respects to Nordic countries than to continental ones.

4.5.2. Tolerance and Cultural Attitudes toward Diversity

Attitudes toward migration and homosexuality are considered here as proxies of how individuals welcome diversity (see table 4.1). In this respect, the items chosen in relation to migration refer more to sociocultural traits (cultural homogeneity) than to socioeconomic traits, and homosexuality is considered only in relation to individuals' freedom to choose the type of relationship they prefer (and not, for instance, in relation to the right to adopt children, which is an issue discussed in the other dimension). The patterns found among clusters and countries in relation to gender equality are also confirmed when (in)tolerance and attitudes toward diversity are taken into consideration. Spain and Portugal belong to the Western European cluster and lie halfway between the two Western subclusters, whereas Italy and (to an even greater extent) Greece display facets quite close to CEE, as is well exemplified by the percentage of people who declared that their national culture is being undermined by immigrants (38.8% in Italy, 58.2% in Greece, 14.8% in Spain, and 15.9% in Portugal) or who would feel uncomfortable having an immigrant as friend, colleague, doctor, family member, manager, or neighbor (48% in Italy, 60% in Greece, 11% in Spain, and 16% in Portugal). Again, if we consider other items that could not be included in the PCA due to missing data, results remain the same: 16.1% of Italians declared being ashamed of having a close family member who is gay/lesbian, as compared with 8.2% for Spaniards.

4.5.3. Social Capital

As shown in the literature cited above, social capital refers to at least three key dimensions: first, to trust and obligations; second, to channels of information;

and third, to norms and effective sanctions. These three dimensions affect a society's efficiency by encouraging coordination and cooperation among individuals or social groups (Coleman 1988).

Nordic countries and the Netherlands represent environments with the highest stocks of social capital (see table 4.1). The rest of Western Europe follows, whereas CEE is quite different. Civicness and general trust in the quality of the political, legal, and institutional environment influence individual outcomes as well as social group interactions, thereby increasing a society's overall effectiveness. While most of the data on trust used in table 4.1 come from the ESS, the information at the bottom of the table comes from an experiment conducted by Cohn et al. (2019) on civic honesty in forty countries around the world. The researchers submitted over seventeen thousand lost wallets with varying amounts of money to public and private institutions and measured whether the recipients contacted the owners to return the wallets. In virtually all countries, citizens were more likely to return wallets that contained more money. The last two rows of the table show the share of wallets reported in the money condition in each country. Although some of the European countries studied in the present chapter were absent from the experiment (Finland, Belgium, Ireland, Austria, Cyprus, and several CEE countries were not included), the picture that emerges from the study by Cohn et al. supports the ESS data and the clustering to a significant extent. In particular, Spain appears to have a higher level of civic honesty compared with other Southern European countries, with Nordic countries (and the Netherlands) and Germany showing the highest level of civic honesty. This finding is particularly relevant, since individuals who feel safe in the surroundings in which they live develop stronger ties within their community. Together with effective norms, this environment facilitates exchange, decreases transaction costs and the cost of information, and encourages the collective management of resources.

4.5.4. Traditional Family Values and Ethical Issues

If we focus on traditional family values and ethical issues linked with religious faith, the two (or three) clusters hold (table 4.2). Northern Europe is the most secularized area, with issues such as abortion and artificial insemination being widely accepted. The rest of Western Europe and Slovenia follow, with a majority of people also approving of these issues. On the other hand, CEE countries are grouped with some of the central-eastern Mediterranean countries, in which a minority of people agree with these ethical questions. Traditional values regarding belief go hand in hand with the role of the family, whose members are linked together by a strong bond and mutual recognition of the value of family culture. This value is confirmed by other items not included in the PCA. For instance, the share of individuals who agree that children have a duty to take care of their parents if they are in need of care is

Table 4.2 Ethical issues,* religion, and attitude toward entrepreneurship

Percentage of individuals who affirm	Cluster 1	Cluster 2.1	Cluster 2.2	Spain	Portugal	Italy	Greece
Ethical issues							
Abortion can be justified (EVS2008)	28.6	64.8	40.6	38.9	26.9	26.8	30.5
Artificial insemination or in-vitro fertilization can be justified (EVS2008)	59.4	79.3	60.1	74.1	56.0	47.8	75.3
Euthanasia can be justified (EVS2008)	30.3	66.3	45.4	56.1	30.0	40.8	21.1
It is important to follow traditions (ESS pooled data 2014–2016)	63.5	43.2	48.3	54.8	41.7	66.3	76.7
Religion in people's life							
They belong to a religious faith (Eurobarometer 2018)	83.8	62.9	69.5	67.3	88.2	87.1	96.3
They belong to the most common religious faith in the country (Eurobarometer 2018)	76.2	48.2	52.7	58.5	83.9	77.3	95.2
They attend at least weekly religious services (EVS2008)	23.6	7.2	16.9	18.5	22.3	32.0	31.1
They attend at least weekly religious services (EVS2017)	21.4	6.1	11.1	18.2	N/A	27.6	N/A
Entrepreneurship							
Individuals perceiving good opportunities to start a business who indicate that fear of failure would prevent them from setting it up (Global Entrepreneurship Monitor [GEM] 2018)	44.4	36.6	36.2	36.2	38.1	51.7	57.8

(continued)

Table 4.2 (continued)

Percentage of individuals who affirm	Cluster 1	Cluster 2.1	Cluster 2.2	Spain	Portugal	Italy	Greece
Social and cultural norms encourage or allow actions leading to new business methods or activities potentially increasing personal wealth and income (mean value)** (GEM 2018)	2.3	3.0	2.8	3.0	2.5	2.1	2.4
Percentage of positive view of entrepreneurship (mean 2016–2018) (Eurobar)	77.0	89.5	80.6	88.6	81.2	64.3	83.9
Percentage of positive view of competition (mean 2016–2018) (Eurobar)	68.5	81.6	75.6	70.2	82.0	57.5	63.5
Percentage of the private sector better placed than the public sector to create new jobs (mean 2016–2018) (Eurobar)	63.3	70.6	66.9	66.7	65.0	51.0	62.0

* Given that we mostly had to use 2008 data for this dimension, we examined correlations between the 2008 and 2017 EVS values at the country level for all countries available in both surveys. The correlations are very high, and the values are as follows: abortion justified, .882; artificial insemination or in-vitro fertilization justified, .900; and euthanasia justified, 850.

**Experts' ratings: 1 = highly insufficient, 5 = highly sufficient

70.1% in cluster 1 (74.8% in Italy, 52.8% in Spain), while it is only 21.1% in cluster 2.1 and 50.6% in cluster 2.2.

4.4.5. Attitudes toward Entrepreneurship

Table 4.2 also shows how the different European countries cluster in relation to entrepreneurial behavior and attitudes. The clusters we find generally fall in line with those found previously in this chapter. In central Northern Europe along with Spain and Portugal, behaviors and attitudes are more supportive of entrepreneurship than in the rest of Southern Europe or—partially—in CEE countries. Among European countries, Italians find themselves in a very difficult situation for several reasons: a very high percentage of individuals believe they have good opportunities to start a business but also indicate that fear of failure would prevent them from doing so; compared to many other European societies, social and cultural norms do not really encourage or allow actions that could lead to new business methods or activities increasing personal wealth and income (as indicated by panels of experts); and a relatively low percentage of adults have a positive view of entrepreneurship and competition and rely on the public sector as an employer more than in many other contexts.

On the one hand, this picture of Italy is surprising given that the country has built a good share of its fortune from dynamic small to midsize enterprises. On the other hand, normative factors related to family ties can explain these differences. Primary ties shape business in Mediterranean countries, where a large share of small to midsize enterprises and microenterprises are family firms. These enterprises and firms represent around 80% of firms in Greece and Spain and about 90% of all companies in Italy, where over 40% of the three hundred largest companies are family-owned (the highest percentage in Europe). The particular relevance of family bonds in Italian businesses is well exemplified by the fact that managers external to the family are less often employed than in other countries: 66% of Italian family businesses are fully managed by family members, while this is the case for only 26% of French family businesses and just 10% of family businesses in the United Kingdom.

However, the roots of economic activity within the family can act as both an economic engine and a limit to company performance. Indeed, beliefs about the importance of family are correlated with the relevance of family ownership, and the capitalization of family firms stems from family funds and the value system (i.e., honesty, credibility, respect, etc.). The personal commitment and engagement of family members within the local community is particularly relevant for the development and functioning of such economic activity.

At the same time, as some scholars have shown, stronger family ties are linked to organizational structures that are geared toward greater self-employment, rely less on external finance, and are more prevalent in traditional and labor-intensive sectors (i.e., manufacturing). These families focus on long-term sustainability more than on renewal and are more reluctant to abandon their traditional core businesses and venture into risky new activities, thereby showing little capacity to adjust to economic changes (Bertrand and Schoar 2006). Additionally, since innovation is tied to management's knowledge and approach, certain characteristics of family firms can work against business development and innovation, such as limited exposure and openness to diverse ideas from outside, a lack of work experience elsewhere, a lack of willingness to adopt outside skills and capabilities, and a limited desire to take risks because all family efforts and resources are concentrated in the business.

4.5. Regional Trends toward Modernization

Data used in this chapter display two diverging paths of modernization within the Mediterranean VoC and differentiate Iberian countries from other Southern European countries. At the same time, some literature indicates that the Southern European countries are traditionally characterized by a high degree of territorial divide in terms of development and economic activities (Molina and Rhodes 2007). Although additional details would exceed the scope of this chapter, it is extremely important reveal intraregional variations that show internal differentiations. In relation to the Italian case, many studies show internal differences regarding social values and behaviors (the most well-known study at the international level is likely that by Putnam et al. [1993], on social capital in the Italian regions).

If we consider the subnational level, at least for the two most populated countries in Southern Europe (i.e., Italy, and Spain), we can aim to answer two sets of questions. First, are both countries highly fragmented internally in terms of social values, and is the level of geographical differentiation within each of them comparable? Second, once we split Italy into two or more different geographical subareas (e.g., northern vs. southern Italy), does a part of Italy show at least some facets that are more similar to Western European countries, such as France, the United Kingdom, or Germany, or does Italy remain quite different?

Table 4.3 helps in answering both sets of questions. Internal differentiation is not really a significant element for Spain, though it is still very strong in Italy. Spaniards are much more territorially homogenous in terms of their social values and attitudes, whereas Italians maintain a strong north-south divide, with northern Italians being closer to other Western Europeans in many respects than are southern Italians. However, even (central-)northern Italians display values and attitudes that are often quite different from those of other Western Europeans.

Table 4.3 Sociocultural values and territorial differentiation in Spain and Italy*

	Gender equality	Intolerance	Social capital	Traditional family values	Entrepreneurship
Spain:	*1.96*	*-1.73*	*-1.17*	*-0.24*	*0.85*
Northwest	1.91	-1.68	-1.22	-0.15	0.81
Northeast (incl. Catalunya)	1.99	-1.70	-1.12	-0.21	0.91
Central (incl. Community of Madrid)	1.90	-1.74	-1.18	-0.27	0.89
South(-east)	1.96	-1.75	-1.16	-0.26	0.84
Italy:	*-1.12*	*1.32*	*-2.17*	*2.04*	*-3.45*
North	-0.60	1.29	-1.15	1.45	-2.90
Central	-0.82	1.31	-1.50	1.92	-3.25
South	-1.55	1.36	-2.95	2.97	-3.82
CEEs, Italy, Greece, and Cyprus	*-1.89*	*2.03*	*-2.65*	*1.49*	*-0.99*
Nordic countries, the Netherlands	*2.81*	*-2.08*	*3.54*	*-3.10*	*1.78*
Western Europe, Slovenia, and Estonia	*0.63*	*-1.00*	*0.05*	*-0.13*	*0.39*

* The indicator of entrepreneurship was calculated only for three items, as data were not available at the subnational level for two of them (GEM items).

4.7. Religion and Secularization

The present chapter examines Southern Europe in a comparative perspective in order to understand whether countries share similar sociocultural facets or are relatively different. As we have seen, differences exist between Iberian countries on the one hand and Italy and Greece on the other hand. Although it is not possible to investigate the roots of such differences in depth in this chapter, it is important examine at least one key variable: the role of religion. Indeed, a major split among VoC is linked to traditional values and family roles, which represent a legacy of deep-rooted societal habits and religious beliefs. Traditional legacies and conservative religious orientations continue to foster a cognitive closure toward diversity and emphasize the significance of gender roles and strong family ties, which influence female labor market participation and discourage gender equality in work and in the household.

Examples of religious influence on economic performance have occurred throughout history, as evidenced in Weber's argument that the rise of capitalism is rooted in Protestant ethics. Economists and sociologists have tested the modernization argument that links economic development to secularization and have revealed both great sociocultural change across countries and the persistence of distinctive cultural traditions (Barro and McCleary 2003; Grief 1994; Rodrik, Subramanian, and Trebbi 2004). Inglehart and Baker (2000) demonstrated that economic development is associated with shifts away from absolute norms and toward increasingly rational and tolerant values, but they also stressed that cultural change is path-dependent and that the broad sociocultural values inherited from religious faiths leave an imprint that endures despite modernization. Thus, although participation in religious practices has decreased over time in all developed countries and an increasing number of individuals have no direct contact with the church today, the impact of living in a society that was historically shaped by once-powerful religious institutions persists and continues to shape national cultures.

For these reasons, the evolution of the relationships between the church and the state and the process of secularization—together with increasing religious diversity—are considered key features of European modernity and are believed to influence sociocultural values within models of capitalism (Therborn 2010).

The church is known to have played a central role in the process of nation-state building and the formation national identity in some countries (i.e., the Orthodox Church in Greece and the Catholic Church in Ireland and Poland) and maintains a high level of sociopolitical legitimacy, presenting itself as the guarantor of a country's unity. On the other hand, in other cases, such as in Spain and (to a lesser extent) in Portugal where the Catholic Church has traditionally been extremely powerful and the closest ally of the government, secular and anticlerical forces emerged with the end of the authoritarian regime and forged a political identity. This is particularly evident in Spain, where the presence of the church in public decision-making arenas was greatly reduced with the process of democratization and religious elites lost their position of social leadership and their role in society (Requena 2005).

As for secularization, this long historical and institutional process led European capitalisms to move away from the idea of a confessional state, thereby distancing the church from political institutions and civil society. However, although secularization is a generalized process, it is not linear; rather, it has manifested in different forms and has tendentially affected Protestant churches more than Catholic or Orthodox churches. In Protestant countries, secularization has been more radical, and institutional distancing between the church and society has gone hand in hand with a loss of the church's influence over customs and social norms (Galland and Lemel 2007). On the other hand, the Catholic and Orthodox Churches have not lost their institutional or cultural influence, which is exercised in both a formal-institutional way and indirect ways in society, for instance, on matters such as patriarchy, abortion, homosexuality, and divorce. Indeed, as some studies have shown, values and attitudes on issues such as fertility and divorce significantly affect female engagement in the labor market (Iversen and Rosenbluth 2010). In these cases, when the church continues to maintain a dominant role, it can inhibit social change (Crouch 1993).

These differences can be considered part of the reason for the split between Portugal, Spain, and central-eastern Mediterranean countries in terms of the importance associated with religion and traditional family values. Table 4.2 displays the relevance of religion in people's lives. Nordic countries are among the least religious nations, followed closely by other Western European countries. However, in central-eastern Mediterranean countries and some CEE countries, religious affiliation and practices are widespread and represent an important part of individual and national identity, even in countries in which communist regimes once repressed religious worship and promoted atheism.

4.8. Conclusion

This chapter aimed at reintroducing the role played by sociocultural factors into the debate on VoC by showing that different sociocultural patterns underlie institutional variations across European countries. While keeping in mind the mutual influence among economic, political, and sociocultural institutions and of the role of policies in affecting sociocultural change, we emphasized the role played by the sociocultural sphere, which is largely overlooked in the literature on capitalist development and in the VoC approach.

We illustrated salient differences among capitalist models in terms of social values, thereby demonstrating why it is highly relevant to consider these dimensions and how much they can add to the scientific debate on Southern European capitalism. More specifically, we highlighted an increasing divergence within Southern European countries. The split runs along the east (Greece and Italy)–west (Spain and Portugal) divide.

Indeed, southern Mediterranean countries are characterized by *differentiated modernization*. Conservative and traditional values and family structures, which used to characterize Southern Europe, have gradually lost social and cultural significance in the western part of Southern Europe, which has become increasingly more tolerant and open and has come to more closely resemble continental and Northern Europe and to separate itself from southeastern countries. These evolving sociocultural attitudes—which began in a context of political and economic restructuring after the dictatorships in Spain and Portugal and continued to evolve throughout the 1990s—have particularly influenced civil society, the role of women, and their access to economic opportunities. Gender roles have changed drastically within a short period of time and have played a significant role in the vast expansion of the female workforce.

This path toward modernization, which is grounded in the expansion of civil rights and liberties, the gradual increase in educational levels, and the steady rise of an active female labor population (even during periods of economic recession), has gone hand in hand and is fully compatible with an economic model based on low productivity and labor-intensive jobs. The expansion of the workforce has taken place mostly in low- and medium-skilled services and in low-productivity sectors (i.e., restoration, construction, tourism) and only little in highly productive service sectors (i.e., communications, finance, business activities). Therefore, modernization has not enhanced a type of development based on innovation and competitive knowledge economy and has not been able to foster productivity growth based on strengthening human capital.

However, our long-term perspective highlighted the persistence of traditional values and the attachment to the patriarchal family found in Italy and Greece, where hostility toward diversity has even increased in the last decade. The persistence of stable gender roles affects female labor market participation, which continues to be particularly low in these countries. This finding means that increasing female human capital and women's average level of education—as is currently under way—is essential albeit not sufficient for female emancipation and participation in the labor market, which is strongly linked to gender roles in society and to household models. Additionally, although the inflow of a young cohort is attaining levels of education in line with the EU Lisbon 2020 target (with at least 85% of the population having earned a secondary-school degree), in Mediterranean countries almost half of the working-age population falls short of this goal.

In these Mediterranean countries, the perception that immigration poses a threat and acts as a limitation to economic development is linked with a low level of general and institutional trust and weak social cohesion. This public sentiment has certainly been influenced by the recent and heavy economic crises and by the growing inadequacy of the Mediterranean welfare model, which is not able to protect against new social risks. Disaffection and distrust influence and legitimize the political and economic choices in these countries.

This context has hampered reforms addressed at supporting the research system, education, and innovation-based firms and has created very few incentives for human capital development or technological innovation, thereby hindering socioeconomic development.

Instead, the sociocultural context continues to support a development model based on the predominance of small firms and self-employment in low- and medium-technology sectors. These latter sectors favored growth until the 1980s in Southern Europe, but with the challenges of the internationalization of markets and the need for upgrading in technology and skills, they have become much less efficient at promoting economic growth. Additionally, the lack of trust in collective endeavors limits the propensity of these firms to cooperate with other firms and to develop public-private partnerships in order to exploit technology and knowledge.

Our analysis revealed that a path toward internal diversification is being followed in Southern European countries in terms of sociocultural structure, but it is unclear whether this divergent trend is linked to other changes and differentiations among these countries (or within the most internally fragmented countries). While southeastern countries seem to be stuck in a low-productivity equilibrium model, a shift toward a different trajectory could be expected from the western part of Southern Europe, which would require these countries to overcome their traditional institutional weaknesses, reduce long-term economic competitiveness, create mechanisms to increase investment and foster their productive capacity in key sectors, and expand research facilities for firms in order to develop an innovation-based economy. The increasing number of highly educated young cohorts, especially in Spain, could lead to such a transformation. Exactly which factors could lead to a further differentiation and what impact they could have from a socioeconomic point of view remain interesting issues for a future research agenda.

PART II

Policies and Processes of Change

Chapter 5

Labor Market (De)Regulation and Wage-Setting Institutions in Mediterranean Capitalism

Alexandre Afonso, Lisa Dorigatti, Oscar Molina, and Arianna Tassinari

5.1. Introduction

Labor market regulations and industrial relations institutions have been assigned a key role in explaining the comparatively poor performance of Mediterranean economies since 1980. According to this view, tightly regulated labor markets and weakly coordinated collective bargaining systems combined with a prominent role for the state are responsible for dualized labor markets, wage-setting practices that undermined competitiveness, and large inequalities (Siebert 1997; Scarpetta 1996; Murtin, de Serres, and Hijzen 2014). These institutional domains have accordingly been the target of recommendations from international organizations to liberalize, deregulate, and decentralize (OECD 1994). These pressures intensified with the run-up to the Economic and Monetary Union (EMU) and membership in the Eurozone, as wage-setting regimes in Southern Europe adopted new mechanisms for coordination, including social pacts, in order to deliver wage restraint and reforms at the margins of the labor market became widespread.

Labor market regulation and wage-setting institutions have certainly been the area where Mediterranean countries have been faced with the greatest amount of pressure during the Eurozone crisis. Indeed, wage-setting and labor market policies have been considered major weaknesses in their economic models once the crisis hit, preventing a swift adjustment of wages to new economic conditions and rising unemployment. In particular, the alleged rigidity in their labor market regulation, the inability of their wage bargaining institutions to deliver wage restraint, and strong patterns of dualization enabling sharp divisions in levels of security between "insiders" and "outsiders" were a major target of reform in the adjustment programs imposed by international financial institutions (in the case of Greece and Portugal) or adopted as part of reform packages by reformist governments to reassure financial markets (in the case of Spain and Italy).

All these reforms, in particular those implemented during the Eurozone crisis, have consolidated a competitive strategy based on the reduction of costs and a more flexible use of labor. Although in the short term they have improved the wage competitiveness of Southern Europe in relation to other Eurozone countries, there is no clear evidence of a positive effect on the growth of exports or the shift toward an export-led growth model (see Baccaro's chapter in this volume; Pérez and Matsaganis 2019). Although from the more orthodox positions of economic liberalism this could be attributed to incomplete reforms, other authors emphasize the limitations of these policies to consolidate a sustainable growth model, given the prevailing structural conditions. In this view, the reforms implemented during the Eurozone crisis would have a negative impact on macroeconomic performance and labor market outcomes because they have eroded the capacity of social actors to govern collective bargaining and therefore wage growth, while the increase in inequalities may jeopardize growth prospects by depressing internal demand.

This chapter provides an overview of the main characteristics of the Mediterranean model of capitalism when it comes to labor market regulation and industrial relations institutions in Southern Europe and highlights reform dynamics and their underlying political economy. We contend that the transformations that have taken place since the 1980s in the labor market and industrial relations regulatory models of Southern European countries are the result of a common impetus for liberalization arising from the twin processes of (neoliberal) economic globalization and European integration. This, however, has not been homogenous in depth but instead has been mediated in each country by domestic political and institutional factors, namely producer group politics and the embeddedness of power resources of industrial relations actors, electoral politics, and institutional path dependencies. Our analysis also underscores how despite the deep transformations that occurred, some of the traits of the "traditional" Mediterranean model persist nonetheless, in particular the central role of the state and of its shadow of hierarchy as factors shaping the regulation of labor markets and industrial relations dynamics. As in many other advanced capitalist economies, however (Howell 2020), this role has shifted from being mostly protective in nature to increasingly acting as an enforcer of liberalization.

The chapter first outlines the main characteristics traditionally associated with the Southern European model of capitalism when it comes to labor market governance and collective bargaining. We then trace the main changes that have taken place since the start of the twenty-first century in state regulation, with a focus on employment protection legislation (second section) and wage-setting institutions (third section). The fourth section explores the political economy of reforms, explaining both commonalities and differences across the four countries. We conclude with a summary of the main dynamics of change and continuity across the areas reviewed.

5.2. The "Traditional" Model of Labor Market and Industrial Relations in Southern Europe

According to classic scholarship (Crouch 1993; Mingione 1995; Ferrera 1996), the Mediterranean model of labor market and industrial relations (IR) encompassed several common features. This section sketches these commonalities, bearing in mind the cross-country and cross-regional heterogeneity *within* the Mediterranean model (Mingione 1995; Karamessini 2008; Marí-Klose and Moreno-Fuentes 2013; Watson 2015).

The first key characterizing feature of the Mediterranean model of capitalism was *extensive state intervention* in the productive system and in the regulation of the labor market (Schmidt 2002; Molina and Rhodes 2007; Emmenegger 2014). The state usually intervened extensively in employment relations through a strong legislative framework; legislative support for and procedural regulation of multiemployer collective bargaining, notably through state-backed extensions of collective bargaining agreements across economic sectors (with the partial exception of Italy); and generous provision of passive insurance-based social protection for workers in open-ended employment. Second, in line with this important role of the state, the two main forms of labor market decommodification that consolidated in Southern Europe were *high employment protection legislation* against dismissal for core (male) workers in open-ended employment and segmented systems of *insurance-based unemployment protection* granting generous safety nets but only to selected components of the labor force. The flipsides of this corporatist-familist protective model were, first, a persistently high incidence of labor market informality, with at least 20–25% of employment estimated to be in the undeclared segment of the economy (Williams and Horodnic 2015, 205); second, segmentation and weak social protection entitlements for the unemployed or those with marginal labor market attachments (Petmesidou 2006; Berton, Ricchiardi, and Sacchi 2012; Mato 2011; Valadas 2017); and third and consequently, high reliance on informal family networks as a source of social protection (Guillén and León 2011).

Pronounced state intervention in the labor market and IR sphere has also historically gone hand in hand with the *organizational weakness of trade unions and employers* (Crouch 1993). Unions and employers' organizations in Southern Europe display indeed a high degree of fragmentation and interorganizational competition, limiting their capacity for autonomous coordination and cooperation (Molina and Rhodes 2007, 225–27). Hence, state intervention in the labor market—for example, through legislative support of collective bargaining institutions or strong statutory job protection legislation—has historically played a compensatory function for the relatively weak autonomous coordinating capacities of social partner organizations (Molina and Rhodes 2007; Emmenegger 2014). Sector-level collective bargaining has been predominant and, except in Italy, supported by mechanisms of legislative extension of sectoral collective bargaining agreements beyond the signatory parties. However, due to the limited density and articulation of IR actors, both horizontal and vertical coordination across sectors and between different bargaining levels have been limited, thus giving rise to either wage drift or sluggish productivity performance.

These factors also contributed to the development of *adversarial systems of industrial relations*. On the one hand, unions and employers' organizations in Southern Europe have historically struggled to aggregate interests internally and to reach long-lasting autonomous compromises with each other. On the other hand, the absence of corporatist structures of interest representation at the national level has meant that the relationships of unions and employers' organizations' with the state in the sphere of politics have been characterized by a mix of confrontation and occasional accommodation and incorporation. Unions and employers' organizations did not play a central role in the historical development and management of welfare state institutions (Andreotti et al. 2001, 49) and have not been routinely incorporated in policymaking through mechanisms of institutionalized corporatist concertation found in Northern Europe. However, such producer groups have been strong enough to act as occasional veto players—either in virtue of their capacity of mobilization and disruption at times of heightened industrial conflict, in the case of unions (e.g., in the late 1970s and early 1980s), or in light of their acquired institutional power resources in policymaking.

To facilitate structural reforms of labor market regulation and coordination in the IR sphere, the state in Southern Europe has thus been occasionally prone to engage in processes of tripartite political exchange (Pizzorno 1978; Molina 2006) with unions and employers to obtain their acquiescence and collaboration in reform processes, overcome veto powers, and attempt to resolve at the macrolevel of policymaking the distributive conflicts that could not be solved in the industrial relations sphere (Molina and Rhodes 2007, 236). Social concertation was used at various junctures to facilitate wage moderation or labor market flexibilization (Pizzorno 1978; Ebbinghaus and Hassel 2000; Hancké and Rhodes 2005; Molina and Rhodes 2007) but always remained on an uncertain institutional footing, driven by political convenience rather than embedded in strong corporatist institutions. One major exception in this pattern has been Greece, where tripartite concertation has never really emerged because organized interests were more tightly controlled by political parties, defeating the purpose of independent concertation (Lavdas 2005).

These features of the Mediterranean model of labor market regulation originated from several parallel processes. Pronounced state intervention and the relative weakness of organized producer groups were legacies of the late process of economic modernization and democratization (Crouch 1993; Andreotti et al. 2001). The shared experiences of authoritarian rule, which lasted in the case of Greece, Portugal, and Spain into the 1970s, favored indeed a monopolization of the social space by the state, stifling the development of autonomous structures of interest representation (Crouch 1993; see also Barreto 1993, 30; Meardi, Gardawski, and Molina 2015, 403). The unwillingness of the state to share its political space was further reinforced by the rivalry between church and state, which originated in the process of nineteenth-century state formation (Crouch 1993, 302–7). Fragmentation in the structures of interest representation was in turn exacerbated by the internal heterogeneity of the productive system, characterized by overlapping structural-sectoral cleavages on the basis of firm size, public or private ownership, and relative sectoral skills intensity (Molina and Rhodes 2007, 233). In addition, in the cases of Portugal, Spain, and Greece, a pattern of inward-looking protectionist late industrialization contributed to generating shared demands among capital and labor for ex ante protection against market forces (Rueda, Wibbels, and Altamirano 2015).

The patterns of state-society relationships and late industrialization described above gave prominence to the role of *statutory* regulation of job protection via legislation—making strong employment protection legislation a central plank of the labor market policy model (Emmenegger 2014). However, statutory regulation only pertained to a limited segment of the labor force. Indeed, as the process of industrialization in Southern Europe was patchy and characterized by regional inequalities, limited areas of urban industrial concentration—such as in northern Italy, the Basque Country and Catalonia in Spain, and Lisbon and Porto in Portugal—emerged against a backdrop characterized by the persisting predominance of small-scale family ownership, which the state sought to protect, and by relative underdevelopment in rural areas. Here, as de-ruralization slowly progressed after World War II, informal employment remained dominant—e.g., in agriculture, construction, tourism, private services, or low-skilled manufacturing, while public-sector employment grew, coming to act as a lifeline to otherwise stagnant local economies.

This process of "incomplete proletarianization" (Mingione 1995) implied that the model of formal labor market regulation developed, especially since the 1970s, primarily as an attempt to acquiesce the mobilization of organized labor, given the nascent but small industrial urban working class. Hence, while introducing generally strong statutory job protection for open-ended employees, state authorities in Southern European countries remained broadly tolerant of employment in the informal economy (Mingione 1995). Informality was key to the viability of family-owned small and medium-size enterprises, enabling them to maintain low labor costs and ensure flexibility in production, and was central to the coping strategies of the population in nonindustrialized areas, allowing them to complement otherwise low incomes and reducing reliance on the welfare state (Mingione 1995). Hence, a segmented model of labor market protections characterized by formally high employment protection legislation for the urban workforce, coexisting with flexibility via informality, became consolidated over time.

Notwithstanding these broad similarities in the formal aspects of labor market and wage-setting regulation, several scholars have highlighted how the operation of the employment-relevant institutions of welfare capitalism—in terms of protective standards and flexibility—was not completely homogenous across Southern European countries. For example, Watson (2015, 7–10) finds that despite formal similarities, the effective stringency of employment protection legislation for individual dismissals in Portugal up to the late 1980s was in practice lower than in Spain, and the level of wage flexibility allowed by the collective bargaining system was higher due to its more substantive de facto fragmentation and decentralization. For this reason, Watson characterizes the post-transition welfare model of Portugal as "liberal" and the Spanish one as "protective." This resulted in higher levels of job creation in the former but also in a higher incidence of poverty and inequality due to the lower protections granted to low-income, low-skilled workers (Watson 2015, 16). On their part, Greece and Italy stand apart from the other two cases for the greater incidence of patronage and clientelism as forces shaping the development of their welfare systems, giving rise to more pronounced patterns of segmentation between sectors and workforce components with regard to protective entitlements and access to state support, what Molina and Rhodes (2007) call "distributive coalitions. Mediterranean countries also display significant variation in their industrial relations systems, making it difficult to speak about a homogeneous Mediterranean model. In particular, Italy stands apart concerning both state intervention in industrial relations, which is fairly limited, and stronger coordination capacity by social partners (Regalia and Regini 1998).

5.2.1. The Liberalization of Employment Protection in Mediterranean Countries

In this section, we present a contextualized outline of the development of employment protection legislation in Mediterranean countries since the 1990s, tracing its main characteristics from the 1980s and 1990s to the important movement of liberalization that has taken place in the wake of the Eurozone crisis of 2010–2014. We identify a clear movement of liberalization in this latter period driven by a push by governments to achieve internal devaluation. As governments, pressured by international institutions and financial markets, were determined to push down labor costs in the wake of the crisis, a flexibilization of employment protection appeared as an important tool to facilitate a decrease in wages.

Employment protection refers to the conditions under which an employment contract may be terminated, such as layoff procedures, possibilities to appeal against unfair dismissals, or required severance payments. Until the Eurozone crisis of 2010–2012, Mediterranean countries displayed higher levels of employment protection—according to the Organization for Economic Cooperation and Development's (OECD) widely used Employment Protection

Legislation index (see table 5.1)—than "core" continental, Nordic, Anglo, and Visegràd countries (Afonso 2019, 944). Compared to other countries in Europe, the common view has been that the Mediterranean model of capitalism put greater emphasis on the protection of *jobs* via employment protection and less on the protection of *individuals* via income maintenance. We could label this *social protection through job security* (Bonoli and Emmenegger 2010).

Besides the historical legacies linked to strong state intervention mentioned above, these high levels of employment protection for people in formal employment should be understood in light of the deficiencies of the formal welfare system. Although unemployment replacement rates in Italy, Spain, Portugal, and Greece have been comparable to other countries, as chapter 6 in this volume shows, the *coverage* of unemployment protection has been low, denoting a real problem to adequately cover individuals out of work. Comparing the number of recipients of unemployment benefits with the number of unemployed, for instance, reveals a discrepancy that is much greater in Mediterranean countries than in Northern Europe (OECD 2018, 190). These gaps in coverage—due to restrictive entitlement rules such as long minimum contribution periods and a sizable informal sector—have particularly affected younger people, families, and women without long and stable contributory periods (Pérez and Rhodes 2015, 179). In theory, rigid employment protection could partially compensate for these deficiencies by making it more difficult for jobs to disappear in the first place. However, of course, income support and job protection are imperfect substitutes. A common view has been that high employment protection disincentivizes employers to hire during upturns if workers cannot be dismissed during downturns. Besides, high employment protection creates high levels of dualization between a more protected—usually male and older—workforce and a less secure—more often young and female—workforce on precarious contracts (Emmenegger et al. 2012).

Employment protection reforms in Southern Europe since the 1980s and up to the Eurozone crisis have been characterized by differentiated paths across forms of employment (permanent or fixed term) and countries. In general, we can identify a dual trajectory characterized by a relative level of stability in protection for permanent employment up until the crisis and a movement of flexibilization at the margins starting earlier and affecting part-time employment.

As mentioned above, strict employment protection legislation emerged at the peak of labor power in the 1970s (in Italy) and periods of democratization (in Spain, Portugal, and Greece). In the Italian case, for instance, the most significant piece of legislation was Article 18 of the Statuto dei lavoratori (Labor Code) adopted in the aftermath of the "hot autumn" of 1969. Following a wave of mobilizations in factories in northern Italy, most notably Turin, trade unions managed to substantially increase employment protection and union power (Pizzolato 2012, 620). Article 18 stipulated that dismissed workers could take their employer to court, where a judge would determine whether the dismissal

Table 5.1 OECD employment protection legislation index (collective and individual dismissals), decade averages

	1990s	2000s	2010–2013
Greece	2.80	2.80	2.31
Italy	2.76	2.76	2.74
Portugal	4.63	4.48	3.75
Spain	2.95	2.36	2.21

Source: OECD.

was justified (by economic reasons or individual misconduct) or not. For firms above fifteen employees, penalties for unfair dismissals included a reinstatement of the worker with payment of foregone wages during the procedure or severance payments equivalent to fifteen monthly wages. Crucially, the choice of compensation rested with the employee. A whole set of other procedures applied for collective dismissals (more than five employees). Because it was not possible to adjust the severity of the sanction for unfair dismissals and because no compensation was provided for fair dismissals, there was an in-built incentive for judges to rule in favor of employees (Hijzen, Mondauto, and Scarpetta 2017, 65). It was the threat of the law rather than its effective use that was dissuasive for employers and increased the cost of dismissals (Ferrera and Gualmini 2004, 158).

Labor power, however, could yield counterintuitive impacts, as the Portuguese example shows. During the forty years of the Estado Novo (1933–1974), social and employment policies were geared toward labor repression and wage restraint under the severe control of the state. The democratic transition process following the so-called Carnation Revolution of 1974, in which the Communist Party played a significant role, was thus driven by a strong desire to catch up and compensate workers. Paradoxically, however, up until the 1990s the resulting employment protection legislation in Portugal proved to be less generous than in neighboring Spain: the strong position of the Communist Party and its allies within the trade union movement weakened mechanisms of political exchange, enabling a form of cooperation between trade unions and government (Watson 2015, 145). On the contrary, party competition between the Socialist Party and the Communist Party (the latter being closely connected to the largest trade union, the General Confederation of the Portuguese Workers) incentivized the socialists to coalesce with the center-right and weaken unions instead (131–32). One element that made job protection less stringent in Portugal was the tolerance for wage arrears, allowing firms to delay the payment of wages sometimes for well over a year (9). If workers sought employment elsewhere, this counted as voluntary separation, and they were not entitled to severance payments. Only after the weakening of the Communist Party in the late 1980s did the employment protection system expand, notably by providing compensation for wage arrears. Nevertheless, if one looks at its actual functioning beyond formal measurements, the Portuguese employment law still remained less protective than the Spanish one, with resulting lower wages but also lower unemployment than in Spain in the 1990s. Watson (2015) argues that the lack of intra-left competition fostered a more stringent legal framework of employment protection. For instance, severance payments for permanent contracts were in practice much higher than in Portugal in spite of lower maximums.

Generally, employment protection in Southern Europe over the 1990s and 2000s was considered too stringent. In the Greek case, for instance, the OECD considered that the high barriers on dismissals may be "contributing to weak labor demand for 'outsiders' and low labor turnover, hindering progress in reducing the large gender/age imbalances in unemployment and hampering innovation activities" (OECD 2007, 22). One specific feature of the Greek employment protection regime was its level of complexity and particularistic nature: for instance, regulations were different for white-collar and blue-collar workers, besides the differences by company size found in other countries. In the early 2000s, regulations included quotas on layoffs (five workers per month for firms up to forty-nine employees and 2% of the workforce per month for larger firms). Severance payments for white-collar workers could reach up to twenty-four months' salary after twenty-eight years of employment, while blue-collar workers could claim 125 daily wages after twenty-five years. Severance payments increased with job tenure (OECD 2001, 66–67)

Over the 1980s and 1990s, which were characterized by high unemployment especially among younger workers, a number of liberalization measures in the area of employment protection legislation were undertaken that targeted young people by loosening regulations to facilitate their entry (Ferrera and Gualmini 2004, 91). In Italy, fixed-term training contracts were introduced in 1984 to allow for the young in particular to enter the workforce while benefiting from training (Adam and Canziani 1998, 9). Firms could also benefit from reduced social security contributions and therefore reduce labor costs by up to 30% on permanent contracts (Adam and Canziani 1998, 13). Article 18 of the Labor Code also became a controversial political issue, with several attempts to revoke it in a referendum in the early 2000s. The reform pressure was eased by low-interest rates in spite of a decade of relative stagnation (Ferrera and Gualmini 2004). In Spain as a consequence of the high unemployment of the 1980s, restrictions on the use of fixed-term contracts with low severance pay were loosened in 1984, which led to an explosion in the proportion of the workforce in temporary employment. The share of fixed-term contracts increased from less than 10% before 1984 to a third of the workforce throughout the 1990s, reaching the highest proportion in Western Europe even after regulatory attempts to limit their use (Ayuso-i-Casals 2004). Meanwhile, protection for permanent contracts remained relatively stable.

The Eurozone crisis was a turning point in the further liberalization of employment protection throughout Southern Europe. Liberalization reforms affected not only workers on the margins but also larger swathes of the core workforce (Afonso 2019). In the context of external conditionality and the need to adjust wages downward, the liberalization of employment protection legislation appeared as an expedient way to accelerate wage devaluation: with lower employment protection, jobs at pay levels set in the boom times could be more quickly replaced by jobs at wages set in a context of high unemployment.

For instance, in 2010 as bond yields on Spanish debt soared, the Spanish Socialist Workers' Party (PSOE) government of José Luis Zapatero reformed the labor code by seeking to balance between liberalization and limiting dualization. The government established a system in which severance payments increased progressively with tenure to reduce dualization and limited the duration of so-called project contracts (*contratos de obra y servicio*) to two years while also extending the list of motives for justified dismissals, thereby reducing severance pay for companies facing economic difficulties. In 2012, the new conservative government led by Mariano Rajoy implemented a much more radical reform of the labor code. The main points of the reform of labor legislation passed in February 2012 were a generalization in contracts with severance payments equivalent to thirty-three days per year with a maximum of twenty-four months' severance pay (vs. forty-five days so far), a facilitation of dismissals for economic causes with a severance payment of a mere twenty days per year. As a whole, average severance payments were cut by two-thirds (García-Pérez, Ignacio, and Jansen 2015, 3).

In Italy, the Fornero Law (92/2012) sought to revoke Article 18. However, after protests the government eventually backtracked, as unions were able to forge an alliance with the left-of-center Partito Democratico and watered down some of the measures, especially those concerning permanent contracts. Matteo Renzi's center-left government (2014–2016) also initiated a number of liberalization reforms framed as a way to overcome the strong dualism of the Italian labor market (Picot and Tassinari 2017). Here again, a reform of Article 18 was on the table, triggering a general strike organized by the biggest trade union confederation, the Italian General Confederation of Labour (CGIL), in December 2014. In spite of resistance from the unions and within his own party, Renzi managed to pass the reform through parliament in a vote of confidence in December 2014. The final version of this reform included the creation of a single contract with increasing tenure, the suppression of contributions of the so-called *cassa integrazione* (compensation fund) in case the company goes bankrupt, and the suppression of the obligation of reintegration of the worker in case of unfair dismissal (Picot and Tassinari 2017, 475).

In Portugal, similarly, the thrust of the reforms implemented was to bring protection for permanent contracts in line with the OECD average and achieve some level of internal devaluation. A major revision of the labor code (Law 23/2012) was adopted in 2012, providing for a decrease by 50% in compensation for extra hours, a reduction in severance payments, a broader understanding of "fair dismissal," fewer holidays, and the introduction of an "hour bank" extending by two hours the maximum duration of the normal working day (Diario da Republica 2012). Severance payments were a particularly important element of reform in this domain, and severance pay was reduced from thirty days per year of seniority to ten, thereby reducing the cost of dismissal of older—and more expensive—workers.

Finally, the country where the extent of liberalization was the greatest was Greece (Afonso 2019). The memorandum of understanding agreed between Greece and its international lenders during the Eurozone crisis outlined measures to "extend the probationary period for new jobs, reduce the overall level of severance payments and ensure that the same severance payment conditions apply to blue- and white-collar workers, to raise the minimum threshold for activation of rules on collective dismissals especially for larger companies, and to facilitate greater use of temporary contracts and part-time work" (European Commission 2010a, 76). Accordingly, the notice period for terminating white-collar permanent contracts was reduced, severance payments were cut by 50% for this category of workers, and thresholds for dismissals were lowered. The threshold for what is considered a collective dismissal (for which justification requirements were more stringent) was increased. Some measures were aimed at fixed-term contracts, making it more difficult to line up fixed-term contracts without justification. Overall, employment protection as measured by the widely used OECD employment protection index declined substantially in all Southern European countries, reaching levels below core European countries such as Germany and France.

5.3. Industrial Relations in Mediterranean Countries

In this section, we present a comparative account of the main developments in industrial relations in Mediterranean countries since the 1990s and focus on two main phases. The first phase runs from the 1990s to the precrisis years, with the most significant developments taking place in the run-up of the EMU in which a common pattern of reform of wage-setting institutions was generally achieved through peak-level coordination with social partners aimed at strengthening coordination and ensuring wage moderation. The second phase, the postcrisis period, instead showed a stronger unilateral state intervention on industrial relations and wage-setting institutions that also entailed pushes for more disorganized decentralization. However, outcomes of these interventions significantly vary across the four countries, strengthening the already existing heterogeneity of the Mediterranean cluster.

5.3.1. Developments Prior to the Crisis

During the 1990s, Mediterranean countries faced the challenge of complying with the Maastricht convergence criteria for entering the EMU. State-sponsored wage coordination in the form of social pacts was a defining feature of these countries' politics of adjustment, which ensured societal support to market-conforming economic policies based on wage restraint, the (organized) decentralization of industrial relations, and strongly controlled public expenditure (Regini 2000; Pochet, Keune, and Natali 2010; Molina 2014). During the 1990s and 2000s, forms of competitive corporatism were shared by Italy, Spain, and Portugal (Ebbinghaus and Hassel 2000; Molina and Rhodes 2007). No pacts were negotiated in Greece despite numerous attempts, but the ad hoc consultation of social partners and the standing bargaining among peak-level employers' and workers organizations on issues including wage setting and wage moderation operated as a functional equivalent to social concertation (Karamessini 2008).

In Italy, reforms of wage-setting institutions started in 1992 with the abolition of the famous wage indexation system *scala mobile*. In 1993, a tripartite agreement defined a comprehensive reform that aimed at the organized decentralization of the collective bargaining system and at fostering an institutionally driven wage moderation (Regalia and Regini 1998; Lucidi and Kleinknecht 2010).

In Portugal, a long series of tripartite agreements characterized the two decades from 1987 to 2009. Their content was strongly influenced by the goal of meeting EMU convergence criteria, with income policy figuring prominently. In Spain, tripartite social dialogue played a fundamental role as a governance mechanism of wage-setting institutions since the return to democracy, although its development trajectory was not linear and was often abandoned. Still, the consolidation of bipartite social dialogue constituted a balance to the more unstable social pacting and established some centralized coordination for wage setting (Molina and Rhodes 2011).

Hence, in the run-up to EMU, wage moderation and the decentralization of wage-setting institutions were reached through social dialogue backed by the active involvement of the state (Molina 2014). However, social pacting entered a phase of crisis after the accession to EMU, particularly in Italy (Hancké and Rhodes 2005; Pochet, Keune, and Natali 2010). A transformed external economic and monetary environment—with weakened incentives for concertation after having met the stringent EMU convergence criteria—combined with changing actors' preferences and strategies—weaker trade unions and increasingly less supportive employers—were identified as the main reasons for the dismissal of tripartite concertation. However, it was with the outbreak of the crisis that social pacting entered a dramatic decline and that state unilateralism resumed as the preferred policymaking mechanism.

5.3.2. Developments during the Crisis

Reforming collective bargaining and wage-setting institutions was a central part of Southern European governments' responses to the crisis with the goal of producing internal devaluation by ensuring downward wage adjustment.

This section examines developments in three different areas: collective bargaining, minimum wages, and employment relations in the public sector. We show that common to all analyzed countries was a tendency toward a stronger intervention of the state in these arenas and the diffusion of a unilateral policymaking style. Still, variation in how national governments intervened in the regulation of collective bargaining and in the setting of minimum wages was also visible—with Greece experiencing the strongest intervention and Italy the more moderate—and, most significantly, the outcome of these interventions. As a consequence, the institutional configuration of wage setting in Mediterranean countries has become more differentiated, particularly with regard to collective bargaining. Stronger similarities are instead visible concerning the way in which national governments addressed employment relations in the public sector.

5.3.2.1. Collective Bargaining Regulation

Governments in Greece, Portugal, and Spain reformed legal regulation of collective bargaining, while in Italy state intervention was significantly more limited, following the tradition of voluntarism characterizing Italian industrial relations (Regalia and Regini 1998). The goal of these reforms was to sustain internal devaluation and ensure the quick adjustment of wages to market conditions. This goal was pursued by different means: promoting the decentralization of wage setting at the firm level by modifying the balance between collective bargaining levels and removing favorability principles, limiting the extension of collective agreements to non-signatory parties and their automatic continuation after expiry, and expanding the legitimate signatories of collective agreements beyond trade unions. According to the Troika, all these rules constituted brakes to internal devaluation because they partially detached wage setting from pure market conditions and contributed to strengthening the power of trade unions.

Importantly, these reforms were in most cases undertaken unilaterally by governments without the involvement of social partners and even in front of significant opposition by trade unions and, to some extent, a cool reception also by employer associations (Bulfone and Afonso 2020; Howell 2020). This strongly differentiates the trajectories of transformation of collective bargaining institutions in Southern European countries (with the exception of Italy) from those taking place in continental and Nordic ones, where reforms of IR institutions have been more marginal and mostly negotiated between the social partners (Marginson 2015).

The most dramatic change was introduced in Greece, where the traditional system of collective bargaining regulation was turned upside down (Katsaroumpas and Koukiadaki 2019). The traditional predominance of sectoral agreements over company-level ones was reverted: the favorability principle was abolished, and company-level agreements now prevail over sectoral ones.

In 2011 the automatic extension of sectoral agreements was suspended, and in 2012 the automatic continuation of the validity of collective agreements was limited to three months. Finally, the law intervened to abolish the bargaining monopoly of trade unions: in 2011 "associations of persons" were entitled to sign company-level agreements in the absence of a company union proving they are supported by three-fifth of the company's workforce.

In Portugal, the most crucial area of intervention regarded the extension of collective agreements. Following the Memorandum of Understanding with the International Monetary Fund in December 2011, which asked for limits to the automatic extension of collective agreements considered to cause downward wage rigidity, more restrictive conditions were introduced by the reform of the Labor Code in 2012. To be extended could be agreements negotiated by organizations representing at least 50% of the sectoral workforce (Addison, Portugal, and Vilares 2016). The duration of collective agreements was reduced from five to three years and their validity after expiry from eighteen to twelve months. Finally, the favorability principle was inverted, with priority given to company-level agreements over sectoral and cross-sectoral ones even though social partners were still allowed to negotiate clauses in higher-level agreements reverting to the favorability principle.

In Spain, statutory intervention concerned both the balance between different collective bargaining levels and the validity of agreements after expiry. Urged by international institutions, Spanish governments pushed for a stronger decentralization of wage negotiation establishing the priority of company collective agreements, easing their capacity to derogate sectoral agreements, and opening the possibility for employers to unilaterally modify terms and conditions agreed (Molina 2014). Moreover, the principle of ultra-activity was modified, limiting to one year the automatic extension of expired agreements (which then cease to exist if not renewed).

Differently from what happened in Greece, Spain, and Portugal, Italian governments exercised relatively few direct interventions on industrial relations, with Article 8 of Law 148/2011 as the only initiative. This provision states that under certain conditions, agreements negotiated at the company or territorial level can derogate from sectoral agreements and even from the law.

In sum, common pressures toward decentralization and liberalization were visible in state intervention in IR in all four countries, although with very different degrees of intensity. Still, significant differences were visible in their actual impact on the collective bargaining system. For example, there has not been a generalized decline in collective bargaining coverage (table 5.2).

Only two countries, Greece and Portugal, witnessed a reduction in coverage rates in the postcrisis period. Still, only in Greece did industry-level bargaining collapse, with coverage rates moving from 100% in 2007 to an estimated 26% in 2016 as a consequence of the combined effects of the removal of the favorability principle, the suspension of extension procedures, and the introduction of new rules on expiry of nonrenewed collective agreements. In

Table 5.2 Collective bargaining coverage in Southern Europe, 2007–2016

	2007	2016
Greece	100	25.5
Italy	80	80
Portugal	86	73.9
Spain	82.9	83.6

Source: OECD.

Portugal coverage rates displayed more stability, with a reduction of 13 percentage points from 2007 to 2016. However, this figure masks deeper effects of the reforms on the functioning of the collective bargaining system. The introduction of more restrictive criteria for extension and the reduction of extension ordinances—which fell from 134 in 2008 to 10 in 2013—blocked the negotiation of new agreements, as Portuguese employers, similarly to their Greek counterparts, proved to be reluctant to negotiate agreements that would not be extended. A remarkable reduction in the number of new collective agreements, which fell from 296 in 2008 to 85 in 2012, and in their coverage, which declined from 66% of eligible workers in 2008 to 10% in 2013, followed suit, with particularly important consequences on wages. The nonrenewal of collective agreements in fact corresponds to a de facto wage freeze, a dimension not captured by relatively stable coverage rates. In Italy and Spain, collective bargaining coverage instead remained rather stable and high, at 80% and 84%, respectively.

Broadly similar were dynamics in company-level agreements. In all countries, this type of agreement shows a very limited take-up and company-level agreements continue to have a fairly limited coverage, ranging from around 20% of workers in Italy (Pedersini 2019), 5% in Portugal (Campos Lima 2019), and 6% in Spain (Pedersini and Leonardi 2018) without any significant increases over the last years. Similarly, the use of opting-out clauses and derogations does not seem to be particularly widespread: they are limited to 2% of Italian firms (CNEL and ISTAT 2016, 115) and to 0.3% of the Spanish workforce (Pedersini and Leonardi 2018, 24). This is deeply connected with the production structure of Southern European countries, which shows the predominance of small companies that, on the one hand, often lack the resources to negotiate autonomously and, on the other, prefer to leave distributional conflict outside the company (Regalia 2020).

Only in Greece are company-level agreements now the predominant form of collective bargaining. Despite being limited in their coverage, they represented 94% of all collective agreements in 2015 (Katsaroumpas and Koukiadakis 2019). Such agreements are predominantly signed by so-called associations of persons, which proved to be much more likely to engage in concession bargaining than trade unions. These pseudo-collective negotiations disguise the "essential sur-render of terms and conditions to the unilateral power of the employer" (Kat-saroumpas and Koukiadakis 2019, 329–30).

In sum, the effects of the reforms introduced during the 2010s were radical in Greece, leading some observers to talk of a "speedy neo-liberalization" (Ko-rnelakis and Voskeritsian 2014, 357), and were significant in Portugal and more limited in Italy and Spain. As we explore in greater detail in the next paragraph, this variation can be explained by considering the responses and strategies developed by social partners (Pedersini and Leonardi 2018) and particularly by employers. The reaction of social partners to governments' unilateral interventions on collective bargaining was in fact common to all Mediterranean countries except, again, Greece. Unsurprisingly, trade unions opposed these initiatives, and employer associations proved less supportive than probably expected, with employer associations in Italy, Spain, and Por-tugal taking action to limit the radical reforms introduced by governments (Bulfone and Afonso 2020).

This does not mean, however, that industrial relations systems did not un-dertake change. On the one hand, employers took advantage of the changing power balance between labor and capital to extract concessions from trade unions. In Italy, for example, Confindustria was able to secure the approval of all trade unions for cross-industry agreements defining rules on the validity of derogatory decentralized agreements, refused by the Italian General Con-federation of Labour (CGIL) in 2009 (Pedersini 2019). Furthermore, as a con-sequence of reforms, the balance of power between social partners seems to have shifted in favor of capital with effects on the content of collective agree-ments. With regard to Spain, Bulfone and Afonso (2020, 20) note that "it is highly likely that collective bargaining now takes place on advantageous terms for the employers, as trade unions are ready to accept worse labor conditions in order to reach an agreement." Similarly, in Italy there are signs of sectoral collective agreements becoming lighter and therefore less able to limit employer discretion and regulate the employment relationship. Concerning some issues (e.g., wages), this trend predates the crisis, but others are strongly connected with crisis-related dynamics, such as the impact of liberalizing labor market reforms on the regulation of atypical contracts in some sectoral collective agreements (Benassi, Dorigatti, and Pannini 2019). With regard to Portugal, Campos Lima (2019) highlights how the standards set by industry-level agree-ments deteriorated over the years and how companies have acquired more discretion, in particular on wage setting and working time flexibility.

5.3.2.2. Minimum Wages

Minimum wages have been another arena of state intervention in Mediterra-nean countries during the crisis, albeit to different extents. Minimum wage levels are historically low in Southern Europe, which is associated with medium to high earnings inequalities and a relatively large number of low-paid workers (Barbieri, Cutuli, and Scherer 2018). Moreover, there are important differences in levels, with Spain exhibiting generally higher levels in statutory minimum wages, especially since the increase in January 2019.

Greece, Portugal, and Spain are the European countries in which the level of minimum wages was reduced the most over the 2010–2013 period. In real terms, minimum wages declined by 29%, 7,% and 6% in Greece, Spain, and Portugal, respectively (Schulten and Müller 2015, 345). This has been accomplished through different means. In Greece in 2012, the level of the minimum wage was cut by 22% for employees above age twenty-five and by 32% for workers younger than age twenty-five. Moreover, since 2013 the Greek minimum wage has been frozen. The cut and the subsequent freeze was accomplished by removing the setting of the minimum wage from social partners' control. Indeed, while prior to the crisis the minimum wage was set by the social partners in the national general collective agreement, Law 4093/2012 and Law 4172/2013 transferred to the government the power to decide on this issue (Katsaroumpas and Koukiadaki 2019, 273).

In Portugal and Spain, the above-mentioned reduction of the minimum wage in real terms was due to the freeze imposed by governments in 2011, which lasted until 2014 in Portugal and 2012 in Spain. In the two countries, setting the level of the minimum wage was already a governmental prerogative (albeit in Spain after a nonbinding consultation with the social partners) (Grimshaw 2010), so nothing changed in this regard.

Italy is one of the few European countries that does not have a statutory minimum wage. Minimum wages are set at the sectoral level by the social partners, which assume a de facto *erga omnes* validity (Pedersini 2019). Provisions for the introduction of a minimum wage were part of the so-called Jobs Act passed during the government of Matteo Renzi (2014), and further proposals were formulated by different political parties since 2018, but with no effect by now.

Since 2015, these trends have been to some extent reversed but with variation across countries. As a consequence, minimum wages in Spain and Portugal are now higher than in 2010 (by 28% and 11%, respectively), while they are still lower in Greece (by 16%) (Eurofound 2019). Moreover, more spaces for negotiations and/or consultation with social partners seem to emerge in those countries where the trend toward state unilateralism intensified. This has been the case in Greece and Portugal, though in the former social partners are still demanding a return to a negotiated minimum wage. However, Spain has witnessed in recent years the preeminence of party-political negotiations over social dialogue when setting minimum wages. This shows that even in a favorable macroeconomic context, the shadow of hierarchy of the state remains key in order to understand developments in relation to industrial relations.

5.3.2.3. Employment Relations in the Public Sector

A last arena of intervention was the public sector. In all countries, the public sector has been a prime target of government austerity policies aimed at fiscal consolidation through a reduction of the public-sector wage bill. This goal was met by intervening on employment levels (introducing more stringent rules concerning turnover) and on wages (cutting or freezing them and/or increasing working time). While these tendencies characterized governments' responses to the crisis all over Europe, they have been particularly significant in Mediterranean countries, with the largest pay bill cuts in Greece, Spain, and Portugal (Bach and Bordogna 2016).

In Greece, any formal and informal collective bargaining was frozen in 2010, and pay cuts were subsequently imposed. In 2010, the government established an across-the-board pay reduction of 10% for wages exceeding €21,600 a year and cut bonuses and Christmas, Easter, and holiday allowances (which were completely abolished in 2012). In 2012, a 12% pay cut was applied to workers in the special wage regimes, which cover judges, diplomats, political appointees, doctors, professors, police, and armed forces. In 2011, weekly working time was increased from 37.5 to 40 hours per week without corresponding wage increases, producing a de facto further cut in wages (Ioannou 2016).

In Italy, legislation first imposed wage moderation (in the 2008–2009 national bargaining round wage increases were limited to half of those agreed to in previous rounds) and then froze wages (and even cut higher-level ones), suspending collective bargaining until 2015, when the Constitutional Court declared this unconstitutional. Collective negotiations were not stopped at the decentralized level, but they were highly discouraged by very tight financial constraints imposed on local administrations (Bordogna 2016).

In Portugal, nominal wages above 1,500 euros were successively cut down between 3.5% and 10% in 2011, 2012, 2013, and 2014. Cuts were extended to wages above 675 euros in 2014, but this measure was declared unconstitutional by the Constitutional Court. In 2011, Christmas bonuses were cut by half and were suspended altogether in 2012, as happened also to holiday bonuses. Again, this decision was later repealed by the Constitutional Court. Working time was increased from thirty-five to forty hours per week in 2013 with no equivalent wage increase. In 2014 and 2015 the central government blocked around five hundred collective agreements signed at the local level between trade unions and local governments that foresaw a return to the weekly working time of thirty-five hours (Campos Lima and Abrantes 2016).

In 2010 Spanish public-sector wages were reduced on average by 5%, with variation according to the occupational scale, and then frozen. Moreover, additional cuts in fringe benefits (such as Christmas and holiday allowances) were imposed in 2012. Working time was increased in 2011 from 35 to 37.5 hours per week without a corresponding wage increase. Estimates set at 15–20% the reduction of average wages of public employees between 2008 and 2014 (Molina 2016, 63).

In all countries, the way in which national governments intervened in public-sector employment relations was marked by strong unilateralism (since in most cases national governments intervened without negotiations with trade unions) and a tendency toward a recentralization of employment relations. This departed from patterns established in the decades preceding the crisis, which on the contrary saw a tendency to expand collective negotiation of employment relations in the public sector and a trend toward more decentralization of bargaining and individualization of wage setting, largely inspired by New Public Management principles (Bach and Bordogna 2016; Molina 2014). A partial exception in this sense is Greece, where working conditions are only partially subject to collective bargaining and public-sector wages are still determined statutorily (Ioannou 2016).

In more recent years, the four countries have shown a certain revitalization of collective bargaining in the public sector and a partial reversal of pay freezes and cuts. In Italy, collective bargaining was resumed in 2017, and collective agreements for all segments of the public sector were signed between the end of 2017 and the beginning of 2018. In Spain, a new framework agreement for working conditions and employment in public administration was signed in March 2018. The agreement establishes a minimum wage increase of 6.1% for public employees over the period 2018–2020 and a maximum of 8.9% conditional upon growth in gross domestic product and the fulfillment of the budget deficit target for 2020. It is the first time that wage increases for public employees will be linked to macroeconomic performance. Also, social dialogue at regional and local levels remains conditional upon administrations meeting deficit objectives.

5.4. Accounting for Trajectories of Change

On the basis of the above discussion, the trajectory of change in the Southern European models of labor market regulation and industrial relations since the 1980s can be summarized as having followed a *common trajectory of liberalization*, albeit with variations—over time and across countries—in the depth and scope of institutional change. In the field of labor market regulation, from the late 1980s and onward until the onset of the financial/sovereign debt crisis a common pattern of "reforms at the margins" resulted in dualization and segmentation of protections, while increased flexibility—especially in the atypical and informal segments of the labor market—was not accompanied by adequate expansions in social safety nets. In industrial relations, the direction of travel until the crisis had, on its part, combined a common pattern of wage moderation—internalized into the structure of collective bargaining and facilitated also through peak-level agreements—with mostly unsuccessful attempts at bargaining decentralization. Both the institutional setup and, to a lesser extent, the functioning of labor market institutions across all Southern

European economies experienced deeper and faster transformations in a liberalizing direction during the decade following the onset of the sovereign debt crisis in 2010. Yet even in the crisis context, several observers have highlighted persisting variation *across* Southern European countries in the depth and scope of liberalization (Picot and Tassinari 2017; Afonso 2019; Bulfone and Tassinari 2020).

How to make sense of these developments? We contend that the transformations that have taken place since the 1980s in the labor market regulatory models of Southern European economies can be understood as a process of variegated and contested institutional change whereby a common impetus for liberalization arising from the twin processes of (neoliberal) economic globalization and European integration has been mediated in each country by domestic political factors, including producer group politics, electoral politics, and institutional path dependencies.

5.4.1. Common Pressures: Globalization and Monetary Integration

As in other advanced capitalist economies (Baccaro and Howell 2017), Southern European countries have been subject since the 1980s to comparable pressures for the liberalization and deregulation of their employment relations and labor market institutions (Gambarotto and Solari 2015, 797–98). Two parallel interconnected processes can be identified as the main drivers of liberalization in Southern Europe: first, increased exposure to globalization, with its associated trends of de-industrialization and progressive financialization of accumulation models since the mid-1980s (Gambarotto and Solari 2015; Dooley 2018), and second and related, the process of integration into the EMU.

Since the mid-1980s, increased exposure to international competition and integration in global value chains generated in Southern European economies strong competitive pressures on several key sectors, especially manufacturing. However, due their late and partial industrialization processes, Southern European countries found themselves facing the challenges of globalization from a particularly disadvantageous semiperipheral position within the global and European political economy (Gambarotto and Solari 2015). Their prevalent specialization in lower value-added productions (with the partial exception of northern Italy) had historically created strong incentives for the state, supported by demands from business groups, to shelter key sectors from excessive competition and guarantee capital profitability through low labor costs and/or tolerance of rules flouting (Gambarotto and Solari 2015, 796). However, integration in the common European market required a progressive liberalization of key sectors and opening up to international competition, thus limiting the coordinating or sheltering role that the state could play in adapting to the pressures of globalization.

Increased economic openness and exposure to international capital flows had several impacts on Southern European economies. Especially in Portugal, Spain, and Greece, access to cheap credit and increased capital inflows accelerated a process of financialization that dislocated investments away from the productive economy and exacerbated domestic demand booms, thus contributing to low productivity growth (Gambarotto and Solari 2015, 804; Dooley 2018). Integration within the EMU also deprived governments of the tool of currency depreciation as a lever of external competitiveness, thus placing an emphasis on the labor market—and particularly on labor costs—as the main channel of adjustment.

During the 1990s, the combination of heightened international competition, stagnating productivity, and a rise in domestic prices generated strong incentives for Southern European employers to demand the flexibilization of labor market protections along with wage moderation and the possibility for flexible adjustment in wage setting to retain external competitiveness. These were important drivers for the processes of labor market deregulation initiated across all Southern European countries from the mid-1980s. Reliance on low labor costs and external numerical flexibility became increasingly internalized by Southern European employers as core components of their competitive strategies.

In the same period, wage moderation also acquired renewed centrality as a macroeconomic policy objective for Southern European policymakers in the process of EMU integration, as containment of inflation was a key criteria for the Maastricht convergence process (Hanckè and Rhodes 2005). Southern European governments were thus compelled to engineer mechanisms of peak-level coordination of wage setting, mostly via headline social pacts, to achieve the goals of wage moderation that labor market actors could not produce fully autonomously (Hanckè and Rhodes 2005). In sum, the competitiveness pressures of globalization and the deflationary pressures inherent in the EMU design gave governments impetus to implement deregulatory structural reforms of labor markets and industrial relations systems to achieve greater labor market flexibility and wage moderation.

These pressures, intrinsic in the design of the EMU, were further reinforced in the context of the Eurozone sovereign debt crisis. As the Southern European crisis experience turned from conjunctural downturn into a severe fiscal-cum-sovereign debt crisis in 2010–2011, structural reforms of labor market regulation and industrial relations became a central target of crisis-responsive adjustment (Cioffi and Dubin 2016; Picot and Tassinari 2017) and a significant component of the policy recommendations leveraged on crisis-struck countries through either the Memoranda of Understanding concluded with the Troika or mechanisms of implicit conditionality (Sacchi 2015). The crisis context therefore empowered Southern European policymakers to pursue liberalization to an unprecedented extent at the expense of organized labor (Cioffi and Dubin 2016; Rutherford and Frangi 2016). According to their stated rationale, liberalizing labor market policy (LMP) reforms aimed at achieving three related objectives: first, facilitate internal devaluation that would supposedly support external competitiveness by lowering labor costs; second, address the unfolding unemployment crisis by, on the one hand, facilitating employment creation and, on the other, encouraging labor market activation; and third, support fiscal consolidation by rationalizing welfare expenditure.

5.4.2. Accounting for Variation: Pressures Mediated by Domestic Political Dynamics

Despite the common pressures and structural trends that lie at its roots, the liberalization of labor market regulation and industrial relations institutions in Southern Europe has been neither seamless nor homogenous. Rather, its trajectory, depth, and scope have been mediated by country-specific configurations of institutional and political factors that have resulted in some nonnegligible differences across countries. Country-specific patterns of variation can be explained in light of three main sets of factors: first, the dynamics of *interest intermediation* between governments and organized producer groups; second, *specific employer preferences*; and third, *electoral politics*. We do not argue for the causal primacy of one set of factors over the others. Rather, we aim to highlight how these combine in mediating and refracting the contested process of neoliberal restructuring.

5.4.2.1. Interest Intermediation and Producer Group Politics

While the state has played an undoubtedly central role as an agent of liberalization in Southern European political economies since the 1980s (Rutherford and Frangi 2016; Howell 2020), its capacity to implement structural reforms has been significantly mediated by the dynamics of *interest intermediation* with organized producer groups and by variations in the balance of power between the actors. In particular, the degree of *government strength* and the *power resources* that *organized producer groups* could rely on to intervene in the policy process have impacted significantly the trajectory of labor market policy and IR change.

Most notably during the process of EMU accession in the 1990s, weak governments—that is, minority or technocratic cabinets or divided coalitions—in Italy, Spain, and Portugal were repeatedly compelled to involve unions and employers' organizations in policymaking via headline social pacts to share the political costs of unpopular labor market, pensions, and welfare reforms and enlist their collaboration in implementation (Avdagic, Rhodes, and Visser 2011). While allowing governments to partly circumvent their potential veto powers, concertation also granted unions and employers' organizations some influence over policy design. Social concertation as an avenue of producer group influence over policy developments was less relevant in Greece, where the main channel of employers' and unions' influence on policymaking were instead their (clientelist) links with the main political parties, which created highly uneven and segmented trajectories of liberalization up to the crisis (Barta 2018).

Notwithstanding the different mechanisms through which they were articulated across countries, the capacity of organized producer groups to leverage influence over the policy process mediated significantly the depth and speed of liberalization in Southern European political economies, resulting in segmentation but also in the resilience of specific institutional forms—such as sectoral collective bargaining—that still retained the overall support of both unions and peak-level employer confederations.

As highlighted above, during the Great Recession formal tripartite concertation lost part of its relevance as a mechanism of political legitimation and socioeconomic adjustment. The far-reaching structural reforms of LMP and IR recalled above were indeed mostly implemented either unilaterally or via cosmetic or symbolic concertation agreements that did not impact meaningfully on reforms' content (Tassinari and Donaghey 2020). This paved the way to more far-reaching liberalization than in the previous two decades. Reasons for this (partial) shift were diversely ascribed to the intensity and urgency of the crisis moment, the severity of exogenous conditionality increasing state autonomy and adversely altering the balance of class power against organized labor, and the progressive loss of strength and legitimacy of Southern European labor movements (Culpepper and Regan 2014; Guardiancich and Molina 2017; Tassinari and Donaghey 2020).

However, the decline of social concertation did not completely eliminate the influence of producer groups over the policy process. Indeed, the resilience of specific *institutional power resources* of unions and employer organizations has continued to mediate the pace of liberalization. For instance, the greater degree of social partners' autonomy in wage setting and collective bargaining in Italy compared to the other three countries has been identified as a key factor accounting for the more limited extent of wage devaluation that Italy experienced during the Great Recession (Afonso 2019) as well as for the persisting (formal) resilience of sectoral collective bargaining despite ongoing pressures for decentralization (Regalia and Regini 2018). This suggests that the capacity of organized labor to mediate liberalization pressures might have shifted from being dependent on its *political* strength to being more contingent on its *institutional* power resources and relative degree of embeddedness in different areas of socioeconomic governance. The progressive erosion of social partners' autonomy in the industrial relations sphere arising from state-driven liberalization might, however, undermine this source of power in the long run.

5.4.2.2. Employer Preferences

The specific *preferences of domestic employers and business actors* have also imparted specific trajectories to the process of liberalization in Mediterranean capitalism. Historically, the fragmentation of domestic employer organizations in the Southern European context limited their influence in shaping systems of labor market regulation and social protection post–World War II (Watson 2015,

22–23). However, although not always fulfilled, their preferences have played a nonnegligible role in accounting for the preservation of specific mechanisms of nonmarket coordination in industrial relations system and labor market governance. For example, as Bulfone and Afonso (2020) show, across Southern Europe domestic employer organizations dominated by small and medium-size enterprises have retained, even in the context of the Great Recession, a preference for preserving various forms of state support for encompassing collective bargaining—in particular sectoral extension mechanisms of collective bargaining agreements—and for maintaining the formal primacy of the sectoral level of collective bargaining over the firm level.

Bulfone and Afonso (2020, 815–17) highlight how Southern European domestic employers' preferences for retaining aspects of encompassing sectoral bargaining arise from both the specific *organizational* interests of employer associations—keen to retain their institutionalized role and competences in sectoral bargaining—and the distinctive *structural* features of the Southern European domestic business landscape. Small and medium-size employers, which make up around 90% of firms in Southern Europe, have indeed retained a preference for sectoral bargaining as a way to eschew the transaction costs associated with firm-level bargaining, avoid having to engage with unions at the workplace, and maintain a level playing field in their respective sectors by avoiding undercutting. Thus, they have sought to accommodate external competitive pressures by aiming to preserve systems of (weakened) sectoral collective bargaining that internalize wage moderation and incorporate *within* sectoral agreements the possibility for substantive firm-level deviations without, however, shifting the legally predominant locus of bargaining while maintaining encompassing coverage.

Employers' varying capacity to enact these preferences, either by influencing the policy agendas of political parties (Moury, Cardoso, and Gago 2019) or via coordinated action with peak-level unions in the industrial relations sphere (Regalia and Regini 2018; Bulfone and Afonso 2020), helps to explain why despite strong attempts at state-induced collective bargaining decentralization, especially during the Great Recession, changes in the predominant level of bargaining have been overall limited. The exception in this respect is Greece, where the almost complete disempowerment of domestic producer groups in the context of the Troika-led adjustment has led to an unprecedented depth of transformation in industrial relations institutions (Kornelakis and Voskeritsian 2014). Whether in the other Southern European countries the mediating influence of domestic employers' preferences will continue to be impactful in this respect is, however, an open question. The forced reorientation of Mediterranean growth models toward exports in the post–Great Recession period (Pérez and Matsaganis 2019) might indeed alter the balance of power between different business segments, possibly increasing the relative influence of export-oriented employers with a more marked preference for bargaining decentralization (Bulfone and Tassinari 2020) and therefore resulting in more path-departing institutional change.

5.4.2.3. Electoral Politics

Alongside producer group politics, *electoral politics* and dynamics of electoral competition have also shaped country-specific trajectories of development of labor market and IR within Southern Europe—both in its phase of consolidation up to the early 1990s and in the successive liberalization period.

Domestic electoral dynamics have also mediated how common exogenous pressures for liberalization have been translated across different Southern European countries in the twenty-first century, including during the Great Recession. In general, it is well established that government partisanship shapes the domestic impacts of exogenous pressures such as bailouts and EU conditionality (cf. Walter 2016). In this regard, extant scholarship highlighted how Southern European center-right governments during the euro crisis, such as in Spain or in Portugal between 2012 and 2015, were generally more keen to pursue far-reaching liberalization of employment protection legislation—both for temporary and open-ended employees—and radical decentralization of collective bargaining than their center-left counterparts, using the crisis as a window of opportunity to disempower labor and fulfill long-standing preferences of employers' groups in dismissal regulation (Cioffi and Dubin 2016; Picot and Tassinari 2017; Branco and Cardoso 2020).

However, differences in the liberalization trajectories observed in the labor market and the industrial relations sphere during the crisis across Southern Europe cannot be explained simply in terms of left-right partisanship differences, as the relative balance of liberalization and regulation has also varied *within* partisan families. For example, the main Italian center-left party, the Partito Democratico, embraced since 2014 a reform agenda combining unprecedented liberalization of employment protection legislation for both temporary and open-ended employees (similar to those implemented by the Spanish and Portuguese center-right cabinets) with an expansion of unemployment benefits coverage in a universalistic direction (Picot and Tassinari 2017). This contrasts with the approach of the Spanish and Portuguese Socialist Parties, which remained instead reluctant to deregulate employment protection legislation for open-ended employees during the Eurozone crisis until forced to do so by exogenous conditionality.

The differing composition of the electoral coalitions and social blocs of reference for governing parties can help to explain the variation observed within party families (Picot and Tassinari 2017; Vesan and Ronchi 2019; Afonso and Bulfone 2020; Bulfone and Tassinari 2020). For example, the Partito Democratico's embrace of employment protection legislation deregulation has been explained in light of the middle-class reorientation it pursued after 2013 and of the increasing weight in its electoral base of social groups privileging liberalizing and social investment measures (Vesan and Ronchi 2019; Bulfone and Tassinari 2020). This in turn decreased the importance of trade unions and traditional working-class constituencies in shaping the party's policy stance. By contrast, the Spanish PSOE and the Portuguese Partido Socialista retained a greater share of traditional working-class voters in their electorate and faced stronger competition from leftist parties with a prolabor, prowelfare stance. Consequently, in the early phases of the crisis the parties remained more resistant to employment protection legislation and collective bargaining liberalization (Bulfone and Tassinari 2020) and in the postcrisis phase advocated various forms of reregulation in LMP and the expansion of prooutsider policies such as generous minimum wages (Branco et al. 2019).

Since 2015, the nonnegligible growth across all four countries of antisystemic challenger parties—of the radical Left in Spain (Podemos), Greece (Syriza), and Portugal (Bloco de Esquerda) and of the populist (M5S) and the radical Right (Lega) variant in Italy—brought to the fore of the political agenda demands for more expansionary social policy and reregulation of elements of labor market regulation (Afonso and Bulfone 2020; Bulfone and Tassinari 2020).

However, the room for maneuver available to Southern European governments to deviate significantly from the dominant trajectory of internal devaluation is narrow in the postcrisis context in light of the imperative of not negatively impacting the fragile prospects of an export-led recovery (Bulfone and Tassinari 2020). The limited scope of policy reversals implemented thus far, even by populist governments such as the Italian M5S-Lega cabinet of 2018–2019 and the PSOE-Podemos cabinet in Spain, demonstrates these limits (Branco et al. 2019).

Finally, in countries characterized by strong clientelist dynamics such as Greece and Italy, political parties' preoccupation with retaining the support of their linked electoral constituencies in specific regions or subsectors of the economy has also shaped the trajectory of LMP change in the face of liberalization pressures. These dynamics account, for example, for the survival of targeted, particularistic forms of labor market protection for powerful electoral groups even at times of liberalization, such as more generous employment protection legislation for senior civil servants in Greece (Matsaganis 2019). Additionally, partisan governments with close linkages to segments of the electorate or to employer groups strongly reliant on informal/undeclared employment practices (e.g., in tourism, agricultures, or textiles), such as Silvio Berlusconi's center-right coalition and the Five Star Movement in southern Italy, have also displayed a higher tolerance for informal employment and an unwillingness to intervene strongly through statutory regulation and law enforcement to suppress these practices. This attitude, akin to what Holland (2017) names a strategy of "forbearance as redistribution," is partly motivated by parties' reluctance to disrupt the livelihoods of informal workers but also by the competitive strategies of employers in key sectors dependent on undeclared work. Tolerance of informal employment, in the Southern European context, might thus also be characterized as a strategy of forbearance as competitiveness.

5.5. Labor Market Outcomes, Wages, and Productivity

The previous sections have shown the trajectories of change in labor markets and employment relations systems of Southern Europe together with those factors accounting for differences behind a common liberalization trend. What have been the outcomes of these reforms? Have they contributed to consolidating and institutionalizing cost-based competitive strategies and internal devaluation? Without pretending to be exhaustive, this section draws a broad picture of commonalities and differences in labor market outcomes, wages, and productivity with a twofold objective: first, analyzing convergence or divergence in labor market and industrial relations outcomes in light of reform trajectories outlined in previous sections, and second, providing a preliminary assessment of their impact on the competitive strategies of Mediterranean countries and, more specifically, on the internal devaluation process.

5.5.1. Employment, Unemployment, and Inequalities

Generally speaking, the broad characteristics of Southern European employment outcomes have been low female employment rates with the notable exception of Portugal, high rates of unemployment among the young and women, and a large informal and precarious sector (Karamessini 2008, 510). Still, these countries diverged in outcomes along the lines of employment and inequality. Namely, Portugal has been characterized for a long time by higher employment but also higher inequality, while the other countries combined a narrower employment base with lower income inequality.

Generally, the employment rate of the working-age population in Mediterranean countries has been lower than the OECD and European Union (EU) averages, with the notable exception of Portugal. In 2019, the employment rate was 56.5% in Greece, 59% in Italy, 63.3% in Spain, and 70.5% in Portugal versus 69.3% in the EU. These lower employment rates in Italy, Spain, and Greece can be accounted for in a large part by lower employment rates for women, which show higher discrepancies than for men. One of the major factors presented in the literature to explain the low participation of women in the labor market has been strong familism (Ferrera 1996; Karamessini 2008). Portugal stands apart from the other Southern European countries in this respect, with above-average rates of labor force participation for women. A major difference seems to be the rate of labor force participation of lower-educated women, who are much more likely to hold a job in Portugal compared to other Southern European countries. In fact, in 2018 Portuguese women with education levels below secondary had the highest employment rates in the EU at 62%, compared to 35% in Greece and Italy, 46% in Spain, and 45% across the EU (see Tavora 2012). This pattern dates back to the 1960s and the mobilization of men in the colonial wars (André 2002). Since the early 2000s there has been a strong increase in female labor force participation in Spain, reaching Portuguese levels at around 70%, while Italy and Greece plateaued at 60%.

Unemployment has also generally been higher in Southern Europe than in the rest of the EU, with notable variation across countries. The extreme case for a long time has been Spain, with a much higher unemployment threshold than other countries. Unemployment in Spain in the 1990s hovered over 20% at its highest point, and even at the height of the construction-led economic boom preceding the financial crisis, unemployment did not get below 8%. In contrast, the lowest unemployment rate in Portugal during the same period was below 4.15%. The Greek case, given the extent of the economic recession it has faced after 2010, also stands out, with a maximum unemployment rate of 27%. Here again, there were stark gender divisions in these differences especially in Spain and Greece, where unemployment rates for women have generally been much higher than for men. In Spain, the average unemployment rate for men has been 14% and 21% for women, even surpassing 30% in the 1990s; in Portugal, the average unemployment has been 7.15% for men and 9.2% for women. The Portuguese labor market has generally been more effective at providing jobs for low-educated women in particular. In Spain, a pattern that is worth noting is the convergence in unemployment rates between men and women in the wake of the financial crisis, as the collapse of the construction sector mostly destroyed jobs held by men.

One last important characteristic of Southern European labor markets has been high levels of segmentation in rights and outcomes across age groups and genders. One central dimension considered in the literature on dualization is the incidence of fixed-term employment as an indicator of the division between a core of relatively protected workers (mostly male and older) in permanent employment and a periphery of precarious workers (disproportionately female and young) in fixed-term employment. These divisions are indeed very important in Mediterranean labor markets. The most extreme case here is Spain, with an extremely high share of fixed-term contracts: at 26.3% in 2019, Spain had the highest proportion of fixed-term employment in the EU; shares in Portugal (20.7%) and Italy (17.1%) were also high, whereas this share in Greece (12.6%) was below the EU average. The incidence of fixed-term employment was particularly high among the young: while the EU average was 43%, fixed-term employment concerned 70% of young Spaniards between ages fifteen and twenty-four in dependent employment and 64% in Portugal and Italy, but this share was only a quarter in Greece. The different levels of fixed-term contracts hide divergent trends among the four Mediterranean countries. The two countries where the liberalization of employment protection legislation was stronger, Spain and Greece, experienced an 18.7% and 6.6% decline, respectively, in fixed-term contracts since 2000. By contrast, Italy and Portugal, where liberalization of employment protection legislation was less intense, experienced a 69% and 4.5% increase, respectively.

Income inequality in Mediterranean labor markets has usually been midway between continental and liberal countries. The Gini coefficient in Mediterranean countries since 2010 has hovered around 0.34 for all countries, compared to 0.27 for Sweden and 0.36 for the United Kingdom. One notable evolution in this area has been the reduction in income inequality in Portugal since 2005. Before 2005, Portugal has higher levels of income inequality than the United Kingdom, mostly due to the much higher share of low-educated women and higher income returns on skills, but since then has mostly converged to levels similar to that of other Mediterranean countries. On a number of indicators of inequality such as Gini, there has been a convergence across countries.

The level and evolution of low-wage earners as a proportion of all employees over the period 2006–2014 shows a mixed picture for Southern Europe (figure 5.1). First, compared to the Eurozone average, Italy, Portugal, and Spain have a below-average low-wage incidence. As a matter of fact, only Portugal before the crisis and Greece both before and afterward have a higher proportion of low-wage earners. Interestingly, the only country where there is no legal minimum wage, Italy, is the one with the lower proportion of low-wage earners. This confirms analyses of the consequences of functional institutional equivalence between legal and negotiated minimum wages with high coverage (Garnero, Kampelmann, and Rycx 2015).

The dynamics in all four Southern European countries are nevertheless different. In the case of the two countries where collective bargaining coverage exhibited a decline, Greece and Portugal, we observe opposite trends. In Greece, there is a sharp increase in 2014 in the percentage of low-wage earners. By contrast, in Portugal there was a reduction between 2006 and 2014. In Spain, the percentage of low-wage earners has increased slightly over the period considered. High collective bargaining coverage is accordingly an important but not sufficient element to reduce the proportion of low-wage earners as shown by the contrasting cases of Greece and Portugal.

5.5.2. Collectively Agreed Wages and Productivity

As we have seen, industrial relations developments prior to the 2008 crisis in all Southern European economies had the aim of achieving wage moderation and a tighter relationship between wages and productivity in collective bargaining. This should have strengthened competitiveness, whose deficit was overwhelmingly attributed to labor costs. How far was this strategy successful? What emerges from a comparison of developments in collectively agreed wages, actual wages, and productivity in the four Mediterranean countries is a clear capacity of wage restraint, particularly evident in the postcrisis period, with the limited

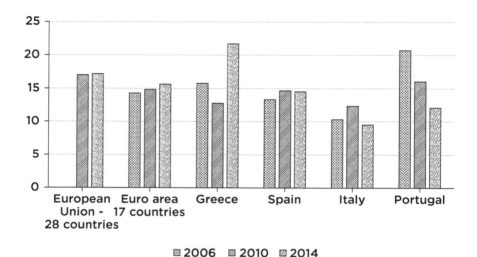

Figure 5.1. Low-wage earners as a proportion of all employees, 2006–2014. Source: Eurostat.

exception of Italy. However, productivity in Southern Europe grew much less than in other EU countries and continued to show a sluggish dynamic, particularly in Greece and Italy. Several authors have highlighted how strategies of internal devaluation (e.g., the liberalization of labor markets, the compression of minimum wages, and the decentralization of collective bargaining institutions) that we have seen at play, although with different intensity, in Mediterranean countries in the wake of the economic and financial crisis may have encouraged firms to focus on forms of low-wage production that tend to further depressing productivity by reducing employers' incentives to invest in productivity-enhancing investments (Lucidi and Kleinknecht 2010; Hall 2018).

In spite of similar trajectories of institutional change in the 1990s, developments in collectively agreed wages, actual wages, and productivity in Southern Europe show the existence of different patterns over the 2000–2008 period (figure 5.2). Italy registered zero or negative productivity increases, with actual and negotiated wages growing in parallel but with a positive wage drift as a consequence of the two-tier bargaining system at place since the early 1990s. In both Portugal and Spain, the early 2000s were also characterized by low increases in actual and negotiated wages. However, while in Spain productivity and wages followed similar dynamics, in the case of Portugal productivity experienced higher increases in relation to actual or negotiated wages since the early 2000s. Finally, though no data on negotiated wages exists for Greece, we can observe how actual wages experienced the highest increases among all four countries in the precrisis period, a trend that changed abruptly in 2010.

In all four countries, the 2008 crisis and reforms implemented during this period had a clear impact on wage-productivity dynamics. However, significant

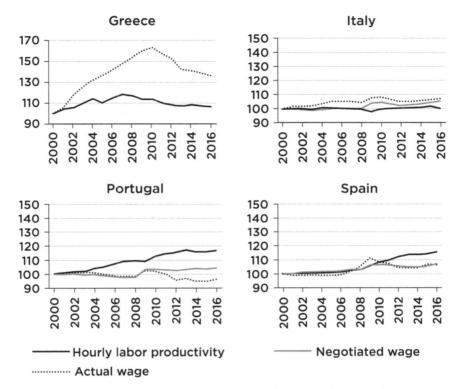

Figure 5.2. Collectively agreed wages, actual wages, and productivity, 2000–2016 (2000 = 100). Source: OECD.

differences can be observed across the countries. In the case of Portugal, the crisis led to a negative wage drift, as negotiated wages have remained rather stable since 2009 but actual wages declined. This is probably related to the decline in collective bargaining coverage registered in the case of Portugal but also to the erosion of the favorability principle and the preeminence of firm-level collective bargaining. In Italy, the crisis led to a narrowing of the gap between actual and negotiated dynamics, with no impact on productivity increases, that remained below those wages. Finally, Spain experienced a sustained increase in labor productivity, while actual and negotiated wages followed very similar trends and grew below productivity.

As a result of these divergent trends in productivity and negotiated and actual wages, we also observed two clearly differentiated patterns in the evolution of real unit labor costs and the adjusted wage share in Southern Europe (figure 5.3). On the one hand, Portugal and Spain have experienced a sustained decline since the early 2000s, with only a temporary halt from 2007 to 2009. On the other side, Italy and Greece experienced an increase in real unit labor costs in the precrisis period. In the aftermath of the crisis,

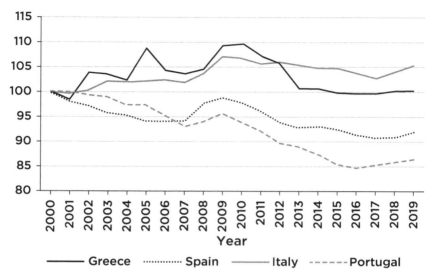

Figure 5.3. Real unit labor costs, 2000–2019 (2000 = 100). Source: AMECO Database.

these two countries registered more moderate declines in real unit labor costs.

5.6. Conclusion

This chapter analyzed the transformation in labor market regulations and industrial relations institutions that occurred in Mediterranean countries since 1980, with a closer focus to developments taking place during the Eurozone crisis. As we have highlighted, far-reaching reforms took place in both arenas, with the Great Recession marking a breakthrough because of both the depth and the number of reforms implemented. As a consequence, labor market and industrial relations institutions have been fundamentally reshaped in these countries. The first question we tried to answer in this chapter was to what extent had all these reforms eroded the contours of a distinctive Mediterranean model of capitalism, that is, whether we are observing substantial stability or change and whether trajectories across the four countries are convergent or divergent.

Despite the transformations that have occurred in labor market regulations, some distinctive features of the Mediterranean model remain in all countries, especially with regard to the intensity of state regulation. However, some of the differences in relation to other European models have been smoothed significantly especially since the 2008 crisis. Particularly notable is the case of duality caused by differences in the regulation of standard contracts and nonstandard contracts, in particular fixed-term contracts. After several years of liberalization at the margins maintaining the protection of standard contracts, in recent years significant changes have been introduced in the regulation of standard employment.

The intensification of statutory intervention as an agent of liberalization has been particularly important in industrial relations, where the state has frequently displaced the social partners in areas such as reforms of collective bargaining, minimum wage, and public-sector employment relations. However, the mechanisms whereby the state has been more active in industrial relations have changed. During the 1990s and early 2000s, the state intervened mostly by promoting peak-level coordination with social partners. With the advent of the 2008 crisis, state intervention shifted toward forms of - stronger unilateralism. Therefore, the central role of the state and the intensity in state regulation is maintained.

While the process of change displays significant similarities across the four countries, however, the outcomes of this change significantly vary. A process of divergence is accordingly taking place, with deregulation of industrial relations being more far reaching in Greece than in any other country, making it more difficult to identify a Mediterranean cluster (Eurofound 2018).

Which factors help to explain the differences in reform trajectories within the Mediterranean cluster? All countries in this cluster have been exposed to similar liberalization pressures as a consequence of the twin processes of monetary integration and deepening globalization. States have played a central role in this process, but their action has been mediated by domestic factors. First, electoral politics is probably the major source of variation precisely because of the gatekeeper role of states in Southern Europe. But rather than left-right partisanship differences, the composition of electoral coalitions and social blocs of reference for governing parties instead explains variations observed within party families in relation to the implementation of a liberalization agenda. Moreover, government actions have also been mediated by the influence of producer groups over the policy process. Even though the stronger unilateral character of state intervention and the decline of social concertation points to a weaker role of trade unions and employer associations, social partners still display a significant influence capacity. In Italy, Portugal, and Spain, in fact, outright liberalization, particularly in the industrial relations sphere, has been resisted by trade unions and, to a remarkable extent, also by employers.

Despite their variation in outcomes, particularly in the industrial relations arena, the process of liberalization since 1980 has contributed to the progressive exhaustion of the domestic demand–led growth models of Southern Europe. The more or less unsuccessful, forced reorientation toward export-led growth after the Great Recession (Pérez and Matsaganis 2019; Baccaro, this volume) has in turn locked in the incentives for Southern European governments to stick to a pathway of internal devaluation and austerity even as crisis pressures partly abated. Those elements of labor market policy and IR liberalization of specific relevance to external competitiveness—especially employment protection legislation deregulation and greater flexibility in collective bargaining at the firm level—have indeed thus far remained untouched in the postcrisis period even when left-wing executives came to power as in Portugal and Greece (Branco et al. 2019), thus testifying to the continuing persistence of liberalization imperatives.

Chapter 6

Southern European Welfare Systems in Transition

Ana M. Guillén, Matteo Jessoula, Manos Matsaganis, Rui Branco, and Emmanuele Pavolini

6.1. Introduction

The idea that a distinct Southern European (SE) welfare model exists within European social protection systems was developed in the 1990s. Ferrera's (1996) seminal article argued that SE countries shared several common traits with respect to both their welfare state architectures and welfare regime configurations. As for the welfare state, the first common trait relates to an institutional structure that has been evolving from a typical Bismarckian occupational approach to a mixed model with the development of Beveridgean universalistic health care systems (or, at least, moving toward universalism) since the 1980s—this coming with an increased role of general revenues in welfare state financing. The second common trait has to do with a highly fragmented[1] corporatist income maintenance system, displaying marked internal polarization along the distributional (i.e., across social groups) and functional (i.e., across welfare sectors) dimensions. Peaks of generosity in the fields of pensions and unemployment protection for core occupational groups actually coexisted with large protection gaps, especially visible in the field of antipoverty and family policies, where underdeveloped social services and the lack of a minimum income safety net were southern trademarks. In other words, these countries presented functional and distributional imbalances in their welfare state architectures, where the prominent role played by cash benefits configured an extreme version of the transfer-centered social protection model typical of continental Europe.

The lack of a national minimum income scheme, the rudimentary character of antipoverty measures for working-age individuals, and the scarcity of social services—for both children and frail elderlies—made reliance on households as welfare providers' key to maintaining social cohesion. Saraceno (1994) called such welfare regime "familialistic by default" in order to emphasize the lack of alternatives to the provision of care by the family—or, better, by women in a strongly gender-biased society and labor market where the division of labor followed the traditional male breadwinner model (with the exception of the Portuguese case). By contrast, reliance on the market had remained limited until the 1990s apart from the health care sector, which already presented elements of a public-private mix.

Several authors have argued that the four unbalanced (and underdeveloped, especially Greece and Portugal) SE welfare states have been facing critical modernization challenges since the 1990s. Actually, these countries needed to launch a thorough process of "institutional adjustment" (Flora 1986) of their welfare architectures in light of the changing "imperatives" of an increasingly globalized economy, population aging, and, last but not least, women's emancipation and entrance into the labor market. All this was at a time when the convergence toward a single European currency and the reduced rate of economic growth typical of postindustrial economies greatly constrained the available resources for welfare state expansion (Ferrera 1996; Fargion 2000). To what extent, then, have the four SE countries been successful in this process of adapting their welfare institutions—vis-à-vis structural transformations—that would imply some kind of welfare "recalibration" (Ferrera, Rhodes, and Hemerijck 2000) along both the functional and the distributive dimensions? Such a question is particularly interesting, since both retrenchment (mainly in the sector of pensions) and expansionary reforms (in the field of antipoverty and family policies) may encounter formidable political obstacles (Natili and Jessoula 2019).

In this chapter, we will address this puzzle outlining national policy trajectories in two different periods—1980–2010 and 2010–2020—in sections 6.2 and 6.4, respectively, while sections 6.3 and 6.5 provide a comparative assessment of welfare state change in the four SE countries. Our conclusions are in section 6.6.

We mostly focus on the core social protection pillars: pensions, labor market policies, social assistance, health care, social care, and family policies.

In sum, although all four countries shared until the 1980s several elements in their social protection systems, they followed in the two decades before the 2007–2008 crisis different paths of development and welfare state modernization. In particular, Spain and Portugal attempted a double process of growth of their social protection systems and institutional recalibration, whereas Italy and Greece were less effective in adjusting their welfare state to structural transformations.

After 2007–2008 SE welfare states started to converge again, although following a downward trajectory. While reforms paths have been partly different across SE countries since 2010, pressures both economic-financial and political—austerity plans and the role of the European Union (EU)—have prompted a process of gradual convergence among the four countries and at the same time, in many respects, a divergence from the rest of Western Europe.

6.2. Reforming Welfare Systems in Southern Europe, 1980s–2000s

6.2.1. Italy: Constrained Recalibration of the Archetypical Southern European Welfare Model

Italy represented the quintessential SE model of welfare, with a mixed welfare state architecture including a universalistic national health care system starting in 1978 and notable functional and distributional imbalances: a hypertrophic pension system attracting a large share of social protection expenditure; underdeveloped policy sectors such as social exclusion, family and labor market/unemployment, extreme regulatory fragmentation with generous rules for some occupational categories coupled with severe protection gaps for others; and, most notably, the lack of a minimum income safety net against poverty. Such a peculiar model of social protection and (protective) labor market regulation emerged over two decades of intense industrialization (mid-1950s–mid-1970s), fast economic growth, relaxed public finances, weak external constraints, and consequent large autonomy of national governments in supporting welfare state expansion using the key levers of public debt and competitive devaluations of the national currency. Against this backdrop, the trigger for expansion was constituted by the peculiar and intense political competition dynamics between the communist and socialist Left (with the allied trade union the Italian General Confederation of Labour) and governing parties, primarily the pivotal Christian Democratic Party, in the framework of a so-called blocked democracy—that is, democracy with no alternation in government (1946–1994) (Jessoula and Alti 2010; Ferrera, Fargion, and Jessoula 2012).

In the early 1990s, this constellation of factors abruptly dissolved. Externally, the run-up to Economic and Monetary Union posed sound constraints on public finances and ruled out currency devaluations aimed at supporting competitiveness, whereas increased international competition hindered the repeated increase of tax/contribution rates. In the context of massive deindustrialization and the expansion of the service sector increasingly relying on atypical and low-paid employment, financing growing social expenditure—mostly due to fast population aging and emerging new social risks—turned into a real challenge for Italian policymakers.

The first trajectory of change since the early 1990s therefore implied the adoption of remarkable cost containment interventions—which had an impact on both the functional and distributive dimensions—in the fields of pensions and health care. Five important reforms in two subsequent waves (1992–1997 and 2004–2007) substantially redesigned the Italian pension system via both parametric and structural measures. As a result, pension expenditure—which had been projected to double its impact on gross domestic product (GDP) by 2030–2040—after reforms was supposed to remain relatively stable in the following decades. This was possible due to the combination of several measures, among which were the change in the calculation formula from an earnings-related system to a much less generous notional defined contribution model and the gradual tightening of eligibility conditions for retirement (both old-age and seniority pensions).

Importantly, cost containment interventions made room for the expansion of private provision in the field of old-age protection since the former were paralleled by structural reforms aimed at reorganizing the pension system on three different pillars: a public and pay-as-you-go pillar and two supplementary "private" pillars based on prefunding.[2]

More room for the market was also created by two key health care reforms in 1993 and 1999, which reorganized the sector in accordance with new principles and guidelines. In an attempt to increase effectiveness and efficiency, the reforms in fact introduced "managed" competition mechanisms between public and private providers, strengthened managerial roles in local health authorities to tackle administrative inefficiency, and, importantly, shared competence in national health service (NHS) governance between the national state and regions.

Whereas retrenchment and reorganizational measures in the field of pensions and health care had been effectively pursued when the global crisis broke out in 2008, the expansionary component of the recalibration process launched in the mid-1990s still lagged behind. Despite comprehensive reform plans and attempts to strengthen protection in the field of unemployment and in anti-poverty policies—which also included the introduction of a pilot minimum income scheme in 1998, subsequently repealed in 2004—Italy still had a rudimentary unemployment benefit system and ineffective active labor market policies (Almps) and residual family policies (especially services) and was without a minimum income safety net against poverty for working-age individuals (Jessoula and Natili 2020). Meanwhile, a thorough process of devolution of power and competence at the regional level had been completed in the fields of active labor market policies and social assistance in addition to health care.

6.2.2. Greece: Unbalanced Growth and Protection Gaps

In Greece, the restoration of democracy and the extension of civil rights to all citizens ushered in a period of welfare state expansion. Moreover, accession to the European Community in 1980, widely seen as a guarantee of political stability, legitimized aspirations for levels of income and social protection comparable to those enjoyed by other Europeans (Petmesidou 1996; Guillén and Matsaganis 2000; Matsaganis 2005a).

Welfare state building took off in 1982 under the newly elected socialist government led by Andreas Papandreou. In the space of a few months, a 40% rise of the minimum wage lifted social insurance minimum pensions and other social benefits indexed to it; noncontributory farmers' pensions doubled in value and eligibility was extended to women, making retired farming couples four times better off; and a pension for the uninsured elderly was introduced for those aged over age sixty-eight with insufficient contributions and low incomes. Pension expansion often degenerated to excess: contributory conditions became lax (in the civil service, a mother could now retire on a full pension after fifteen years); manual work declined while "hard and arduous occupations," conferring the right to early retirement, proliferated; and invalidity pensions reached 34% of all new pensions (in 1984). The creation of a national health system in 1983 was a decisive if incomplete step toward establishing universal health coverage. Social assistance remained low-key and fragmented, with new disability benefits introduced to cover additional categories. In social care, a nationwide network of open care centers was created, reducing old people's isolation and dependence. The poverty rate fell from 20.4% to 17.9% (Tsakloglou and Mitrakos 2006).

In the 1990s, the minimum age required for eligibility to the social pension was lowered to sixty-five, new higher benefits targeted to families with three or more children were introduced, and the maximum duration of unemployment benefits was extended from six to twelve months (Sotiropoulos 2004b). From 1996 under the socialist "modernizing" government led by Costas Simitis, pension reform was high on the agenda but was effectively abandoned in 2001 in the face of stiff opposition from unions and the majority of public opinion (Featherstone 2005; Matsaganis 2007). An income-tested pension supplement introduced in 1996 enabled the government to escape an earlier pledge to restore the link of minimum pensions to the minimum wage. A guaranteed minimum income scheme was briefly considered but rejected (Matsaganis 2005b). Meanwhile, the number of disability benefit recipients quadrupled, divided into ten different categories with twenty-two subcategories, in an absurd manifestation of "microcorporatist" political exchanges and patronage. Social expenditure grew faster than the economy, averaging 20.1% of GDP in 1996–2003 (Sotiropoulos 2004b).

When the Eurozone crisis broke out, the Greek welfare state was no longer under-resourced: social spending had grown to 24.8% of GDP. Yet, its traditional traits—an inefficient health service, an unsustainable pension system, and a "rudimentary social assistance regime" (Gough 1996, 13)—were left intact, combining "unparalleled peaks of generosity reserved for the protected core of the labor market" and "vast gaps of protection" (Ferrera 1996, 29). Liberal professionals and employees in the civil service, the public utilities, and banks enjoyed generous pensions and superior health insurance. At the other extreme, nonstandard workers and their families were de facto disenfranchised from contributory social insurance, most households received little or no family benefits even if poor, public assistance with housing costs was limited, and a social safety net of last resort continued to be unavailable (Matsaganis 2011).

6.2.3. Portugal: Modernization and Recalibration toward a Mature Welfare State

The Portuguese welfare state also expanded and consolidated late relative to other Western European countries. Since the transition and consolidation of democracy, a hybrid architecture was set up: occupational-based social security, universal public health services, social assistance and social care (once left to families), and increased means-tested public provision in partnership with civil society. A guaranteed minimum income was created in 1996, one of several departures from the SE model (Ferrera 1996). Despite dual labor markets and fragmented social protection regimes, the fragmentation into distinct schemes is closer to continental standards. Also, Portugal evinced a pattern of low unemployment and high employment, including high female employment (59% in 1983 to 75% in 2007) (Karamessini 2008).

In the transition from a political economy with large nationalized sectors and public employment to a market-based liberal economy, policies prioritized job security and low unemployment, leading to tardy and weaker unemployment protection and lower wages. With the 1986 EU accession and the 1989 constitutional revision (triggering a vast privatization program), the shift to an open market orientation was concluded, and a new social policy phase ensued as the welfare state consolidated the protection for traditional social risks and expanded new social rights and policies.

From the 1990s up to the Great Recession, under mostly center-left governments (1995–2001 and 2005–2011) there was rapid catch-up convergence in social expenditure for material and personal coverage. Portugal followed a recalibration path: rebalanced social protection across risks and social categories, reformed old social policies (retrenchment and cost containment in pensions and health care), and protected new social risks (expansion of social needs coverage through new noncontributory benefits), stressing employment activation, defamiliarization, social inclusion, and antipoverty services.

Pensions underwent retrenchment and cost containment. From 1990 to 2010 pensions rose from 39% to 49% of total social protection expenditure, a result of constrained maturation. In the 1990s the minimum contributory period was lengthened, the retirement age for women was raised to that of men (sixty-five), and early retirement was penalized. The generous reference period in 1993 (best five of the last ten years) gave way to the whole contributory career in 2002. The 2007 reform indexed pensions in payment to a new sustainability factor, adjusting the retirement age to life expectancy, which "reduced dramatically the generosity of benefits" in the long run (Pereirinha and Murteira 2019, 437). The forecasted drop in net replacement rate for sixty-five-year-old workers with forty years of contributions from 94% in 2008 to 70% in 2048 could contain expenditures below the EU average (from 9.7% to 5.5% GDP) (European Commission 2010b).Created in 1979, the NHS replaced Bismarckian health insurance for workers and dependents varying across socio-professional groups with a Beveridgean social-democratic political logic of tax-based universal public provision. The architecture was completed with the Health Framework Law (1990) and the Statutes of the NHS (1993). Reforms since the 1990s sought administrative and financial decentralization, cost containment and efficiency gains, and privatization and individual responsibility. Contracts between the state and public hospitals separated financing from service provision, public/private partnerships reduced the state's delivery role, there were higher user charges and lower public contributions to drug costs and generic drug contained costs, and generous tax expenditures fostered out-of-pocket expenses and private health insurance (Pereirinha and Murteira 2016; Branco and Costa 2019). A large private sector and generous health insurance schemes for public servants and other subsystems meant that the NHS was never fully fledged. In addition to the NHS, occupational subsystems covered 16% of the population, and 26% was covered by private insurance (Guillén and Petmesidou 2008; Simões et al. 2017).

Increasing needs-based, noncontributory protection was a salient component of the recalibration. The social pension created in 1974 and social unemployment assistance created in 1985 were limited efforts. It was only with the guaranteed minimum income in 1996 that a truly universal system of social protection was set up, the first of its kind in Southern Europe (Matsaganis et al. 2003). Guaranteed minimum income was designed as an antipoverty means-tested social transfer geared toward activation and reintegration. In 2002 it was retrenched (tighter access and means testing) and renamed Social Insertion Income (SII) by the center-right executive. The socialist executive again expanded this component in 2005 by creating the solidarity benefit for low pensions known as the Solidarity Supplement for the Elderly (CSI) and partially reversing the changes in the SII (Pereirinha et al. 2020).

Unlike other SE countries, precocious high levels of female full-time employment and comparative higher poverty and weaker family services made welfare dependent on intensive labor market participation, overburdening women in salaried work with unpaid care (Silva 2003). Countering such limitations, from 1995 the trend in family policy has been expansion with defamiliarization of social care for children and the elderly while improving work-family balance. Parental leave and family allowances were recalibrated and expanded, as were services for the elderly, children, and people with disabilities whose coverage was vastly increased. Family allowances, once contributory, universal, and uniform, became a noncontributory resident entitlement directed at low-income families (Pereirinha and Murteira 2019). Parental leaves were greatly extended for women and men. Since 2009, on top of a compulsory initial parental leave for fathers and mothers, the maximum benefit can be granted only to both, favoring gender equality in care. Preschool for five-year-old has become nearly universal, and kindergarten coverage has met the Barcelona target of 33%. However, family cash benefits became stingy and means-tested. At the same time, albeit heavily subsidized, the expanding network of social services was run in partnership with private providers, with distortions in cost, efficiency, and access (Branco 2017).

6.2.4. Spain: Overcoming Historical Legacies through Europeanization

The Spanish welfare state expanded dramatically starting in the late 1970s. Peculiar to Spain among Southern European economies is that European governance had a pronounced impact on reform of the welfare state before the crisis so that a deep process of Europeanization took place (Moreno and Serrano 2011; Guillén and Álvarez 2004; Guillén, Álvarez, and Adão e Silva 2003). This is hardly surprising when taking into account the intense devotion for the EU among Spanish citizens and socioeconomic actors, which only diminished at the peak of the Great Recession.

The strategy of reform of the Spanish welfare state since its transition to democracy (1975–1982) consisted of closing protection gaps and attaining a welfare state tailored along the lines of the most developed ones within the EU, especially the social democratic model regarding welfare services (Guillén 2010). In particular, on the one hand the strategy starting in the 1980s pursued the consolidation/universalization of the coverage of "old risks" coupled with rationalizing redistribution and regulatory homogenization starting in the early 1990s, coinciding with the Maastricht Treaty and fiscal discipline. On the other hand, a clear effort may be ascertained in the expansion of protection of "new social risks" without attaining the level of the most developed welfare states and with a clear break during the 2008–2012 economic crisis. In parallel, the Spanish welfare state underwent a very deep process of decentralization to the regions. Devolution was precisely one of the main variables contributing to increased attention to new risks at the regional level, such as policies related to minimum income and social care. While the political will to reform was present and public preferences were clearly in its favor, competition among regions was key to the swift spread of expansionary reform.

As to old risks, the contributory income maintenance system was based on occupational principles and financed through a mix of social contributions and a small share of tax on income, including all pensions, unemployment benefits, and sick leave transfers.

The retirement pension system remained mainly public, managed by the national/central government (i.e., not devolved to the regions). It was also highly redistributive due, among other reasons, to the existence of maximum and minimum retirement pensions. Almost one-fifth of all pensioners enjoyed top-ups to reach the minimum pension. The reform strategy followed by the different governments since the transition to democracy included an upgrade of the lowest pensions; a rationalization of the system based on parametric changes aimed at lowering replacement rates, which started very early (1985) compared to other EU member states and has been repeatedly pursued (1997, 2002, and 2007); and the convergence (or in some cases integration) of all occupational schemes to the conditions enjoyed by workers belonging to the general scheme for salaried employees. Such has been the case of part-timers (reformed in the late 1990s) and, just before the advent of the crisis, of self-employed and domestic service workers. The strategy of coverage universalization included also since the late 1980s the introduction of noncontributory old-age and invalidity "social" pensions targeted toward citizens not having completed the minimum contributory period of fifteen years to access the public system. Furthermore, since 1995 the pension system has been reformed in accordance with the recommendations of the so-called Toledo Pact, an agreement reached by all political parties in parliament and subscribed also by the social partners and the banking sector.

Among old risks, the health care system consisted of an NHS of universal, social democratic character (introduced in 1986) and financed out of general taxation. The NHS was also devolved to the autonomous regions, which enjoyed full competencies. In a comparative perspective, the Spanish health care system looked both equitable and efficient and enjoyed the support of the vast majority of the economic and social actors (Petmesidou, Pavolini, and Guillén 2014).

If the strategy of reform of the welfare state was focused on closing protection gaps and attaining a welfare state tailored along the lines of the most developed ones within the EU, as tables 6.1 to 6.3 show, old risks were still much better covered in financial terms than new social risks at the end of the period under analysis, which resulted in a comparative lower protection of risks within the active age interval and in the domain of care policies.

6.3. Welfare Recalibration and Institutional Adjustment until the Great Recession: A Comparative Assessment

In summarizing the policy developments outlined in the four national cases, it is important to remember that in the 1980s there were some intragroup differences with regard to the overall welfare state maturity and the relevance of both functional and distributive imbalances, as Ferrera (1996) had already acknowledged.

As shown in table 6.1, in the early 1980s Portugal and Greece still presented an underdeveloped social protection system, whereas Spain had a semideveloped one. Only Italy had a relatively mature welfare state, mostly as result of the time lag in both full industrialization and political authoritarianism, which lasted until the 1970s in Greece, Portugal, and Spain, in contrast to the 1940s democratic transition in Italy.

The distribution of resources along the functional dimension—that is, across the various welfare state sectors—was particularly unbalanced in the cases of Greece and Italy, which showed a peculiar concentration of expenditure in the field of old-age protection (see table 6.2), although Ferrera (1996) argued that Spain and Portugal would soon become heavy pension spenders as well. Finally, not only functional imbalances but also distributional ones affected the four countries differently, according to the same pattern: more in Italy and Greece, less in Spain and Portugal.

Against such a backdrop, the first trend between the 1980s and the 2000s concerned both catching up and convergence in terms of total social protection expenditure. Whereas Italy reached expenditure levels similar to (if not higher than) Western Europe (EU-15), the other three countries started an accelerated process of welfare state expansion toward the EU-15 average. This converging pattern lasted until the onset of the 2007–2009 Great Recession: in 2010, social protection expenditure as a percentage of GDP had practically reached the EU-15 average in Greece and was above in Italy and below but not too distant in Spain and Portugal. Considering per capita expenditure, the situation was only partly different: in 2010, per capita expenditure was around the EU-15 average in Italy and below by 22% in Spain and by 29–33% in Greece and Portugal. Although the differences were still wide, Spain, Portugal, and Greece had mostly filled the gap compared to the early 1980s. Moreover, in light of the +134% public social protection expenditure increase in Western European countries in 1980–2010, SE figures are remarkable: the growth was only slightly lower in Italy (+127%) but much higher in Spain (+195%) and especially in Greece (+268%) and Portugal (367%). For the latter three countries, both the entrance into the EU in the 1980s and a delayed process of industrialization and modernization provided favorable conditions for welfare state expansion, which was mainly triggered by the institutionalization and consolidation of democratic political dynamics.

If we shift from overall expenditure levels to its composition by function, we find that despite the adoption of severe retrenchment reforms during the 1990s—especially in Italy (cf. Jessoula 2009)—the functional profile of the Italian and Greek welfare states remained greatly unbalanced in favor of pensions (table 6.2). This was not the case, however, in Spain and Portugal, where the share of total resources devoted to old-age protection was in line with the EU-15 average and remained so over time until the 2000s.

Among SE countries, partly different trends could be observed in the two traditionally underdeveloped fields of antipoverty (housing and social assistance) and family programs over the three decades considered here. In the social assistance sector, expenditures remained well below the EU-15 average in the four countries, but a tendency toward stronger antipoverty measures started to materialize in Portugal and Spain mostly as a consequence of the establishment of the first minimum income schemes at the national (Portugal) and regional (Spain) levels (see table 6.2). In a similar vein, investment in family policies remained limited in the four countries—and the gap with the EU-15 average persisted around 5–6% in 2010—despite the adoption of the first expansionary interventions in Spain, the only country presenting a relevant expenditure increase in the field, from 3.1% (1980) to 5.7% (2010) of total social protection expenditure (see table 6.2).

To sum up, although the typical SE underinvestment in family and antipoverty policies continued, a divide appeared between Portugal and Spain on the

Table 6.1 Public and mandatory private social protection expenditure in Southern Europe over time (1980–2018)

		UE-15	Italy	Spain	Greece	Portugal
In percentage of GDP	1980	18.6	18.2	15.0	9.9	9.7
	1990	21.0	22.2	19.2	15.7	12.4
	2000	22.0	23.8	19.5	17.8	18.9
	2010	26.8	28.4	24.7	25.5	24.7
	2018	24.6	27.9	23.7	23.5	24.6
Per head, at constant prices (2010) and constant purchasing power parities (PPP) (2010), in US dollars	1980	4333	4339	2681	1955	1449
	1990	5974	6693	4429	3168	2515
	2000	7640	8412	5740	4329	4921
	2010	10140	9849	7902	7193	6765
	Var. 1980–2010	+134.0%	+127.0%	+194.7%	+267.9%	+366.9%
	Var. 2010–2017*	+5.7%	−0.6%	−4.8%	−15.7%	+0.2%
Per head expenditure in Southern Europe compared to the EU-15 average (in percentage of PPP)	1980	100.0	100.1	61.9	45.1	33.4
	1990	100.0	112.0	74.1	53.0	42.1
	2000	100.0	110.1	75.1	56.7	64.4
	2010	100.0	97.1	77.9	70.9	66.7
	2017*	100.0	88.8	67.5	55.1	60.7

* Data from Eurostat online database (indicator: spr_exp_sum).
Source: OECD online SOCX database (https://stats.oecd.org/).

Table 6.2 Social expenditure by function over time (percentage of total social expenditure), 1980–2015

		EU-15	Greece	Italy	Portugal	Spain
Old age and survivors	1980	39.5%	52.6%	51.4%	37.8%	40.7%
	1990	39.5%	60.4%	56.1%	39.1%	41.0%
	2000	39.8%	57.3%	60.8%	41.7%	44.4%
	2010	39.3%	55.7%	58.5%	48.9%	39.5%
	2015	41.5%	65.2%	57.9%	55.3%	47.0%
Health	1980	26.0%	31.9%	29.4%	30.7%	26.5%
	1990	23.6%	20.9%	25.7%	28.8%	24.9%
	2000	24.6%	25.1%	23.1%	31.3%	25.0%
	2010	26.8%	25.9%	24.8%	27.7%	27.3%
	2015	26.3%	18.3%	22.7%	24.4%	26.4%
Family	1980	10.5%	3.0%	5.7%	6.5%	3.1%
	1990	9.4%	4.1%	3.9%	5.5%	1.6%
	2000	9.8%	4.6%	4.9%	5.2%	4.8%
	2010	9.8%	4.0%	4.8%	5.6%	5.7%
	2015	9.4%	4.1%	6.6%	4.9%	5.0%
Housing and social assistance	1980	2.6%	0.6%	0.0%	0.4%	0.3%
	1990	3.1%	3.3%	0.1%	0.3%	0.9%
	2000	3.4%	0.3%	0.6%	1.3%	1.5%
	2010	3.7%	0.2%	0.8%	1.2%	1.6%
	2015	4.0%	0.4%	0.8%	0.7%	1.3%
Invalidity	1980	17.0%	9.7%	10.3%	21.8%	15.6%
	1990	15.0%	7.6%	10.6%	20.2%	11.6%
	2000	13.1%	8.0%	6.6%	13.9%	12.0%
	2010	11.2%	7.3%	6.8%	8.9%	10.1%
	2015	11.0%	7.3%	6.8%	8.3%	9.7%

Source: OECD online SOCX database (https://stats.oecd.org/).

one hand, the two countries that had started to modernize and recalibrate their welfare states, and Greece and Italy on the other hand, still presenting the main traits of the traditional model.

Nevertheless, with regard to the cash transfer bias characterizing SE, the gap with the rest of Europe did not disappear. In a phase when also continental European countries (with the partial exception of Austria) dramatically geared their welfare states toward the expansion of services, the only SE countries following a similar trend (although less robustly) were Spain and Portugal, as the share of social transfers on total social protection expenditure shows (see table 6.3).

Turning to welfare entitlements (table 6.4), again Portugal and Spain on the one hand and Greece and Italy on the other had developed different unemployment and pension protection systems. In the early 1980s, Greece and Italy already had more generous pension schemes than the other two countries and the EU-15 average, whereas the opposite applied to unemployment benefits,

Table 6.3 Social expenditure by type of expenditure: Percentage of expenditure on cash transfers in total social protection expenditure over time (1980–2015)

	1980	1990	2000	2010	2015
EU-15 average	65.4%	64.7%	61.2%	59.2%	60.0%
Greece	67.2%	72.4%	72.8%	72.6%	79.9%
Italy	69.0%	71.7%	71.1%	70.0%	72.1%
Portugal	69.0%	66.0%	62.7%	67.1%	70.9%
Spain	71.5%	68.8%	64.7%	60.9%	64.4%

Source: OECD online SOCX database (https://stats.oecd.org/).

being more generous and covering a larger part of the active population in Spain and Portugal. In this respect, however, data in table 6.4 show that intra-group differences were going down due to both pay-as-you-go pension scheme maturation in Portugal and Spain and incremental reforms of unemployment benefit systems in Italy and Greece.

Overall, considering the national trajectories illustrated above and the comparative data presented here, we can argue that the four Mediterranean countries fit the ideal type of the SE welfare model to a different extent. The starting points were different in the early 1980s, but welfare state evolution in the following three decades, until the 2008 global shock, is a story of quite different patterns of change: welfare state expansion and consolidation with only modest retrenchment interventions in the three countries with a less-developed social protection system (Greece, Portugal and Spain), in contrast with welfare state growth followed by relevant retrenchment measures in Italy. However, welfare state expansion in the three former countries did not follow the same route, with both Portugal and Spain being more effective in pursuing the expansionary recalibration agenda in the fields of family and antipoverty policies vis-à-vis a more traditional policy trajectory in Greece, similar to that in Italy.

Interestingly, especially in Italy and Spain, other important changes concerned the constellation of actors involved in welfare state governance (i.e., the politico-institutional dimension of recalibration), with a growing role for private providers and subnational (mainly regional) levels of government especially in the fields of health care and social assistance/family policies.

6.4. Welfare State Responses to Multiple Crises and Beyond

6.4.1. Italy: From Harsh Austerity to Modest Signs of Comprehensive Recalibration

Soon after the 2008 global shock, Italian governments adopted three main anti-crisis packages in 2009, 2010, and 2011, followed by two important reforms aimed

Table 6.4 Generosity of social protection systems (1980–2010)

		EU-15	Greece	Italy	Portugal	Spain
Pension generosity index	1980	10.8	14.6	12.6	N/A	10.7
	1990	12.2	15.3	14.3	10.2	12.3
	2000	12.3	14.6	14.3	10.9	13.6
	2010	13.2	14.5	14.3	15.0	13.9
Unemployment benefits' generosity index	1980	9.5	4.6	3.3	6.8	9.6
	1990	9.9	5.5	3.3	10.0	11.2
	2000	10.2	6.0	4.9	10.7	10.8
	2010	9.9	7.3	5.7	10.6	11.7
Percentage of the labor force insured for unemployment risk	1980	64.6	48.0	46.0	60.0	56.0
	1990	64.6	52.0	N/A	67.0	66.0
	2000	70.5	52.0	N/A	70.0	72.0
	2010	61.1	63.0	N/A	69.0	76.0
Unemployment insurance: replacement rate single (%)	1980	46.7	37.4	4.7	55.0	87.8
	1990	54.7	46.5	20.0	78.7	89.5
	2000	57.4	48.8	41.6	79.0	75.3
	2010	59.3	49.7	55.0	77.6	80.0
Unemployment insurance: replacement rate family (%)	1980	53.2	46.0	12.5	63.9	86.4
	1990	61.4	58.1	28.6	75.8	90.8
	2000	65.3	63.2	49.5	79.2	73.6
	2010	68.7	64.8	66.9	77.1	76.8

Source: Comparative Welfare Entitlements Dataset, Version 2017-09 (http://cwed2.org/).

at flexibilizing the labor market in 2012 and 2014. In the first wave, reforms were mostly prompted by formal EU fiscal governance rules as well as "informal conditionality" mechanisms imposed by the European Central Bank after the onset of the sovereign debt crisis in the spring of 2010 (Jessoula 2013; Sacchi 2015), which progressively restricted room for national actors' maneuvering.

Whereas in health care there were severe cuts but no major reform, pensions soon came back to the top of the political agenda, and substantial retrenchment reforms were adopted in 2009, 2010 and 2011. Differently from those enacted in the first two waves, the reforms of the third wave implied radical measures for both the magnitude of change and the timing of its implementation. The aim was in fact to reduce the cost burden in the very short term, regain credibility on the financial markets, and especially reassure the European Central Bank, which then started to purchase Italian bonds on the secondary market to block speculation. Pension indexation was temporarily frozen, the phasing in of the notional defined contribution formula was accelerated, and, most importantly, eligibility conditions were severely tightened for both old-age and seniority pensions: the pensionable age for women passed from sixty years in 2010 to sixty-five in 2012 (for public employees) and to sixty-seven (in the public and the private sector) in 2019, a unique case for rapidity in the EU.

The 2014 labor market reform called the Jobs Act represented a critical watershed between the first and the second phases of the reform. In combination with the 2012 reform, the act radically redesigned the institutional architecture of Italian employment policies, pursuing flexibilization by putting an end to the protective regime against dismissals guaranteed by Article 18 of the Workers' Statute, which had been introduced in 1970. As partial compensation of such a move, the reforms modernized and strengthened the Italian unemployment benefit system, making it more inclusive—especially for atypical workers, who were previously de facto excluded from ordinary unemployment insurance—as well as more generous in terms of duration and replacement rates. Despite the upgrade, when compared to the traditional model developed in the post–World War II decades, insecurity in the Italian labor market has increased due to the remarkable flexibilization of employment relationships.

Increased insecurity, poverty, and material deprivation rates and the emergence of the National Alliance Against Poverty, bringing together thirty-three social organizations, as well as changing political dynamics due to the appearance of a new competitor, the Five Stars Movement (5SM), calling for the introduction of a citizenship income led to a stepwise process of expansion of antipoverty measures, which ultimately culminated in the establishment of a national minimum income scheme in 2018, the Inclusion Income (Reddito di Inclusione), after two decades of debates, attempts to path departure, and policy reversals (Jessoula and Natili 2020). Subsequently, the Citizenship Income (Reddito di Cittadinanza) scheme replaced the Inclusion Income scheme in 2019: compared to the latter, the Citizenship Income scheme is endowed with more budgetary resources (7.0 billion in 2019, of which €6.3 billion was for the monetary component and the rest for strengthening active labor market policies), is more generous and inclusive, and has longer duration and stricter conditionality rules for beneficiaries.

Improvements in cash transfers to tackle unemployment/poverty were not matched, however, by similar developments in services in the field of employment policies (at least until 2019, although the development of active labor market policies had been evoked since 1997 in accordance with a flexicurity approach) or in family policies, which actually constitute the weak spot of the reform (or recalibration) process. Very limited progress has in fact been visible in services for both early childhood education and care, where coverage remains modest (28.6% in 2019), and long-term care, where the relatively high (1.7% of GDP) Italian expenditure has been prevalently absorbed (55% of the total) by the main social provision, a universalistic cash transfer, the Companion Allowance (Indennità di accompagnamento), of around 530 euros per month provided to all dependent individuals.

Inertia in developing care services thus implies the persistence of a substantial burden on households especially on women's shoulders (mothers and grandmothers), suggesting at least a partial continuation of the SE model in Italy despite the relevant changes since 2010.

6.4.2. Greece: Drastic Retrenchment of Core Programs and a Bolstered Social Safety Net

In October 2009 the socialist government, fresh from its electoral triumph earlier that month, announced that earlier fiscal data had been misreported. The budget deficit as a share of GDP for 2008 was corrected from 3.7% to 12.5% (later revised to 15.6%). The new figures stunned public opinion in Europe and shocked markets worldwide. The yield on ten-year government bonds spiraled out of control, from below 5% in October 2009 to nearly 30% in April 2010. In early May 2010 faced with the prospect of bankruptcy, the country was forced to accept a bailout in return for massive fiscal consolidation and structural reforms, supervised by the European Commission, the International Monetary Fund, and the European Central Bank, collectively known as the Troika (Matsaganis 2018a).

Social spending declined dramatically (by 19% in the 2009–2013 period). However, with the economy in free fall, the size of the Greek welfare state increased in relative terms (to 28.1% of GDP in 2012).

The effects of austerity on the welfare state were asymmetric. In the 2010–2014 period, pension benefits were cut in nominal terms, from 15% to as much as 45% in real terms. Nonetheless, total expenditure on pensions, driven by rising recipient numbers, continued its upward trend. Predictably, the growth in pensions spending crowded out other components of Greek welfare to a still greater extent than had always been the case. Structural reforms attempted to rein in pension spending, raising the age of retirement and unifying entitlements across categories. The 2010 reform was Scandinavian in structure but at extremely modest benefit levels, providing a tax-funded quasi-universal first tier and a contribution-related second tier (Matsaganis and Leventi 2011). The new system was due to come into force in January 2015, but the general election of that month brought in an anti-austerity government, led by Alexis Tsipras, which repealed the 2010 reform and promised to reverse cuts. That never happened. The Tsipras government's own reform, in 2016, further reduced accrual rates, especially for those with a long work history, and reinstated the sharp division between those with an adequate contributory record and those without, leaving the latter less protected than under the 2010 reform.

Spending cuts were deeper still in the case of health. Public health expenditure declined by 46% in real terms between 2009 and 2014 (OECD 2019b). In part, this was associated with successful efforts to eliminate waste (e.g., in prescriptions), long overdue policy initiatives aimed at shifting the balance from hospital to primary care, and efforts to move from fragmented social insurance to a universal health service, as the 1983 reform had aspired but never quite achieved. However, austerity undermined the reforms, and access to essential services suffered (Petmesidou 2020).

As the recession heightened the need for social protection, austerity weakened the welfare state's capacity to respond. This can be seen most clearly in the area of income support for the unemployed. On the negative side, contributory unemployment insurance was cut, and its maximum duration was limited to four hundred days over four years. On the positive side, unemployment insurance was extended to the self-employed (on strict terms), and access to means-tested unemployment assistance was broadened (though the benefit rate was left unchanged). The net result of all these changes was reduced coverage. Between 2010 and 2014 the number of jobless workers doubled, but the number of unemployment benefit recipients fell by almost 30% (Matsaganis 2018b).

Attempts to strengthen the social safety net were more successful in other policy areas. School meals were provided to a larger number of children, a childcare voucher was made available for families meeting the income test, and the Home Help program was fully restored. A noncategorical income-tested child benefit was created in 2013 and was made more generous (though also more narrowly targeted) in 2018. A means-tested housing benefit was introduced in 2019. Last but not least, a guaranteed minimum income scheme was launched nationwide in 2017 (Matsaganis 2020). As a result of these changes, hundreds of thousands of poor families received income support from the government for the first time ever.

6.4.3. Portugal: A Risky Retreat of a Maturing Welfare State

Under formal conditionality, Portugal enacted retrenchment and structural reforms to improve short-term fiscal imbalances and long-term economic competitiveness through internal devaluation. Social policy was deployed to balance the budget and correct structural factors impairing competitiveness and growth. Pensions and health care saw harsh austerity and retrenchment, not structural reform. Goals in family and social safety net policies and the political principles underpinning state intervention also changed (Silva and Pereira 2017). As a matter of fact, without paradigmatic changes, austerity in pensions and health care can trigger a recessive evolution, for cuts in public provision endanger universal access (Guillén and Pavolini 2017).

The Memorandum of Understanding (MoU) did not feature a pension structural reform. Pensions underwent rising cyclical austerity: nominal cuts, indexation freeze (with the exception of the lowest), increased taxation, and ad hoc tax levies. Pensions above €1,500 suffered steep, progressive cuts. The budget law for 2012 hiked the "extraordinary solidarity levy" with 25% and 50% rates for the highest pensions. One of the Vacation and Christmas subsidies was cut for pensions between €600 and €1,100, and both subsidies were cut for those above €1,100 (later the Constitutional Court vetoed these cuts). Still, the executive passed a comprehensive reform in early 2014: an immediate one-year increase in the statutory retirement age to sixty-six, a convergence of the public-sector General Retirement Fund rules and benefits with the General Social Security Regime by changing the replacement rate, and a new "extraordinary" levy on public-sector pensions. After the court annulled the new levy and General Retirement Fund convergence rules, the executive renounced all ambitious reforms. From 2010 to 2015, pensioners' income fell sharply: gross monthly pensions of €500 incurred net losses of €3,000, those of €1,000 lost €10,000, and those of €3,000 lost €32,300 (Louçã et al. 2016).

The MoU sought to tackle segmentation, "generous" unemployment benefits, and long-term unemployment. Cuts in benefit value and duration slashed income security in unemployment by 25% from 2010 to 2013 (Moreira et al. 2015), hitting both insiders and outsiders. Other measures trying to broaden access and coverage only barely offset the drop in income security. Reforms did not fix segmentation or long-term unemployment. From 2007 to 2014 as the maximum duration of benefit for the most vulnerable and with the lowest entitlement dropped, the gap widened relative to the most entitled to unemployment protection (European Commission 2016b). Worryingly, coverage remained low (47% in 2015) due to the increasing number of long-term unemployed who were no longer eligible for benefits (46% in 2015) (Pereirinha and Murteira 2019).

The MoU sought to rein in NHS public expenditure and debt. Reforms focused on drug expenditure, user charges, operational and staff costs, and occupational subsystems (Pereirinha and Murteira 2016). Drug spending cuts relied on administrative price controls and revised reference pricing, price regulation of generic drugs, new prescription practices, and rising co-payments for drugs (Petmesidou et al. 2014). User charges rose on average by 115% from 2011 to 2014, hiking revenue from €68 million in 2010 to €175 million in 2013. However, the scope of exemptions to those in dire social and economic need was expanded for about 40% of users (Tribunal de Contas 2014). Salaries, career progressions, and recruitment were frozen, generating personnel shortages. Cutbacks in management staff and overtime pay in addition to reorganization and rationalization of the hospital network (about one thousand beds were eliminated) reduced operational costs. A budget cut starved the various subsystems for civil servants.

Economic support to families and the social safety net had been hit since 2010 with more stringent formulas and means-testing. The MoU sought to cut €430 million in social assistance noncontributory benefits through stricter eligibility via means-testing in SII, CSI (differential benefit for low pensions), and family allowance. The SII was the hardest hit by expenditure cuts and tighter means-testing: from over five hundred thousand recipients in 2010 to less than three hundred thousand in 2015 (Pereirinha et al. 2020). From 2009 to 2014 the benefit value dropped by one-third, as did the number of recipient families especially those with children. After a freeze from 2010 to 2012, the CSI reference value was cut in 2013, which, given its differential nature, cut expenditures but also the coverage of the low-pension elderly poor: in the Troika's final year beneficiaries dropped 23.2% (Louçã et al. 2016). Family allowances were retrenched by excluding higher income brackets, harsher means-testing, and ending the thirteen-month subsidy and the increase for lower-income brackets. From 2010 to 2014 expenditure shrank by over 30%, with over five hundred thousand fewer recipients (Silva and Pereira 2017). In sum, reforms lowered protection and restricted access, leading to fewer beneficiaries, while household incomes plummeted and unemployment rose sharply. Family policy was reoriented from a long rise of noncontributory benefits and services to a more residual approach coupled with a delegation of protection to civil society organizations. The 2011 Social Emergency Plan, signed by the executive and the peak welfare organization, the National Confederation of Solidarity Institutions, opened social services such as social solidarity canteens and funerals to the Santas Casas da Misericórdia (Holy Houses of Mercy) and the Private Institutions of Social Solidarity.

6.4.4. Spain: Europeanization of the Welfare State in Crisis

The strategies followed to reform Spanish welfare during the crisis have been highly influenced by both EU conditionality and decisions made by national political elites. The former had the effect of reducing the policymaking process to almost just two internal actors, the executive and the Ministry of Finance, due to the extreme shortage of time for negotiations and even less for reaching consensuses coupled with a deep fall in trust in public institutions (Guillén and Pavolini 2017).

Rapid population aging and massive unemployment together with Bank of Spain warnings and EU conditionality all contributed to generating significant pressure for pension reform during the crisis. Legislation passed in 2011 raised the statutory retirement age from sixty-five to sixty-seven years and increased the number of salaried years from fifteen to twenty-five. The reform is to be gradually implemented up to 2026. This phased-in character is similar to most new regulations adopted in other EU countries (Natali and Stamati 2014). Further, a demographic sustainability factor was introduced into the pension system in 2013 (cf. Pérez-Díaz and Rodríguez 2014, 141–60), starting from 2021. What the history of pension reforms in Spain demonstrates is that despite rationalization, Spain remains one of the most solid pillars of the welfare state (though by no means comparable to those of Italy and Greece).

In health care the institutional framework has remained in place during the crisis. The strategy has been centered on budgetary cuts. A further rationalization of the costs of pharmaceutical services was enacted in 2010. In addition, the only existing co-payments, namely those for over-the-counter drugs, were reformed in 2012. Pensioners, previously exempted, are now subject to those co-payments. Still, these co-payments have been tuned to income levels (the active population was subject to these co-payments before, even when unemployed). Budgetary cuts resulted in the closing down of services such as operating theaters and emergency units and in growing waiting lists, with different intensities depending on the autonomous region (Petmesidou et al. 2014). Regulation on access was also reformed in 2012 through a re-adoption of the social insurance principle and the exclusion of irregular immigrants. Nonetheless, this never became a reality due to lack of implementation by the regions and was formally reverted to universal access in July 2018.

Family protection policies, reconciliation, and long-term care, which constitute a much weaker aspect of the Spanish welfare state in comparative terms, also underwent either cuts or, in the latter case, implementation delays during the crisis (Léon and Pavolini 2014; Moreno Fuentes and Marí-Klose 2013).

The third pillar of the Spanish welfare state bears a liberal (means-tested) character and is also financed through general taxation. This pillar includes minimum income, noncontributory unemployment subsidies, housing and emancipation allowances, and tax breaks. Some of these policies are managed by the national government, in particular when they are part of the social security system of income maintenance (family allowances, unemployment transfers, and subsidies), but in general they have either been created from scratch at the regional level (e.g., minimum income schemes and/or social salaries) or devolved to the regional/municipal levels. What they all have in common is their low protection and redistributive capacity in terms of very low income thresholds for eligibility and the meager amount of transfers. Despite sustained efforts at their reinforcement, they still constitute the Achilles' heel of the Spanish welfare state. It is yet to be seen what the effects will be of the May 2020 Minimum Living Income (Ingreso Mínimo Vital) scheme, introduced in May 2020.

As for family support and reconciliation (parental leaves are in force but are nonremunerated) and despite recent enlargement of daddy leaves, comparative underdevelopment has been due to idiosyncratic reasons. So far, no government in Spain has taken the risk of being compared with the dictatorship, self-proclaimed as most keen on family support and probirth interventions.

To sum up, during the crisis while the pension reform was parametric and phased-in, budgetary cuts were applied to the social democratic and liberal pillars. Indiscriminate cuts to the universal pillar (mainly in health care and impeding agile implementation of the 2006 law on universal long-term care) followed the logic of less for all but, in reality, meant less for the worst off due to their lower capacity to resort to market services (Guillén and González Begega 2019).

6.5. Closer Than Ever but Further Away from Everybody Else? Southern European Welfare States after the Global Crisis

As shown in section 6.3, between the 1980s and the 2000s different policy trajectories had appeared across the four SE countries: two of them, Spain and Portugal, had not only expanded their welfare states but also started a process of institutional recalibration—with modest but significant improvements especially in the fields of social assistance, family, and reconciliation policies—whereas Italy and Greece were less effective in adjusting their social protection systems to structural transformations despite the adoption of severe cost containment measures in Italy and substantial welfare expansion in Greece.

Since 2007–2008, however, the multiple crises and subsequent austerity measures have hit Southern Europe harder than most other European countries. Three main questions therefore emerge. First, can we identify a similar reform trajectory in the four countries since 2010? Second, have the economic crisis and austerity been a driver for further differentiation among the SE welfare states or, to the contrary, for a stronger isomorphism in their institutional design and functioning? Third, did the crises push SE welfare states closer to or further from the other European countries presenting different welfare arrangements?

Our analysis shows that what has taken place is a process of gradual convergence among the four countries and at the same time, in many respects, a divergence from the rest of Western Europe.

As for the latter point, it must first be noted that three SE countries registered a reduction in the level of per capita public social protection expenditure between 2010 and 2017 (see table 6.1): relatively limited in Italy (−0.6%), more severe in Spain (−4.8%), and dramatic in Greece (−15.7%). Only in Portugal was there practically no change. Meanwhile, a strong increase in per capita expenditure occurred in the EU-15 (+5.7%). The overall outcome is that the gap in the per capita social protection expenditure between the average EU-15 figure and the four SE countries has grown for the first time after thirty years of convergence, reaching dramatic peaks in Portugal and Greece—which spent almost half of the EU-15 average on a per capita basis in 2017—and partly in Spain. Italy has also become a country with a per capita expenditure quite below the EU-15 average.

Austerity measures have affected all welfare state sectors: those protecting against old social risks (pensions and health care primarily) and against the new social risks as well. As for health care, the cuts have been draconian in Southern Europe: per capita expenditure grew in real terms between 2010 and 2017 by almost 8% in EU-15 while dropping by around 6% in Portugal, 9% in Italy, 12% in Spain, and 35% in Greece. The gap in per capita public health care expenditure has thus reached dramatic peaks in Greece, where each citizen receives the equivalent of around 40% of what an average Western European receives in terms of health care expenditure, and Portugal (52%) but also Spain (62%) and Italy (69%), which are all far larger than health care expenditures in the rest of Western Europe.

Although pension reforms were key ingredients of reform packages in all four countries, the magnitude of cuts and cost containment interventions was higher in Greece and Italy, whereas the newly developed (especially care) policies for families and children were more severely cut in Spain and Portugal, and minimum income generosity was reduced in the latter case. The result is that looking at aggregate expenditure, SE countries increasingly look like pension welfare states (less so Spain, more so the other three), especially when compared with EU-15 figures (see table 6.2). At the same time, the parallel cuts in the recently developed sectors in Spain and Portugal and the expansionary interventions—especially in the field of antipoverty policies—in Italy and Greece have made the institutional architecture of the four SE welfare states more similar than before the global crisis.

Finally, cash transfers play an even bigger role than in the past and nowadays a lot more than in the 1980s and 1990s. Southern Europe (with the exception of Spain) constitutes an extreme version of the transfer-centered model of social protection typical of continental Europe, as Ferrera (1996) argued (see table 6.3). In the critical field of early childhood education and care services for children below three years of age, however, intragroup differences persist, with coverage remaining very modest in Greece (20.5%) and Italy (28.6% in 2019), far from the Barcelona target of 33%—set already in 2000—and lower than in Spain (45.8%) and Portugal (47.5%). Similarly, per capita expenditure for in-kind benefits for families and children was in 2016 still incomparably lower in Greece (20 euros in purchasing power parity ppp]) and Italy (57 euros ppp) than in Spain (185 euros ppp), with Portugal representing an intermediate case (88 euros ppp).

6.6. Conclusion

Adopting a comparative perspective on SE welfare states over four decades provides many insights. Although all four countries shared some basic common elements in the past, up to the 2007–2008 crisis they followed different paths of development and modernization of their social protection architectures. In particular, Spain and Portugal actively implemented reforms more in line with a continental European approach and started a double process of growth of their social protection systems and institutional recalibration. Italy and Greece were less effective in adjusting their welfare state to structural transformations. Italy adopted mostly retrenchment policies with few hints of recalibration, whereas the substantial welfare expansion in Greece was not also used to transform its social protection architecture, missing the goal of coping with functional and distribution imbalances. The 2007–2008 crisis and the following austerity plans have proven to be a great equalizer for SE welfare states are but following a downwards trajectory. National governments and European institutions have considered SE social protection systems as one of the main culprits for the lack of competitiveness of SE capitalism, together with labor market regulation and wage-setting procedures. Most of the structural reforms requested by the EU and implemented by national elites had to do with these institutions. The outcome has been a wave of deep policy changes, which have tried to adjust SE social protections. However, the outcomes are questionable. First, the reforms have slowed down recalibration attempts in Spain and Portugal. Second, the cuts have been so severe as to push back by decades the Greek social protection system, putting at risk some of its key functional goals. Third, the overall result has been a stronger convergence than ever among the four SE countries toward a partially reduced but still quite imbalanced welfare state.

This was the state of social protection in SE when the COVID-19 pandemic arrived in the spring of 2020. The pandemic found SE welfare states already in great difficulties after a decade of cuts, especially in relation to service provision. Elderly care, health care, and family policies had to face in both Spain and Italy an unprecedented and terrible challenge. They had to cope with the health-related crisis but also the ensuing socioeconomic turmoil with limited resources and, even more importantly, limited room to maneuver. The upcoming years will tell us if this time, differently from what happened in the aftermath of the 2007–2008, these countries and the EU will be able to develop a different and more reasonable strategy to cope with external shocks not just based on structural reforms mainly and mostly cutting down only social protection expenditures.

Notes

1. Institutional fragmentation refers to the presence of several schemes for the various professional categories, with huge variations in financing and eligibility rules as well as in benefit formulas.

2. For details on pension reforms in Italy, see Jessoula and Raitano (2017) and Jessoula (2018).

Chapter 7

How to Adjust?

Italy and Spain at the Test of Financial Integration and Crisis

Fabio Bulfone and Manuela Moschella

7.1. Introduction

Since 1990 Italy and Spain have witnessed profound changes in the main features of their financial sectors. The financial system of both countries was shaken at its foundations by two waves of economic shocks originating twenty years apart. The first wave dates back to the early 1990s, when the deepening of the Single Market required European countries to converge on a set of reforms modeled on the Anglo-American paradigm of shareholders' capitalism (Deeg and Pérez 2000; Rangone and Solari 2012). This process occurred at a time when both countries were also making efforts to tighten their budgets in order to qualify for membership in the Economic and Monetary Union (EMU) (Hancké, Rhodes, and Thatcher 2007). Participation in the Single Market and the EMU called for a radical reshaping of the financial sector of both countries. Until then, Italy and Spain had shared an inward-looking, highly segmented, heavily regulated, and largely state-controlled banking sector. These features hampered the efficiency of credit provision. As a result, Italian and Spanish banks trailed behind their counterparts from the United Kingdom, France, and the Netherlands in terms of both size and profitability (Tortella, Garcia, and Ruiz 2013; Messori 2002). Throughout the 1990s and early 2000s a twin process of privatization and concentration led to the near disappearance of direct state ownership, a drastic reduction in the number of domestic credit institutions, and the emergence in both countries of internationally competitive banking groups.

The second shock to domestic financial systems came on the back of the 2010 Eurozone sovereign debt crisis. The sudden stop of capital inflows from core Eurozone member states coupled with the dramatic increase of governmental borrowing costs called into question the viability of the demand-led growth model on which Italy and Spain had relied, albeit with diverging fortunes, in the pre-crisis period (Hall 2018; Johnston and Regan 2018). The crisis had a particularly profound impact on the banking sector. In Spain, the burst of the housing bubble burdened the balance of domestic lenders with an enormous pile of nonperforming loans (NPLs), putting many savings banks on the brink of bankruptcy. In Italy, NPLs grew massively as a result of a double-dip recession coupled with the instability of sovereign bond yields, triggering a series of banking crises.

The aim of this chapter is to compare the way in which Italy and Spain adjusted their domestic financial systems to the challenges brought about first by the European Single Market and Monetary Union and then by the European sovereign debt crisis. How did the process of adjustment materialize? How were the costs distributed among different domestic actors? What was the institutional outcome of this process? How similar or different have Italy and Spain become as a result of it? Is it still possible to consider them contiguous models of capitalism? We will answer these questions by testing the predictions derived from existing analyses of the Mediterranean model of capitalism.

In terms of the *dynamic* of adjustment, following Molina and Rhodes (2007) we expect it to be decisively influenced by state actors. As Molina and Rhodes argue, in Mediterranean countries state actors are decisive in fostering coordination by mediating between the demands of fragmented interest groups. When faced with an economic shock, they would pay out rents to selected economic groups, turning crises into distributive struggles between vested interests (Hassel 2014). In terms of the *outcome* of the process of adjustment, there is agreement in the literature that the state-led pattern of adjustment characterizing Mediterranean countries leads to institutional outcomes that are inferior in their performance to those achieved by other continental and Anglo-Saxon models (Amable 2003; Hancké, Rhodes, and Thatcher 2007; Molina and Rhodes 2007), particularly in the case of Italy (Schmidt 2002; De Cecco 2007). In fact, the compensatory role (Hancké, Rhodes, and Thatcher 2007, 16) often taken by the government tends to favor clientelistic practices that benefit well-connected insiders to the detriment of overall economic efficiency (Molina and Rhodes 2007). In terms of the *comparison* between Italy and Spain, in both countries the process of adjustment involved deregulatory reforms leading to a downsizing of the direct role of the state in the economy and a shift toward more liberal practices. However, according to the literature, this pattern of deregulation is expected to have a more profound impact on Spain due to the combined presence of strong governments and a unified capital front coalescing around large domestic service companies and foreign multinationals (Pérez 1997; Molina and Rhodes 2007). Instead, change is expected to be slower and resistant to deregulation in Italy due to the weakness of the executives coupled with the fragmentation of the entrepreneurial front (Molina and Rhodes 2007). To sum up, the existing literature expects state actors to play a decisive role in shaping the pattern of adjustment in both countries, with adjustment leading to suboptimal outcomes due to a tendency by state actors to protect vested interests, and also expects Spain to reform its domestic market more swiftly and extensively than Italy. In the remaining of the chapter we test the validity of these claims by analyzing the trajectory of reform of the financial sector in the two countries.

This chapter mainly focuses on the banking sector, although when covering the first wave of reforms of the 1990s we broaden our scope to include corporate governance at large, as such comprehensive focus is necessary to understand the underlying logic of that transformation. Two features make banking a particularly promising angle for studying patterns of adjustment to exogenous shocks in Italy and Spain. First, banking is a strategically important sector serving a critical function for the economic development of a country. This is particularly true in countries characterized by a continental corporate model where, due to the underdevelopment of the stock exchange, "banks control capital that is essential for economic growth and employment; banks finance government debt; states can use banks to influence the allocation of capital in the economy; and banks are often used for public and social purposes" (Deeg 2012, 2). Second, due to the dynamics mentioned above, banking is perhaps the sector in which domestic structures came under the most intense level of exogenous pressure, thereby making adjustment all the more needed.

The remainder of the chapter is organized as follows. Section one presents the main features that characterized the Spanish and Italian banking sectors until the 1980s. Section two describes how the two countries adapted to the wave of financial liberalization inspired by the European Union (EU) and the EMU-related budgetary constraints in the 1990s. Section three looks at the pattern of adjustment to the Eurozone crisis and the consequent banking crisis. The last section concludes by comparing the findings of the two case studies and reflecting on continuities/discontinuities in the processes and outcomes of adjustment in Mediterranean countries.

7.2. The Financial Sector in Spain and Italy: A Bird's-Eye View

7.2.1. Spain

Until the late 1980s Spain had a heavily regulated banking sector characterized by geographical branching restrictions, legal separation between commercial and savings banks (*cajas de ahorro*), regulated interest rates levels, and a state-directed circuit of privileged credit allocation (Pérez 1997). The commercial segment was dominated by seven banks owned by prominent families from their region of origin, collectively known as the Big Seven.[1] Already strong in the 1930s, the Big Seven further increased their wealth and power during the Francisco Franco dictatorship (1939–1975) when they became a crucial ally of the government. In exchange for their financing of Franco's autarkic policies, the Big Seven were allowed to operate as a state-sanctioned self-regulated cartel (Aguilera 1998). For this reason, some authors have argued that the Franco dictatorship and the Big Seven were tied together by a relationship of mutual dependence, sustained reciprocity, and reciprocal accommodation (Binda 2013; Pérez 1997).

Despite their dominant position in the Spanish market, the Big Seven were very small by European standards, trailing behind their competitors from Germany, France, and the United Kingdom. In 1985 only the largest among them—barely—made the Top 100 in the Global Banking Ranking (Tortella, Garcia, and Ruiz 2013, 153). This lack of size was motivated by two factors: weak competition in the domestic market and low levels of internationalization (Tortella, Garcia, and Ruiz 2013). Unlike in Italy, state ownership in the banking sector was restricted to the savings banks segment, and commercial banks were allowed to provide long-term credit and own shares in nonfinancial firms. The Franco dictatorship had established a system of state-led selective credit allocation aimed at supporting strategic sectors modeled on France, which remained in place until the late 1970s. The seven largest domestic banks thus emerged as the pivotal actors in Spanish corporate governance, owing to the regulatory protection they continuously enjoyed during the Franco dictatorship and after democratization (Pérez 1997). The strength of the private banking cartel was mirrored by the relative weakness of family-owned nonfinancial firms (Etchemendy 2004). Spanish manufacturing firms were hampered in their development by a shortage of patient capital, be it in the form of credit or equity. On one hand, the Big Seven imposed high interest rates for their credit, thereby severely curtailing the borrowing capacity of manufacturing firms. On the other hand, when the Big Seven invested in the manufacturing industry, they treated their industrial holdings as short-term financial investments that could be easily sold in a procyclical fashion. This investment pattern still characterizes Spanish banks in 2021, as confirmed by their decision since the mid-2000s to dispose of most of their nonfinancial holdings (Bulfone 2017, 451–52). The consequent ownership instability weakens manufacturing firms, preventing the emergence of a strong bank-industry relationship like in Germany (Deeg and Pérez 2000; Tortella, Garcia, and Ruiz 2013).

Moving to the analysis of corporate practices in general, Spain was characterized by a continental corporate model with concentrated ownership, low stock market capitalization, widespread cross-shareholding and dense interlocking directorates, and an almost nonexistent market for corporate control (Aguilera 2004; Gutierrez and Surroca 2014). State ownership was also widespread, in particular in the manufacturing sector, as a result of the industrial crisis that followed the second oil shock (Pérez 1997). Many state-owned firms fell under the umbrella of a large cross-sector conglomerate, the Instituto Nacional de Industria (National Institute of Industry), modeled on the Italian example (Aguilera 2004).

7.2.2. Italy

Similarly to Spain, the Italian banking industry was repressed by heavy state regulation. The sector was divided into three types of credit institutions that could not compete with each other: commercial, savings, and cooperative banks. Unlike in Spain, state ownership was pervasive across all segments (Deeg 2005). Still, in the early 1990s the state owned, directly or indirectly via the industrial conglomerate Istituto per la Ricostruzione Industriale (Institute for Industrial Reconstruction), commonly known as IRI, a stake in all the largest commercial banks and the main investment bank (Mediobanca), and appointed the board of most local savings banks and public-law banks (Messori 2002, 189). In 1991 state-owned banks collected 90% of deposits and gave 90% of all loans (McCann 2007, 108). Widespread state ownership dated back to the Great Depression that began in 1929, when the three largest investment banks went bankrupt and were taken over by the state. Initially meant as a short-term emergency measure, state ownership became a permanent solution. Both local savings banks and large credit institutions were highly politicized in their board appointments, and credit was mostly allocated according to political rather than economic criteria (Deeg and Pérez 2000). The sector was fragmented along regional lines due to rigid branching restrictions, leading to the mushrooming of a myriad of local state-owned credit institutions (Hallerberg and Markgraf 2018). Low concentration coupled with a weak capacity to penetrate foreign markets made Italian banks small by European standards.

Italian banks, like their Spanish peers, provided the main channel of financing for nonfinancial firms while the stock market was very narrow (Bulfone 2017, 450; Deeg and Pérez 2000). Only a few special credit institutions were allowed to provide long-term loans to industry, while most banks had to restrict their activity to short-term lending. Furthermore, the 1936 Banking Law, modeled on the Glass-Steagall Act, prevented credit institutions from acquiring stakes in nonfinancial firms (Barca 2010). These regulatory restrictions prevented the emergence of a close bank-industry relationship, confining banks to a rather marginal role in Italian corporate governance. The only exception to the overall weakness of the banking sector was the investment bank Mediobanca, which by virtue of being the only credit institution allowed to own shares in nonfinancial firms played a pivotal role as the arbiter of the shareholder alliances linking the main family blockholders (Amatori and Colli 2000).

The weakness of the bank-industry nexus was compounded by the prevailing corporate governance practices. As in Spain, Italy was until the 1990s characterized by a very high degree of ownership concentration among listed firms. Most large private firms were owned by family blockholders whose fortunes originated in the manufacturing sector. Through the widespread deployment of control-enhancing measures such as pyramidal ownership, cross-shareholding, and shareholder alliances, prominent families such as the Agnellis and the Pirellis managed to progressively diversify their activity across many manufacturing and service sectors (Barca 2010). The extreme degree of ownership concentration coupled with the lack of adequate legal protection made the Italian corporate system highly exploitative of minority shareholders (Melis 2000). Along with blockholder domination, the other major feature of Italian corporate governance pre-1990 was the widespread diffusion of state ownership. Nearly all the large domestic firms that were not family owned had the state as the largest shareholder. State ownership spanned very diverse sectors from banking, to car making, from food production to steel, from energy to chemicals (Deeg 2005). As anticipated, many state-owned firms were organized under the giant industrial conglomerate IRI that in 1985 employed nearly half a million people.

7.3. Adapting to Financial Liberalization: From the Single Market to the Common Currency

Since the mid-1980s, Italy and Spain were both called to implement a set of liberalizing reforms aimed at adjusting their corporate systems to the global push toward shareholders' capitalism, the growing competition for the attraction of foreign direct investment inflows, and the need to implement liberalizing measures emanating from the EU while meeting the EMU budgetary targets (Hancké, Rhodes, and Thatcher 2007; Deeg and Pérez 2000).[2] This liberalizing package centered on three goals: banking liberalization, privatization, and the adoption of shareholder-protective corporate legislation. However, despite the imposition of a (gradual) opening to foreign competition of their domestic markets, domestic economic authorities retained some room of maneuver to regulate their industry. Anticipating the content of this section, they would use it to support a process of sheltered consolidation among domestic banks aimed at favoring the emergence of credit institutions with a sufficient size to play an active role in the European market. The governments of Italy and Spain also engaged in such an industrial policy effort, triggering a state-led restructuring of their domestic banking industries (Deeg 2012).

Banking liberalization started in Spain already in 1977 with the dismantling of the state-directed privileged credit allocation system, gaining further pace in the 1980s during the negotiations for the country's accession to the European Economic Community (EEC) (Pérez 1997). In 1985 branching restrictions on commercial banks were removed, in 1987 the government lifted interest rate ceilings, while in 1989 branching freedom was extended to the retail segment as well. This process of liberalization was meant to foster domestic competition and strengthen the most efficient domestic banks. However, liberalization was not accompanied by an opening of the Spanish market to foreign investors. Instead, coherently with the expectations from the literature

(Molina and Rhodes 2007), Spanish authorities engaged in an effort aimed at sheltering domestic banks from foreign competition during the process of consolidation (Deeg 2012). In the context of the negotiations for the EEC accession, the government agreed to the establishment of an interim period lasting until 1992 during which the Bank of Spain could limit the acquisition of banking shares by foreign credit institutions (Pérez 1997). The Spanish government and the Bank of Spain exploited this window of opportunity to actively promote a wave of consolidation among the Big Seven. To this end, the government granted generous tax exemptions for capital gains resulting from banking mergers (Tortella, Garcia, and Ruiz 2013). As a result, between 1988 and 2000 the Big Seven went down to three, with Santander and Banco Bilbao Vizcaya Argentaria (BBVA) emerging as the two domestic leaders and the smaller Banco Popular retaining its independence. Since the start of the twenty-first century, Santander and BBVA have progressively acquired a dominant position also in Latin America and in the European market, graduating to the rank of European champions (Santander is ranked fourth in the Eurozone in terms of assets, while BBVA is ranked eleventh). Santander and BBVA were joined in their Latin American forays by other Spanish service multinationals such as Telefonica, Endesa, and Iberdrola (Tortella, Garcia, and Ruiz 2013). BBVA and, less often, Santander act as reference shareholders in these other utilities along with the savings bank La Caixa (Bulfone 2019, 2020).

The savings banks segment also underwent a process of state-led restructuring. In 1988 the government lifted the geographical constraints to the activity of savings banks, allowing them to expand their branch network to the national scale. However, they kept the savings banks segment separate from commercial banking (Deeg 2012). As a result of the progressive devolution of powers from the central government to the regional level that took place after democratization, control over the board of savings banks has shifted from the central government to the autonomous regions, all this without altering their status of nonprofit public institutions (Deeg and Donnelly 2016). Consequently, the parliaments of the autonomous regions could exert strong political influence over the credit activities of local savings banks (Hallerberg and Markgraf 2018). In a dynamic coherent with the pattern of clientelistic-prone, state-led adjustment described by Molina and Rhodes (2007), saving banks' suboptimal corporate governance structure significantly contributed to mismanaged investment decisions that culminated in an excessive exposure to the construction sector (Tortella, Garcia, and Ruiz 2013). As discussed at greater length in the next section, while initially this strategy paid high dividends, allowing Spanish banks to increase their domestic market share from 32% in 1977 to over 50% in 2000 (Cárdenas 2013, 10–11), their decisive role in fueling the housing bubble coupled with their excessive reliance on borrowing from the wholesale market put savings banks in a particularly fragile position when the crisis hit (Deeg and Donnelly 2016).

In Italy banking liberalization had to wait until the early 1990s, when the main reforms were implemented amid a situation of profound economic and political crisis. Public debt was spiraling out of control due to the huge losses piled up by state-owned firms, the political system had been shaken at its foundations by the discovery of a widespread bribery scandal, and the lira had been ejected from the European Monetary System. To make matters worse, Italy needed a radical effort of fiscal consolidation to meet the stringent Maastricht budgetary targets and qualify for EMU membership (Deeg 2005). In this context, a restricted group of reform-minded technocrats from the treasury and the Bank of Italy, in association with moderate left-wing political forces, took advantage of the political void to engineer a series of liberalizing reforms of the corporate governance legislation, the labor market, the pension system, the banking industry, and the state-owned sector (Amatori and Colli 2000; Culpepper 2007; Quaglia 2004). This reformist agenda had the explicit goal of moving Italian capitalism closer to the Anglo-American corporate models by diffusing shareholding and deepening the stock market. The reformist attitude of the center-left/technocratic alliance does not easily fit with the view of Molina and Rhodes (2007), according to which state actors in Mediterranean countries tend to intervene in the market in a way to protect established domestic interests. Instead, at least until the late 1990s the center-left/technocratic alliance saw the opening of Italian corporate practices as a way to challenge the power of traditional family blockholders (Cioffi and Höpner 2006; Culpepper 2007; McCann 2007).

The liberalization of banking featured among the core pillars of the center-left/technocrats' reformist agenda. The first important piece of legislation in this regard was the Amato Law of 1990, named after Treasury Minister Giuliano Amato, that transformed all banks into joint-stock companies (Deeg 2005). The second watershed moment in the process of banking consolidation was the Banking Law of 1993. Motivated by the need to transpose the European banking passport provisions into Italian legislation, the Banking Law ended market segmentation between credit institutions and allowed banks to own shares in nonfinancial firms, issue bonds, and extend medium- and long-term credit to industry (Deeg and Pérez 2000). While since then banks have progressively acquired important participation in nonfinancial firms, this did not result in the emergence of the strong bank-industry network found in other continental corporate models. In fact, Italian banks mostly acted as passive investors without engaging in the active monitoring of their nonfinancial holdings (Simoni 2020, 11).

To facilitate the privatization of community-owned banks (i.e., savings banks owned by provinces or regions), the Amato Law gave the control of local savings banks to not-for-profit banking foundations. Specifically, the Italian government fostered the creation of eighty-eight community-owned nonprofit foundations to take over the capital of the newly privatized banks as *temporary* trustees. Although the foundations were meant to address the limited availability of credit, they ultimately became exclusive owners of the newly privatized banks. The problem is that foundations were far from having abandoned the investee banks despite past legislative attempts—the Ciampi Law (No. 461/1998) and the Decree Law (No. 153/1999)—to induce foundations to relinquish control of their holdings. As of the end of 2014, for instance, "only one fourth of the foundations have disinvested fully from their original banks" (Jassaud 2014, 7). Furthermore, in several banks foundations "control bank Boards with an even smaller share of ownership, often through shareholders' agreements" (Jassaud 2014, 5). This ownership structure, which grants foundations a controlling shareholder position, allows them (and the political interests they represent) to influence the composition of the investee bank's governance and thus the bank's operations. The decision by the Italian government to award banking shares to politically connected banking foundations seems in line with the *process* of proinsider state-led adjustment identified by the literature on Mediterranean capitalism (Molina and Rhodes 2007; Schmidt 2002). However, when looking at this adjustment pattern in terms of its economic *outcome*, the picture appears more nuanced. In fact, while in some cases such as that of the large lender Monte dei Paschi, analyzed below, the excessive prominence of a banking foundation led to credit misallocation and political interferences, in other instances, such as those of Unicredit and Intesa-Sanpaolo analyzed below, banking foundations played a decisive role in speeding up the process of banking consolidation and improving the efficiency of the credit system (Inzerillo and Messori 2000).

Banking liberalization came hand in glove with the privatization of most state-owned credit institutions. By 2001 direct state ownership had fallen to negligible levels (0.12% of total banking assets) (Messori 2002, 184). Liberalization and privatization were the necessary premises to the consolidation of the banking industry, which the reformers encouraged in order to help the emergence of banking groups with a sufficient size to expand in the European market, thereby preventing the foreign colonization of the sector. The first merger between large domestic banks took place in 1997 when the savings bank Cariplo merged with the commercial bank Banco Ambrosiano Veneto to create Banca Intesa. This was followed by a wave of mergers that shook the Italian banking sector at its foundations. Between 1990 and 2004 there were 627 mergers involving 55% of total banking activities and 78% of the banking groups. By the end of 2004 the Italian banking sector was composed of 82 banking groups, 67 banks, and 435 cooperatives, down from 1,156 banks in 1990 (Messori and Hernández 2005, 140–41).

Higher concentration coupled with tougher competition had a positive impact on the performance of domestic credit institutions (Messori 2002). Crucially, the wave of banking consolidation led to the emergence of two large and internationally competitive European banking champions Unicredit and Intesa-Sanpaolo, which both featured banking foundations as their main shareholders. As of 2017 both banks ranked in the Eurozone top ten in terms of assets. Their growth was the result of a strengthening on the domestic market, in particular by Intesa-Sanpaolo, coupled with a successful penetration of foreign markets mainly in Central and Eastern Europe, though Unicredit developed as well an important presence on the German market (Deeg 2012). The government and the Bank of Italy played a decisive role in fostering and shaping the outcome of banking consolidation by sheltering domestic banks from foreign competition, granting generous fiscal incentives in case of banking mergers, and helping the rise of outward-looking and at times politically close banking managers (Quaglia 2013).

While Spain and Italy had a similar approach in reforming their banking sector, the reform of the corporate system at large led to divergent outcomes. While Spain acquired some Anglo-Saxon corporate features, Italian corporate practices remained largely unchanged (Aguilera and Garcia-Castro 2012; Bulfone 2017). This aligns with predictions by Molina and Rhodes (2007) that market liberalization is likely to have a more profound impact on Spain than on Italy due to the presence of a more cohesive and outward-looking capital alliance. In particular, Spain witnessed a sizable deepening of the stock market, with market capitalization peaking in 2007 at 122% of GDP, a figure close to the level of countries such as the United States and the United Kingdom. Although stock market capitalization declined dramatically as a result of the crisis and the burst of the housing bubble, it still stood at 67% of GDP in 2017. The wave of privatization led also to the near disappearance of direct state ownership among listed firms, another feature typical of the Anglo-Saxon model. Furthermore, the process of privatization led to a further opening of Spanish capitalism to foreign investment. In fact, while governments of all political persuasions protected the domestic ownership of large banks and utilities, state-owned manufacturing firms such as the car maker Seat were directly sold to foreign multinational enterprises (Etchemendy 2004).

The implementation of a similar package of corporate reforms had instead a negligible impact on corporate practices in Italy, with the country still displaying many traits of the continental model. Stock market capitalization remains comparatively low and even declined after the crisis, standing at 36% of GDP in 2017. Similarly, the ownership pattern among listed firms remains extremely concentrated. Even though some manufacturing groups were dissolved due to the dramatic impact of the crisis, family blockholders still control a large share of blue-chip companies, thereby preventing the development of an active market for corporate control. Despite the fact that Italy underwent one of the largest privatization waves worldwide, the pace of the sell-offs slowed down since the early 2000s, and the state remains the controlling shareholder in many large firms (Bulfone 2017). Hence, as Culpepper (2007, 799) aptly summarized commenting on the liberalizing effort of the 1990s, "The most important result is that the effort failed." As anticipated, the only reform that had a lasting impact on Italian corporate practices was the liberalization of banking, which triggered a wave of consolidation and the emergence of two large European players: Unicredit and Intesa-Sanpaolo.

Even though the wave of reforms had a different impact on Italian and Spanish corporate practices, this growing heterogeneity is nevertheless the result of the very same dynamic: the exploitation of liberalizing reforms by powerful corporate insiders (Bulfone 2017; Deeg and Pérez 2000). In Italy, traditional blockholding families took advantage of the wave of privatizations to acquire the control of state-owned firms active in sheltered sectors such as transports and telecommunications. At the same time, the widespread use of shareholder agreements allowed them to retain control over their diversified business groups, thereby preventing the deepening of the stock exchange and the diffusion of ownership. Similarly, in Spain the deepening of stock market capitalization was essentially driven by Santander and BBVA and by the utilities and large building companies in which large domestic banks had invested (Deeg and Pérez 2000; Bulfone 2017). Hence, rather than opening Italian and Spanish corporate governance to new actors, in line with the intuitions of Molina and Rhodes (2007), the wave of liberalizing reforms further strengthened its insider-dominated nature.

7.4. Spain and Italy at the Test of the Crisis

The recent global financial crisis and the ensuing Eurozone sovereign debt crisis provide a further test to assess how processes of adjustment takes place in Spain and Italy and with what consequences. Indeed, the crisis required policymakers in both countries to make important decisions on how to fix the problems of domestic banks and how to allocate the costs of the resolution of banking crises. An examination of how governments responded to the banking crisis thus offers a glimpse into the continuities/discontinuities of processes of adaptation in the two Mediterranean countries.

7.4.1. Spain

As the global financial crisis originating in the United States spread across advanced economies, the Spanish banking sector initially seemed sufficiently resilient to weather the impending storm (Quaglia and Royo 2015). A traditional retail-oriented focus and robust regulation were key for the initial positive performance. However, the disruptions in the wholesale credit markets and the burst of the housing bubble, with the attendant sharp economic downturn, brought to the surface the problems that had been accumulating in the Spanish financial system. Indeed, as the economy entered recession and construction activity collapsed, the crisis vividly revealed the poor lending decisions and suboptimal practices that had characterized Spanish banks during the preceding economic upswing.

The reckoning was particularly dramatic for savings banks, as their politicized corporate governance had contributed to weakening their stability (Hallerberg and Markgraf 2018). Indeed, empirical evidence shows that while increasing in size, savings banks had shifted the focus of their activity toward profit maximization (García-Cestona and Surroca 2008). This in turn led them to favor risky lending practices in the construction and real estate sectors (Cárdenas 2013).[3] The distinct traits of Spanish corporate governance also contributed to the buildup of risks. For instance, empirical evidence indicates that saving banks whose chairperson was a political appointee have had a significantly worse performance than other financial institutions (Cuñat and Garicano 2010). The turn for the worse became clearly visible in the pronounced deterioration of credit quality: in less than three years since 2007, saving banks' NPLs soared from about 1% to almost 10% of gross loans (IMF 2012b, 12).

How did Spanish authorities react to the growing difficulties of a crucial banking segment? In line with the expectations developed at the beginning of this section, Spanish public authorities played a key role in supporting the necessary adjustment. This dynamic is not particularly surprising or distinctive to Mediterranean countries, as fearing repercussions on the real economy, virtually all governments in advanced economies rushed in support of domestic credit institutions during the crisis. However, the modalities of public interventions are revealing of some features of the Mediterranean type of adjustment as originally conceptualized by Molina and Rhodes (2007).

Indeed, the center-left government led by José Luis Zapatero and the Bank of Spain initially reacted to the problems emerging in the savings bank segment by adopting measures aimed at improving liquidity and favoring mergers and acquisitions instead of strengthening the solvency of troubled lenders (Banco de España 2017, 107). The initial crisis management strategy was supported through the establishment in 2009 of the Fund for the Orderly Restructuring of the Banking Sector, which was designed to provide funds to viable credit institutions to favor domestic consolidation while at the same time directly intervening to rescue weaker lenders. In line with past practices of adjustment and with the expectations derived from Molina and Rhodes (2007), this strategy allowed the saving banks and their political patrons to preserve the status quo. As Otero-Iglesias, Royo, and Wechsler (2017, 205), write, "the *cajas* were more than pleased to play along [with the proposed governmental strategy] because it enabled them to continue with business as usual." Furthermore, "the local and regional governments were also happy because they would remain in control." Indeed, local governments retained the last word over merger decisions involving local banks. For instance, in the region of Galicia, Galician saving banks resisted their acquisition by the Catalan La Caixa, and Madrid also blocked the merger of Bankia and Caixabank for political reasons (Otero-Iglesias et al. 2017, 206).

As the problems continued mounting, the Spanish authorities pushed ahead with forced consolidations of the *cajas* segment. The expectation was that the acquisition of weaker banks by stronger competitors would favor the emergence of more solid entities, better placed to attract private capital. However, these expectations went largely unfulfilled. The case of Bankia is instructive in this respect, revealing the failure of the strategy put in place by Spanish authorities as well as the features of a model of adjustment benefiting insiders by allowing them to retain power and procrastinate regarding necessary transformations. Established in 2010, Bankia resulted from the merger of Caja Madrid, Bancaja, and five other smaller *cajas*. Reflecting the continuing influence of political ties in the savings sector, Rodrigo Rato, former minister of finance under the José María Aznar conservative government and former International Monetary Fund (IMF) managing director, became head of the newly created entity. However, despite the managerial shake-up, since Bankia remained firmly under political control, little was done to address the existing distorted lending practices. Bankia's troubles were finally revealed when the incoming conservative executive led by Mariano Rajoy in 2012 put in place new provisioning demands. As a result, the €305 million profit initially reported for 2011 turned into a €3 billion loss, forcing government authorities to use public funds to rescue the bank (Santos 2014, 37–38). Bankia's troubles, however, are emblematic of a wider trend in the adjustment process, with Spanish public authorities postponing the necessary reforms to protect the *cajas* and their political patrons. However, this protection of selected economic interests came at a heavy cost. "Procrastination from 2007 till 2012 meant that banking losses were much larger than if the authorities had intervened earlier on" (Otero-Iglesias et al. 2017, 195).

It was in this context that the problems in the banking sector intersected with the deterioration of the Eurozone sovereign debt markets and the economic downturn. Indeed, in few other Eurozone countries did the crisis hit the real economy as badly as in Spain as well as Italy. For instance, unlike France and Germany, in the first quarter of 2012 output in Spain had not yet recovered its precrisis level, with domestic demand hovering 13% below the 2007 peak due to the collapse in private consumption and investment (IMF 2012a, 8).

In June 2012, Spain requested financial assistance from the European Financial Stability Facility.[4] As detailed in the Memorandum of Understanding on Financial Sector Policy Conditionality, this assistance was mainly directed at supporting banking restructuring and recapitalization. Not surprisingly, the saving banks were the main recipients of public aid given the losses they had accumulated over the preceding years (Committee on the Global Financial System 2018, 15). Apart from shoring up savings banks, the main result of the European-supported adjustment program was to trigger a wave of banking consolidation. Between 2008 and 2016 the number of domestic credit institutions fell from 195 to 125, with savings banks going down from 45 to 2 (Committee on the Global Financial System 2018, 15). The EU intervention was also crucial in the case of Banco Popular, the only member of the Big Seven that had retained its independence and the first bank to be solved under the EU Single Resolution Mechanism in 2017. Santander agreed to acquire its rival for the symbolic price of €1 after EU authorities declared the Madrid-based lender "failing or likely to fail."[5]

The radical restructuring and consolidation of the Spanish banking sector as well as the speed in managing the crisis of Banco Popular, especially when compared to the Italian banking crises discussed below, are in line with Molina and Rhodes's (2007) expectation that Spain is inclined to major jumps in the adjustment process. However, unlike in Molina and Rhodes's analysis, the intensity of the transformations of the Spanish banking sector has less to do with features of the political system. Rather, two factors stand out when comparing the Spanish trajectory of adjustment with that of Italy. The first factor concerns the nature of the banking crisis, which in Spain was more systemic and concentrated in one segment than in Italy. The dire state of the Spanish savings banking sector created the conditions for more radical reforms than those implemented in Italy. The second factor relates to the fact that Spain had to enter the EU financial assistance program to shore up its banking sector. This direct influence by EU authorities was in turn decisive in shaping the process of consolidation. As Otero-Iglesias et al. (2017, 195) note, for instance, "In the Spanish case restructuring occurred not because one of the key groups was substantially weakened, but because in the context of the monetary union external (European actors) forced policy changes when the Spanish banking crisis threatened the entire euro project." Although in Italy the adjustment process was not as radical as in Spain, the EU would still play a similar albeit less profound role in the process.

7.4.2. Italy

In Italy, the impact of the global financial crisis was relatively modest at the beginning of the downward cycle. The resilience of the Italian banking system has been attributed to a number of factors including the traditional business model, characterized by a relatively high reliance on retail lending, strong customer relationships, and very limited exposure to toxic assets (Financial Stability Board 2011, 9). Former Italian finance minister Giulio Tremonti nicely captured what back then looked like a strength of the system, noting that "Italian banks do not speak English" (as reported in Quaglia 2009).

However, the shockwaves of the crisis eventually hit Italy too, although without triggering a full-fledged banking crisis of an entire segment as in Spain. Indeed, at the onset of the financial crisis, Italian banks suffered the deterioration of global market conditions. As the Bank of Italy summarizes, "Italian banks, in particular the biggest banks, faced difficulties in raising funding in international markets" (Banca d'Italia 2009, 201).

It was in this context that Italian domestic authorities introduced a number of measures to support the resilience of the banking system. Along with the provision of liquidity and bank deposit guarantees, bank recapitalization became a critical measure.[6] Indeed, by injecting public funds into banks that were no longer able to raise sufficient private capital or were forced to cut back their operations to serve outstanding obligations, the Italian government, like other governments around the world, aimed at halting panic and avoiding the adverse feedback loop with the real economy. In particular, the Ministry of Finance was authorized to subscribe special equity instruments (*obbligazioni bancarie speciali*) issued by sound banks committed to maintaining their credit to small and medium-size enterprises (Decree-Law 185 of 2008, converted into Law 2/2009), the so-called Tremonti bonds.

Although Italian policymakers' interventions were largely in line with those adopted in other European countries to save the banking sector (see, e.g., Woll 2014), the Italian recapitalization policy is nonetheless distinctive in some crucial respects that reflect the expectations developed at the beginning of this chapter about patterns of adjustment in Mediterranean economies. Specifically, the Italian government opted for an indirect intervention in the banking sector by acquiring banks' debt (rather than equity) and by avoiding punitive measures for domestic bankers (Moschella 2011). In Tremonti's words, "capital injected into the banks won't be the type of capital active in the management of the bank. Rather, it will be a capital that will exhaust its role in the form of preference shares, that is to say, shares that do not contemplate the possibility for the government to directly act within the bank" (Tremonti 2008). In other words, rather than imposing a pattern of adjustment on domestic banks, the government preferred to coordinate with them a process leading to the restoration of functioning capital and credit markets. Furthermore, the Italian legislation did not contemplate punitive measures for the CEOs of domestic banks in need of recapitalization. Rather, in an attempt to reassure domestic banks, Prime Minister Silvio Berlusconi explained that government intervention would take place "without the imposition of punitive conditions for managers and shareholders" (Il Sole 24 ore 2008). In short and in line with past practices of economic adjustment, Italian policymakers orchestrated adjustment by shielding banks from the most severe adjustment costs.

The similarities with past practices of adjustment continued to be visible as the banking crisis worsened in 2016–2017. As with previous executives, the center-left government of Matteo Renzi tried to orchestrate private-sector–led rescues and shield the banking industry from the costs of adaptation to new EU rules on banking resolution. In particular, as the crisis morphed from a financial to a sovereign debt crisis, Italian banks suffered from the so-called doom loop due to the growing weight of domestic government bonds in their balance sheets. According to European Central Bank (ECB) data, for instance, the stock of government bonds in the portfolios of Italian banks rose from 182.9 billion euros at the end of 2007 to a peak of 463.9 billion in May 2015 (Codogno and Monti 2018). Given their exposure, banks became increasingly affected by the turmoil in the market of Italian government bonds. To make matters worse, their financial strength was seriously dented by the economic downturn associated with the double-dip recession (in 2008–2009 and again in 2011–2013). Between the second quarter of 2011 and the first quarter of 2013, GDP fell by more than 5 percentage points in Italy, as compared with just 1 point in the rest of the Eurozone. In this context, many businesses and households found themselves unable to pay back their loans, thus bringing to daylight all the vulnerabilities of the very same lending practices that had allowed Italian banks to limit their losses during the initial phase of the crisis. Indeed, the growing difficulties that Italian households and firms confronted quickly translated into troubles for Italian banks' profitability and the quality of their portfolios.

Nowhere is this effect more clearly visible than in the rise of NPLs, which tripled between 2007 and 2015. Among Italian banks, *banche popolari* (popular banks) were hit particularly hard by the economic downturn (Moschella 2016). The profitability of banking foundations "has [also] been heavily impaired by the downturn in banks' profits" (Jassaud 2014, 14). Since 2008, the crisis has eroded the value of banking foundations' investments by 41% from its peak in 2006 (Filtri and Guglielmi 2012, 6). The weakness of this market segment is well illustrated in an IMF assessments of the stability of the Italian financial sector. According to the IMF (2013, 30), "Banks with a significant presence of banking foundations—defined as those in which foundations control at least 20 percent of shares—are the weakest link of the system."

The large domestic lender Monte dei Paschi (MdP) offers the most emblematic example of these "weak links" as well as of the risks associated with direct political interference in lending activities. Indeed, MdP's problems date back to its acquisition of Banca Antonveneta for €9 billion in 2007. This massively overpriced acquisition, finalized on the eve of the global subprime crisis, gave MdP the largest corporate loan book relative to its size in Italy and substantially weakened its capital base. In 2009, the bank took €1.9 billion of state capital injection in the form of Tremonti Bonds. In 2013, the bank took a second bailout worth €3.9 billion (the so-called Monti Bonds). In the meantime, MdP did several (nonpublic) derivatives deals with Deutsche Bank and Nomura in order to keep its huge losses off the balance sheet. The weaknesses of MdP were sharply brought into the spotlight when the bank came under direct supervision from the ECB at the end of 2014 following the creation of the Single Supervisory Mechanism (SSM).

By the same time, the problems in other Italian banks also came to light. The comprehensive asset quality review undertaken by the ECB in October 2014 revealed that nine out of the twenty-five banks failing the ECB stress tests were based in Italy. Following multiple interventions by the government between January and September 2014, only four of them were actually in need of recapitalization, namely Banca Popolare di Milano, Banca Popolare di Vicenza, MdP, and Banca Carige (Banca d'Italia 2014, 26).

The structural problems of the Italian banking system became vividly manifest at a time when the introduction of new EU rules on banking resolution had made the managing of domestic banking crises particularly difficult for member states. In particular, the impending entry into force of the Bank Recovery and Resolution Directive considerably reduced the room of maneuver available to local authorities. These challenges were most forcefully exposed at the end of 2015 when the government decided to rescue four small lenders—Banca Etruria, Cariferrara, Carichieti, and Banca Marche—anticipating the entry into force of tougher EU rules imposing the bail-in of depositors with over €100,000.[7] Indeed, the rescue agreement formulated by the Renzi government spared depositors and senior bondholders of the four banks but allowed thousands of junior debtholders and shareholders to be wiped out. Italian policymakers' interventions at the end of 2015 were nonetheless only the harbinger of the difficulties that the same policymakers were about to face in a context where traditional practices of adjustment were increasingly constrained by EU rules and institutions.

The management of the crisis of two Veneto banks—Banca Popolare di Vicenza and Veneto Banca—is revealing in this respect (Moschella and Quaglia 2020). To deal with the growing weaknesses of the two banks, Italian policymakers operated on different fronts. To start with, in line with the usual logic of adjustment according to which Italian policymakers tend to protect selected actors from the costs of adaptation, the government passed a law decree setting up a guarantee scheme on senior tranches of NPLs. The scheme, which was offered to all Italian banks, allowed them to sell their NPLs to special-purpose vehicles, which issued bonds to fund the purchases through securitization. To make the bonds appealing and cheaper to issue, a state guarantee was offered on senior tranches. The banks paid a fee to prevent the guarantee from qualifying as state aid.

In spite of these measures, in March 2017 the ECB-SSM sent a letter to the two Veneto banks (Popolare Vicenza and Veneto Banca) demanding a €6.4 billion capital increase. In the attempt to support its banking sector, the Italian authorities expressed serious reservations about the ECB's request and were inclined to contemplate the merger of the two banks, a solution that was met with opposition from the ECB-SSM (Davi 2017). In June 2017 the ECB declared that Popolare Vicenza and Veneto Banca were failing or likely to fail, opening the application of national insolvency rules for winding them down. At the same time, the Italian government asked the ECB for permission to provide state aid to the two banks, arguing that they fulfilled critical functions for the economy. In June 2017, the Italian authorities sought a buyer for the two banks. Eventually the only bid came from Intesa-Sanpaolo, which made a symbolic offer of €1 for each bank that was accepted by the Italian authorities. Around the same time, the Italian government injected €20 billion of public money into the Monte dei Paschi after the failure of the private recapitalization plan.[8]

like in Spain, the Italian process of adjustment to the financial and sovereign debt crisis largely confirms the persistence of the model theorized by Molina and Rhodes (2017), namely a process by which public authorities play a key role in shielding domestic societal actors from necessary adjustment costs. Similar to what we found in the Spanish case, this pattern of adjustment was disrupted by interventions from the EU authorities, albeit to a minor extent than in Spain. In line with the expectations derived from Molina and Rhodes's work, the process of adjustment has been significantly less deep and extensive in Italy than in Spain. This different magnitude is in turn due to the different nature of the crises affecting the two countries.

7.5. Conclusion

In this chapter, we examined how Spain and Italy have transformed their financial systems since the early 1990s. In particular, we compared the process of adaptation taking place in the two Mediterranean countries following the deepening of the European Single Market and the adoption of the EMU in the 1990s and the burst of the Eurozone sovereign and banking crisis in the 2010s. We found the dynamic of adjustment and its outcome to be broadly in line with the expectations we drew from the comparative study by Molina and Rhodes (2007). To start with, our analysis indicates that public authorities played a decisive role in shaping financial adaptation in both countries and consistently over time. In the 1990s, Spanish and Italian state actors superseded to a radical overhaul of their financial and corporate systems characterized by a twin process of privatization and consolidation. Later, they would take a leading role in addressing the multiple banking weaknesses affecting their financial sector in the context of the Eurozone crisis.

Coherently with Molina and Rhodes (2007) as well as Hassel (2014), public authorities of both countries often prioritized the protection of politically connected insiders. This sort of clientelistic dynamic of crisis adjustment is evident when looking at the inefficient governance practices and the pervasive political intrusions characterizing Spanish savings banks in the precrisis period as well as at the role played by banking foundations in the governance of many Italian banks. It is not a coincidence that Spanish savings banks and Italian credit institutions dominated by a single banking foundation were the most severely affected during the Eurozone crisis. The attempt to protect vested interests also helps explain why governments in both countries were slow to react to the Eurozone sovereign and banking crisis. This procrastination aggravated financial instability and contributed weakening economic recovery.

However, our analysis also suggests that the state-led adjustment characterizing Mediterranean countries can at times pinpoint financial stability and create the condition for supporting real economic activity. One prominent example of such positive dynamics has been the emergence of large and highly internationalized European banking champions such as Santander, BBVA, Intesa-Sanpaolo, and Unicredit. During the Eurozone crisis none of these banks required assistance from their government. Instead they played an important countercyclical role, purchasing large amounts of sovereign bonds and intervening in the resolution of the crises affecting smaller domestic lenders. This unexpected success, mirrored by the good performance of other Mediterranean service multinationals such as Telefonica and Enel calls for a more comprehensive assessment of patterns of state-led restructuring in Southern Europe (Bulfone 2020).

Finally, our analysis sheds some light on the *outcome* of the process of financial adjustment. In both countries the transformation of the financial system was particularly profound, arguably more significant than in other policy areas examined in this book. In a dynamic common to other European countries, this transformation came as a response first to the EU-led banking liberalization and later to the Eurozone crisis. Despite this similarity, however, our analysis reveals important difference across the two case studies. In particular, in line with Molina and Rhodes (2007), Spain seems to be implementing EU-driven deregulatory reforms more radically and profoundly than Italy. This is particularly evident when looking at the overhaul of the savings banks segment superseded by Spanish authorities during the crisis. Instead, Italian authorities responded to the banking crisis, combining attempts to resist to EU influence with one-off emergency measures. This observation points to two important preliminary findings that should be tested across other domains. First, Spain seems to be capable of adapting its domestic institutions to the EU influence better than Italy, which in turn explains the solid growth performance achieved in the precrisis and postcrisis periods. Second, Spain adapts by following a clearly neoliberal trajectory characterized *both* precrisis and postcrisis by processes of financial liberalization, privatization, and consolidation, which led among other things to the disappearance of the alternative banking segment (Deeg and Donnelly 2016). While this capacity for adaptation has arguably made the Spanish banking sector less crisis-prone than its Italian counterpart, the consolidation of the savings banks segment further reduced the already limited borrowing options available to small and medium-size enterprises. This pattern of neoliberal adaptation in Spain and a resistance to adapt in Italy deserves to be studied further and across different policy areas (Pérez and Matsaganis 2018; Picot and Tassinari 2017). More importantly, the differences highlighted here call for caution in applying the label "Mediterranean capitalism" to both Spain and Italy.

Notes

1. The Big Seven were Banesto, Bilbao, Central, Vizcaya, Hispano Americano, Banco Popular, and Santander.

2. Starting in the late 1970s the European Commission engaged in an effort of market integration of the banking industry marked by watershed moments such as the First Banking Directive (77/780/EEC) and the Second Banking Directive (89/646/EEC). The two directives allowed credit institutions authorized in a country that was part of the European Economic Community (forerunner of the EU) to operate on the entire European market without further authorization and under a common regulatory framework. Banking liberalization was completed by the lifting of capital controls and the Financial Service Action Plan of 1999. The removal of most barriers to competition at the European level opened the scope for a wave of cross-border consolidation among European firms.

3. For a detailed analysis of the relationship between local politicians, regional and municipal savings banks, and constructors, which would go beyond the scope of this study, see Cárdenas (2013) and Tortella, Garcia, and Ruiz (2013).

4. In November 2012, responsibility for providing financial support was transferred to the European Stability Mechanism.

5. Single Resolution Board, Banco Popular, available at https://srb.europa.eu/en/content /banco-popular.

6. In particular, the government introduced government guarantees and swaps for bank liabilities (Decree Law 157 of 2008, converted into Law 190/2008) to increase the liquidity in the system and allowed the Ministry of Finance to purchase nonvoting shares issued by banks that the Bank of Italy deems to be undercapitalized (Decree Law 155 of 2008, converted into Law 190/2008). Finally, a state guarantee was introduced to protect depositors against bank failures until October 2011 (Decree Law 155 of 2008).

7. See, for instance, James Politi, "Eurozone Austerity Fanning Populist Flames, Says Renzi," *Financial Times*, December 21, 2015, https://www.ft.com/content/08ba78f8-a805-11e5 -955c-1e1d6de94879.

8. Subordinated bondholders suffered losses due to burden sharing, but retailers were to be partly compensated by the bank for approximately €1.5 billion.

Chapter 8

Human Capital Formation, Research and Development, and Innovation

Luigi Burroni, Sabrina Colombo, and Marino Regini

8.1. Introduction

All the economies of the Mediterranean countries have proven incapable of responding to the globalization of the 1990s—and to the European Union's (EU) eastward expansion in the 2000s—by making a transition toward a "knowledge economy" based on highly qualified human capital and research-based innovation, unlike the economies of continental and Northern Europe. In particular, despite some internal diversities, four Mediterranean countries— Greece, Italy, Portugal, and Spain—have shared a model based on weak knowledge-intensive industries and low labor productivity. This low productivity is due, as seen in the introduction to this book, to a stronger presence of low-productivity sectors, such as construction and tourism, than other countries, and to the fact that even the high-productivity and knowledge-intensive sectors have a lower productivity in the Mediterranean countries than in others.

This chapter covers the role of institutional factors that are behind the low productivity and the low development of the so-called knowledge economy in the Mediterranean countries, concentrating on the analysis of some of these institutional factors with a focus on two dimensions that a large amount of literature has shown have direct links to labor productivity.

The first dimension refers to the supply and demand of human capital. Productivity was already shown to be directly linked to human capital and workers' skills by Robert Barro (2001) and by Paul Romer and Robert Lucas (2015), who showed a direct tie, above all in the sphere of innovation activities, between levels of schooling and economic growth. More recent works have assessed scientific skills to explain the difference in the prosperity of various countries through the availability of knowledge capital. And many works of comparative political economy have highlighted the importance that education, training, and skills have in shaping the different models of capitalism (Savvides and Stengos 2009; Hanushek and Wößmann 2015; Thelen 2014; Busemeyer and Trampusch 2012).

The second dimension that will be taken into consideration instead concerns investment in research and development (R&D) and in innovation. Extensive literature has underlined the importance of this type of both public and private investment for competitiveness and the development of innovation activities in various models of capitalism (Block 2008; Hall and Soskice 2001; Ramella 2013; Mazzucato 2013; Iversen and Soskice 2019; Weiss 2013).

Hence, this chapter focuses on these two institutional arenas—human capital formation and innovation policies—with an analysis of firms' competitive strategies, the supply and demand of human capital, and innovation and development policies. In order to better understand the main features of Mediterranean countries in a comparative perspective, we compare Italy, Spain, Portugal, and Greece with three countries that come closest to the "ideal types" of different models of capitalism, namely Germany for continental capitalism, Sweden for the Northern European model, and the United Kingdom for Anglo-Saxon capitalism. This analysis will highlight that the inability of the four Mediterranean countries to make a transition toward a knowledge economy has been displayed in one or more of the following ways:

- A marked weakness in the supply and demand of research-based innovation by companies and by the economic system more generally, which includes the production system and the private and public service supply system, and a greater importance of low-productivity sectors (section 8.2);
- Lack or unsuitability of the demand as well as the supply of highly qualified human capital as provided by the advanced training and higher education systems (section 8.3);
- Policies of moderate efficacy that have not been able to support or promote corporate investment in innovation, with little done to promote innovation and that little done badly, a characteristic shared by the four Mediterranean countries but with recent signs of diversification contrasting Greece and Italy on one hand with Spain and Portugal on the other (section 8.4); and
- Lack of coordination mechanisms between the supply and demand of innovation and skills (section 8.5).

As we will see, this set of factors has prevented the affirmation—and the reproduction—of a model based on a "high road" to development, with high innovation and high productivity. In the conclusion (section 8.6), some hypotheses will be formulated as to the reasons leading toward this model, while we will leave to the concluding chapter of the volume the task to explain why the Mediterranean countries have continued to make policies with little inclination to support a shift toward the "high road."

8.2. Companies' Competitive Strategies and the Features of the Production System

A first and very important element of weakness of the four Mediterranean political economies is given by the fact that the private firms invest very little in R&D and mainly places its trust in informal and incremental product and process innovation mechanisms. These might have been a competitiveness factor until the mid-1990s, but today they are proving less and less suited to competing at an international level.

This low level of expenditure has gone hand in hand with a reorganization of the economy that has favored the so-called non-tradable sectors, such as tourism and the building industry. While these labor-intensive sectors can give rise to a sizable growth in employment in periods of international growth (such as in Spain before the 2008 slump), they are highly exposed to the international economic situation and remain characterized by low-skill and low-productivity labor. At the same time, the low degree of corporate investment in R&D has not fostered a technological upgrade in the less labor-intensive sectors. Hence, this has yielded low labor productivity in those sectors too.

As far as the low level of expenditure on R&D is concerned, the case of Italy is almost an ideal type. According to the annual Eurostat Community Innovation Survey, which sums up the whole spectrum of possible innovation activities, among the EU members, Italy is classified as a "moderate innovator." While recent years have seen remarkable improvements in some components of the index (for example, in the amount of human resources and in the quality of the research system), the private sector remains very much behind in terms of the percentage of companies with workers involved in R&D and in R&D expenditure (Bugamelli and Lotti 2019). According to Andrews, Criscuolo, and Gal (2015), in Italy the knowledge and innovation "diffusion machine" has broken down. This is the result of the presence of a few highly innovative internationalized companies capable of operating on the frontier of efficiency and an immense number of small firms that seem incapable of drawing benefit from the knowledge spillovers or adopting the innovations developed by the market leaders. Indeed, small companies are less likely to have the internal resources to support the risks and costs of innovative projects (Pagano and Schivardi 2003) and can also lack the ability to absorb new technologies.

But as anticipated, low expenditure in R&D is characteristic of all four Mediterranean countries, not just Italy. Indeed, already in the mid-1990s, compared to investment in Sweden, Spanish companies invested around one-sixth of the amount, Italy around one-fifth, and Greece and Portugal around one-twentieth. Over time, corporate investment as a percentage of gross domestic product (GDP) has increased by a great deal: from 1995 to 2016 it quadrupled in Greece, in Portugal it increased by six times, and even in Spain and Italy it almost doubled. However, the starting point was very low in all four countries, and despite these increases, the distance from Sweden and Germany has remained extremely large: in 2015, business enterprise R&D expenditure as a percentage of GDP was 0.7 in Italy, 0.6 in Portugal and Spain, and 0.3 in Greece, against 1.9 in Germany and 2.2 in Sweden.

The lesser inclination to invest in R&D activities also emerges from the data on the staff in private companies employed in R&D activities: for every one thousand employees, the numbers employed in R&D are twenty in Sweden and thirteen in Germany against nine in Italy, six in Spain, five in Portugal, and three in Greece.

At the same time, the accumulation of knowledge-based capital is lower than in other developed countries: in 2016 intangible investments as a percentage of GDP accounted for 2.7% in Italy and 2.9% in Spain, against 3.6% in Germany.

The low investment in R&D is linked to the type of production structure in the four Mediterranean countries, made up of small and medium-size companies that often do not have the resources to make investments in R&D. This type of enterprise is therefore little inclined to invest in formal laboratory facilities and in general to spend on activities to explore the technological frontiers, while there is a greater drive to purchase new machinery and equipment and to invest human resources in informal activities aimed at on-site innovation in response to the clientele's requirements (Onida 2019).

In substance, the Mediterranean countries follow a particular type of innovation road. Even in the most advanced sectors, both process and product innovation—defined in these sectors as technological craftsmanship (Biagiotti and Burroni 2004)—is often incremental. However, it is an innovation model that has come under pressure in recent years, owing to the increasing importance of innovation heavily based on companies' in-house activities or research applied in partnership with external institutions. This is also the case in the most traditional manufacturing activities: suffice it to think of nanotechnology research and the impact on the textile sector or of new materials and innovation in household goods and activities.

This is another reason why the Mediterranean countries are weaker in terms of the development of knowledge-intensive activities and products as shown by, for example, the analysis of the MIT Media Lab Economic Complexity Index (ECI), which measures the knowledge intensity of an economy. As can be seen in figure 8.1, the most knowledge-intensive country in Europe is Germany, followed by Sweden and the United Kingdom. The ECI values are much lower for Italy, Spain, and above all Greece and Portugal.

Besides, if we are to look at another indicator, patent yield, it can be seen that the Mediterranean countries perform less well than the other European countries. Already at the start of the 1990s, Sweden and Germany had much higher patent intensity levels than the Mediterranean countries, but since the mid-1990s—not coincidentally the years when the productivity gap widened—the difference in patent-intensity growth became enormous. On one hand, Germany and Sweden saw the share of patents per inhabitant grow at an

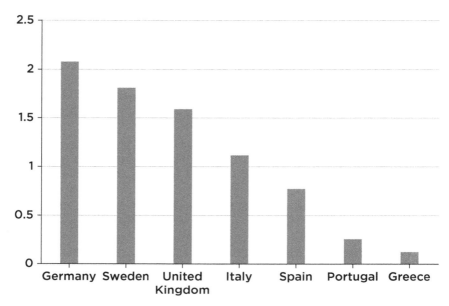

Figure 8.1. Economic Complexity Index (2017). Source: Elaborations on data from the Observatory of Economic Complexity (OEC). Note: The Economic Complexity Index measures the relative knowledge intensity of an economy by considering the knowledge intensity of the products it exports.

incredibly fast rate; on the other, the growth in Italy was practically zero, despite having a higher patent-intensity level than the other Mediterranean countries. Of the four Mediterranean countries, the patent quota only grew in Spain but at a very moderate rate. The result of this different growth path is a very marked distance between the share of patents per inhabitant in Sweden and Germany—326 and 274 patents, respectively, per one million inhabitants in 2016—and the Mediterranean countries, where the number of patents per one million inhabitants was 78 in Italy, 35 in Spain, 19 in Portugal, and 15 in Greece.

Naturally, the presence of a high patent quota as well as the ECI index points to just some aspects of innovation, namely the more "formalized" dimension, which does not, however, represent all of its possible forms. Nonetheless, these aspects offer important indications relating to the main characteristics of the Mediterranean countries' production organization.

Hence, the development of activities exposed to competition, such as manufacturing, has been very different in the Mediterranean countries compared to countries such as Germany, whose competitiveness is based on large companies and institutionalized industrial relations as well as on the role of big banks and proactive state policies. Moreover, since the 1990s the production structure in Germany has invested a lot in in-house R&D and in team relations between the large companies, research bodies, and institutions. The two pillars supporting the development of an important part of the manufacturing in Mediterranean countries instead consisted of small and medium-size companies and the possibility of exporting thanks to the presence of a weak currency.

As of the mid-1990s and early 2000s, however, three processes have taken place that have made this balance very unstable. The first was the increase in international competition and the arrival of producers with a much greater ability to accommodate higher costs than the companies in the Mediterranean countries, a factor that helped to undermine the strategy centered around exports of medium-quality, low-price products. Second, at the start of the 2000s entry to the Eurozone further reduced the space for cost competition, and hence it became necessary to upgrade the competitive strategies and center them more around product quality. Finally, the downturn in the consumer goods markets following the events of September 11, 2001, helped to make this realignment even more necessary. The 2007–2008 financial crisis, with its long-term effects, also came to bear on this difficult scenario. To remedy this difficult situation, investments in innovation would have been necessary. However, as we will see, these found no corporate or government support in any of the four Mediterranean countries.

It is in this frame that already during the 1990s a marked process of industrial restructuring began, leading to a large reduction in manufacturing activities in all four Mediterranean countries and to a development model centered around a specific variant of the "low road." It was a variant characterized by a shift from activities exposed to international competition toward nontradable activities, such as commerce, construction, and tourism. Employment in these areas grew greatly during the 1990s up to the 2007 crisis.

From this point of view, Spain, where national policies explicitly supported low-productivity activities, is a very interesting case. In this country too, the start of the 1990s was an important watershed marking the start of constant and pronounced economic growth. This was linked, as López and Rodríguez (2011) note, to a series of factors: low-interest rates that fostered domestic, mainly private, debt; EU policies that promoted the liberalization of large segments of the Spanish economy; and privatizations in Latin America that enabled the large Spanish companies to make important investments, also thanks to the buying power of the euro. These contextual factors paired up with a regulation of the real estate market that fostered significant long-term growth in this sector. With roots going back to the 1950s, these policies were also confirmed by the series of governments that took up the reins after the end of the dictatorship. Indeed, policies to support the construction sector met with transversal consensus, from the Partido Socialista Obrero Español (Spanish Socialist Workers' Party) to the Partido Popular. Hence, until the end of the 1990s, it was precisely the economic policy and local government interventions—as shown, for example, by the important 1998 law on the National Building Plan—

that strengthened the local administrations' room for maneuver in support of the building sector. These measures led to mass investments in building in both the urban and metropolitan areas and in other areas of the country such as the Mediterranean coast, together with the construction of infrastructures that at times far outstripped their effective potential use (López and Rodríguez 2011). It was a sector that therefore grew thanks to the support of politics, propelled further by mass private foreign investments, mainly from Germany, France, and the United Kingdom, and by the market of second homes both for investment and most of all tourism purposes. To conclude, for a long time low productivity was not a significant problem for the development of the Spanish economy. Quite the opposite, it was the development of very labor-intensive sectors, such as building, that led to an enormous increase in employment: the overall numbers of the employed went from 12.5 million in 1995 to 15.5 million in 2000 and 20.6 million in 2007, when the arrival of the recession struck these very same sectors hard.

Even though the case of Spain is the ideal-type example of this road, specialization in non-tradable sectors was a route taken by all four Mediterranean countries. Tourist activities, for example, are much more developed in the Mediterranean countries. Direct employment in tourism in 2015 accounted for around 13% of the total employment in Spain, 10% in Portugal and Greece, and 8% in Italy, against 3% in Sweden and 4% in the United Kingdom. Not surprisingly, the share of GDP stemming from tourist activities was also much higher in the Mediterranean countries: indeed, tourism accounted for over 12% in Portugal, 11% in Spain, and 6% in Greece and Italy, against 4% in Germany and 2.7% in Sweden (see supplementary table 8.A at https://hdl.handle .net/1813/103543). As a matter of fact, this sector followed an anticyclical trend during the recession: a postcrisis lowering of prices together with an increase in terrorism in many North African countries fostered the growth of tourism after the 2008 economic downturn.

From this point of view, Italy constitutes a bit of an exception. Here too the crisis factors recalled above played an important role, and there was a reduction in manufacturing activities. But this happened above all in the regions in the south of Italy, where so-called protoindustrial districts had arisen at the end of the 1980s (Burroni and Trigilia 2001) in a context characterized, however, by weak local institutions and the presence of a hidden economy that formed a sort of iron cage, slowing down the realignment and increasing the decline of these areas. Even the recent growth in activities linked to the promotion of cultural resources or agricultural production has not managed to counterbalance this lack of realignment, fostering the growth of regional inequalities. On the contrary, in some areas of the center-north—where the institutional context was characterized by greater resources, more robust medium-size companies, collective actors with cooperative behavior, and local governments that made policies to support competitiveness—there were local and regional factors that at least in part made up for the absence of national policies, contributing to the resilience of a large part of the highly export-oriented traditional Italian manufacturing. All the same, in these areas sustainment of these realignment processes called out for a strong national policy in strategic sectors. Instead, there was none. This is why it can be said that the low road characterizing the other three countries also plays an important role in the case of Italy as a whole, albeit with significant local exceptions.

Hence, what emerges is a Mediterranean capitalism model characterized by low development in innovation activities, which has undermined the competitive edge of all four countries. Low-productivity activities, such as those in the non-tradable sectors, are more developed, in some cases driven to grow by the economic crisis. Furthermore, a marked feature of the Mediterranean countries is the hidden economy, which is more developed in low-productivity activities such as building, trade, and tourism. In fact, the percentage of irregular employment on total employment is around 33% in Greece, 27% in Spain, 19% in Italy, and 12% in Portugal, against just 10% in Germany and 8% in Sweden. As to the contribution of the hidden economy to GDP, it is estimated to be around 23% in Greece, 21% in Italy, and 19% in Portugal and Spain, against 13% in Germany and Sweden (see supplementary table 8.B at https://hdl.handle.net /1813/103544).

Hence, a picture is formed of a production model that on the whole has followed a low road to development centered around low investment in R&D activities, with comparably limited economic innovation, high specialization in the nontradable sectors, and a large hidden economy. While this production model may have contributed to creating political consensus, it has definitely not favored the transition toward the knowledge economy more typical of advanced capitalist systems such as Germany and Sweden. It is in this context that the companies' lack of demand for qualified human capital and innovation has become consolidated over time.

8.3. The Supply and Demand of Skills and Human Capital

The European Labour Force Survey data show that for over twenty years most European countries have consistently increased the share of people employed in knowledge-intensive professional positions (i.e., managers, professionals, and technicians), while the share of those employed at medium to low professional levels has dropped substantially. For instance, in Germany the former increased from 40.7% in the 1997–2007 period to 43.9% in the following decade, and the increase has been even greater in the United Kingdom (from 40.2% to 47%) and Sweden (from 42.6% to 49%).

On the contrary, in most Mediterranean countries only a very small rise in the most highly qualified professional figures has taken place over this period. On one hand, at the end of the 1990s their share in all four countries was already lower than in most countries in continental and Northern Europe (just over 30% or less, such as in the case of Portugal). On the other hand, the increase over twenty years has not brought the share of high professional level employees in line with the European trends. Portugal differs from this trend, as it has recorded strong growth in the skill level of the workers in its economy over time. However, Portugal started from much lower percentages of highly skilled workers than in the other Mediterranean countries (see supplementary table 8.C at https://hdl.handle.net/1813/103545).

If we consider the possible effect of the economic crisis that began in 2008, these data suggest that the crisis has split the European countries in two: countries where over time qualified human capital has become increasingly strategic for the economy (the continental and Northern European countries) and countries where qualified human capital does not seem to be fundamental to the companies' competitive strategies (the Mediterranean countries).

The use of highly skilled human capital in the Mediterranean countries is below the European average in the technology- and knowledge-intensive sectors too. In these sectors, the employment rate of highly skilled workers in all four countries under consideration is around 15%. Between 2008 and 2018 this figure experienced a very small rise (1% or 2% except in Portugal), while over the same ten years the European average rose by at least 3% (15% in 2008, 18% in 2018).

We have seen that the weakness of the demand for highly qualified workers reflects to a large extent a fragile industrial structure and the scarcity of adequate investments in innovation. But the companies' delays also reflect the lack of labor supply, particularly in the qualified work segment. According to the results of the 2012 Programme for the International Assessment of Adult Competencies (PIAAC) survey, in Italy workers' digital as well as language and mathematical skills are among the lowest of the countries considered, and the percentage of highly qualified employed people is far below average. This means that despite the low demand for qualified labor, there is nevertheless a lack of qualified labor supply. It is a sort of mismatch between labor supply and demand that has been getting worse since 2010 (Guerrieri 2019, 54).

The inadequacy in the supply of highly qualified human capital can be seen in both quantitative terms (in the form of the percentage of population with a high level of schooling) and qualitative terms (in the form of the skills of young people accessing the highest levels of the education system). The data relating to both these aspects would seem to contrast the situation of some Mediterranean countries with that of others. Nevertheless, these data need to be interpreted with care.

According to Eurostat data, the rate of the population ages thirty to thirty-five with tertiary qualifications is very low in Italy (27.8%) and Portugal (33.5%), while in Spain and Greece it is quite high (42.4% and 44.3%, respectively), above the EU-28 average (40.7%). Furthermore, the share of the population ages twenty-five to thirty-four with a PhD is lower than the 1.4‰ EU-28 average in Greece (0.5‰), Portugal (0.8‰) and Italy (1.0‰), but it is higher in Spain (1.5‰).

Nevertheless, even in the Mediterranean countries that seem to perform better, it must be asked how far we are speaking of overeducation due to a range of factors (Ansell and Gingrich 2017). According to the Education and Training Monitor (European Commission 2017b), the employment rate of recent tertiary graduates (ages twenty to thirty-four, having left education one to three years before the reference year) is lower than the EU-28 average (78.2%) in all four Mediterranean countries, with a minimum of 49.2% in Greece and a maximum of 73.8% in Portugal. This leads us to think that the choice of many young Greeks and Spaniards to carry on studying to tertiary level is guided not so much by the perception of a demand for highly qualified human capital as by the paucity of this demand: instead of becoming a NEET (in neither employment nor education and training), a condition particularly widespread among young Italians, these young people prefer to find a sort of stopgap solution. The trend in tertiary educational attainment during the crisis seems to confirm this hypothesis. In the ten years between 2008 (the year when the crisis began) and 2018, the rate of the population ages thirty to thirty-five with tertiary qualifications increased in Italy by 8.6 points (from 19.2% to 27.8%), quite in line with the European average, which went up from 31.1% to 40.7%. In Spain, from the 2008 starting figure—already an extremely high 41.3%—the increase was just 0.9%. Instead, in Greece and Portugal that period saw a dramatic increase of, respectively, 18.6% (from 27.7% to 44.3%) and 11.9% (from 21.6% to 33.5%). Besides, the Education and Training Monitor (European Commission 2017b) reveals how in Greece this led to the emigration of large numbers of highly qualified people and how in Spain 37% of graduates work in jobs that do not require a university education, the highest percentage in the whole of the EU.

A telltale sign of the lack of policy design and strategy in the Mediterranean countries by political and economic actors can be spotted in the dimensions of the tertiary vocational sector. As is well known, in the economically most advanced countries, the traditional elitist university started to transform into a "mass" university in the 1960s (Trow 1974). In Europe, this was also supported by an ideology of equal access to higher education for all. In the continental and Nordic countries, this thrust was mainly interpreted as a request to expand access to higher positions in the labor market. The main response to the pressure of the "numbers" was to differentiate the higher education system by dividing it into two separate "tracks," one typically academic, the other vocational (Teichler 1988); that is, a highly professionalizing tertiary education channel was created alongside the traditional academic one. In Germany in the 1970s, followed by Austria and Switzerland, *Fachhochschulen* (universities of applied sciences) were set up alongside the universities. Similar solutions were adopted in the same period in The Netherlands and Belgium as well as in Sweden and

Finland. An alternative way of responding to the same problem of "numeric pressure" was to create "short cycles" of tertiary education within the university system but with a highly vocational bent. This was the solution adopted in various countries and above all in France with the establishment of the *Instituts Universitaires de Technologie* in 1966.

Instead, in Italy—like in other countries of Southern Europe where higher education was seen more as a status symbol than an effective tool to train human capital for use in the labor market—a similar solution to the French one was attempted in 1965. However, it was blocked in parliament. Hence, a single channel of access was maintained, at the price of having to lower standards. It was only in 2010 that the *Istituti Tecnici Superiori* (higher technical education institutions) were finally established, with the participation of local economic actors. Strongly directed toward precise vocational opportunities, however, they have only been capable of attracting less than 1% of the total number of students registered in tertiary education—such a tiny percentage that one might say a vocational channel still does not exist.

On the other hand, in Spain the short cycles of tertiary education gradually became very popular, so much so that the percentage of students on these courses today amounts to no less than 19.5% of the total tertiary students (the highest percentage in the EU after the 19.8% in France), making an important contribution to the country's high rate of tertiary attainment. However, it is more difficult to establish if these short cycles are of a sufficient quality to provide the economic system with the type of human capital that is needed. The very low rate of employment among graduates in this country and the extremely high percentage of those with a job that does not require a tertiary qualification lead to serious doubts in this regard.

The experiences in Portugal and Greece are different. The higher education system developed there is in certain ways more similar to the German one. In Greece there are fourteen universities of applied sciences, ten of which are large in size (ETER 2019). As for Portugal, with thirteen universities, fifteen polytechnics, and five other institutions, there is effectively a two-track public tertiary system. Nevertheless, flexible regulations and growing competition to attract students has ended up making the boundaries between the university and polytechnic courses quite blurred (as has also been the case in Germany). Hence, despite its appreciable size, the vocational track in this country has ended up not adequately performing the function of matching the tertiary education courses to the training needs of the human capital required by the economic system.

Now, dealing with the inadequacy of the human capital supply in qualitative rather than quantitative terms—that is, in the form of the skill levels of the young people accessing the higher levels of the educational system—we again have to note the great differences among the four Mediterranean countries. The 2015 PISA (Programme for International Student Assessment) survey indicates that fifteen-year-olds in Italy, and even more so in Greece, are among the least skilled in mathematics, sciences, and reading skills, a long way behind their Asian and Northern European peers. Instead, the performance of fifteen-year-olds in Spain and Portugal is better than the European average, above all in sciences and reading skills. Nevertheless, in this sense Italy's learning delay hides situations that differ profoundly in geographical terms, as shown by the 2018 INVALSI (Italian national assessment system) data (Gavosto 2019). While the regions in the northeast show comparable results to those of the best European systems, in the south the results make bleak reading. Not only that, while the results from the schools in the northeast are very similar, in the south they vary a great deal. This is a clear sign of less equality among the southern schools depending on the quality of the teachers and the class composition criteria, which often favor social origin (Gavosto 2019).

8.4. Innovation and Development Policies

The inability of the four Mediterranean countries to make a transition to the knowledge economy has therefore depended on a range of factors, which may or may not have been jointly present in each country. The first aspect is the production system structure and the companies' competitive strategies, alongside a shift in the economy toward the low-productivity and labor-intensive sectors. The second aspect is the shortcomings in the supply and demand of human capital. But in order to understand how these factors led to the Mediterranean countries' inability to move toward a knowledge economy, they must be related to the characteristics of the economic and political actors responsible for coordinating and promoting the adjustment processes. In other words, we must look at the public policies for development and innovation.

As we saw in the second section, the structure of the existing production system set the economies of the Mediterranean countries far apart from those of other countries. Hence, a different set of incentives was required to make the transition to a knowledge economy. Nevertheless, the economic and political actors were guided by logics not very consistent with the needs of their production systems.

In particular, as far as state intervention and policies are concerned, three elements characterize the relationship between state action and innovation development in the Mediterranean countries (Schmidt 2002; Amable 2003; Featherstone 2008). The first relates to the presence of an administrative/bureaucratic machine that constrained and slowed down the development processes. The second relates to the low level of expenditure on innovation policies. The third element is the scarce effectiveness of the public policies, in particular those concerning innovation. Let us look at these elements one by one.

As far as the weight of the administrative machine is concerned, in the Mediterranean countries there is a system of rules, authorizations, and restrictions that has a significant—and by no means virtuous—impact on processes linked to economic competitiveness (see Capano and Lippi, this volume). According to the Global Competitiveness Index Historical Dataset of the World Economic Forum, Italy and Greece are the countries where the public administration machine is seen as the greatest hindrance to the economic arena, but Portugal and Spain record high levels for this indicator too (see supplementary table 8.D at https://hdl.handle.net/1813/103547).

If we are to look at the overall expenditure on the economy, it can be noted how the four Mediterranean countries spend less than other countries to create services for competitiveness: in fact, in 2017 the state spent around 1,835 euros per capita for these services in Sweden against 587 euros in Greece, which become 953 for Spain, 970 for Portugal, and 1,000 for Italy (see supplementary table 8.E at https://hdl.handle.net/1813/103548).

Naturally this is the overall spending, regardless of the production sectors, and includes expenditure for manufacturing, farming, etc. Therefore, it is important to look at how the governments spend for R&D activities, which are of more direct interest for this work. As we saw in the introduction to this book, the overall spending on R&D in the Mediterranean countries is far lower than in the other advanced economies and on average did not grow during the Great Recession, as was the case in almost all the other European countries including those of Eastern Europe, which started from very low levels. In truth, the Mediterranean countries have been spending less on R&D than the other countries since the beginning of the 1990s, albeit with some differences: Spain and Portugal saw their spending grow from the mid-1990s until 2009; nevertheless, they remained a long way behind Germany and Sweden. The low level of expenditure is therefore a historical characteristic that has been strengthened by the growing search for macroeconomic stability through austerity, leading to a sharp reduction in public spending, alongside the reorganization of welfare, labor, and development policies.

The spending differential between the countries that spend more and those that spend less, which has remained substantially constant in time, produces cumulative effects. In the period 2000–2013 alone, the amount of state spending in support of R&D activities in Sweden was $4,600 per capita and in Germany almost $3,800, while in Greece the figure was just $1,200 and in Portugal less than $1,800 (see supplementary table 8.F at https://hdl.handle.net/1813/103549).

Hence, this confirms less state commitment to supporting innovation activities, a weakness that also combines with a low diffusion of financial risk tools and venture capital. Few collective goods for innovation produced by policies, together with low investment on the part of companies and fewer possibilities of turning to private credit, might have hindered the development of high-tech and innovation activities on the part of a production structure characterized mainly by small and medium-size companies. Indeed, these firms have fewer internal resources for innovation than the large companies of continental and Anglo-Saxon capitalism and therefore would need greater institutional support to foster high-tech development (Ramella 2013; Burroni, Gherardini, and Scalise 2019). These shortcomings help explain why all four Mediterranean countries record very low values for the innovative capacity indicators that we saw in the first part of this chapter.

Looking at the quantity of expenditure on R&D offers important elements for an understanding of the main weaknesses of the Mediterranean countries. But this is not enough. It is also very important to investigate the spending capacity in qualitative terms, in other words, the capacity of the public machine to come up with effective policies. In this way one can observe that not only is there little spending on innovation policies in Mediterranean capitalism but also that what spending exists is done badly. If we are to take the indicators relating to the quality of governance, which refer to the effectiveness of the state action as a whole, it can be remarked that the four Mediterranean countries have lower values than Sweden, the United Kingdom, and Germany for all of the dimensions taken into consideration in table 8.1.

In these institutional contexts the public actors have been less able to offer quality public services and to formulate and implement effective policies. Not only that, the executives are less credible, with low capacity to promote policies for private-sector development and scarce capacity to create a context that penalizes irregular behavior. All of these factors belong to institutional contexts that do not foster innovation.

Table 8.1 Quality of public governance (2017)

	Government effectiveness	Regulatory quality	Rule of law
Greece	0.31	0.24	0.08
Italy	0.50	0.70	0.32
Portugal	1.33	0.91	1.13
Spain	1.03	0.94	1.01
Germany	1.72	1.78	1.61
Sweden	1.84	1.80	1.94
United Kingdom	1.41	1.71	1.68

Source: Elaborations on World Bank data.

Note: *Government effectiveness* reflects perceptions of the quality of public services, the quality of the civil service and the degree of its independence from political pressures, the quality of policy formulation and implementation, and the credibility of the government's commitment to such policies. *Regulatory quality* reflects perceptions of the ability of the government to formulate and implement sound policies and regulations that permit and promote private-sector development. *Rule of law* Reflects perceptions of the extent to which agents have confidence in and abide by the rules of society, in particular the quality of contract enforcement, property rights, the police, and the courts, as well as perceptions regarding the likelihood of crime and violence, see http://info.worldbank.org/governance/wgi/.

Table 8.2 Policy performance (2017)

	Overall policy performance	Economic policies	Research and innovation	Education
Germany	7.4	7.6	8.0	6.6
Greece	4.5	4.1	3.8	4.3
Italy	5.7	5.7	4.6	5.0
Portugal	5.7	5.4	4.5	5.5
Spain	5.9	5.6	4.5	5.8
Sweden	8.2	8.1	9.4	7.2
United Kingdom	7.0	6.8	6.1	6.6

Source: Elaborations on Bertelsmann Stiftung sustainable governance database (https://www.sgi-network.org).

Things get no better if we take into consideration the effectiveness of the public policies in some areas of intervention discussed in this chapter. Indeed, the effectiveness of economic and education policies is lower in all four Mediterranean countries than in Germany, Sweden, and the United Kingdom. The biggest gap in terms of performance is found, however, precisely in the policies to promote R&D activities (table 8.2).

The road that all four Mediterranean countries have followed in order to deal with these inefficiencies has produced more problems than solutions. The response to the dual pressure given by the attempt to limit public spending and reduce the inefficiencies of the administrative machine has been linear spending cuts and regulations aimed at reducing public employment through indirect tools such as blocking turnover. However, none of these has resulted in an effective reorganization of the administrative machine; indeed, paradoxically, it has helped to further reduce the efficacy of the state action.[1]

8.5. The Lack of Coordination Mechanisms between Supply and Demand

A further element of weakness has to do with the shortage of mechanisms coordinating the supply and demand of skills and the supply and demand of knowledge and innovation.

As far as competences are concerned, on one hand the capacity of the education and training system to provide the necessary skills has been limited by the scarce amount of resources invested in it (only in Portugal is the percentage of GDP spent on education higher than the EU-28 average, while in the other three countries it is far lower). On the other hand, in all the Mediterranean countries the production structure still tips very much in favor of low-skilled labor-intensive industries and micro and small firms that require little technological innovation. This setup leads to negative interactions between supply and demand. The more innovative companies are discouraged from investing in new technologies and demanding highly educated workers due to the difficulty in finding such workers with suitable skills.

This may seem at odds with the general increase in tertiary enrollments that has taken place in Mediterranean countries. Ansell and Gingrich (2017, 424), for instance, argue that in Southern Europe "graduates enter low-skill employment that neither uses their skill-set nor pays them a graduate premium"; that is, the mismatch between supply and demand is caused by underemployment due to the lack of demand for graduates. However, several surveys of employers' needs and hiring forecasts (e.g., Excelsior in Italy)[2] signal a different type of mismatch. As regards Italy in particular, it is the widespread opinion that this country presents

> one of the most alarming levels in Europe of misalignment between the degree programs chosen by young people and labor market needs, a sort of skills mismatch. This is because the composition of the graduates by field goes in quite a different direction from what is requested by the companies and the knowledge economy. . . . In short, in this country labor supply and demand do not match, with workers who are either over- or underqualified for the jobs on offer. It is a mismatch that discourages investment in human capital, also because many brilliant graduates have started to leave the country *en masse*, making the professional resources available even more scarce. (Guerrieri 2019, 54–55, our translation)

It is a vicious circle between insufficient demand and inadequate supply that limits economic growth (Sestito 2017).

Let's now turn to the mismatch between supply and demand of innovation and knowledge. In the previous section, we saw the state expenditure in support of R&D and innovation, but we did not dwell on the specific type of policy instruments used. In particular, two different types of instrument can be distinguished: those aimed at promoting collaboration between public organizations (universities, research centers, agencies specialized in the production of knowledge, etc.) and private companies, often defined as "collaborative RDI programmes" (European Commission 2013), and measures aimed at giving direct support to companies through tax incentives or individual funding.

As far as the first instrument is concerned, connection policies in support of activities with a high added value prove to be particularly well established in the countries with the highest growth in productivity such as Germany and Sweden, with large investments in policies aimed at promoting the collaboration between public organizations and private companies. They are policies that fund development agencies, specific arrangements aimed at fostering private cofunding of public research, measures dedicated toward technology transfer, and other interventions aimed at strengthening the relationship between public institutions and private actors and involving the latter in the knowledge production phase. Among the measures to promote competitiveness are also those in support of local clusters. One such example is the German GO-Cluster Programme, which funds thematic regional clusters aimed at holding public and private research together. Therefore, they are policies that concentrate on connections among actors, which have progressively and increasingly involved large companies, fostering their active participation. In this model, such companies can be defined as *embedded large firms*; that is, they are part of a network of partnerships with subcontractors and with public and private institutions that work in the research sector.

Instead, the road of direct support to single companies through tax incentives is different. These incentive tools have advantages and disadvantages. The main advantage is the speed and simplicity of the procedure to allocate the funds, which is often completely automatic; at the same time, these measures promote additional private expenditure in R&D activities. However, some studies have underlined that the incentives are more effective at promoting the arrival of direct foreign investments than the growth of local companies. At the same time, entrepreneurs often use incentive measures to do things they would have done anyway, and therefore they do not manage to spark any hidden energies or prompt interventions that would not have been done without public funding.

Existing data suggest that the four Mediterranean countries are more specialized in the second type of policy, namely support for innovation in companies through tax incentive instruments, and less in policies aimed at promoting connections between knowledge-creating institutions and companies (see supplementary tables 8.G at https://hdl.handle.net/1813/103550 and 8.H at https://hdl.handle.net/1813/103551). This may have further weakened the effects of the policies recalled in section 8.4.

8.6. Final Considerations

At the start of this chapter we asked whether some institutional factors may have hindered the transition of Mediterranean countries toward a knowledge economy while instead fostering a "low road" to development characterized by low innovation and productivity. We set out to investigate whether these factors were linked to two important institutional arenas, that of human capital and investment in R&D.

The analysis we performed led us to highlight some aspects that it is useful to briefly recall here.

First, we saw how all four Mediterranean countries feature low investment by companies in R&D activities, which is also linked to a large presence of small and medium-size companies. Innovation has continued to follow a more traditional, incremental path that is largely unable to take advantage of the great deal of progress being made in the field of research. For these reasons, low investment in R&D is associated with a low development of knowledge-intensive activities, low patent intensity, and low levels of competitiveness in the innovation sectors.

At the same time, all four Mediterranean countries prove to be strongly specialized in nontradable activities, such as consumer services, tourism, and construction, which in periods of good international weather also fostered important growth in employment, albeit in work with a low degree of skills and productivity. This specialization did not come about out of the blue, but it was often explicitly supported by public policies, as the Spanish case clearly shows.

In the face of such features of the production organization and of companies' strategies, we highlighted shortcomings in terms of both the supply and demand of human capital. As far as demand is concerned, from the 1990s to date there has been little increase in the most highly skilled employees in all four Mediterranean countries, in the same way as there is little circulation of these figures within the labor market. As far as supply is concerned, some of the workers' skills—for example, digital skills—prove to be far lower than those of other European countries, and the analysis we carried out emphasizes precisely this both qualitative and quantitative lack of qualified labor.

Another important point that emerged from the analysis is the type of public policies put into practice in the four Mediterranean countries since the beginning of the 1990s. In contexts characterized by small and medium-size companies, which often do not have the resources to make technological investments, the state has not acted as a functional substitute to make up for this shortcoming. In other words, even though the companies in the Mediterranean countries had a greater need for industrial policies, the state has intervened less than in countries such as Sweden and Germany since the start of the 1990s. This strategy has created a significant cumulative disadvantage for companies in the Mediterranean countries, even though some differences and signals of change can be seen, above all in Portugal and Spain.

These shortcomings combine with a worse performance by the administrative machine. Therefore, the state has not only spent less on policies for human capital and innovation but has often spent its money worse than the other countries taken into consideration here.

Finally, we have seen how the problems recalled above have been further bolstered by a lack of coordination mechanisms aimed at creating connections between the supply and demand of skills and the supply and demand of innovation.

It remains to be understood why in the four Mediterranean countries politics has not been able to effectively deal with these problems even when their negative effects on development appeared evident. As far as the inadequate provision of highly educated human capital is concerned, one answer might be path dependency. In fact, "the comparative perspective teaches us that political actors have significant room to maneuver as long as the higher education systems are still in their infancy. Once the systems have developed in a particular direction . . . path dependencies prevail and radical policy change become increasingly costly for governing parties" (Garritzmann 2017, 416).

However, this is a question that concerns all the aspects touched on in this book and will therefore be dealt with more appropriately in the concluding chapter.

Notes

1. The logic has often been to expect an efficient reorganization following the reduction of funds, with the idea that streamlining resources automatically leads the administration to reorganize in order to do more with less. Hence, the upshot should be to increase the "productivity" and efficiency of work in the public sector.

2. "Project Excelsior," Unioncamere, https://excelsior.unioncamere.net/.

Conclusion

Mediterranean Capitalism between Change and Continuity

LUIGI BURRONI, EMMANUELE PAVOLINI, AND MARINO REGINI

1. Introduction

In order to study Mediterranean capitalism, this volume has combined the traditional varieties of capitalism (VoC) approach with some of its more recent findings as well as other streams of the comparative political economy (CPE) literature. The chapters have therefore looked at key institutional dimensions such as corporate governance, labor market regulation and industrial relations, social protection, human capital formation, and support to innovation. However, the chapter authors have considered other approaches and variables as well, from growth models to the supranational regulation of the Eurozone, from the role of the state and public bureaucracies to sociocultural values.

This concluding chapter focuses on four key issues. First, it provides a clearer and more articulated view of the specificities of Mediterranean capitalism and the ways it has changed over time. Second, this conclusion answers the question of why Southern European (SE) countries share difficulties in being competitive and finding a stable growth pattern in the global economy. Third, it sets the agenda for research on an emerging topic: why these countries find it hard to change their path. Finally, this chapter provides a set of arguments on what might happen to these four countries in the future and whether they will stick together or are likely to follow different paths.

2. What Type of Capitalism? A Look at the Institutional Features of Southern European Political Economies over Time

A first goal of the volume was to provide a more nuanced vision of what SE political economies are. In this respect, we have focused on the main institutional dimensions considered in the VoC literature: corporate governance, labor market regulation and industrial relations, social protection, and human capital formation and innovation. As the volume has shown, analyzing these institutions over thirty years can provide not only an updated and stylized view but also helps to understand what changes have happened and where they have taken place.

Table C1 summarizes the core features and main findings presented in previous chapters of the book and reframes them in relation to the well-known coordinated market economies–liberal market economies (CME-LME) typology (Hall and Soskice 2001). The table shows the traditional characteristics of the Mediterranean model, the extent to which this model resembles an LME or CME ideal type, and how it has evolved over time (especially since the Great Recession).

Overall, the SE economies appear to have traditionally adopted a peculiar (or weak, depending on the institutional dimensions considered) version of the CME model. Rather than being a hybrid model with difficulties in exploiting institutional complementarities, the Mediterranean variety of capitalism has traditionally followed the CME path but without adopting all of its features, thus creating its own version of this model.

In the past, when a few aspects of an LME model were present they were mostly unintended consequences of specific policies. For instance, the highly dualized labor market and social protection systems were more the outcome of the main political actors' preference to focus on insiders (and grant them generous coverage) than the willingness to create a liberalized labor market for outsiders. A dualized social protection and labor market system was a stable and traditional facet in SE well before it became a policy option in other European regions in the last quarter of the century.

What has happened in recent decades, especially since the onset of the economic crisis in 2007–2008 and the following austerity plans, is a partial reconfiguration of this model, especially with regard to social protection and labor market regulation. The reformers' goals were to promote internal devaluation through a reduction in (direct and indirect) labor costs while at the same time de-dualizing the welfare system and the labor market and trying to recalibrate both. Given that the latter goal has been much less successful than the former, the overall outcome has been a shift toward a more liberal labor market and social protection system to a level not witnessed in previous decades (when liberalization mostly took place at the margins of the system). Therefore, the SE political economies are currently far more at risk of lacking institutional complementarities than a decade ago, having increasingly become a mix between an LME and a CME model without an overall defined design.

Moreover, a typical and traditional characteristic of SE political economies, namely the pivotal role of the state, has regained strength and centrality since 2007–2008 compared to the previous two decades, when attempts had been made to make way for corporatist arrangements and social dialogue in certain policy fields. In social protection, labor market regulation, industrial relations,

Table C.1 Southern European institutional features over time

	Model's traditional characteristics	LME vs. CME model	Changes over time (since 2007)
Labor market regulation and wage setting	Medium-high level of labor market protection (for insiders)	*Weak version of CME model* (strong dualization between "outsiders" and "insiders," with state intervention and a fragmented and an often adversarial industrial relations system)	*Still a weak version of CME shifting toward an LME model with renewed state protagonism* (labor market dualism not overcome, plus a context of overall liberalization of labor market contracts; stronger intervention of the state in the arena of industrial relations and wage setting and the diffusion of a unilateral policymaking style)
Social protection	Medium-high level of social expenditure mostly concentrated on "old social risks"	*Weak version of CME model* (strong dualization between "outsiders" and "insiders" and between different types of social risk)	*Still a weak version of CME shifting toward an LME model with renewed state protagonism* (limited recalibration between social groups and risks and cuts to social expenditure that may jeopardize social rights)
Corporate governance	Self-financing and banking as main source of firms' funding	*Peculiar version of CME model* (without a strong institutionalized firm-bank relationship but with local "social capital" and political intermediation as the base of the interaction)	*Still a peculiar version of the CME model* (no institutionalization) but with the crisis of part of the banking system due to the Eurozone architecture (interbank markets and Eurozone governance)
Human capital formation, R&D, and support to innovation	Medium- to low-skilled human capital; low investment in (incremental) innovation	*Weak version of CME model* (limited investment in skill formation and R&D)	*Still a weak "traditional" version of CME model* (incapable of fostering the transition toward a "knowledge economy" as CMEs have more recently done)

and corporate governance, central governments have increasingly acted in a unilateral way. Our findings partially go in the same direction to what Hassel (2014) suggests in relation to the legacy of state intervention in SE, namely that it tends to inspire a distinctive pattern of adjustment in which, in the face of economic challenges, firms and producer groups turn to the state for protection rather than change their practices. The paradox is that the introduction of structural reforms trying to liberalize the SE political economies has required strong state intervention. A second paradox is that this (renewed) high level of statism finds limitations in the presence of a weak state, characterized on one hand by an inefficient and often ineffective public administration and on the other hand by its inability to provide some form of coordination to ensure the needed institutional complementarities (as Capano and Lippi, this volume, show). The result is a model where the SE states have been very active in directly regulating some fields (social protection, labor market, industrial relations, and corporate governance) but have been unable or unwilling to support change in others (skill formation and support to innovation).

While these are the overall features and trends in the SE political economies, it is necessary to observe individual institutions more closely, starting with those that have changed the most.

2.1. Labor Market Regulation and Wage-Setting Institutions

SE countries have historically shared, at least in part, similar labor market regulation and wage-setting institutions. One traditional trait of this Mediterranean pattern was pronounced state intervention in the sphere of labor market and collective bargaining regulation. The industrial relations system was characterized by a fragmented and often adversarial structure, with unstable patterns of confrontation and cooperation between the state and organized interest groups. Also, the confrontation hinged around job security rather than individual rights-based entitlements to social protection as the main safeguard against labor market risks. Finally, the system was characterized by a high degree of segmentation in the types and levels of protection granted to different workforce components, with entitlements skewed toward (male) workers in open-ended employment to the detriment of labor market outsiders. In this respect, the segmentation increased even more in the 1990s following a wave of reforms in the four countries aimed at creating more flexible labor markets. These reforms changed the regulation at the margins (Regini 2000), not touching the working conditions of those employed in the core sectors but reducing the outsiders' employment protection.

These institutions have been affected by changes since the onset of the crisis. In the period under investigation, labor market regulation and unemployment protection systems were a key component of the overall reform strategy adopted in SE, with attempts made to transform their whole way of functioning. These changes were mostly implemented through unilateral decision-making methods rather than facilitated by processes of tripartite concerta-tion with the social partners. They departed from the trajectory of dualization that had characterized the reforms in the 1990s, aiming to achieve liberaliza-tion and deregulation that directly targeted labor market insiders rather than only focusing on interventions at the margins. They also aimed to achieve a recalibration of the social protection system by reducing entitlements for in-siders and correspondingly strengthening the protections and forms of support available to labor market outsiders by, for example, extending the coverage of unemployment benefits or active labor market policies. However, hitherto the weight of adjustment between the liberalizing and recalibrating compo-nents of the crisis-induced reforms has been asymmetrical and skewed in favor of the former. Hence, labor market dualism and social protection seg-mentation have not been overcome and persist within a context of globally reduced labor market protection levels.

In addition, industrial relations institutions have been significantly trans-formed since 2008 toward stronger state intervention in the wage-setting arena and the diffusion of a unilateral policymaking style, especially in three policy areas: collective bargaining, the minimum wage, and employment relations in the public sector. Variations can be seen in the way in which the national governments have intervened in the four SE countries in the regulation of col-lective bargaining and the setting of minimum wages, with Greece experienc-ing the highest levels of intervention and Italy the most moderate, whereas stronger similarities can be seen in the way in which national governments have addressed employment relations in the public sector.

2.2. Social Protection Institutions

In relation to social protection institutions, SE countries have traditionally been described in the literature as a peculiar mixed model, with functional imbalances (some social risks covered more than others) and distributional imbalances (some social groups covered more than others) in the way their so-cial protection systems worked. However, during the 1990s and up to the crisis in the late 2000s, the trajectories of the four countries started to diverge, with a territorial diversification between the two Iberian countries on one hand and Italy and Greece on the other. Only in these latter two countries did the tradi-tional type of SE welfare state hold rather well, whereas in Spain and Portugal there were signs of departure from the path. The austerity plans following the crisis started in 2007 proposed similar reforms, which fostered a process of progressive convergence among the four countries and at the same time, in many respects, a divergence from the rest of Western Europe. Economic cuts, especially in the provision of welfare services, and a limited capacity to address the functional and distributional imbalances inherited from the past meant that the attempt to recalibrate the SE welfare states often transformed into a partial retrenchment more than anything else. In the field of social protection too, the state—and governments in particular—made a strong comeback in the last decade, often fostering (quasi)-unilateral reforms while leaving aside parliaments and social partners (Guillén and Pavolini 2015).

2.3. Corporate Governance

Hence, social protection and labor market institutions underwent major changes, especially during the period of austerity, in terms of both regulation and how policy decisions were made. The field of corporate governance also witnessed changes but at two different times: in the early 1990s and then in the years after the Great Recession. Like in CMEs, in the SE countries banks traditionally shared a pivotal role in their political economies, being by far the most important source of credit for nonfinancial firms. Despite having a banking-dominated financial system, the SE countries had not been able to develop such a strong bank-industry relationship as in CMEs such as Germany. In Spain, the commercial segment was traditionally dominated by a limited number of banks owned by prominent families whose domestic strength was mirrored by the political weakness of the manufacturing firms, hampered in their development by a shortage of patient capital in the form of credit or equity. Instead, in Italy the banks were prevalently state-owned.

The SE banks have continued to play a central role during the process of banking liberalization since the early 1990s, thanks to the protagonism of governments and the national central banks. In the 1990s, Spanish and Italian state actors promoted a radical overhaul of their financial and corporate systems through a twin process of privatization and consolidation. The public authorities of both countries often prioritized the protection of politically connected insiders. This state-led adjustment in the banking sector fostered the emergence of a few highly competitive and internationalized credit institutions, legitimately seen as European champions. These banks retained a strong retail focus and did not engage in risky market-based investment operations. Instead, they played an important countercyclical role by purchasing large amounts of sovereign bonds and intervening to resolve the crises affecting smaller domestic lenders. The initial impact of the global financial crisis was relatively modest in both Italy and Spain, primarily due to the low exposure of their banking systems to toxic products. However, both banking sectors came increasingly under pressure with the unfolding of the crisis and in particular following the deterioration of economic conditions and strains in the sovereign debt market. In this respect, the traditional analysis on institutions regulating corporate governance needs to be integrated by looking at the workings of cross-border financial markets and in particular interbank markets, given the fact that the four SE countries are part of the Eurozone. Indeed, monetary union has created a very particular set of incentives for banks to channel credit within the Eurozone (as Pérez, this volume, argues). Moreover, the Eurozone's governance model has had a strong influence on national-level corporate governance in SE. Monetary union created incentives for banks in the Eurozone's core economies in continental Europe to channel lending to other Eurozone areas such as SE. Yet from 2008 on, the Eurozone's governance model—in particular the failure of the European Central Bank to clarify its position as a lender of last resort coupled with the adoption of procyclical austerity measures—produced an accelerating reversal of or put an abrupt halt to these capital flows and the fragmentation of the interbank markets. This left the SE governments in the situation of having to address the consequences for their domestic financial institutions, which in turn had to take on greater holdings of sovereign debt and vastly increasing levels of public debt.

2.4. Human Capital Formation and Innovation

Among the set of institutions considered so far, those supporting human capital formation and innovation have been the least affected by changes in recent decades. The four SE countries have proven incapable of making a transition toward a knowledge economy based on highly qualified human capital and research-based innovation, unlike many CMEs in continental and Northern Europe. In particular, the four SE countries have continued to adopt a model based on weak knowledge-intensive industries and low labor productivity. In this respect, two sets of institutions have worked badly: those in charge of providing the human capital needed by a knowledge economy and those responsible for investment in research and development (R&D) and for support to innovation. SE has a structural problem with a marked weakness in the supply and demand of research-based innovation by companies due to the characteristics of the firms (the strong presence of small to medium-size enterprises, often in low-productivity, nontradable sectors such as consumer services, tourism, and construction requiring a low degree of skills and productivity). Innovation has continued to follow a more traditional and incremental path, while the CMEs in continental and Northern Europe have instead been successful in adapting their political economies in order to exploit radical innovations.

A further factor has been the lack of demand as well as the unsuitability of the supply of highly qualified human capital. Policies have largely been unable to promote corporate investment in innovation, and the few public resources invested have not been spent effectively. In contexts characterized by small to medium-size enterprises, which often do not have the resources to make technological investments, the state has not acted as a functional substitute to make up for this shortcoming. Despite the companies in SE's greater need for industrial policies, the state has intervened less than in the CMEs, and its bureaucracy has been less efficient in implementing the policies. Finally, the lack of coordination mechanisms connecting the supply and demand of skills and the supply and demand of innovation have been a further obstacle.

It is important to underline that many of these outcomes are the result of explicit public policies (e.g., supporting low-productivity, nontradable sectors as a source of strategic specialization). In this respect, for decades the SE political economies adopted an unstable consumption-led growth model in which the main demand contributing to growth was household consumption, fueled by the expansion of household and/or state debt (see Baccaro, this volume). Its instability came from the tendency to accumulate foreign debt through sustained current account deficits, a phenomenon magnified by the Eurozone's institutional design, as underlined above. After the 2007–2009 crisis, international pressures pushed the SE political economies in the direction of an export-led growth model, so far with limited success for reasons discussed in the next section.

3. Why SE Economies Share Difficulties in Being Competitive and Finding a Stable Growth Pattern

The introduction to the volume argued that one feature of Mediterranean capitalism is its unstable growth (with recurrent peaks and troughs) and the fragile bases of this growth in the medium term, in comparison with different types of capitalism, including the Central and Eastern European (CEE) model. This book has attempted to clarify the reasons behind these difficulties. As seen in the introduction, the two main explanations offered in the international debate are based on the following factors: the (bad) functioning of supply-side institutions (namely social protection, labor market regulation, and industrial relations) and the peripheral position of SE economies in the Eurozone. A third explanation, less present in the literature and in the political debate, points to the low degree of investment in R&D and highly skilled human capital in SE. Our starting hypothesis was that the third and in part the second factors hold most explanatory power. The book's findings confirm our hypothesis, underlining the interplay between the second and third types of explanation.

The reforms of recent decades have mainly attempted to transform the institutions regulating social protection and the labor market. However, so far these reforms have not been able to provide the expected results in terms of growth and competitiveness. Why? Apart from reasons related to the lack of policies fostering human capital accumulation and innovation and the failure to recognize the role that the Eurozone's institutional design can play, which will be discussed below, a policy approach based on reforming social protection and labor market-related institutions falls short for several reasons discussed in this book. First, the approach that was successful in CEE, based on exports and liberalization, can only partially work for SE: a quasi-total dismantlement of the labor market, social protection, and industrial relations institutions in SE would have unbearable social and political consequences in the medium term, as we have already seen with the rise of both right- and left-wing populist movements in some Mediterranean countries. A strategy has been pursued based on internal devaluation through a reduction in (direct and indirect) labor costs, but this can hardly go so far as to make SE—at least Italy and Spain—competitive in these respects with CEE countries, not to mention other emerging economies worldwide. Second, as the growth model approach clearly shows, a strategy based only on fostering supply-side reforms as a core driver for growth will most likely result in failure. In SE, the export sector is too small and of limited technological sophistication. Therefore, the SE countries tend to produce intermediate goods for global supply chains or low value-added services for international customers (e.g., tourism). An export-led growth model could only be successful if the technological content of production improved, but this would require a huge investment in R&D and human capital accumulation, a point we will come back to shortly.

The second explanation, based on the peripheral position of SE economies in the Eurozone, has proven more convincing, although it requires a more nuanced specification than is usually the case in the literature and the public debate. The chapter in this volume by Sofia Pérez goes exactly in this direction, showing that the difficulties of SE countries cannot simply be ascribed to the usual suspects (domestic supply-side factors such as labor market institutions, wage dynamics, and social protection systems). An important role is played by cross-border capital markets in interaction with the Eurozone's governance rules, which subsequent to the monetary union produced large capital inflows into the economies of SE through interbank markets, followed by the acute reversal of this trend from 2008 on. The rules of the game of monetary union have created incentives for banks in the Eurozone's core economies to channel lending from the core and the rest of the world to the Eurozone periphery. Yet since 2008, the Eurozone's governance model has left SE financial institutions in the position of having to take on greater holdings of sovereign debt and vastly expanding levels of public debt. In countries that had joined the Eurozone with a high level (Italy and Greece) or rising level (Portugal) of public debt, fiscal policy was constrained by the Stability and Growth Pact, and their governments were forced to take countercyclical measures. On the other hand, those countries that had joined the Eurozone with a particularly low level of public debt (such as Spain) did not face such constraints, instead experiencing a seemingly virtuous cycle of falling public debt and rapid growth.

However, an explanation focusing mostly on supranational factors risks overlooking the fact that some of the economic difficulties in SE were already at work before monetary union or would probably have occurred even without it. For instance, slow productivity growth and high public debt in Italy and Greece as well as high rates of unemployment in Spain were present even before these countries joined the Eurozone, while the real estate bubble and the bank crisis in Spain were likely to have happened anyway, though possibly at different times and to different degrees. As this book shows (see Burroni, Colombo, and Regini as well as Pavolini and Scalise, this volume), we must also look at other internal factors in SE countries: on one hand the unsatisfactory investment in R&D and human capital and on the other the type of sociocultural values characterizing some of them (Italy and Greece) and how these can support economic growth.

The low degree of innovation in SE economies stems from a set of reasons, among which the scarcity of investment in R&D and highly skilled human capital is especially important. These countries are all underspecialized in high-tech sectors and have large numbers of small and medium-size enterprises. In these respects, the gap from the rest of continental and Northern Europe has increased over time.

Sociocultural values have also played a role. In this respect, there has been an increasing differentiation between Spain and Portugal on one hand and Italy and Greece on the other. The conservative and traditional values and family structures that used to characterize all of SE are gradually losing their social and cultural significance in the southwestern area, which has become more tolerant and open, closer to continental and Northern European societies. In the eastern part of SE, sociocultural modernization seems to have slowed down compared not only to Spain and Portugal but also to the whole of Western Europe (see the next two sections on this topic). The result is a social environment that has been less friendly and supportive toward several potential drivers of economic growth: women's and migrants' labor market participation, tolerance and acceptance toward diversity and innovation, and social and institutional trust.

4. Factors Inhibiting Policy Change: Why Have Wrong and Ineffective Policies Been Fielded for Such a Long Time?

The story of other political economies in Europe in recent decades is one of a partial departure from their traditional path, as many CMEs show with their successful attempt to become more export-led economies widely based on innovation. As already underlined in the previous section, this is not the story of SE. What are the reasons behind the consolidation of an unsuccessful model of political economy? And how can we identify the factors that have inhibited a change in policy strategy in the four countries? What has characterized SE in the last three decades is not a lack of legislative innovation but rather its ineffectiveness. SE has witnessed an ongoing process of reforms since the 1990s. However, these reforms have often pursued contradictory objectives and have often ended up, especially in countries such as Italy and Greece, aggravating the lack of a consistent trajectory of development (Simoni 2012). In this respect, institutional path dependence has played a very important role. There is a long and important tradition within CPE studies, rooted in institutionalist approaches, that argues how difficult it is to break with path dependence. However, the latter can still be achieved through incremental change (Streeck and Thelen 2005). Germany can be considered an example of a partial departure from the path of its original political economy model (Streeck 2009; Baccaro and Benassi 2017).

Recent research, especially in the field of political science, has focused on the relationship between political economy models and partisan politics, highlighting the influence of polity on policies. For example, it has been shown that Westminster systems have had a greater propensity to put in place regulatory and distributive policies that are more attentive to economic competitiveness than social cohesion, while the opposite has occurred in consensual democracies (Lijpart 1999; Iversen and Soskice 2006; Trigilia 2019). Beramendi et al. (2015) defined the SE model of capitalism as capture-oriented capitalism, where the most important position belongs to two groups: small businesses, which hinder state involvement in the economy, and organized insiders, which support consumption policies tailored to their interests. The outcome, with some exceptions, is a public administration characterized by a low level of efficiency, with the family becoming a functional alternative to public intervention in the fields of income maintenance and services provision. In this system, left-oriented parties promoted the expansion of services trying to create a coalition between organized labor and sociocultural professionals, while right-oriented parties sought a coalition between the petit bourgeois, business owners, and liberal professionals. The 2007–2009 economic crisis and the consequent push for austerity reduced the capacity of these two political strategies to achieve social cohesion or to promote investment-oriented policies. In this context, center-right coalitions pushed for tax reduction and internal devaluation, as many chapters of the book emphasized, and this hindered the search for a development path based on innovation and growth in high added-value activities.

Although these are important theses, particularly fruitful in explaining the differences between CMEs and LMEs, the role of polity seems less useful in explaining the trajectories of the four Mediterranean countries for several reasons. Other authors emphasize that politics and, more generally, actors' decisions play a role in explaining economics crises. For instance, Bosco (2018) showed how the strong conflict between the Partido Socialista Obrero Español (Spanish Socialist Workers' Party) and the Partido Popular in Spain hindered the possibility for an institutional cooperation aimed at facing the impact of the economic crisis in that country. By this point of view, the economic and political crisis—along with the territorial and the institutional ones—mutually reinforced themselves, reducing the possibility to recover from the crisis. Finally, a potentially perverse role of the relationship between society and politics has been underlined in recent work on corruption. Focusing on the Italian case, for instance, Capussela (2018) has showed the perverse relationship between corruption and clientelism on the one hand and development policies on the other.

However, it is important to take into account other processes in the analysis of the relationship between politics and sound socioeconomic policies. Many of the policies analyzed in this volume are not the outcome of partisan politics; in fact, they do not play a big role in the electoral agenda and are not part of the exclusive worldview of right- or left-wing governments. The contents of innovation policies, for example, are decided within arenas in which highly organized interests dominate a policy process that is shielded from public debate and characterized by negotiation between different policy networks according to a model that has been defined as "quiet politics" (Culpepper 2011, xv). Moreover, these policies were implemented during the 1990s, when a sort of consensual democracy based on social pacts emerged in Italy, Spain, and Portugal (Regini 2000), and in more recent years by governments that acted in a more unilateral way. Finally, for a long time the Mediterranean countries have shared an electoral system that is more similar to the proportional type than to the Westminster system, yet despite this feature the differences from the CMEs are remarkable. Thus, the question of why wrong or ineffective policies have been followed for such a long time cannot find a clear-cut answer in this perspective.

A more fruitful approach to shed light on this question is to focus on some specificities shared by the SE countries. In particular, we will focus on four main factors that have inhibited policy change: demand-side problems, supply-side weaknesses, the social consensus of middle-road policies, and international pressures.

4.1. Demand-Side Problems

The first factor is related to the demand for education and innovation policies. In SE, education and innovation policies have remained underdeveloped for several reasons, one of them being the lack of an adequate demand. This phenomenon is related to several variables: (1) the structure of manufacturing activities and the economic actors involved in them, (2) the large share of self-employed workers, (3) the great diffusion of the shadow economy, and (4) persistent territorial disparities that make it difficult to create powerful coalitions supporting reforms.

1. SE economies are characterized by a type of manufacturing mainly based on small to medium-size enterprises, whose competitiveness is based on neither research and innovation nor a highly skilled workforce. According to Eurostat data, in 2017, around half of the workers in manufacturing not just in Germany (55%), Sweden (48%), and the United Kingdom (45%), but also in Poland (45%) were employed in large companies with at least 250 employees. This share drops to 31% in Spain and is even lower in Italy (27%), Portugal (22%), and Greece (21%), the latter countries showing a relatively higher share of workers in very small enterprises.

This feature has created a low demand for such collective goods as education, R&D, and innovation, discouraging governments from investing in them.

The Italian case is ideal-typical of this trend. The two pillars around which Italian manufacturing developed are family-based firms and small to medium-size enterprises. These firms are clustered in territorial systems characterized by a high degree of sectoral specialization in mature sectors—such as textiles and clothing, leather, and furniture—but also in the machine tools industry, where in the past local small-firm systems were competitive thanks to their high level of specialization, high labor flexibility, the weak Italian currency (lira), and high inflation that despite increasing the costs of raw materials contributed to making products more competitive for export. This kind of local system (the industrial district) was characterized by low levels of schooling: local vocational secondary schools (*istituti tecnici*) played the most important role in providing technical skills, while workers with tertiary degrees were few and not crucial for the firms' competitiveness. The key human resources in this kind of firm were the entrepreneurs themselves, who were required to perform a plurality of functions—productive, commercial, administrative, etc.—calling on outside consultants but often employing very few personnel (Regini 1997). In this kind of local system, which continues to be relevant in the Italian economy, local competitiveness was possible even within a national political economy that was not particularly efficient. Trigilia (1996) defined this as "private dynamism with public disorder." But a specific demand for national policies fostering innovation or investments in education never emerged.

2. The second factor reinforcing this vicious circle on the demand side is the high share of self-employed workers, especially in Italy and Greece. In 2018, 22% of workers in Italy and 30% in Greece were self-employed, whereas this figure was around 10% in Sweden, Germany, and France and only partially higher in the United Kingdom (15%). In this respect, Spain and Portugal (both around 16%) are closer to continental and Northern Europe than Italy and Greece. The high proportion of independent workers has favored a demand for more incentive-related public support, a decrease in taxation or deregulation, and a reduction in bureaucratic fulfillments rather than a demand for investment in R&D or education.

3. The third variable is the large share of the irregular economy. All the SE countries are characterized by a sizable shadow economy, accounting for 23% of GDP and 33% of total employment in Greece, 21% and 19% in Italy, 19% and 12% in Portugal, and 18% and 27% in Spain (the highest values in the EU-28). As is well known, shadow economies spread in institutional systems characterized by highly labor-intensive activities—such as agriculture, tourism, and the construction industry—in which the demand for R&D and education is low.

4. Finally, still on the demand side, the role played by far-reaching territorial disparities should not be underestimated. These territorial disparities are particularly strong in Italy and Spain. This leads to very different policy needs for different areas, from highly developed regions such as Lombardy and Catalonia to the more backward Calabria and Andalusia. These clashing needs

do not favor the establishment of coherent national policies, with governments that remain "stuck in the middle" and unable to create a systemic and coherent policy framework. And the resulting policy framework can explain why both developed and backward regions perceive of themselves as places that are left behind by the national political choices (Rodríguez-Pose 2017).

4.2. Supply-Side Weaknesses

Besides the problems on the demand side, the supply side has also demonstrated significant weaknesses. The above-mentioned demand-side framework has not given policymakers any strong incentives to create policies to upgrade national competitive strategies. Thus, no changes in the national political economy have been steered by governments of any color. Additionally, three of these weaknesses have been fostered by the low levels of public administration efficiency. The first is related to the scarce institutional capacity to not only make public policies—as seen in the previous section—but also regulate market competition: the average value of the World Bank's governance indicators on regulatory quality and rule of law are 1.8 and 1.9 for Sweden, and 1.8 and 1.6 for Germany; but only 0.9 and 1.1 for Portugal, 0.9 and 1 for Spain, 0.7 and 0.3 for Italy, and 0.2 and 0.1 for Greece. This twofold poor capacity to promote effective policies in the fields of education and innovation and in effective market competition is one of the major constraints of what has been defined as the "middle-income trap" (Kharas and Kohli 2011; Iversen and Soskice 2019). Second, what is usually overlooked in the literature is that a public administration's low institutional capacity hinders not only an efficient implementation of competitiveness policies but also the policy design phase. This is quite relevant, because many development policies are "quiet politics": they are not part of the electoral agenda and are often planned by small policy networks with a stronger technical rather than political component, wherein the public component plays a very important role. Thus, the public administration's low institutional capacity also creates notable constraints in the supply of sound policies.

This low capacity to produce effective collective goods has triggered consensus toward a decrease in public expenditure and a reduction of taxes, reducing the possibility of investing in education and innovation policies. These supply-side weaknesses have also been reinforced by the role played by the social partners at the national level, in particular by employers' associations: they strongly pushed for a flexible labor market and a reduction in labor costs more so than toward investments in education and R&D.

Furthermore, the political culture widespread in SE has not been particularly attentive to progrowth investments. Italy is a good case in point: in an interview released in July 2010 to the *European Voice* (a newspaper in the *Economist* Group), Silvio Berlusconi—at the time both a foremost entrepreneur and Italy's prime minister—asked "why should we pay scientists when we make the most beautiful shoes in the world?" And his question was accompanied by the caption "Italy's prime minister explains why it is OK to cut spending on research and development." More recently, the populist parties of the center-right coalition also emphasized the importance of reducing public spending and taxes rather than the need for more structural and proactive investments. As regards Spain, one can quote José Luis Arrese, the Spanish minister of housing under the Francisco Franco regime, who said at the end of the 1950s, "Queremos un país de propietarios y no de proletarios" (We want a country of owners, not of proletarians), showing long-term support for the building industries. This support also continued in recent decades and partially hindered the development of a more innovation-oriented political economy.

4.3. Social Consensus

The policies adopted as a consequence of this political culture did produce social consensus, which in turn hindered policy diversification and new sets of policies: they fostered a model that—in a period of good weather for the international economy—favored the growth of young people and women in employment. The sociocultural context described above continues to sustain a development model based on the predominance of small firms and self-employment specialized in low- and medium-technology sectors. Additionally, a lack of trust in collective endeavors has always limited the propensity of these firms to cooperate and develop public-private partnerships to exploit technology and knowledge.

The social consensus was also due to the policymakers' attention to supporting profits from real estate. This created benefits for middle-class homeowners, a category that is significant in all four SE countries. As emphasized, the middle road is characterized by medium-high specialization in low added-value and labor-intensive activities such as tourism and construction. According to the World Economic Forum Global Competitiveness Index for total activities, Spain ranks twenty-third among all the countries studied, and Italy ranks thirtieth. But if we focus on the global competitiveness index for tourist activities, Spain comes in first and Italy eighth. In 2015, tourist activities accounted for 6% of GDP in Italy and Greece, 11% in Spain, and 12% in Portugal as well as for 8% of total employment in Italy, 10% in Portugal and Greece, and 13% in Spain. Prior to the COVID-19 pandemic, Barcelona and Milan were among the twenty most visited cities in the world, with more than nine million tourists per year. Along with manufacturing activities, the construction industry plays an important role, especially in the Spanish case. This high degree of specialization in labor-intensive activities favored a notable employment growth during the 1990s: in Spain, total employment rose from 12.5 million in 1995 to 15.5 million in 2000 and 20.6 million in 2007.

All this made support for this low added-value and high labor-intensive model particularly interesting for policymakers for several reasons. First and foremost, it resulted in widespread electoral consensus: a model based on the expansion of construction favored an increase in real estate yields, meeting the interests of the "average voter." Second, the model created significant tax revenues for local governments through taxation on property (Carballo-Cruz 2011). Finally, the model contributed to high employment growth in countries characterized by low employment rates and a low level of labor market participation. Thus, in SE countries a nexus emerged between the creation of new jobs, the promotion of private investments, and the production of political consensus. On the one hand this sustained the reproduction of policies to support the middle road, while on the other it hindered the establishment of new policies addressed toward promoting diversification in new activities characterized by high innovation and added value.

4.4. The Role of International Pressures

Finally, the role of international pressures should not be underestimated, especially in the last decade. Despite the rhetoric of promoting the transition toward a so-called knowledge economy, the measures undertaken by the European Commission substantially pushed the four SE countries toward a specific type of structural reform, which led to a containment of public spending and an increase in labor flexibility. This push favored linear cuts in public spending, concentrated on institutional sectors such as education that are particularly expensive for the public budget, and hindered investments in R&D. On the contrary, these linear cuts were compatible with all the policies implemented by the SE countries, in particular the support for a process of flexibilization at the margins.

In conclusion, the four above-mentioned factors—problems on the demand and supply sides of policies, the social consensus for middle-road policies, and international pressures—supported a model of political economy that hindered investment in innovation and was conducive to the consolidation of low value-added activities. These measures, as we have underlined, did not support a consolidation of the business system, a marked growth in productivity, or the emergence of strategic sectors based on R&D and innovation. All this has left Mediterranean countries stuck in the middle, without the competitive strengths of the high road based on high wages, high skills, high cooperation, and high product quality but at the same time far from a low road based on low wages, low worker involvement, and low product quality.

5. One Model, Different Trajectories?

The analyses presented in this book show that the SE political economies share a set of commonalities in terms of the socioeconomic institutions regulating their capitalist systems, although with a certain level of variation between the different countries. For this reason, the concept of Mediterranean capitalism can still be useful in CPE even though it must be handled with care. But what about the coming years? Can we expect the four Mediterranean economies to stick together in the future too? Or is there the possibility that the differences among the SE countries will increase and they will follow different paths in the future and increasingly diverge?

The book provides mixed answers to these questions. As we have already emphasized, the diversification between the four countries appears to be limited, especially when we compare their characteristics with those of other models of capitalism, such as the continental and Nordic ones: all four countries still feature some common elements, such as the prevalence of sectors with low added value, a lesser capability to respond to new social risks, and scarce support for labor productivity. Moreover, signs of policy differentiation were at play before the 2007–2009 crisis, but the austerity plans implemented in the following decade acted as a great equalizer.

At the same time, however, we have also seen significant differences in many arenas, which seem to indicate centrifugal forces in the SE cluster. For example, the chapter by Capano and Lippi shows that the four countries have followed similar paths of reforms to improve the institutional capacity of their public administration, but the results have been different. On the one hand, Portugal and Spain have gradually adjusted to exogenous change and preserved some ability to respond to economic and societal pressures. On the other hand, Greece and Italy have increasingly shifted toward a bad performance and loss of capacity. The reasons for this bifurcation are manifold, but two seem particularly important: policy legacy and political commitment and governance supporting policy capacity.

Moreover, the analysis by Pavolini and Scalise (this volume) highlights an increasing divergence in terms of sociocultural values within the SE countries. Again, the split runs along the east (Greece and Italy)–west (Spain and Portugal) divide. Evolving sociocultural attitudes, which started in a context of political and economic restructuring after the dictatorships in Spain and Portugal and continued throughout the 1990s, have particularly influenced civil society as well as the role of women and their access to economic opportunities. Gender roles changed drastically within a short period of time, playing a significant role in the great expansion of the female workforce. This path of modernization, grounded on the expansion of civil rights and liberties, the gradual increase in educational levels, and the steady rise in the female-active population (even during periods of economic recession) has progressed hand in hand and is fully compatible with an economic model based on low-productivity and labor-intensive jobs. The expansion of the workforce has mostly happened in low- and medium-skilled services and low-productivity sectors (i.e., catering, construction, and tourism) and little in highly productive service sectors (i.e., communications, finance, and business-related activities). Despite the widespread social consensus, here modernization has not promoted a type of development based on innovation and the knowledge economy, nor has it been able to unlock productivity growth by strengthening human capital.

On the contrary, the long-term perspective highlights the persistence of traditional values and attachment to the patriarchal family in Italy and Greece, where hostility toward diversity has even grown in the last decade. The persistence of stable gender roles affects women's labor market participation, which continues to be particularly low in these countries. This means that raising female human capital and education levels—as is indeed happening—is essential to but not sufficient for women's emancipation and participation in the labor market, which is strongly linked to gender roles in society and household models. Here, the perception that immigration is a threat and limit to economic development is linked to a low level of general and institutional trust and weak social cohesion. This public sentiment has certainly been influenced by the severe economic crisis and the growing inadequacy of the Mediterranean welfare model, which is no longer able to protect against new social risks. Despite this, references to the past, to the authority of tradition, and the shared feeling of distrust continue to exercise a particular influence on the cultural climate. The disaffection and distrust are manifested through attachment to the stability of social environments that influence and legitimize the political and economic choices in these countries. It is a context that slows down reforms aimed at supporting the research system, education, and innovation-based firms and creates very few incentives for human capital development and technology innovation, thus hindering socioeconomic development. Instead, the sociocultural context continues to uphold a development model based on the predominance of small firms and self-employment specialized in low- and medium-technology sectors, which favored growth in these fields until the 1980s. However, with the challenges of globalization and the need to upgrade both the technology and the skills employed, they have become much less efficient in promoting development. Additionally, the lack of trust in collective endeavors limits these firms' propensity to cooperate and develop public-private partnerships to exploit technology and knowledge.

A process of diversification can also be found in the labor market and industrial relations fields. Portugal tended to be characterized by higher levels of employment but also higher income inequality, while the other countries combined a smaller employment base with lower income inequality. In particular, a clear cleavage formed in recent years, with Portugal scoring good results in terms of employment and unemployment rates, followed by Spain and, at a great distance, by Italy and Greece. In 2019, the activity rate (ages fifteen to sixty) and employment rate (ages twenty to sixty four) were, respectively, 75.5% and 76.1% in Portugal, 73.8 and 68.0 in Spain, 68.4 and 61.0 in Greece, and 65.7 and 63.5 in Italy, while female activity and employment rates were 72.9 and 72.7 in Portugal, 69.0 and 62.1 in Spain, 60.4 and 51.3 in Greece, and 56.5 and 53.8 in Italy. A partially different frame emerges when looking at total and long-term unemployment, where the difference between Portugal and the other three countries is greater. Afonso, Dorigatti, Molina, and Tassinari (this volume) show that in terms of dualization—measured by fixed-term employment—this process has been particularly intense in Spain, followed by Portugal, Italy, and Greece, while the liberalization process shows more blurred results, achieving a high level in Spain and Greece and a lower intensity in Portugal and Italy. At the same time, labor market flexibilization was more similar in Portugal and Spain, where it started at the end of the 1980s. A process of diversification also emerges by looking at the evolution of real unit labor costs or the adjusted wage, with Portugal and Spain experiencing a sustained decline since the early 2000s, while Italy and Greece experienced an increase in real unit labor costs in the precrisis period and a more moderate decline in its aftermath.

Bulfone and Moschella (this volume) show that in terms of the outcome of the process of financial adjustment, Spain seems to have implemented EU-driven deregulatory reforms more radically and profoundly than Italy. This is particularly evident when looking at the overhaul of the savings banks segment that was superseded by the Spanish authorities during the crisis. Instead, the Italian authorities responded to the banking crisis by combining attempts to resist EU influence with one-off emergency measures. This observation confirms that Spain seems to be capable of adapting its domestic institutions to EU influences better than Italy, which in turn explains the solid growth performance achieved in the precrisis and postcrisis periods. Spain followed a clearly neoliberal trajectory characterized, both precrisis and postcrisis, by processes of financial liberalization, privatization, and consolidation, which led among other things to the disappearance of the alternative banking segment (Deeg and Donnelly 2016).

As regards policies for innovation and human capital investment, Burroni, Colombo, and Regini (this volume) show that the difference among SE countries is less clear-cut in this field. Looking at the government-financed Gross Domestic Expenditure on R&D (GERD), in 2017 Portugal had the highest government-financed GERD as a percentage of GDP (0.54), followed by Spain (0.47), Italy (0.44), and Greece (0.43). Italy, on the other hand, has a higher level of economic complexity of its production structure, followed by Spain, Portugal, and Greece. Italy also had the highest per capita cumulative expenditure in R&D—public and private—for the period 2000–2013, followed by Spain, Portugal, and Greece.

These differences are often still in an embryonic stage and as yet have not given rise to a clear and stable cleavage in the SE political economy. However, many—though not all—of them seem to confirm that Portugal and Spain share more common features, while Greece and Italy stand apart.

But what kind of elements could have favored the emergence of these different trajectories? In their chapter about the appearance of different trajectories in the labor market and industrial relations fields, Afonso, Dorigatti, Molina, and Tassinari refer to such factors as electoral politics, the presence of social blocks, and the role and influence of social partners: the different configuration of the four countries in terms of these variables has promoted a diverse liberalization process. Beside these factors, some of the elements emerging in the various chapters have had the effect of fostering diversification through what could be called "facilitating factors," that is, playing an important role in support of the processes relayed above and creating favorable conditions for change.

First, compared to the cases of Italy and Greece, in the 1990s Spain and Portugal embarked upon a series of investments to be made in infrastructure. These investments were in order to keep up with the Joneses, namely with countries such as France. This was a way of confirming that at this point the postdictatorship modernization had been more than accomplished and of making the two countries full-fledged European partners. This factor may have driven Spain to overinvest in some fields such as high-speed railways (with a population of around sixty million inhabitants, Italy has about one thousand kilometers of high-speed tracks compared to twenty-seven hundred kilometers in Spain, with forty-five million inhabitants) (Beria et al. 2018) or in the airport system. Investments in these types of infrastructure also led to spillovers in complementary segments, such as high-tech, to a greater extent than in Italy. At the start of the 1990s, Italy instead was in a very different situation, with a political crisis and a macroeconomic system in turmoil. As a result, it could not carry out investments of such a size, given that its priorities were very different (incomes policies, welfare reforms, etc.).

In second place, at the start of the 1990s both Spain and Portugal were lacking a solid manufacturing base. Instead, Italy had a large manufacturing base that remained competitive (owing to the weak currency and thanks to the "flexible specialization" model of production) despite the lack of specific policies. Greece at least in one big manufacturing sector—shipbuilding—followed a competitive strategy that hinged little on innovation. The result was that if Spain and Portugal wanted to support activities that fostered endogenous competitiveness, they had to invest in new sectors such as R&D, given that rebuilding the manufacturing base was not very feasible. Instead, in Italy and Greece these sectors could still continue to be competitive with few investments in education and innovation at the national level.

Besides, the bigger presence of manufacturing companies in Italian regions with a great deal of independent resources for generating industrial policies such as Lombardy, Piedmont, and Emilia Romagna may paradoxically have prevented a strong voice from reaching the national government and fostered the escape route of supporting regional innovation policies, helping us to understand why the lack of national policies had a relatively marginal effect on the competitiveness of the companies in these areas. These circumstances may have led Portugal as well as Spain to invest more in R&D and human resources at the national level compared to Italy, while Greece lagged behind.

Finally, an important factor is the different political culture in the four countries. Indeed, in Spain and Portugal there have been no long lasting antistate parties such as the Lega, with supporters convinced that domestic devaluation and lowering taxes was the best route to follow. Even the Vox party in Spain originated rather recently and did not have a strong hold on the dynamics studied in this book, while the Lega and Forza Italia already appeared on the political scene at the start of the 1990s.

6. Which Way Out? The "Long and Winding Road" to Competitiveness for Mediterranean Capitalism

As we have seen, for the SE economies a high road to development, based on highly skilled human capital, innovation, and great social cohesion, is severely hindered by their somewhat peripheral position in the Eurozone and especially by their low innovation capacity. However, a low road, based on export-led growth, low wages, and low worker involvement, is also barred to them, as their social models cannot be dismantled further to what has already been done by the austerity policies without resulting in incalculable social and political costs. Mediterranean capitalism would seem to lack all the institutional competitive advantages available in different ways and to varying extents in other European economies. Hence, what lies ahead for SE political economies?

If the apparently straightforward solution of more and more structural reforms—on which the Troika has long insisted as the only solution to the problem of the competitiveness of SE economies—simply cannot bring the expected results in the long run, what way out can there be without inflicting enormous social and political costs? It seems clear that no effective solutions can be found without dealing with two key problems discussed in this volume: the SE economies' position in the Eurozone and especially their level of investment in R&D and human capital, which does not encourage innovation or a transformation of the production system. It is far from easy to overcome these two crucial shortcomings in the SE political economies. To quote The Beatles, it would imply a very "long and winding road." Yet, it may be the only road ahead.

The SE economies are unlikely to overcome their peripheral position in the Eurozone by simply imitating the "good practices" of the core economies, as the structural reforms rhetoric would assume. For Italy and Spain, which are two of the largest economies in the Eurozone, it might be possible (in accordance with France and with a benevolent eye from Germany, as recently happened with the Next Generation EU plan) to try to change the power relations in the EU economic policy. For Portugal and Greece, on the other hand, given the much smaller size of their economies, threatening to leave the Eurozone would not have the same impact and could even be welcomed by some EU countries. But in either case, the political and institutional processes would be extremely complex and full of unpredictable consequences.

On the other hand, the very low level of investment in R&D and human capital that hampers innovation is so intimately connected to the economic structure of the SE countries that no incentive could possibly convince the entrepreneurs to radically change this situation. Also, as Pérez (2014, 25) notes regarding Italy and Spain, "social model features . . . may have affected productivity by contributing to the pattern of sectoral investment in the two economies. It is possible that a regulatory regime offering a particularly high level of flexibility at the margins coupled with high dismissal costs for individuals on indefinite contracts might skew investment towards sectors that are not intensive in sector-specific skills or in high skills."

Given these structural conditions, the only solution to the low level of private investment in R&D and skill formation that hampers innovation would be an extraordinary effort by the SE states to compensate for the poor performance of their business sectors with a substantial and well-directed increase in public expenditure in this field. So far, the main government policies have focused on the reduction of public expenditure rather than on research funding, advanced training, and the provision of public goods for innovation. The 2007–2009 crisis could have been the right time for a strategic rethinking of development policies (Donatiello and Ramella 2017), but this opportunity has been missed.

Yet, if there are any countries that badly need neo-Keynesian economic policies and a very proactive state role (Mazzucato 2013), it would be the SE countries. Of course, high public debts are a major problem, and this is why, besides the current EU financial support, selective investments are needed whereby states act in strategic rather than short-sighted ways. This is a question of not just the size but also the quality of social expenditure, which should aim to support innovation and competitiveness through human capital development. Therefore, it is the question of institutional capability that makes this task extremely demanding (Burroni and Scalise 2017; Capano, Regini, and Turri 2016; Capano and Lippi, this volume), and it is on this that the scholars and policymakers should focus their attention.

In this respect, the COVID-19 pandemic and the Next Generation EU plan can represent a dramatic and fundamental turning point for the SE political economies and the EU as a whole. In the short run, the four SE countries risk being the most severely hit by the consequences of the crisis in socioeconomic terms. The forecasts show that in 2020 and 2021 not just Spain and Italy but also the two SE countries less hit by the pandemic—Greece and Portugal—will probably be among the economies with the worst drop in GDP in the whole EU. The structural weaknesses described in this book provide enough evidence of the reasons why these forecasts might be correct.

In the medium term, had the policies requested by the European institutions and the other member states resembled the ones adopted after the 2007–2009 crisis, the result would have been a serious risk of collapse for the SE political economies. On the other hand, a robust neo-Keynesian approach, such as the one inspiring and implied by both the European Central Bank and the Next Generation EU plan, can be very helpful not just to contain the negative socioeconomic consequences of the pandemic but also to bolster a modernization agenda in many policy fields.

In other words, for all its atrocity, the pandemic could turn out to be a window of opportunity to substantially improve Mediterranean capitalism and to bring SE countries closer to the core European political economies.

References

Adam, Paula, and Patrizia Canziani. 1998. "Partial De-regulation: Fixed-Term Contracts in Italy and Spain." Center for Economic Performance, https://cep.lse.ac.uk/pubs/download/dp0386.pdf.

Addison, John T., Pedro Portugal, and Hugo Vilares. 2016. "Unions and Collective Bargaining in the Wake of the Great Recession: Evidence from Portugal." *British Journal of Industrial Relations* 55, no. 3: 551–76.

Afonso, Alexandre. 2019. "State-Led Wage Devaluation in Southern Europe in the Wake of the Eurozone Crisis." *European Journal of Political Research* 58, no. 3: 938–59.

Afonso, Alexandre, and Fabio Bulfone. 2020. "Electoral Coalitions and Policy Reversals in Portugal and Italy in the Aftermath of the Eurozone Crisis." *South European Society and Politics* 24, no. 2: 233–57.

Aguilera, Ruth V. 1998. "Directorship Interlocks in Comparative Perspective: The Case of Spain." *European Sociological Review* 14, no. 4: 319–42.

Aguilera, Ruth. 2005. "Corporate Governance and Employment Relations: Spain in the Context of Western Europe." In *Corporate Governance and Labour Management: An International Perspective*, eds. A. Pendleton and H. Gospel, 197–225. Oxford: Oxford University Press.

Aguilera, Ruth, and Roberto Garcia-Castro. 2012. "A Decade of Corporate Governance Reforms in Spain (2000–2010)." In *The Convergence of Corporate Governance Promise and Prospects*, ed. Abdul Rasheed and Toru Yoshikawa, 187–211. Basingstoke, UK: Palgrave Macmillan.

Alba, Carlos R. 2001. "Bureaucratic Politics in Spain." In *Politicians, Bureaucrats and Administrative Reform*, ed. Guy B. Peters and Jon Pierre, 89–100. London: Routledge.

Alba, Carlos R., and Carmen Navarro. 2011. "Administrative Tradition and Reforms: In Spain: Adaptation versus Innovation." *Public Administration* 89, no. 3: 783–800.

Albert, Michel. 1991. *Capitalisme contre capitalisme*. Paris: Edition du Seuil.

Álvarez, Ignacio, Jorge Uxó, and Eladio Febrero. 2018. "Internal Devaluation in a Wage-Led Economy: The Case of Spain." *Cambridge Journal of Economics* 43, no. 2: 335–60.

Amable, Bruno. 2003. *The Diversity of Modern Capitalism*. Oxford: Oxford University Press.

Amatori, Franco, and Andrea Colli. 2000. "Corporate Governance: The Italian Story." Unpublished paper, Bocconi University, https://www.researchgate.net/profile/Andrea_Colli3/publication/267771741_Corporate_Governance_The_Italian_Story/links/55b89ba608aed621de05ef23.pdf.

André, Isabel Margarida. 2002. "At the Centre on the Periphery? Women in the Portuguese Labour Market." In *Women of the European Union: The Politics of Work and Daily Life*, ed. Maria Dolors García-Ramon and Janice Monk, 153–70. New York: Routledge.

Andreotti, Alberta, Soledad Marisol Garcia, Aitor Gomez, Pedro Hespanha, Yuri Kazepov, and Enzo Mingione. 2001. "Does a Southern European Model Exist?" *Journal of European Area Studies* 9, no. 1: 43–62.

Andrews, Dan, Chiara Criscuolo, and Peter N. Gal. 2015. *Frontier Firms, Technology Diffusion and Public Policy*. Paris: OECD Publishing.

Ansell, Ben, and Jane Gingrich. 2017. "Mismatch: University Education and Labor Market Institutions." *PS: Political Science & Politics* 50, no. 2: 423–25.

Antenucci, Fabrizio, Matteo Deleidi, and Walter Paternesi Meloni. 2019. "Demand and Supply-side Drivers of Labour Productivity Growth: An Empirical Assessment for G7 Countries." Working Papers 0042, ASTRIL-Associazione Studi e Ricerche Interdisciplinari sul Lavoro.

Anzoategui, Diego, Diego Comin, Mark Gertler, and Joseba Martinez. 2016. "Endogenous Technology Adoption and R&D as Sources of Business Cycle Persistence." *American Economic Journal: Macroeconomics* 11, no. 3: 67–110.

Araújo, Joaquim Filipe. 2002. "NPM and the Change in Portuguese Central Government." *International Public Management Journal* 5, no. 3: 223–36.

Arenilla Sàez, Manuel. 2017. "Cuatro décadas de modernización vs. reforma de la Administración pública en España" [Four Decades of Modernization vs. Reform of the Public Administration in Spain]. *Methaodos: Revista de Ciencias Sociales* 5, no. 2: 302–217.

Avdagic, Sabina, Martin Rhodes, and Jelle Visser, eds. 2011. *Social Pacts in Europe: Emergence, Evolution and Institutionalization*. Oxford: Oxford University Press.

Ayuso-i-Casals, Joaquin. 2004. *Fixed-Term Contracts in Spain: A Mixed Blessing*. Brussels: European Commission, Directorate-General for Economic and Financial Affairs.

Baccaro, Lucio, and Chiara Benassi. 2017. "Throwing Out the Ballast: Growth Models and the Liberalization of the German Industrial Relations." *Socio-Economic Review* 15, no. 1: 85–115.

Baccaro, Lucio, and Massimo D'Antoni. 2020. "Has the "External Constraint" Contributed to Italy's Stagnation? A Critical Event Analysis." MPIfG Working Paper 20/9. Cologne: Max Planck Institute for the Study of Societies.

Baccaro, Lucio, and Chris Howell. 2017. *Trajectories of Neoliberal Transformation: European Industrial Relations after the 1970s*. Cambridge: Cambridge University Press.

——. 2018. "Unhinged: Industrial Relations Liberalization and Capitalist Instability." MPIfG Discussion Paper 17/19. Cologne: Max Planck Institute for the Study of Societies.

Baccaro, Lucio, and Jonas Pontusson. 2016. "Rethinking Comparative Political Economy: The Growth Model Perspective." *Politics & Society* 44, no. 2: 175–207.

——. 2018. "Comparative Political Economy and Varieties of Macroeconomics." MPIfG Discussion Paper 18/10. Cologne: Max Planck Institute for the Study of Societies.

——. 2019. "Social Blocs and Growth Models: An Analytical Framework with Germany and Sweden as Illustrative Cases." Unpublished paper, University of Geneva.

——. 2021. "European Growth Models before and after the Great Recession." In *Growth and Welfare in Advanced Capitalist Economies: How Have Growth Regimes Evolved?*, ed. Anke Hassel and Bruno Palier, 98–134. Oxford: Oxford University Press.

Bach, Stephen, and Lorenzo Bordogna. 2016. "Emerging from the Crisis: The Transformation of Public Sector Employment Relations?" In *Public Service Management and Employment Relations in Europe: Emerging from the Crisis*, ed. Stephen Bach and Lorenzo Bordogna, 1–28. New York: Routledge.

Ban, Cornel. 2016. *Ruling Ideas: How Global Neoliberalism Goes Local*. Oxford: Oxford University Press.

——. 2019. "Dependent Development at a Crossroads? Romanian Capitalism and Its Contradictions." *West European Politics* 42, no. 5: 1041–68.

Ban, Cornel, and Oddný Helgadóttir. 2019. "Financialization and Growth Regimes." Unpublished paper, Copenhagen Business School.

Banca d'Italia. 2009. *Relazione Annuale sul 2008*. Rome: Banca d'Italia.

———. 2014. *Rapporto sulla stabilità finanziaria 2/2014*. Rome: Banca d'Italia.

Banco de España. 2017. *Report on the Financial and Banking Crisis in Spain, 2008–2014*. Madrid: Banco de España.

Barbieri, Paolo, Giorgio Cutuli, and Stefani Scherer. 2018. "In-work poverty in un mercato del lavoro duale: Individualizzazione riflessiva dei rischi sociali o stratificazione della diseguaglianza sociale?" *Stato e mercato* 38, no. 3: 419–60.

Barca, Fabrizio. 2010. *Storia del capitalismo italiano*. Rome: Donzelli Editore.

Barreto, José. 1993. "Portugal: Industrial Relations under Democracy." In *Industrial Relations in the New Europe*, ed. Anthony Ferner and Richard Hyman, 395–425. Oxford: Blackwell.

Barro, Robert J. 2001. "Human Capital and Growth." *American Economic Review* 91, no. 2: 12–7.

Barro, Robert J., and Rachel M. McCleary. 2003. "Religion and Economic Growth across Countries." *American Sociological Review* 68, no. 5: 760–81.

Barta, Zsófia. 2018. *In the Red: The Politics of Public Debt Accumulation in Developed Countries*. Ann Arbor: University of Michigan Press.

Barth, James R., Gerard Caprio Jr., and Ross Levine. 2013. "Bank Regulation and Supervision in 180 Countries from 1999 to 2011." *Journal of Financial Economic Policy* 5, no. 2: 111–219.

Barzelay, Micheal, and Raquel Gallego. 2010. "The Comparative Historical Analysis of Public Management Policy Cycles in France, Italy, and Spain: Symposium Introduction." *Governance* 23, no. 2: 209–23.

Behringer, Jan, and Till van Treeck. 2019. "Income Distribution and Growth Models: A Sectoral Balances Approach." *Politics & Society* 47, no. 3: 303–32.

Béland, Daniel. 2016. "Ideas and Institutions in Social Policy Research." *Social Policy and Administration* 60, no. 6: 734–50.

Belke, Ansgar, and Christian Dreger. 2011. "Current Account Imbalances in the Euro Area: Catching up or Competitiveness?" Discussion Papers of DIW Berlin No. 1106. Berlin: DIW-German Institute for Economic Research.

Benassi, Chiara, Lisa Dorigatti, and Elisa Pannini. 2019. "Explaining Divergent Bargaining Outcomes for Agency Workers: The Role of Labour Divides and Labour Market Reforms." *European Journal of Industrial Relations* 25, no. 2: 163–79.

Benigno, Gianluca, Nathan Converse, and Luca Fornaro. 2015. "Large Capital Inflows, Sectoral Allocation, and Economic Performance." International Finance Discussion Papers No. 1132. Washington, DC: Board of Governors of the Federal Reserve System.

Benigno, Gianluca, and Luca Fornaro. 2014. "The Financial Resource Curse." *Scandinavian Journal of Economics* 116, no. 1: 58–86.

Beramendi, Pablo, Silja Häusermann, Herbert Kitschelt, and Hanspeter Kriesi, eds. 2015. *The Politics of Advanced Capitalism*. New York: Cambridge University Press.

Beria, Paolo, Raffaele Grimaldi, Daniel Albalate, and Germá Bel. 2018. "Delusions of Success: Costs and Demand of High-Speed Rail in Italy and Spain." *Transport Policy* 68: 63–79.

Bertelsmann Stiftung. 2018. "Policy Performance and Governance Capacities in the OECD and EU." https://www.bertelsmann-stiftung.de/en/publications/publication/did/policy-performance-and-governance-capacities-in-the-oecd-and-eu-2018/.

Berton, Fabio, Matteo Richiardi, and Stefano Sacchi. 2012. *The Political Economy of Work Security and Flexibility: Italy in Comparative Perspective*. Bristol, UK: Policy Press.

Bertrand, Marianne, and Antoinette Schoar. 2006. "The Role of Family in Family Firms." *Journal of Economic Perspectives* 20, no. 2: 73–96.

Biagiotti, Andrea, and Luigi Burroni. 2004. "Between Cities and Districts: Local Software Systems in Italy." In *Changing Governance of the Local Economies*, ed. Colin Crouch, Patrick

Le Galès, Carlo Trigilia, and Helmut Voelzkow, 283–305. Oxford: Oxford University Press.

Binda, Veronica. 2013. *The Dynamics of Big Business: Structure, Strategy, and Impact in Italy and Spain*. New York: Routledge.

Blanchard, Olivier. 2007. "Current Account Deficits in Rich Countries." NBER Working Paper No. 12925. https://www.nber.org/system/files/working_papers/w12925/w12925.pdf.

———. 2012. *Macroeconomics*. London: Pearson.

Blanchard, Olivier, and Francesco Giavazzi. 2002. "Current Account Deficits in the Euro Area: The End of the Feldstein-Horioka Puzzle?" *Brookings Papers on Economic Activity* 2: 147–86.

Blanchard, Olivier, Jonathan D. Ostry, Atish R. Gosh, and Marcos Chamon. 2015. "Capital Flows: Expansionary or Contractionary?" *American Economic Review* 106, no. 5: 565–69.

Blyth, Mark. 2002. *Great Transformations: Economic Ideas and Institutional Change in the Twentieth Century*. Oxford: Oxford University Press.

Block, Fred. 2008. "Swimming against the Current: The Rise of a Hidden Developmental State in the United States." *Politics & Society* 36, no. 2: 169–206.

Bohle, Dorothee. 2017. "The End of 'Buying Time'? Capitalism and Democracy in East Central Europe before and after the Financial Crisis." *Wirtschaft und Gesellschaft* 44, no. 4: 585–606.

Bohle, Dohrothee, and Béla Greskovitz. 2012. *Capitalist Diversity on Europe's Periphery*. New York: Cornell University Press.

Bolgherini, Silvia, and Cristina Dallara, eds. 2016. *La retorica della razionalizzazione: Il settore pubblico italiano negli anni dell'austerity*. Bologna: Istituto Cattaneo.

Bolgherini, Silvia, and Andrea Lippi. 2021. "Oblique-Change Matters: 'Bradyseismic' Institutional Change in Local Government." *Italian Political Science Review* 51: 117–135.

Boltho, Andrea, and Wendy Carlin. 2013. "EMU's Problems: Asymmetric Shocks or Asymmetric Behavior?" *Comparative Economic Studies* 55, no. 3: 387–403.

Bonoli, Giuliano, and Patrick Emmenegger. 2010. "State–Society Relationships, Social Trust and the Development of Labour Market Policies in Italy and Sweden." *West European Politics* 33, no. 4: 830–50.

Bordogna, Lorenzo. 2016. "Italy: The Uncertainties of Endless Reform: Public Service Employment Relations Confronting Financial Sustainability Constraints." In *Public Service Management and Employment Relations in Europe: Emerging from the Crisis*, ed. Stephen Bach and Lorenzo Bordogna, 84–111. New York: Routledge.

Borio, Claudio, and Piti Disyatat. 2015. "Capital Flows and the Current Account: Taking Financing (More) Seriously." BIS Working Papers No. 525, Bank of International Settlements.

Bosco, Anna. 2018. *Le quattro crisi della Spagna*. Bologna: Il Mulino.

Bourdieu, Pierre. 1986. "The Forms of Capital." In *Handbook of Theory and Research for the Sociology of Education*, ed. John Richardson, 241–58. Westport, CT: Greenwood.

Bowles, Samuel, and Robert Boyer. 1995. "Wages, Aggregate Demand, and Employment in an Open Economy: An Empirical Investigation." In *Macroeconomic Policy after the Conservative Era: Studies in Investment, Saving and Finance*, ed. G. Epstein and H. Gintis, 143–71. Cambridge: Cambridge University Press.

Boyer, Robert, and Yves Saillard, eds. 2002. *Regulation Theory: The State of the Art*. London: Routledge.

Branco, Rui. 2017. "Entre Bismarck e Beveridge: Sociedade Civil e Estado Providência em Portugal (1960–2011)." *Análise Social* 224, no. 52: 534–38.

Branco, Rui, and Daniel Cardoso. 2020. "The Politics of Change: Coalitional Politics and Labour Market Reforms during the Sovereign Debt Crisis in Portugal." *Journal of Social Policy*, 1–19, https://doi.org/10.1017/S0047279420000653.

Branco, Rui, Daniel Cardoso, Ana M. Guillén, Stefano Sacchi, and David Luque Balbona. 2019. "Here to Stay? Reversals of Structural Reforms in Southern Europe as the Crisis Wanes." *South European Society and Politics* 24, no. 2: 205–32.

Branco, Rui, and Eda Costa. 2019. "The Golden Age of Fiscal Welfare: Tax Expenditures and Inequality in Portugal (1989–2011)." *New Political Economy* 24, no. 6: 780–97.

Briguglio, Damiano, Lazaros Dimitriadis, Virginia Maestri, and Gianluca Papa. 2019. "Private Investment in Italy." European Economy Discussion Papers No. 108. Luxembourg: Publications Office of the European Union.

Broner, Fernando, Tatiana Didier, Aitor Erce, and Sergio L. Schmukler. 2013. "Gross Capital Flows: Dynamics and Crises." *Journal of Monetary Economics* 60, no. 1: 113–33.

Bruff, Ian. 2008. *Culture and Consensus in European Varieties of Capitalism.* Basingstoke, UK: Palgrave Macmillan.

Brunnermeier, Markus, José De Gregorio, Philip R. Lane, Hélèn Rey, and Hyun Song Shin. 2012. "Banks and Cross-Border Capital Flows: Policy Challenges and Regulatory Responses." VoxEU.org, October 7, https://voxeu.org/article/banks-and-cross-border-capital-flows-policy-challenges-and-regulatory-responses.

Bugamelli, Matteo, and Francesca Lotti. 2019. "Il ristagno della produttività." In *Inclusione, crescita, produttività. Un'agenda per l'Italia*, ed. Paolo Guerrieri and Carlo Dell'Aringa, 65–98. Bologna: Il Mulino.

Buiter, Willem H. 2008. "Lessons from the 2007 Financial Crisis." CEPR Discussion Paper No. DP6596. https://ssrn.com/abstract=1140525.

Bulfone, Fabio. 2017. "Insider Job: Corporate Reforms and Power Resources in France, Italy and Spain." *Socio-Economic Review* 15, no. 2: 435–59.

———. 2019. "The State Strikes Back: Industrial Policy, Regulatory Power and the Divergent Performance of Telefonica and Telecom Italia." *Journal of European Public Policy* 26, no. 5: 752–71.

———. 2020. "New Forms of Industrial Policy in the Age of Regulation: A Comparison of Electricity and Telecommunications in Italy and Spain." *Governance* 33, no. 5: 93–108.

Bulfone, Fabio, and Alexandre Afonso. 2020. "Business against Markets: Employer Resistance to Collective Bargaining Liberalization during the Eurozone Crisis." *Comparative Political Studies* 53, no. 5: 809–46.

Bulfone, Fabio, and Arianna Tassinari. 2020. "Under Pressure. Economic Constraints, Electoral Politics and Labour Market Reforms in Southern Europe in the Decade of the Great Recession." *European Journal of Political Research*, https://ejpr.onlinelibrary.wiley.com/doi/epdf/10.1111/1475-6765.12414.

Burroni, Luigi, and Gemma Scalise. 2017. "Quando gli attori contano: Agency, eredità storiche e istituzioni nei modelli di capitalismo." *Stato e mercato* 37, no. 1: 133–72.

Burroni, Luigi, Alberto Gherardini, and Gemma Scalise. 2019. "Policy Failures in the Triangle of Growth. Labour Market, human Capital and Innovation in Spain and Italy." *South European Society and Politics* 24, no. 1: 29–52.

Burroni, Luigi, and Carlo Trigilia. 2001. "Italy: Economic Development through Local Economies." In *Local Production Systems in Europe. Rise or Demise?*, ed. Colin Crouch, Patrik Le Galès, Carlo Trigilia, and Helmut Voelzkow, 46–78. Oxford: Oxford University Press.

Busemeyer, Marius R. 2015. *Skills and Inequality: The Political Economy of Education and Training Reforms in Western Welfare States.* Cambridge: Cambridge University Press.

Busemeyer, Marius R., and Christine Trampusch, eds. 2012. *The Political Economy of Collective Skill Systems.* Oxford: Oxford University Press.

Buti, Marco, and Nicolas Carnot. 2012. "The EMU Debt Crisis: Early Lessons and Reforms*." *Journal of Common Market Studies* 50, no. 6: 899–911.

Campbell, John. 2004. *Institutional Change and Globalization.* Princeton, NJ: Princeton University Press.

Campos Lima, Maria da Paz. 2019. "Portugal: Reforms and the Turn to Neoliberal Austerity." In *Collective Bargaining in Europe: Towards an Endgame*, ed. Torsten Mueller, Kurt Vandaele, and Jeremy Waddington, 483–504. Brussels: ETUI.

Campos Lima, Maria da Paz, and Manuel Abrantes. 2016. *Country Report: Portugal*. DIADSE—Dialogue for Advancing Social Europe. Amsterdam: University of Amsterdam. https://www.cesis.org/admin/modulo_projects/upload/files/DIADSE_Portugal%20Report.

Capano, Giliberto. 1992. *L' improbabile riforma*. Bologna: Il Mulino.

———. 2003. "Administrative Traditions and Policy Change: When Policy Paradigms Matter; The Case of Italian Administrative Reform during the 1990s." *Public Administration* 81, no. 4: 781–801.

Capano, Giliberto, Marino Regini, and Matteo Turri. 2016. *Changing Governance in Universities: Italian Higher Education in Comparative Perspective*. London: Palgrave Macmillan.

Capussela, Andrea Lorenzo. 2018. *The Political Economy of Italy's Decline*. Oxford: Oxford University Press.

Carapeto, Carlos, and Fatima Fonseca. 2005. *Administração Pública*. Lisboa: Ediçãp Sílabo.

Carballo-Cruz, Francisco. 2011. "Causes and Consequences of the Spanish Economic Crisis: Why the Recovery Is Taken So Long?" *Panoeconomicus* 58, no. 3: 309–28.

Cárdenas, Amalia. 2013. "The Spanish Savings Bank Crisis: History, Causes and Responses." IN3 Working Paper Series. http://dx.doi.org/10.7238/in3wps.v0i0.1943.

Cassese, Sabino. 2019. "Che cosa resta dell'amministrazione pubblica?" *Rivista Trimestrale di Diritto Pubblico* 1: 1–12.

Castles, Francis, Stephan Leibfried, Jane E. Lewis, Herbert Obinger, and Christopher Pierson, eds. 2010. *The Oxford Handbook of the Welfare State*. Oxford: Oxford University Press.

Cesaratto, Sergio. 2015. "Alternative Interpretation of a Stateless Currency Crisis." *Cambridge Journal of Economics* 4, no. 4: 977–98.

Chen, Ruo, Gian-M. Milesi-Ferretti, and Thierry Tressel. 2012. "External Imbalances in the Euro Area." IMF Working Paper 12/236. Washington, DC: International Monetary Fund. https://www.imf.org/en/Publications/WP/Issues/2016/12/31/External-Imbalances-in-the-Euro-Area-40027.

Cioffi, John W., and Kenneth A. Dubin. 2016. "Commandeering Crisis: Partisan Labor Repression in Spain under the Guise of Economic Reform." *Politics & Society* 44, no. 3: 423–53.

Cioffi, John W., and Martin Höpner. 2006. "The Political Paradox of Finance Capitalism: Interests, Preferences, and Center-Left Party Politics in Corporate Governance Reform." *Politics & Society* 34, no. 4: 463–502.

Claessens, Stijn, and Laura Kodres. 2014. "The Regulatory Responses to the Global Financial Crisis: Some Uncomfortable Questions." IMF Working Paper 14/46. Washington, DC: International Monetary Fund. https://www.imf.org/external/pubs/ft/wp/2014/wp1446.pdf.

Claeys, Grégory, Maria Demertzis, Konstantinos Efstathiou, Inês Gonçalves Raposo, Alexander Lehmann, and David Pichler. 2017. "Analysis of Developments in EU Capital Flows in the Global Context." Final Report Bruegel FISMA/2016/032/B1/ST/OP. Brussels: European Commission. https://op.europa.eu/en/publication-detail/-/publication/400319a7-148d-11e9-81b4-01aa75ed71a1.

CNEL and ISTAT. 2016. *Progetto CNEL-ISTAT sul tema 'Produttività, struttura e performance delle imprese esportatrici, mercato del lavoro e contrattazione integrativa': Report intermedio*. Rome: Consiglio Nazionale dell'Economia e del Lavoro, Istituto Nazionale di Statistica.

Codogno, Lorenzo, and Mara Monti. 2018. "A Stylised Narrative of Italian Banking Problems." LUISS School of European Political Economy Policy Brief, September 19.

https://sep.luiss.it/sites/sep.luiss.it/files/A%20Stylised%20Narrative%20of%20Italian%20Banking%20Problems-Codogno-Monti.pdf.

Coeurdacier, Nicolas, and Philippe Martin. 2009. "The Geography of Asset Trade and the Euro: Insiders and Outsiders." *Journal of the Japanese and International Economies* 23, no. 2: 90–113.

Cohn, Alain, Michel André Maréchal, David Tannenbaum, and Christian Lukas Zünd. 2019. "Civic Honesty around the Globe." *Science* 365, no. 6448: 70–73.

Coleman, James. 1988. "Social Capital in the Creation of Human Capital." *American Journal of Sociology* 94: S95–S120.

———. 1990. *Foundations of Social Theory.* Cambridge, MA: Harvard University Press.

Committee on the Global Financial System. 2018. "Structural Changes in Banking after the Crisis." CGFS Papers No. 60.

Constacio, Vítor. 2012. "Contagion and the European Debt Crisis." *Financial Stability Review* 16: 109–21. https://EconPapers.repec.org/RePEc:bfr:fisrev:2011:16:10.

Copelovitch, Mark, Jeffry Frieden, and Stefanie Walter. 2016. "The Political Economy of the Euro Crisis." *Comparative Political Studies* 49, no. 7: 811–40.

Corkill, David. 2014. "The Portuguese Economy: The Impact of Membership to the European Monetary Union." In *Portugal in the European Union: Assessing Twenty-Five Years of Integration Experience,* ed. Laura C. Ferreira-Pereira London, 63–81. Routledge.

Corte-Real, Isabel. 2008. "Public Management Reform in Portugal: Successes and Failures." *International Journal of Public Sector Management* 21, no. 2: 205–29.

Crespo Gonzalez, Jorge, and Pastor G. Albaladejo, eds. 2002. *Administraciones Pùblicas Espanolas.* Madrid: McGraw Hill.

Crouch, Colin. 1993. *Industrial Relations and European State Traditions.* Oxford, UK: Clarendon.

Culpepper, Pepper D. 2007. *"Eppure, non si muove*: Legal Change, Institutional Stability and Italian Corporate Governance." *West European Politics* 30, no. 4: 784–802.

———. 2011. *Quiet Politics and Business Power: Corporate Control in Europe and Japan.* New York: Cambridge University Press.

Culpepper, Pepper D., and Aidan Regan. 2014. "Why Don't Governments Need Trade Unions Anymore? The Death of Social Pacts in Ireland and Italy." *Socio-Economic Review* 12, no. 4: 723–45.

Cuñat, Vicente, and Luis Garicano. 2010. "Did Good Cajas Extend Bad Loans? Governance, Human Capital and Loan Portfolios." FEDEA Working Papers 2010–08.

Davi, Luca. 2017. "Capire la vicenda banche venete: Tra Roma e Bruxelles; Tutti i punti chiave." *Sole 24 Ore,* May 26.

De Cecco, Marcello. 2007. "Italy's Dysfunctional Political Economy." *West European Politics* 30, no. 4: 763–83.

Deeg, Richard. 2005. "Remaking Italian Capitalism? The Politics of Corporate Governance Reform." *West European Politics* 28, no. 3: 521–48.

———. 2012. "Liberal Economic Nationalism and Europeanization: The Rise of Spanish and Italian Banks." APSA 2012 Annual Meeting Paper. https://ssrn.com/abstract=2106606.

Deeg, Richard, and Shawn Donnelly. 2016. "Banking Union and the Future of Alternative Banks: Revival, Stagnation or Decline?" *West European Politics* 39, no. 3: 585–604.

Deeg, Richard, and Sofia A. Pérez. 2000. "International Capital Mobility and Domestic Institutions: Corporate Finance and Governance in Four European Cases." *Governance* 13, no. 2: 119–53.

De Grauwe, Paul. 2013. "The Political Economy of the Euro." *Annual Review of Political Science* 16, no. 1:153–70.

Del Pino, Eloísa. 2017. "The Spanish Welfare State from Zapatero to Rajoy: Recalibration to Retrenchment." In *Politics and Society in Contemporary Spain,* ed. Bonnie N. Field and Alfonso Botti, 197–216. Dordrecht: Springer.

Demertzis, Maria, André Sapir, and Guntram B. Wolff. 2019. "Promoting Sustainable and Inclusive Growth and Convergence in the European Union." Bruegel Policy Contribution Issue No. 7.

Demirgüç-Kunt, Asli, and Enrica Detragiache. 1998. "The Determinants of Banking Crisis in Developing and Developed Countries." *IMF Staff Papers* 45, no. 1: 81–109.

Diario da Republica. 2012. "Lei 23/2012" (Law No. 23/2012). *Diário da República,* no. 121/2012, Series I, June 25. https://dre.pt/web/guest/pesquisa/-/search/178501/details/normal?q=23%2F2012.

Di Giulio, Marco, and Giancarlo Vecchi. 2019. "Multi-Level Policy Implementation and the Where of Learning: The Case of the Information System for School Buildings in Italy." *Policy Sciences* 52, no. 1: 119–35.

DiMaggio, Paul J., and Walter W. Powell. 1983. "The Iron Cage Revisited: Institutional Isomorphism and Collective Rationality in Organizational Fields." *American Sociological Review* 48, no. 2: 147–60.

Di Mascio, Fabrizio, and Alessandro Natalini. 2014. "Austerity and Public Administration: Italy between Modernization and Spending Cuts." *American Behavioral Scientist* 58, no. 12: 1634–56.

——. 2016. "The Reform of the Public Administration: Centralization and Reorganization." *Italian Politics: Governing under Constraint* 31, no. 1: 155–73.

Di Mascio, Fabrizio, Davide Galli, Alessandro Natalini, Edoardo Ongaro, and Francesco Stolfi. 2017. "Learning-Shaping Crises: A Longitudinal Comparison of Public Personnel Reforms in Italy, 1992–2014." *Journal of Comparative Policy Analysis* 19, no. 2: 119–38.

Dølvik, Jon Erik. 2009. "Percorsi nordici di trasformazione del mercato del lavoro." *Stato e Mercato* 9: 217–34.

Dølvik, Jon Erik, Jørgen Goul Andersen, and Juhana Vartiainen. 2015. "The Nordic Social Models in Turbulent Times: Consolidation and Flexible Adaptation." In *European Social Models from Crisis to Crisis*, ed. Jon Erik Dølvik and Andrew Martin, 246–86. Oxford: Oxford University Press.

Dølvik, Jon Erik, and Andrew Martin, eds. 2015. *European Social Models from Crisis to Crisis*. Oxford: Oxford University Press.

Donatiello, Davide, and Francesco Ramella. 2017. "The Innovation Paradox in Southern Europe. Unexpected Performance during the Economic Crisis." *South European Society and Politics* 22, no. 2: 157–77.

Dooley, Neil. 2018. *The European Periphery and the Eurozone Crisis: Capitalist Diversity and Europeanisation*. London: Routledge.

Dore, Ronald P. 1987. *Taking Japan Seriously*. Stanford, CA: Stanford University Press.

Draghi, Mario. 2014. "Unemployment in the Euro Area." Speech delivered at the Annual Central Bank Symposium, Jackson Hole, August 22.

Ebbinghaus, Bernhard. 2003. "Ever Larger Unions: Organisational Restructuring and Its Impact on Union Confederations." *Industrial Relations Journal* 5: 446–60.

Ebbinghaus, Bernhard, and Anke Hassel. 2000. "Striking Deals: Concertation in the Reform of Continental European Welfare States." *Journal of European Public Policy* 7, no. 1: 44–62.

Eisenstadt, Shmuel N. 1966. *Modernization: Protest and Change*. Englewood Cliffs, NJ: Prentice Hall.

Emmenegger, Patrick. 2014. *The Power to Dismiss: Trade Unions and the Regulation of Job Security in Western Europe*. Oxford: Oxford University Press.

Emmenegger, Patrick, Silja Häusermann, Bruno Palier, and Martin Seeleib-Kaiser. 2012. *The Age of Dualization: The Changing Face of Inequality in Deindustrializing Socities*. Oxford: Oxford University Press.

Emter, Lorenz, Martin Schmitz, and Marcel Tirpak. 2018. "Cross-Border Banking in the EU since the Crisis: What Is Driving the Great Retrenchment?" European Central Bank Working Paper No. 2130.

Eppinger, Peter S., Nicole Meythaler, Marc-Manuel Sindlinger, and Marcel Smolka. 2018. "The Great Trade Collapse and the Spanish Export Miracle: Firm-Level Evidence from the Crisis." *World Economy* 41: 457–93.

Esping-Andersen, Gøsta. 1990. *The Three Worlds of Welfare Capitalism.* Princeton, NJ: Princeton University Press.

Etchemendy, Sebastián. 2004. "Revamping the Weak, Protecting the Strong, and Managing Privatization: Governing Globalization in the Spanish Takeoff." *Comparative Political Studies* 37, no. 6: 623–51.

ETER. 2019. "Dual vs. Unitary Systems in Higher Education, European Commission." The ETER Project, No. 3/2019.

Eurofound. 2018. *Measuring Varieties of Industrial Relations in Europe: A Quantitative Analysis.* Luxembourg: Publications Office of the European Union.

———. 2019. *Minimum Wages in 2019: Annual Review.* Luxembourg: Publications Office of the European Union.

European Commission. 2010a. "The Economic Adjustment Programme for Greece." Directorate-General for Economic and Financial Affairs Occasional Papers No. 76.

———. 2010b. *Joint Report on Pensions: Progress and Key Challenges in the Delivery of Adequate and Sustainable Pensions in Europe; Country profiles.* Luxembourg: Publications Office of the European Union.

———. 2013. "Lessons from a Decade of Innovation Policy: What Can Be Learnt from the INNO Policy." Enterprise and Industry Report. Luxembourg: European Union.

———. 2016a. *Regional Innovation Scoreboard.* Brussels: Publications Office of the European Union.

———. 2016b. *Employment and Social Developments in Europe, 2015.* Luxembourg: Publications Office of the European Union.

———. 2017a. "Investment in the EU Member States: An Analysis of Drivers and Barriers." European Economy Institutional Paper No. 062.

———. 2017b. *Education and Training Monitor 2017.* Luxembourg: Publications Office of the European Union.

Evans, Peter, and John D. Stephens. 1988. "Studying Development since the Sixties: The Emergence of a New Comparative Political Economy." *Theory and Society* 17: 713–45.

Fargion, Valeria. 2000. "Timing and the Development of Social Care Services in Europe." *West European Politics* 23, no. 2: 59–88.

Featherstone, Kevin. 2005. "'Soft' Coordination Meets 'Hard' Politics: The European Union and Pension Reform in Greece." *Journal of European Public Policy* 12, no. 4: 733–50.

———. 2008. *"Varieties of Capitalism" and the Greek Case: Explaining the Constraints on Domestic Reform?* London: Hellenic observatory Papers on Greece and Southeast Europe no. 11. https://www.lse.ac.uk/Hellenic-Observatory/Assets/Documents/Publications/GreeSE-Papers/GreeSE-No11.pdf?from_serp=1.

———. 2015. "External Conditionality and the Debt Crisis: The 'Troika' and Public Administration Reform in Greece." *Journal of European Public Policy* 22, no. 3: 295–314.

Felipe, Jesus, and Utsav Kumar. 2014. "Unit Labor Costs in the Eurozone: The Competitiveness Debate Again." *Review of Keynesian Economics* 2, no. 4: 490–507.

Ferrera, Maurizio. 1996. "The 'Southern Model' of Welfare in Social Europe." *Journal of European Social Policy* 6, no. 1: 17–37.

Ferrera, Maurizio, Valeria Fargion, and Matteo Jessoula. 2012. *Alle radici del welfare all'italiana: Origini e futuro di un modello sociale squilibrato.* Venezia: Marsilio Editore.

Ferrera, Maurizio, and Elisabetta Gualmini. 2004. *Rescued by Europe? Social and Labour Market Reforms in Italy from Maastricht to Berlusconi.* Amsterdam: Amsterdam University Press.

Ferrera, Maurizio, Martin Rhodes, and Anton Hemerijck. 2000. *The Future of Social Europe: Recasting Work and Welfare in the New Economy.* Oeiras: Celta Editora.

Filtri, Andrea, and Antonio Guglielmi. 2012. *Italian Banking Foundations.* Milano: Mediobanca Securities.

Financial Stability Board. 2011. "Peer Review of Italy." FSB Review Report, January 27.

Flassbeck, Heiner, and Costas Lapavitsas. 2015. *Against the Troika: Crisis and Austerity in the Eurozone.* London: Verso.

Flora, Peter, ed. 1986. *Growth to Limits: The Western European Welfare State since World War II.* Berlin: de Gruyter.

Franks, Jeffrey R., Bergjkit B. Barkbu, Rodolphe Blavy, William Oman, and Hanni Schoelermann. 2018. "Economic Convergence in the Euro Area: Coming Together or Drifting Apart?" IMF Working Paper 18/10. Washington, DC: International Monetary Fund.

Frenkel, Roberto, and Martin Rapetti. 2009. "A Developing Country View of the Current Global Crisis: What Should Not Be Forgotten and What Should Be Done." *Cambridge Journal of Economics* 33, no. 4: 685–702.

Gabrisch, Hubert, and Karsten Staehr. 2014. "The Euro Plus Pact: Cost Competitiveness and External Capital Flows in the EU Countries." European Central Bank Working Paper 1650/2014. https://it.scribd.com/document/212648988/Gabrisch-and-Staehr-2014 -ECB-WP.

Galland, Olivier, and Yannick Lemel. 2007. *Valeurs et cultures en Europe.* Paris: La decouverte.

Gallego, Raquel, and Michael Barzelay. 2010. "Public Management Policymaking in Spain: The Politics of Legislative Reform of Administrative Structures, 1991–1997." *Governance* 23, no. 2: 277–96.

Gambarotto, Francesca, and Stefano Solari. 2015. "The Peripheralization of Southern European Capitalism within the EMU." *Review of International Political Economy* 22, no. 4: 788–812.

García-Cestona, Miguel, and Jordi Surroca. 2008. "Multiple Goals and Ownership Structure: Effects on the Performance of Spanish Savings Banks." *European Journal of Operational Research* 187, no. 2: 582–99.

García-Pérez, José Ignacio, and Marcel Jansen. 2015. "Assessing the Impact of Spain's Latest Labour Market Reform." *Spanish Economic and Financial Outlook* 4, no. 3: 5–15.

Garnero, Andrea, Stephan Kampelmann, and Francois Rycx. 2015. "Sharp Teeth or Empty Mouths? European Institutional Diversity and the Sector-Level Minimum Wage Bite." *British Journal of Industrial Relations* 53, no. 4: 760–88.

Garritzmann, Julian L. 2017. "The Partisan Politics of Higher Education." *PS: Political Science & Politics* 50, no. 2: 413–17.

Gaulier, Guillarme, and Vincent Vicard. 2013. "The Signatures of the Euro-Area Imbalances: Export Performance and the Composition of ULC Growth." COMPNET Policy Brief 02/2013. Frankfurt: European Central Bank.

Gavosto, Andrea. 2019. "Investire in istruzione." In *Inclusione, crescita, produttività: Un'agenda per l'Italia,* ed. Paolo Guerrieri, and Carlo Dell'Aringa, 567–97. Bologna: Il Mulino.

Girardi, Daniele, and Riccardo Pariboni. 2020. "Autonomous Demand and the Investment Share." *Review of Keynesian Economics* 8, no. 3: 428–53.

Glyn, Andrew. 2006. *Capitalism Unleashed: Finance Globalization and Welfare.* Oxford: Oxford University Press.

Goldstein, Andrea. 2003. "Privatization in Italy 1993–2002: Goals, Institutions, Outcomes, and Outstanding Issues." CESifo Working Paper Series No. 912. https://papers.ssrn.com /sol3/papers.cfm?abstract_id=396324

Gough, Ian. 1996. "Social Assistance in Southern Europe." *Southern European Society and Politics* 1, no. 1: 1–23.

Gourinchas, Pierre-Olivier, Hélène Rey, and Kai Truempler. 2012. "The Financial Crisis and the Geography of Wealth Transfers." *Journal of International Economics* 88, no. 2: 266–83.

Granovetter, Mark. 1978. "Threshold Models of Collective Behavior." *American Journal of Sociology* 83, no. 6: 1420–43.

——. 1985. "Economic Action and Social Structure: The Problem of Embeddedness." *American Journal of Sociology* 91: 481–510.

Grief, Avner. 1994. "Cultural Beliefs and the Organization of Society: A Historical and Theoretical Reflection on Collectivist and Individualistic Societies." *Journal of Political Economy* 102, no. 5: 912–50.

Grimshaw, Damian. 2010. "What Do We Know about Low Wage Work and Low Wage Workers? Analysing the Definitions, Patterns, Causes and Consequences in International Perspective." Technical Background Report prepared for the Global Wage Report, International Labour Organization.

Gros, Daniel. 2012. "Macroeconomic Imbalances in the Euro Area: Symptom or Cause of the Crisis." CEPS Policy Brief.

Guardiancich, Igor, and Oscar Molina, eds. 2017. *Talking through the Crisis: Social Dialogue and Industrial Relations Trends in Selected EU Countries.* Geneva: International Labour Organization.

Guerrieri, Paolo. 2019. "Introduzione: Per una crescita inclusiva; Analisi e proposte:" In *Inclusione, crescita, produttività: Un'agenda per l'Italia,* ed. Paolo Guerrieri and Carlo Dell'Aringa. 9–62. Bologna: Il Mulino.

Guillén, Ana M. 2010. "Defrosting the Spanish Welfare State: The Weight of Conservative Components." In *A Long Good-Bye to Bismarck: The Politics of Welfare Reforms in Continental Welfare State,* ed. Bruno Palier, 183–206. Amsterdam: Amsterdam University Press.

Guillén, Ana M., and Santiago Álvarez. 2004. "The EU's Impact on the Spanish Welfare State: The Role of Cognitive Europeanisation." *Journal of European Social Policy* 14, no. 3: 285–300.

Guillén, Ana M., Santiago Álvarez, and Pedro Adão e Silva. 2003. "Redesigning the Spanish and Portuguese Welfare States: The Impact of Accession into the European Union." *South European Society and Politics* 8, no. 1: 231–69.

Guillén, Ana M., and Sergio González Begega. 2019. "Spain: Economic Crisis and the Politics of Welfare under Austerity." In *Welfare and the Great Recession: A Comparative Study,* ed. Stefán Ólafsson, Mary Daly, Olli Kangas, and Joakim Palme, 97–114. Oxford: Oxford University Press.

Guillén, Ana M., and Margarita León. 2011. *The Spanish Welfare State in European Context.* Ashgate, UK: Aldershot.

Guillén, Ana M., and Manos Matsaganis. 2000. "Investigating the 'Social Dumping' Hypothesis in Southern Europe: Welfare Policies in Greece and Spain during the Last 20 Years." *Journal of European Social Policy* 10, no. 2: 120–45.

Guillén, Ana M., and Emmanuele Pavolini. 2015. "Welfare States under Strain in Southern Europe: Overview of the Special Issue." *European Journal of Social Security* 17, no. 2: 147–57.

——. 2017. "Spain and Italy: Regaining the Confidence and Legitimacy; Advance Social Policy." In *After Austerity: Welfare State Transformation in Europe after the Great Recession,* ed. Peter Taylor-Gooby, Heejung Chung, and Benjamin Leruth, 136–54. Oxford: Oxford University Press.

Guillén, Ana M., and Maria Petmesidou. 2008. "The Public-Private Mix in Southern Europe: What Changed in the Last Decade?" In *Welfare State Transformations,* ed. Martin Seeleib-Kaiser, 56–78. London: Palgrave Macmillan.

Gumbrell-McCormick, Rebecca, and Richard Hyman. 2013. *Trade Unions in Western Europe: Hard Times, Hard Choices.* Oxford: Oxford University Press.

Gutiérrez, Isabel, and Jordi Surroca. 2012. "Revisiting Corporate Governance through the Lens of the Spanish Evidence." *Journal of Management & Governance* 18: 989–1017.

Hale, Galina, and Maurice Obstfeld. 2016. "The Euro and the Geography of International Debt Flows." *Journal of European Economics Association* 14, no. 1: 115–44.

Hall, Peter A. 2012. "The Economics and Politics of the Euro Crisis." *German Politics* 21, no. 4: 355–71.

———. 2014. "Varieties of Capitalism and the Euro Crisis." *West European Politics* 37, no. 6: 1223–43.

———. 2018. "Varieties of Capitalism in Light of the Euro Crisis." *Journal of European Public Policy* 25, no. 1: 7–30.

Hall, Peter A., and Daniel W. Gingerich. 2009. "Varieties of Capitalism and Institutional Complementaries in the Political Economy." *British Journal of Political Science* 39, no. 3: 449–82.

Hall, Peter A., and David Soskice, eds. 2001. *Varieties of Capitalism: The Institutional Foundations of Comparative Advantage.* Oxford: Oxford University Press.

Hallerberg, Mark, and Jonas Markgraf. 2018. "The Corporate Governance of Public Banks before and after the Global Financial Crisis." *Global Policy* 9, no. 51: 43–53.

Hamilton, Gary. 1994. "Civilization and the Organization of the Economy." In *The Handbook of Economic Sociology*, ed. Neil Smelser and Richard Swedberg. Princeton, NJ: Princeton University Press.

Hamilton, Gary G., and Nicole W. Biggart. 1988. "Market, Culture and Authority: A Comparative Analysis of Management and Organization in the Far East." *American Journal of Sociology* 94: 52–94.

Hancké, Bob. 2013. *Unions, Central Banks and EMU: Labour Market Institutions and Monetary Integration in Europe.* Oxford: Oxford University Press.

Hancké, Bob, and Martin Rhodes. 2005. "EMU and Labor Market Institutions in Europe: The Rise and Fall of National Social Pacts." *Work and Occupations* 32, no. 2: 196–228.

Hancké, Bob, Martin Rhodes, and Mark Thatcher, 2007. *Beyond Varieties of Capitalism: Conflict, Contradictions, and Complementarities in the European Economy.* Oxford: Oxford University Press.

Hanushek, Erik, and Ludger Wößmann. 2015. *The Knowledge Capital of Nation.* Cambridge, MA: MIT Press.

Hardiman, Niamh, Calliope Spanou, Joaquim Filipe Araújo, and Muiris MacCarthaigh. 2019. "Tangling with the Troika: 'Domestic Ownership' as Political and Administrative Engagement in Greece, Ireland, and Portugal." *Public Management Review* 21, no. 9: 1265–86.

Hassel, Anke. 2014. "The Paradox of Liberalization: Understanding Dualism and the Recovery of the German Political Economy." *British Journal of Industrial Relations* 52, no. 1: 57–81.

Hijzen, Alexander, Leopoldo Mondauto, and Stefano Scarpetta. 2017. "The Impact of Employment Protection on Temporary Employment: Evidence from a Regression Discontinuity Design." *Labour Economics* 46: 64–76.

Hlepas, Nikolaos-K. 2003. "Local Government Reform in Greece." In *Reforming Local Government in Europe: Closing the Gap between Democracy and Efficiency*, ed. Norbert Kersting and Angelika Vetter, 221–39. Berlin: Springer.

———. 2010. "Incomplete Greek Territorial Consolidation: From the First (1998) to the Second (2008–09) Wave of Reforms." *Local Government Studies* 36, no. 2: 223–249.

———. 2012. "Local Government in Greece." In *Local Government in the Member States of the European Union: A Comparative Legal Perspective*, ed. Ángel Manuel Moreno, 257–81. Madrid: Instituto Nacional de Administracion Publica.

Hlepas, Nikos K., and Theodore N. Tsekos. 2018. "Greek Municipalities before and during the Austerity Era: Imposed Policies, Local Resistances and Unsuccessful Reforms." In *Local Public Services in Times of Austerity across Mediterranean Europe*, ed. Andrea Lippi and Theodore N. Tsekos, 49–71. London: Palgrave.

Hobza, Alexandr, and Stefan Zeugner. 2014. "Current Accounts and Financial Flows in the Euro Area." *Journal of International Money and Finance* 48, part B: 291–313.

Holland, Alisha C. 2017. *Forbearance as Redistribution: The Politics of Informal Welfare in Latin America.* Cambridge: Cambridge University Press.

Hopkin, Jonathan, and Mark Blyth. 2012. "What Can Okun Teach Polanyi? Efficiency, Regulation and Equality in the OECD." *Review of International Political Economy* 19, no. 1: 1–33.

Höpner, Martin. 2018. "The German Undervaluation Regime under Bretton Woods, 1950–1973: How Germany Became the Nightmare of the World Economy." MPIfG Discussion Paper 19/1. Cologne: Max Planck Institute for the Study of Societies.

Höpner, Martin, and Mark Lutter. 2018. "The Diversity of Wage Regimes: Why the Eurozone Is Too Heterogeneous for the Euro." *European Political Science Review* 10, no. 1: 71–96.

Howart, David, and Lucia Quaglia. 2015. "The Political Economy of the Euro Area's Sovereign Debt Crisis: Introduction to the Special Issue of the *Review of International Political Economy*." *Review of International Political Economy* 22, no. 3: 457–84.

Howell, Chris. 2020. "Rethinking the Role of the State in Employment Relations for a Neoliberal Era." In *Work, Employment and Society,* https://doi.org/10.1177/001979392090 4663.

Il Sole 24 ore. 2008. "Berlusconi: 'Governo nelle banche, ma senza punire i manager.'" *Il Sole 24 ore,* October 29, https://st.ilsole24ore.com/art/SoleOnLine4/Finanza%20e%20 Mercati/2008/10/Berlusconi-banche-mercati.shtml?uuid=ef11f8e6-a5ae-11dd-bd0e -74972eef3b4a&DocRulesView=Libero&correlato.

IMF. 2012a. "Spain: 2012 Article IV Consultation." IMF Country Report No. 12/202, July. Washington, DC: International Monetary Fund.

———. 2012b. "Spain: The Reform of Spanish Savings Banks Technical Notes." IMF Country Report No. 12/141, June. Washington, DC: International Monetary Fund.

———. 2013. "Italy: Financial System Stability Assessment." IMF Country Report No. 13/300 Washington, DC: International Monetary Fund.

Inglehart, Ronald, and Wayne E. Baker. 2000. "Modernization, cultural change, and the persistence of traditional values." *American Sociological Review* 65, no. 1: 19–59.

Inzerillo, Ugo, and Marcello Messori. 2000. "Le privatizzazioni bancarie in Italia." In *Le privatizzazioni italiane,* ed. Sergio De Nardis, 119–90. Bologna: Il Mulino.

Ioannou, Christos A. 2016. "Greece: Public Service Employment Relations; Adjustments and Reforms." In *Public Service Management and Employment Relations in Europe. Emerging from the Crisis,* ed. Stephen Bach and Lorenzo Bordogna. New York: Routledge.

Iversen, Torben, and Frances Rosenbluth. 2010. *Women, Work, and Politics: The Political Economy of Gender Inequality.* New Haven, CT: Yale University Press.

Iversen, Torben, and David Soskice. 2006. "Electoral Institutions and the Politics of Coalitions: Why Some Democracies Redistribute More Than Others." *American Political Science Review* 100, no. 2: 165–81.

———. 2019. *Democracy and Prosperity.* Princeton, NJ: Princeton University Press.

Iversen, Torben, David Soskice, and David Hope. 2016. "The Eurozone and Political Economic Institutions." *Annual Review of Political Science* 19, no. 1:163–85..

Jassaud, Nadèg. 2014. "Reforming the Corporate Governance of Italian Banks." IMF Working Paper 14/181. Washington, DC: International Monetary Fund.

Jessoula, Matteo. 2009. *La politica pensionistica.* Bologna: Il Mulino.

———. 2013. "The 'Vincolo Esterno' Thesis Revisited: Irresistible Forces, Movable 'Objects' in Italian Pension Reforms." Paper presented at the 20th International Conference of Europeanists, Amsterdam, June 25–27.

———. 2018. "Pension Multi-pillarisation in Italy: Actors, 'Institutional Gates' and the New Politics' of Funded Pensions." *Transfer: European Review of Labour and Research* 24, no. 1: 73–89.

Jessoula, Matteo, and Tiziana Alti. 2010. "Italy: An Uncompleted Departure from Bismarck." In *A Long Goodbye to Bismarck? The Politics of Welfare Reform in Continental Europe,* ed. Bruno Palier, 157–79. Amsterdam: Amsterdam University Press.

Jessoula, Matteo, and Marcello Natili. 2020. "Explaining Italian 'Exceptionalism' and Its End: Minimum Income from Neglect to Hyper-politicization." *Social Policy & Administration* 54, no. 4: 599–613.

Jessoula, Matteo, and Michele Raitano. 2017. "Italian Pensions from 'Vices' to Challenges: Assessing Actuarial Multi-pillarization Twenty Years On." In *The New Pension Mix in Europe: Recent Reforms, Their Distributional Effects and Political Dynamics*, ed. David Natali. 33–69. Brussels: Peter Lang.

Johnston, Alison, Bob Hancké, and Suman Pant. 2014. "Comparative Institutional Advantage in the European Sovereign Debt Crisis." *Comparative Political Studies* 47, no. 13: 1771–800.

Johnston, Alison, and Aidan Regan. 2016. "European Monetary Integration and the Incompatibility of National Varieties of Capitalism." *JCMS: Journal of Common Market Studies* 54, no. 2: 318–36.

———. 2018. "Introduction: Is the European Union Capable of Integrating Diverse Models of Capitalism?" *New Political Economy* 23, no. 2: 145–59.

Kalantzis, Yannick. 2015. "Financial Fragility in Small Open Economies: Firm Balance Sheets and the Sectoral Structure." *Review of Economic Studies* 82, no. 3: 1194–222.

Kalemli-Ozcan, Sebnem, Elias Papaioannou, and José-Luis Peydró. 2010. "What Lies beneath the Euro's Effect on Financial Integration? Currency Risk, Legal Harmonization, or Trade?" *Journal of International Economics* 81, no. 1: 75–88.

Karamessini, Maria. 2008. "Still a Distinctive Southern European Employment Model?" *Industrial Relations Journal* 39, no. 6: 510–31.

Katsaroumpas, Ioannis, and Aristea Koukiadaki. 2019. "Greece: 'Contesting' Collective Bargaining." In *Collective Bargaining in Europe: Towards an Endgame*, ed. Torsten Mueller, Kurt Vandaele, and Jeremy Waddington, 267–93. Brussels: ETUI.

Kharas, Homi, and Harinder Kohli. 2011. "What Is the Middle Income Trap, Why Do Countries Fall into It, and How Can It Be Avoided?" *Global Journal of Emerging Market Economies* 3, no. 3: 281–89.

Kickert, Walter. 2007. "Public Management Reforms in Countries with a Napoleonic State Model: France, Italy and Spain." In *New Public Management in Europe: Adaptation and Alternatives*, ed. Christopher Pollitt, Sandra van Thiel, and Vincent Homburg. 26–51. London: Palgrave.

———. 2011. "Distinctiveness of Administrative Reform in Greece, Italy, Portugal and Spain." *Public Administration* 89, no. 3: 801–18.

Knibbe, Merijn. 2019. *Macroeconomic Measurement versus Macroeconomic Theory*. London: Routledge.

Kohl, Sebastian. 2018. "More Mortgages, More Homes? The Effect of Housing Financialization on Homeownership in Historical Perspective." *Politics & Society* 46, no. 2: 177–203.

Kollmann, Robert, Marco Ratto, Werner Roeger, Jan in 't Veld, and Lukas Vogel. 2015. "What Drives the German Current Account? And How Does It Affect Other EU Member States?" *Economic Policy* 30, no. 81: 47–93.

Kornelakis, Andreas, and Horen Voskeritsian. 2014. "The Transformation of Employment Regulation in Greece: Towards a Dysfunctional Liberal Market Economy." *Industrial Relations* 69, no. 2: 344–65.

Kranendonk, Henk, and Johan Verbruggen. 2008. "Decomposition of GDP Growth in Some European Countries and the United States." *De Economist* 156, no. 3: 295–306.

Kristensen, Peer Hull, and Kari Lilja. 2011. *Nordic Capitalisms and Globalization: New Forms of Economic Organization and Welfare Institutions*. Oxford: Oxford University Press.

Kuhlmann, Sabine, and Hellmut Wollmann. 2014. *Introduction to Comparative Public Administration: Administrative Systems and Reforms in Europe*. Cheltenham, UK: Edward Elgar.

Ladi, Stella. 2014. "Austerity Politics and Administrative Reform: The Eurozone Crisis and Its Impact upon Greek Public Administration." *Comparative European Politics* 12, no. 2: 184–208.

Lampropoulou, Manto. 2017. "Administrative Reforms and the Eurozone Crisis: A Comparative Study of Greece and Portugal." *International Journal of Social Sciences* 3, no. 2: 336–61.

———. 2018. "Policy Responses to the Eurozone Crisis: A Comparative Analysis of Southern European Administrations." *Public Policy and Administration* 35, no. 3: 289–311.

Lampropoulou, Manto, and Giorgio Oikonomou. 2018. "Theoretical Models of Public Administration and Patterns of State Reform in Greece." *International Review of Administrative Science* 84, no. 1: 101–21.

Lane, Philip R.. 2013. "Capital Flows in the Euro Area," European Economy - Economic Papers 2008 - 2015, 497, Directorate General Economic and Financial Affairs (DG ECFIN), European Commission.

Lane, Philip R., and Agustín S. Benetrix. 2013. "Fiscal Cyclicality and EMU." *Journal of International Money and Finance* 24: 164–73.

Lane, Philip R., and Peter McQuade. 2013. "Domestic Credit Growth and International Capital Flows." *Scandinavian Journal of Economics* 116, no. 1: 218–52.

Lane, Philip R., and Gian Maria Milesi-Ferretti. 2005. "The International Equity Holdings of Euro Area Investors." The Institute for International Integration Studies Discussion Paper Series No. 104. Dublin: Trinity College.

Lavdas, Kostas A. 2005. "Interest Groups in Disjointed Corporatism: Social Dialogue in Greece and European 'Competitive Corporatism.'" *West European Politics* 28, no. 2: 297–316..

Lavoie, Marc, ed. 2009. *Introduction to Post-Keynesian Economics*. London: Palgrave.

Lavoie, Marc, and Engelbert Stockhammer. 2013. *Wage-Led Growth*. London: Palgrave.

León, Margarita, and Emmanuele Pavolini. 2014. "Social Investment or Back to Familism: The Impact of the Economic Crisis on Family and Care Policies in Italy and Spain." *South European Society and Politics* 19, no. 3: 353–69.

Liddle, Joyce. 2009. "Regeneration and Economic Development in Greece: De-industrialisation and Uneven Development." *Local Government Studies* 35, no. 3: 335–54.

Lijphart, Arend. 1999. *Patterns of Democracy*. New Haven, CT: Yale University Press.

Lippi, Andrea, and Theodore N. Tsekos, eds. 2018. *Local Public Services in Times of Austerity across Mediterranean Europe*. London: Palgrave.

Louçã, Francisco, João Ramos de Almeida, José Luis Albuquerque, and Vitor Junqueira, eds. 2016. *Segurança Social: Defender a Democracia*. Lisbon: Bertrand.

López, Isidro, and Emmanuel Rodríguez. 2011. "The Spanish Model." *New Left Review* 69: 5–29.

Lucas, Robert E., Jr. 2015. "Human Capital and Growth." *American Economic Review* 105, no. 5: 85–8.

Lucidi, Federico, and Alfred Kleinknecht. 2010. "Little Innovation, Many Jobs: An Econometric Analysis of the Italian Labour Productivity Crisis." *Cambridge Journal of Economics* 34, no. 3: 525–46.

Magone, José M. 2011. "The Difficult Transformation of the State and Public Administration in Portugal." *Public Administration* 89, no. 4: 756–82.

Manaresi, Francesco, and Nicola Pierri. 2018. "Credit supply and productivity growth," *Temi di discussione (Working Papers) Banca d'Italia* no. 1168: 1–84

Marginson, Paul. 2015. "Coordinated Bargaining in Europe: From Incremental Corrosion to Frontal Assault?" *European Journal of Industrial Relations* 21, no. 2: 97–114.

Marí-Klose, Pau, and Francisco Javier Moreno-Fuentes. 2013. "The Southern European Welfare Model in the Post-Industrial Order." *European Societies* 15, no. 4: 475–92.

Masciandaro, Donato, Rosaria Verga Pansini, and Marc Quintyn. 2013. "The Economic Crisis: Did Supervision Architecture and Governance Matter?" *Journal of Financial Stability* 9, no. 4: 578–96.

Mato, F. Javier. 2011. "Spain: Fragmented Unemployment Protection in a Segmented Labour Market." In *Regulating the Risk of Unemployment: National Adaptations to Post-Industrial Labour Markets in Europe*, ed. Jochen Clasen and Daniel Clegg. Oxford: Oxford University Press.

Matsaganis, Manos. 2005a. "Fighting with the Hands Tied behind the Back: Anti-poverty Policy without a Minimum Income." In *Welfare State Reform in Southern Europe: Fighting Poverty and Social Exclusion in Greece, Italy, Spain and Portugal*, ed. Maurizio Ferrera, 152–72. London: Routledge.

——. 2005b. "The Limits of Selectivity as a Recipe for Welfare Reform: The Case of Greece." *Journal of Social Policy* 34, no. 2: 235–53.

——. 2007. "Union Structures and Pension Outcomes in Greece." *British Journal of Industrial Relations* 45, no. 3: 537–55.

——. 2011. "The Welfare State and the Crisis: The Case of Greece." *Journal of European Social Policy* 21, no. 5: 501–12.

——. 2018a. "Making Sense of the Greek Crisis, 2010–2016." In *Europe's Crises*, ed. Manuel Castells, Oliveir Bouin, Joao Caraça, Gustavo Cardoso, John Thompson, and Michel Wieviorka, 49–69. Cambridge, UK: Policy Press.

——. 2018b. "Income Support Policies and Labour Market Reform under Austerity in Greece." In *Labour Market Policies in the Era of Pervasive Austerity: A European Perspective*, ed. Sotiria Theodoropoulou, 43–68. Bristol, UK: Policy Press.

——. 2019. "Greece: The Crisis, Austerity and Transformations of Welfare." In *Welfare and the Great Recession: A Comparative Study*, ed. Stefán Ólafsson, Mary Daly, Olli Kangas, and Joakim Palme, 83–96. Oxford: Oxford University Press.

——. 2020. "Safety Nets in (the) Crisis: The Case of Greece in the 2010s." *Social Policy and Administration* 54, no. 4: 587–98.

Matsaganis, Manos, Maurizio Ferrera, Luís Capucha, and Luis Moreno. 2003. "Mending Nets in the South: Anti-poverty Policies in Greece, Italy, Portugal and Spain." *Social Policy & Administration* 37, no. 6: 639–55.

Matsaganis, Manos, and Chrysa Leventi. 2011. "Pathways to a Universal Basic Pension in Greece." *Basic Income Studies* 6, no. 1: 1–20.

Matthijs, Matthias. 2016. "The Euro's 'Winner-Take-All' Political Economy: Institutional Choices, Policy Drift and Diverging Patterns of Inequality." *Politics & Society* 44, no. 3: 393–422.

Mazzucato, Mariana. 2013. *The Entrepreneurial State: Debunking Public vs. Private Sector Myths.* London: Anthem.

McCann, Dermot. 2007. "Globalization, European Integration and Regulatory Reform in Italy: Liberalism, Protectionism or Reconstruction?" *Journal of Modern Italian Studies* 12, no. 1: 101–17.

McPhilemy, Samuel. 2014. "Integrating Rules, Disintegrating Markets: The End of National Discretion in European Banking?" *Journal of European Public Policy* 21, no. 10: 1473–90.

Meardi, Guglielmo, Juliusz Gardawski, and Oscar Molina. 2015. "The Dynamics of Tripartism in Post-Democratic Transitions: Comparative Lessons from Spain and Poland." *Business History* 57, no. 3: 398–417.

Melis, Andrea. 2000. "Corporate Governance in Italy." *Corporate Governance* 8, no. 4: 347–55.

Melis, Guido. 1996. *Storia dell'amministrazione italiana.* Bologna: Il Mulino.

Messori, Marcello. 2002. "Consolidation, Ownership Structure and Efficiency in the Italian Banking System." *Banca Nazionale del Lavoro Quarterly Review* 55, no. 221: 177–17.

Messori, Marcello, and Bethel Hernández. 2005. "The Bank Takeover Bids and the Role of the Bank of Italy." *Italian Politics* 21: 139–62.

Mian, Atif, and Amir Sufi. 2011. "House Prices, Home Equity-Based Borrowing, and the US Household Leverage Crisis." *American Economic Review* 101, no. 5: 2132–56.

Milesi-Ferretti, Gian Maria, and Céderic Tille. 2011. "The Great Retrenchment: International Capital Flows during the Global Financial Crisis." Hong Kong Institute for Monetary Research Working Paper No. 382011.

Milio, Simona. 2007. "Can Administrative Capacity Explain Differences in Regional Performances? Evidence from Structural Funds Implementation in Southern Italy." *Regional Studies* 41, no. 4: 429–42.

Mingione, Enzo. 1995. "Labour Market Segmentation and Informal Work in Southern Europe." *European Urban and Regional Studies* 2, no. 2: 121–43.

Mjøset, Lars. 2011. "Nordic Political Economy after Financial Deregulation: Banking Crisis, Economic Experts and the Role of neo-liberalism. " In *The Nordic Varieties of Capitalism (Comparative Social Research*, Vol. 28), ed. Lars Mjøset. 365–420. Bingley: Emerald Group Publishing Limited.

Molina, Oscar. 2006. "Trade Union Strategies and Change in Neo-corporatist Concertation: A New Century of Political Exchange?" *West European Politics* 29, no. 4: 640–64.

———. 2014. "Self-Regulation and the State in Industrial Relations in Southern Europe: Back to the Future?" *European Journal of Industrial Relations* 20, no. 1: 21–36.

———. 2016. "Spain: Rationalization without Modernization: Public Service Employment Relations under Austerity." In *Public Service Management and Employment Relations in Europe: Emerging from the Crisis*, ed. Stephen Bach and Lorenzo Bordogna, 57–83. New York: Routledge.

Molina, Oscar, and Martin Rhodes. 2007. "The Political Economy of Adjustment in Mixed Market Economies: A Study of Spain and Italy." In *Beyond Varieties of Capitalism*, ed. Bob Hancké, Martin Rhodes, and Mark Thatcher, 223–52. Oxford: Oxford University Press.

———. 2011. "Spain: From Tripartite to Bipartite Pacts." In *Social Pacts in Europe: Emergence, Evolution and Institutionalization*, ed. Sabina Avdagic, Martin Rhodes and Jelle Visser, 174–200. Oxford: Oxford University Press.

Monnet, Éric, Stefano Pagliari, and Shahin Vallée. 2014. "Europe between Financial Repression and Regulatory Capture." Bruegel Working Paper 2014/08.

Moreira, Amilcar, Angel Alonso-Domínguez, Cátia Antunes, Maria Karamessini, Michele Raitano, and Miguel Glatzer. 2015. "Austerity-Driven Labour Market Reforms in Southern Europe: Eroding the Security of Labour Market Insiders." *European Journal of Social Security* 17, no. 2: 202–25.

Moreno, Luis, and Amparo Serrano. 2011. "Europeanization and Spanish Welfare: The Case of Employment Policy." In *The Spanish Welfare State in European Context*, ed. Ana M. Guillén and Margarita León, 39–58. Farnham, Surrey, UK: Ashgate.

Moreno Fuentes, Francisco Javier, and Pau Marí-Klose, eds. 2013. "The Southern European Welfare Model in the Post-industrial Order: Still a Distinctive Cluster?" *The Mediterranean Welfare Regime and the Current Crisis*, special issue of *European Societies* 15, no. 4: 475–92.

Morlino, Leonardo. 1998. *Democracy between Consolidation and Crisis: Parties Groups and Citizens in Southern Europe*. Oxford: Oxford University Press.

Moschella, Manuela. 2011. "Different Varieties of Capitalism? British and Italian Policies in Response to the Sub-prime Crisis." *Comparative European Politics* 9, no. 1: 76–99.

———. 2016. "A New Governance for Banks: The Short- and Long-Term Drivers of the Italian Financial Sector Reform." *Italian Politics* 31, no. 1: 174–94.

Moschella, Manuela, and Lucia Quaglia. 2019. "European Banking Union to the Rescue? How Supranational Institutions Influenced Crisis Management in Italy." *South European Society and Politics* 24, no. 4: 421–40.

Moury, Catherine, Daniel Cardoso, and Angie Gago. 2019. "When the Lenders Leave Town: Veto Players, Electoral Calculations and Vested Interests as Determinants of

Policy Reversals in Spain and Portugal." *South European Society and Politics* 24, no. 2: 177–204.

Murtin, Fabrice, Alain de Serres, and Alexander Hijzen. 2014. "Unemployment and the Coverage Extension of Collective Wage Agreements." *European Economic Review* 71: 52–66.

Natali, David, and Furio Stamati. 2014. "Reassessing South European Pensions after the Crisis: Evidence from Two Decades of Reforms." *South European Society and Politics* 19, no. 3: 309–30.

Natili, Marcello, and Matteo Jessoula. 2019. "Children against Parents? The Politics of Intergenerational Recalibration in Southern Europe." *Social Policy & Administration* 53, no. 3: 343–56.

Navarro, Carmen, and Esther Pano. 2018. "Spanish Local Government and the Austerity Plan: In the Eye of the Perfect Storm." In *Local Public Services in Times of Austerity across Mediterranean Europe*, ed. Andrea Lippi and Theodore N. Tsekos, 95–114. London: Palgrave.

Nieto García, Alejandro. 2014. "Informe de 2013 de la Comisión para la Reforma de las Administraciones Pública." *Mediterráneo Económico* 25: 97–115.

OECD. 1994. *The OECD Jobs Study*. Paris: OECD Publishing.

——. 2001. *OECD Economic Surveys: Greece 2001*. Paris: OECD Publishing.

——. 2007. *Economic Policy Reforms 2007: Going for Growth*. Paris: OECD Publishing. https://read.oecd-ilibrary.org/economics/economic-policy-reforms-2007_growth-2007-en.

——. 2015. *OECD Country Surveys: Spain 2014*. Paris: OECD Publishing.

——. 2018. *OECD Employment Outlook 2018*. Paris: OECD Publishing.

——. 2019a. *Government at a Glance*. Paris: OECD Publishing.

——. 2019b. *Greece: Country Health Profile 2019; State of Health in the EU*. Paris: OECD Publishing.

Onaran, Özlem, and Giorgos Galanis. 2014. "Income Distribution and Growth: A Global Model." *Environment and Planning A* 46, no. 10: 2489–513.

Ongaro, Edoardo. 2010a. *Public Management Reform and Modernization: Trajectories of Administrative Changes in Italy, France, Greece, Portugal and Spain*. Cheltenham, UK: Edward Elgar.

——. 2010b. "The Napoleonic Administrative Tradition and Public Management Reform in France, Greece, Italy, Portugal and Spain." In *Tradition and Public Administration*, ed. Martin Painter and Guy B. Peters, 174–190. Basingstoke, UK: Palgrave Macmillan.

Onida, Francesco. 2019. "Per una nuova politica industriale." In *Inclusione, crescita, produttività: Un'agenda per l'Italia*, ed. Paolo Guerrieri and Carlo Dell'Aringa, 299–335. Bologna: Il Mulino.

Opello, Walter C., Jr. 1983. "Portugal's Administrative Elite: Social Origins and Political Attitudes." *West European Politics* 6, no. 1: 63–74.

Otero-Iglesias, Miguel, Sebastián Royo, and Federico Steinberg Wechsler. 2017. "War of Attrition and Power of Inaction: The Spanish Financial Crisis and Its Lessons for the European Banking Union." *Revista de Economía Mundial* 46: 191–214.

Pagano, Patrizio, and Fabriano Schivardi. 2003. "Firm Size Distribution and Growth." *Scandinavian Journal of Economics* 105, no. 2: 255–74.

Pagoulatos, George. 2003. *Greece's New Political Economy*. London: Palgrave.

Pagoulatos, George, and Christos Triantopoulos. 2009. "The Return of the Greek Patient: Greece and the 2008 Global Financial Crisis." *South European Society and Politics* 14, no. 1: 35–54.

Papaconstantinou, Panagiota, Athanasios G. Tsagkanos, and Costas Siriopoulos. 2013. "How Bureaucracy and Corruption Affect Economic Growth and Convergence in the European Union: The Case of Greece." *Managerial Finance* 39, no. 9: 837–84.

Parrado, Salvador. 2008. "Failed Policies but Institutional Innovation through 'Layering' and 'Diffusion' in Spanish Central Administration." *International Journal of Public Sector Management* 21, no. 2: 230–52.

Parsons, Talcott. 1964. *Social Structure and Personality*. New York: Free Press of Glencoe.

Paraskevopoulos, Christos J. 2017. "Varieties of Capitalism, Quality of Government, and Policy Conditionality in Southern Europe: Greece and Portugal in Comparative Perspective." Hellenic Observatory Papers on Greece and Southeast Europe, GreeSE Paper No. 117, http://eprints.lse.ac.uk/85330/1/GreeSE_117.pdf.

Pavolini, Emmanuele, Margarita León, Ana M. Guillén, and Ugo Ascoli. 2015. "From Austerity to Permanent Strain? The EU and Welfare State Reform in Italy and Spain." *Comparative European Politics* 13, no. 1: 56–76.

Pedersini, Roberto. 2019. "Italy: Institutionalisation and Resilience in a Changing Economic and Political Environment." In *Collective Bargaining in Europe: Towards an Endgame*, ed. Torsten Mueller, Kurt Vandaele, and Jeremy Waddington, 337–59. Brussels: ETUI.

Pedersini, Roberto, and Salvo Leonardi. 2018. "Breaking through the Crisis with Decentralisation? Collective Bargaining in the EU after the Great Recession." In *Multi-employer Bargaining under Pressure: Decentralisation Trends in Five European Countries*, ed. Roberto Pedersini and Salvo Leonardi, 7–37. Bruxelles: ETUI.

Pereirinha, José António, Francisco Branco, Elvira Pereira, and Maria Inês Amaro. 2020. "The Guaranteed Minimum Income in Portugal: A Universal Safety Net under Political and Financial Pressure." *Social Policy & Administration* 54, no. 4: 1–13.

Pereirinha, José António, and Maria Clara Murteira. 2016. "The Portuguese Welfare System in a Time of Crisis and Fiscal Austerity." In *Challenges to European Welfare Systems*, ed. Klaus Schubert, Paloma de Villota, and Johanna Kuhlmann, 587–613. Cham: Springer.

———. 2019. "The Portuguese Welfare System: A Late European Welfare System under Permanent Stress." In *Routledge Handbook of European Welfare Systems*, ed. Sonja Blum, Johanna Kuhlmann, Klaus Schubert, 424–44. London: Routledge.

Pérez, Sofia A. 1997. *Banking on Privilege: The Politics of Spanish Financial Reform*. Ithaca, NY: Cornell University Press.

———. 2014. "Eurozone Crisis and Social Models: What We Can Learn from Italy and Spain." CES Papers, Open Forum No. 20, 2013–2014, http://aei.pitt.edu/67194/1/CES_OFWP_20.pdf.

———. 2017. "Banking Regulation, Supervision and Crises in the Eurozone: from Decentralized Governance to Banking Union," *GEGI Working Paper* 1/2017, Boston University Global Economic Governance Initiative.

———. 2019. "A Europe of Creditor and Debtor States: Explaining the North/South Divide in the Eurozone." *West European Politics* 42, no. 5: 989–1014.

———. 2021. "Competitiveness Revisited: Labour Costs, Financial Flows and the case of Italy." *German Politics*, doi.org/10.1080/09644008.2021.1913724.

Pérez, Sofia A., and Manos Matsaganis. 2018. "The Political Economy of Austerity in Southern Europe." *New Political Economy* 23, no. 2: 192–207.

———. 2019. "Export or Perish: Can Internal Devaluation Create Enough Good Jobs in Southern Europe?" *South European Society and Politics* 24, no. 2: 259–85.

Pérez, Sofia A., and Martin Rhodes. 2015. "The Evolution and Crises of the Social Models in Italy and Spain." In *European Social Models from Crisis to Crisis*, ed. Jon Erik Dølvik, and Andrew Martin, 177–213. Oxford: Oxford University Press.

Pérez-Díaz, Víctor, and Juan Carlos Rodríguez. 2014. *Entre desequilibrios y reformas: Economía política, sociedad y cultura entre dos siglos*. Madrid: FUNCAS.

Petmesidou, Maria. 1996. "Social Protection in Greece: A Brief Glimpse of a Welfare State." *Social Policy and Administration* 30, no. 4: 324–47.

———. 2006. "Tracking Social Protection: Origins, Path Peculiarity, Impasses and Prospects." In *Social Policy Developments in Greece*, ed. Elias Mossialos. 25–54. Ashgate, UK: Aldershot.

———. 2020. "Health Policy and Politics." In *Oxford Handbook of Modern Greek Politics*, ed. Kevin Featherstone and Dēmētrēs A. Sōtēropoulos, 505–20. Oxford: Oxford University Press.

Petmesidou, Maria, and Ana M. Guillén. 2014. "Can the Welfare State As We Know It Survive? A View from the Crisis-Ridden South European Periphery." *South European Society and Politics* 19, no. 3. 295–307.

Petmesidou, Maria, Emmanuele Pavolini, and Ana M. Guillén. 2014. "South European Healthcare Systems under Harsh Austerity: A Progress–Regression Mix?" *South European Society and Politics* 19, no. 3: 331–52.

Picot, Georg, and Arianna Tassinari. 2017. "All of One Kind? Labour Market Reforms under Austerity in Italy and Spain." *Socio-Economic Review* 15, no. 2: 461–82.

Pizzolato, Nicola. 2012. "'I Terroni in Città': Revisiting Southern Migrants' Militancy in Turin's 'Hot Autumn.'" *Contemporary European History* 21, no. 4: 619–34.

Pizzorno, Alessandro. 1978. "Political Exchange and Collective Identity in Industrial Conflict." In *The Resurgence of Class Conflict in Western Europe since 1968*, Vol. 2, *Comparative Analyses*, ed. Colin Crouch and Alessandro Pizzorno, 277–98. London: Macmillan.

Pochet, Philippe, Maarten Keune, and David Natali. 2010. *After the Euro and Enlargement: Social Pacts in the EU*. Bruxelles: ETUI/OSE.

Pollitt, Christopher, and Geert Bouckaert. 2011. *Public Management Reform: A Comparative Analysis; New Public Management, Governance and the Neo-Weberian State*. Oxford: Oxford University Press.

Putnam, Robert D., Robert Leonardi, and Raffaella Nanetti. 1993. *Making Democracy Work: Civic Traditions in Modern Italy*. Princeton, NJ: Princeton University Press.

Quaglia, Lucia. 2004. "Italy's Policy towards European Monetary Integration: Bringing Ideas Back In?" *Journal of European Public Policy* 11, no. 6: 1096–111.

——. 2009. "The Response to the Global Financial Turmoil in Italy: 'A Financial System That Does Not Speak English.'" *South European Society and Politics* 14, no. 1: 7–18.

——. 2013. "The Europeanisation of Macroeconomic Policies and Financial Regulation in Italy." *South European Society and Politics* 18, no. 2: 159–76.

Quaglia, Lucia, and Sebastián Royo. 2015. "Banks and the Political Economy of the Sovereign Debt Crisis in Italy and Spain." *Review of International Political Economy* 22, no. 3: 485–507.

Rajan, Raghuram G. 2010. *Fault Lines: How Hidden Fractures Still Threaten the World Economy*. Princeton, NJ: Princeton University Press.

Ramella, Francesco. 2013. *Sociologia dell'innovazione economica*. Bologna: Il Mulino.

Rangone, Marco, and Stefano Solari. 2012. "From the Southern-European Model to Nowhere: The Evolution of Italian Capitalism, 1976–2011." *Journal of European Public Policy* 19, no. 8: 1188–1206.

Rebora, Gianfranco. 1999. *Un decennio di riforme*. Rome: Guerini.

Regalia, Ida. 2020. *Regulating Work in Small Firms: Perspectives on the Future of Work in Globalised Economies*. London: Palgrave MacMillan.

Regalia, Ida, and Marino Regini. 1998. "Italy: The Dual Character of Industrial Relations." In *Changing Industrial Relations in Europe*, 2nd ed., ed. Richard Hyman and Anthony Ferner, 459–503. Malden, MA: Blackwell Publishers.

——. 2018. "Trade Unions and Employment Relations in Italy during the Economic Crisis." *South European Society and Politics* 23, no. 1: 63–79.

Regini, Marino. 1997. "Social Institutions and Production Structure: The Italian Variety of Capitalism in the 1980s." In *Political Economy and Modern Capitalism: Mapping Convergence and Diversity*, ed. Colin Crouch and Wolfgang Streeck, 102–16. London: Sage.

——. 2000. "Between De-regulation and Social Pacts: The Responses of European Economies to Globalization." *Politics & Society* 28, no. 1: 5–33.

——. 2014. "Models of Capitalism and the Crisis." *Stato e Mercato* 100, no. 1: 21–44.

——. 2018. "Il mutamento del modello sociale europeo." In *Europa. Culture e società*, Vol. 3, ed. Marc Lazar, Mariuccia Salvati, and Loredana Sciolla, 165–73. Rome: Istituto della Enciclopedia Italiana Treccani.

Reis, Ricardo. 2013. "The Portuguese Slump-Crash and the Euro-Crisis." *Brookings Papers on Economic Activity*, 143–93.

Remes, Jaana, Jan Mischke, and Mekala Krishnan. 2018. "Solving the Productivity Puzzle: The Role of Demand and the Promise of Digitization." *International Productivity Monitor, Centre for the Study of Living Standards* 34: 28–51.

Requena, Miguel. 2005. "The Secularization of Spanish Society: Change in Religious Practice." *Southern European Society and Politics* 10, no. 3: 369–90.

Rocha Oliveira, J. A., and Joaquim Filipe Ferraz Esteves de Araujo. 2007. "Administrative Reform in Portugal: Problems and Prospects." *International Review of Administrative Sciences* 73, no. 4: 583–96.

Rodrigues, Miguel, and César Madureira. 2010. "Portugal—Highly Centralised Despite European Pressures." In *Regional Governance in EU-Staaten*, ed. Roland Sturm and Jurgen Dieringer, 255–68. Opladen: Verlag Barbara Budrich.

Rodríguez-Pose, Andrés. 2017. "The Revenge of the Places That Don't Matter (and What to Do about It)." *Journal of Regions, Economy and Society* 11, no. 1: 189–209.

Rodrik, Dani. 2014. "When Ideas Trump Interests: Preferences, Worldviews, and Policy Innovations." *Journal of Economic Perspectives* 28, no. 1: 189–208.

Rodrik, Dani, Arvind Subramanian, and Frencesco Trebbi. 2004. "Institutions Rule: The Primacy of Institutions over Geography and Integration in Economic Development." *Journal of Economic Growth* 9, no. 2: 131–65.

Rothstein, Bo. 2012. *The Quality of Government: Corruption, Social Trust and Inequality in International Perspective*. Chicago: University of Chicago Press.

Rothstein, Bo, and Jan Teorell. 2008. "What Is Quality of Government? A Theory of Impartial Government Institutions." *Governance* 21, no. 2: 165–90.

Rueda, David, Erik Wibbels, and Melina Altamirano. 2015. "The Origins of Dualism." In *The Politics of Advanced Capitalism*, ed. Pablo Beramendi, Silja Hausermann, Herbert Kitschelt, and Hanspeter Kriesi, 89–111. Cambridge: Cambridge University Press.

Rutherford, Tod, and Lorenzo Frangi. 2016. "Overturning Italy's Article 18: Exogenous and Endogenous Pressures, and Role of the State." *Economic and Industrial Democracy* 39, no. 3: 439–57.

Sacchi, Stefano. 2015. "Conditionality by Other Means: Eu Involvement in Italy's Structural Reforms in the Sovereign Debt Crisis." *Comparative European Politics* 13, no. 1: 77–92.

Santos, Tano. 2014. "Antes del Diluvio: The Spanish Banking System in the First Decade of the Euro." In *After the Flood: How the Great Recession Changed Economic Thought*, ed. Edward L. Glaeser, Tano Santos, and E. Glen Weyl, 153–208. Chicago: University of Chicago Press.

Sapir, André. 2005. "Globalisation and the Reform of European Social Models." *Journal of Common Market Studies* 44, no. 2: 369–90.

Saraceno, Chiara. 1994. "The Ambivalent Familism of the Italian Welfare State." *Social Politics* 1, no. 1: 60–82.

Saraceno, Chiara, and Wolfgang Keck. 2010. "Can We Identify Intergenerational Policy Regimes in Europe?" *European Societies* 12, no. 5: 675–96.

Savvides, Andreas, and Thanasis Stengos. 2009. *Human Capital and Economic Growth*. Stanford, CA: Stanford University Press.

Scarpetta, Stefano. 1996. "Assessing the Role of Labour Market Policies and Institutional Settings on Unemployment: A Cross-Country Study." *OECD Economic Studies*, no. 26, 1996/1: 43–98.

Scharpf, Fritz. 2011. "Monetary Union, Fiscal Crisis and the Preemption of Democracy." MPlfG Discussion Paper 11/11. Cologne: Max Planck Institute for the Study of Societies. https://www.mpifg.de/pu/mpifg_dp/dp11-11.pdf.

———. 2012. "Legitimacy Intermediation in the Multilevel European Polity and Its Collapse in the Euro Crisis." MPIfG Discussion Paper 12/6. Cologne: Max Planck Institute for Social Studies.

Schäuble, Wolfgang. 2011. "Why Austerity Is Only Cure for the Eurozone." *Financial Times*, September 5, https://www.ft.com/content/97b826e2-d7ab-11e0-a06b-00144feabdc0.

Schelkle, Waltraud. 2017. *The Political Economy of Monetary Solidarity.* Oxford: Oxford University Press.

Schmidt, Torsten, and Lina Zwick. 2015. "Uncertainty and Episodes of Extreme Capital Flows in the Euro Area." *Economic Modelling* 48, no. C: 343–56.

Schmidt, Vivien A. 2002. *The Futures of European Capitalism.* Oxford: Oxford University Press.

———. 2007. "Bringing the State Back into the Varieties of Capitalism and Discourse Back into the Explanation of Change." Pittsburgh: Center for European Studies Working Paper Series 152: 1–31. http://aei.pitt.edu/9281/.

———. 2008. "Discursive Institutionalism: The Explanatory Power of Ideas and Discourse." *Annual Review of Political Science* 11: 303–26.

Schneider, Friedrich. 2003. "Privatisation in OECD Countries: Theoretical Reasons and Results Obtained." CESifo DICE Report 3. https://www.cesifo.org/DocDL/dicereport3-03-research-reports-1.pdf.

Schulten, Thorsten, and Torsten Müller. 2015. "European Economic Governance and Its Intervention in National Wage Development and Collective Bargaining." In *Divisive Integration: The Triumph of Failed Ideas in Europe—Revisited,* ed. Steffen Lehndorff, 331–63. Bruxelles: ETUI.

Sepe, Stefano. 1995. *Amministrazione e Storia: Problemi della evoluzione degli apparati statali dall'Unità ai giorni nostri.* Rimini: Maggioli.

Sestito, Paolo. 2017. "Riforma della contrattazione: Tra rischi di deflazione e gap di competitività." In *Salari, produttività, disuguaglianze,* ed. Carlo Dell'Aringa, Claudio Lucifora and Tiziano Treu. 381–400. Bologna: Il Mulino.

Siebert, Horst. 1997. "Labor Market Rigidities: At the Root of Unemployment in Europe." *Journal of Economic Perspectives* 11, no. 3: 37–54.

Silva, Pedro Adão. 2003. "Building a Welfare State in a Context of Austerity: The Portuguese Case." In *Portugal: Strategic Options in a European Context,* ed. Fatima Monteiro, Jose Albuquerque Tavares, Miguel Glatzer, and Angelo Cardoso, 107–28. Boston: Lexington Books.

Silva, Pedro Adão, and Mariana Trigo Pereira. 2017. "O Estado Social Português: Entre a maturação e os constrangimentos externos." In *Política Comparada: O Sistema Político Português numa Perspectiva Comparada,* ed. Conceição Pequito Teixeira, 403–30. Cascais: Principia.

Simões, Jorge de Almeida, Augusto Goncalo Figueiredo, Ines Fronteira, and Cristina Hernandez-Quevedo. 2017. "Portugal: Health System Review." *Health Systems in Transition* 19, no. 2: 1–184.

Simoni, Marco. 2012. *Senza alibi: Perché il capitalismo italiano non cresce più.* Venezia: Marsilio Editore.

———. 2020. "Institutional Roots of Economic Decline: Lessons from Italy." *Italian Political Science Review/Rivista Italiana di Scienza Politica* 50, no. 1: 1–16.

Sinn, Hans-Werner. 2014. "Austerity, Growth and Inflation: Remarks on the Eurozone's Unresolved Competitiveness Problem." *World Economy* 37, no. 1: 1–13.

Smelser, Neil J. 1959. *Social Change in the Industrial Revolution: An Application of Theory to the British Cotton Industry.* Chicago: University of Chicago Press.

Sotiropoulos, Dimitri A. 2004a. "South European Public Bureaucracies in Comparative Perspective." *West European Politics* 27, no. 3: 405–22.

———. 2004b. "The EU's Impact on the Greek Welfare State: Europeanization on Paper?" *Journal of European Social Policy* 14, no. 3: 267–84.

———. 2006. "Old Problems and New Challenges: The Enduring and Challenging Functions of Southern European State Bureaucracies." In *Democracy and the State in the New Southern Europe*, ed. Nikiforos Diamandouros, Demetres A. Sotiropoulos, and Richard Gunther, 197–234. Oxford, Oxford University Press.

———. 2012. "The Paradox of Non-reform in a Reform-Ripe Environment: Lessons from Post-authoritarian Greece." In *From Stagnation to Forced Adjustment: Reforms in Greece, 1974–2010*, ed. Haridimos Tsoukas, George Pagoulatos, and Stathis N. Kalyvas. London: Hurst.

Spanou, Calliope. 2001. "(Re)shaping the Politics-Administration Nexus in Greece: The Decline of a Symbolic Relationship?" In *Politicians, Bureaucrats and Administrative Reform*, ed. Guy B. Peters and Jon Pierre. London: Routledge.

———. 2008. "State Reform in Greece: Responding to Old and New Challenges." *International Journal of Public Sector Management* 21, no. 2: 150–73.

———. 2012. "The Quandary of Administrative Reform: Institutional and Performance Modernization." In *From Stagnation to Forced Adjustment: Reforms in Greece, 1974–2010*, ed. Haridimos Tsoukas, George Pagoulatos, and Stathis N. Kalyvas, 171–94. London: Hurst.

———. 2014. "La haute fonction publique hellénique: La permanence du provisoire." *Revue Française d'Administration Publique* 151–52: 645–61.

———. 2015. "Administrative Reform and Policy Conditionality in Greece." *Administration and Public Employment Review* 1: 31–54.

Spanou, Calliope, and Dimitri A. Sotiropoulos. 2011. "The Odyssey of Administrative Reforms in Greece, 1981–2009: A Tale of Two Reform Paths." *Public Administration* 89, no. 3: 723–37.

Spiegel, Mark M. 2009. "Monetary and Financial Integration: Evidence from the EMU." *Journal of the Japanese and International Economies* 23, no. 2: 114–30.

Stinchcombe, Arthur L. 1965. "Social Structure and Organizations." In *Handbook of Organizations*, ed. James P. March, 142–93. Chicago: Rand McNally.

Stockhammer, Engelbert. 2015a. "Rising Inequality as a Cause of the Present Crisis." *Cambridge Journal of Economics* 39, no. 3: 935–58.

———. 2015b. "Neoliberal Growth Models, Monetary Union and the Euro Crisis: A Post-Keynesian Perspective." *New Political Economy* 21, no. 4: 365–79.

Storm, Servaas. 2017. "The New Normal: Demand, Secular Stagnation, and the Vanishing Middle Class." *International Journal of Political Economy* 46, no. 4: 169–210.

Storm, Servaas, and C.W.M. Naastepad. 2012. *Macroeconomics beyond the Nairu*. Cambridge, MA: Harvard University Press.

Streeck, Wolfgang. 1997. "Beneficial Constraints: On the Economic Limits of Rational Voluntarism." In *Contemporary Capitalism: The Embeddedness of Institutions*, ed. Robert J. Hollingsworth and Robert Boyer, 197–219. Cambridge: Cambridge University Press.

———. 2009. *Re-forming Capitalism: Institutional Change in the German Political Economy*. Oxford: Oxford University Press.

———. 2012. "How to Study Contemporary Capitalism?" *European Journal of Sociology* 53, no. 1: 1–28.

———. 2015. "German Hegemony: Unintended and Unwanted." https://wolfgangstreeck.com/2015/05/15/german-hegemony-unintended-and-unwanted/.

Streeck, Wolfgang, and Kathleen Thelen. 2005. *Beyond Continuity: Institutional Change in Advanced Political Economies*. Oxford: Oxford University Press.

Summers, H. Lawrence. 2014. "U.S. Economic Prospects: Secular Stagnation, Hysteresis, and the Zero Lower Bound." *Business Economics* 49, no. 2: 65–73.

Tassinari, Arianna, and Jimmy Donaghey. 2020. "Social Partnership through and beyond the Crisis." In *Reimagining the Governance of Work and Employment*, ed. Dionne Pohler, 113–42. Ithaca, NY: Cornell University Press.

Tavora, Isabel. 2012. "Understanding the High Rates of Employment among Low-Educated Women in Portugal: A Comparatively Oriented Case Study." *Gender, Work & Organization* 19, no. 2: 93–118.

Teichler, Ulrich. 1988. *Changing Patterns of the Higher Education System: The Experience of Three Decades*. London: Jessica Kingsley Publishers.

Therborn, Göran, ed. 2010. *Handbook of European Societies: Social Transformations in the 21st Century*. Berlin: Springer.

Thelen, Kathleen. 2014. *Varieties of Capitalism and the New Politics of Social Solidarity*. New York: Cambridge University Press.

Tokarski, Pawel. 2019. "Divergence and Diversity in the Euro Area: The Case of Germany, France and Italy." Stiftung Wissenschaft und Politik SWP Research Paper No. 6. Berlin: German Institute for International and Security Affairs.

Toniolo, Gianni. 2013. "An Overview of Italy's Economic Growth." In *The Oxford Handbook of the Italian Economy since Unification*, ed. Gianni Toniolo, 3–36. Oxford: Oxford University Press.

Torres, Lourdes, and Vicente Pina. 2004. "Reshaping Public Administration: Spanish Experience Compared to UK." *Public Administration* 82, no. 2: 445–64.

Tortella, Gabriel, J. Garcia Ruiz, and José Luis Ruiz, eds. 2013. *Spanish Money and Banking: A History*. Cham: Springer.

Tremonti, Giulio. 2008. "Informativa del Ministro dell'Economia e delle Finanze al Parlamento sugli sviluppi della crisi finanziaria in atto." *Roma*, October 9.

Tribunal de Contas. 2014. "Acompanhamento dos Mecanismos de Assistência Financeira a Portugal." Report No. 27/2014, 2nd. ed.

Trichet, Jean Claude. 2011. "Competitiveness and the Smooth Functioning of EMU." Speech delivered at European Central Bank, Liège, February 23.

Trigilia, Carlo. 1995. "Dinamismo privato e disordine pubblico. Politica, economia e società locali". In *Storia dell'Italia Repubblicana*, Vol. II, Tomo I, 713–77. Turin: Einaudi.

——. 2016. "Tipi di democrazia e modelli di capitalismo: Un'agenda di ricerca." *Stato e Mercato* 107: 183–213.

——. 2019. "Capitalismo e democrazia politica: Crescita e uguaglianza si possono conciliare?" *Rivista Il Mulino* 2: 177–95.

Trow, Martin. 1974. "Problems in the Transition from Elite to Mass Higher Education." In *The General Report on the Conference on Future Structures of Post-Secondary Education*, 55–101. Paris: OECD Publishing.

Tsakalotos, Eukleidis. 1998. "The Political Economy of Social Democratic Economic Policies: The PASOK Experiment in Greece." *Oxford Review of Economic Policy* 14, no. 1:114–38.

Tsakloglou, Panos, and Theodoros Mitrakos. 2006. "Inequality and Poverty in the Last Quarter of the Twentieth Century." In *Social Policy Developments in Greece*, ed. Elias Mossialos and Maria Petmesidou, 126–46. Aldershot, UK: Ashgate.

Tsekos, Theodore N. 2013. "Structural, Functional, and Cultural Aspects of the Greek Public Administration and Their Effects on Public Employees' Collective Action." *Comparative Labor Law Policy Journal* 34, no. 2: 457–78.

Ufficio di Valutazione del Senato della Repubblica Italiana. 2018. *The Impact of Cohesion Policies in Europe and Italy*. Rome: Senato della Repubblica. http://www.senato.it/service /PDF/PDFServer/BGT/01083823.pdf.

Valadas, Carla. 2017. "A Changing Labour Market under the Intensification of Dualization: The Experience of a Southern European Society." *Social Policy & Administration* 51, no. 2: 328–47.

Vasileva-Dienes, Alexandra, and Vivienne A. Schmidt. 2019. "Conceptualising Capitalism in the Twenty-First Century: The BRICs and the European Periphery." *Contemporary Politics* 25, no. 3: 255–75.

Vecchi, Giancarlo. 2020. "Le politiche di riforma amministrativa." In *Le politiche pubbliche in Italia*, ed. Gilberto Capano e Alessandro Natalini, 26–41. Bologna: Il Mulino.

Verney, Susannah. 2009. "Flaky Fringe? Southern Europe Facing the Financial Crisis." *South European Society and Politics* 14, no. 1: 1–6.

Vesan, Patrik, and Stefano Ronchi. 2019. "The Puzzle of Expansionary Welfare Reforms under Harsh Austerity: Explaining the Italian Case." *South European Society and Politics* 24, no. 3: 371–95.

Walter, Stefanie. 2016. "Crisis Politics in Europe: Why Austerity Is Easier to Implement in Some Countries Than in Others." *Comparative Political Studies* 49, no. 7: 841–73.

Watson, Sara. 2015. *The Left Divided: The Development and Transformation of Advanced Welfare States.* Oxford: Oxford University Press.

Weiss, Linda. 2013. *America Inc. Innovation and Enterprise in the National Security State.* Ithaca, NY: Cornell University Press.

Wierts, Peter, Henk Van Kerkhoff, and Jakob De Haan. 2014. "Composition of Exports and Export Performance of Eurozone Countries." *Journal of Common Market Studies* 52, no. 4: 928–41.

Williams, Colin C., and Ioana A. Horodnic. 2015. "Explaining the Prevalence of Illegitimate Wage Practices in Southern Europe; An Institutional Analysis." *South European Society and Politics* 20, no. 2: 203–21.

Woll, Cornelia. 2014. *The Power of Inaction: Bank Bailouts in Comparison.* Ithaca, NY: Cornell University Press.

Zahariadis, Nikolaos. 2013. "Leading Reform amidst Transboundary Crises: Lessons from Greece." *Public Administration* 91, no. 3: 648–62.

Zemanek, Holger, Ansgar Belke, and Gunther Schnabl. 2010. "Current Account Balances and Structural Adjustment in the Euro Area." *International Economics and Economic Policy* 7: 83–127.

Contributors

Alexandre Afonso is an associate professor of public policy at Leiden University. His research areas are labor markets, the welfare state, and immigration. He has published in journals such as *Socio-Economic Review, Comparative Political Studies,* and the *European Journal of Political Research.* He is currently writing a book on immigration policy and the welfare state under contract with Oxford University Press.

Lucio Baccaro is director of the Max Planck Institute for the Study of Societies in Cologne. His current research is on the comparative and international political economy of growth models. He also has an ongoing interest in comparative labor relations. He is a coauthor, with Chris Howell, of *Trajectories of Neoliberal Transformation* (Cambridge University Press, 2017).

Rui Branco is an associate professor in the Department of Political Studies, NOVA University of Lisbon, Portugal. His research focuses on comparative social and labor policies, fiscal welfare, and inequality. He has published in journals such as the *Journal of Comparative Politics,* the *Journal of Social Policy, New Political Economy,* and *South European Society and Politics.*

Fabio Bulfone is a postdoctoral researcher at the Max Planck Institute for the Study of Societies in Cologne. His research focuses on Southern European capitalism, industrial policy, labor markets, and industrial relations. He has published in the *Socio-Economic Review,* the *European Journal of Political Research,* the *Journal of European Public Policy, Governance,* and *Comparative Political Studies,* among others.

Luigi Burroni is a professor of economic sociology at the University of Florence. Since 2014 he coordinated two research projects funded by the European Commission on the political economy of Southern Europe, compared to other models of capitalism, in the fields of labor market regulation and innovation. His recent works on Mediterranean capitalism have been published in the *European Journal of Industrial Relations, Economy and Society, EPC-Government and Policy, Socio-Economic Review*, and *Stato e Mercato*. Among his books are: *Capitalismi a confronto. Istituzioni e regolazione dell'economia nei paesi europei* (Il Mulino 2016) and *Economy and Society in Europe: a Relationship in Crisis?* (Elgar 2012, with M. Keune and G. Meardi).

Giliberto Capano is a professor of political science and public policy at the University of Bologna. His research focuses on governance dynamics and performance in higher education, policy design and policy change, policy instruments' impact, the social role of political science, and leadership as an embedded function of policymaking.

Sabrina Colombo is an associate professor of economic sociology in the Department of Social and Political Studies at the University of Milan. Her research is focused on the study of industrial relations, the sociology of work, and higher education.

Lisa Dorigatti is an assistant professor of labor and economic sociology in the Department of Social and Political Studies at the University of Milan. Her research is in the area of comparative employment relations and labor sociology, with a specific focus on trade unions, precarious work, and organizational restructuring. Her writing was published in, among others, the *British Journal of Industrial Relations, Industrial and Labor Relations Review*, the *European Journal of Industrial* Relations, and *Work, Employment and Society*.

Ana M. Guillén is a professor of sociology at the University of Oviedo (Spain) and the director of PROMEBI, Promoting Work and Welfare in Europe. Her research interests include comparative social protection and labor policies, Europeanization, and European integration.

Matteo Jessoula is an associate professor of political science and comparative welfare states at the University of Milan. He has published several contributions on policy developments and political dynamics in the fields of pensions, minimum income schemes, employment policies, and European Union social governance.

Andrea Lippi is a professor of political science and public policy in the Department of Political and Social Sciences, University of Florence, and the scientific coordinator of the Public Policy area at the Scuola Nazionale dell'Amministrazione. His research interests range from public policy to public administration with a special focus on governance, reforms, and evaluation.

Manos Matsaganis is a professor of public finance at the Polytechnic University of Milan. His current research focuses on technological change and the future of work, the changing fortunes of the middle class in Southern Europe, and the transformations of the European social model after the Eurozone crisis and COVID-19.

Oscar Molina is a professor in the Department of Sociology of the Autonomous University of Barcelona. His main research interests are in the areas of comparative industrial relations, trade unions and neocorporatism, social pacts and policy concertation, comparative political economy, and labor markets.

Manuela Moschella is an associate professor of the international political economy at the Scuola Normale Superiore, Italy. Her research is focused on the politics of macroeconomic and financial regulatory choices at the domestic, European, and international levels. Her recent articles have appeared in the *Journal of Common Market Studies*, the *Journal of European Public Policy, New Political Economy, Public Administration, Review of International Political Economy*, and *West European Politics* other journals.

Emmanuele Pavolini is a professor of economic sociology at the University of Macerata. His research interests are mainly in two fields: (1) comparative welfare state studies, with a special focus on Southern European welfare states; and (2) labor market and economic development. He has coedited a volume on *The Italian Welfare State in European Perspective: A Comparative Analysis* (Policy Press 2016, with U. Ascoli) and has published in several journals, including *Social Policy and Administration; Journal of European Public Policy; International and Comparative Social Policy; Work, employment and society; Comparative European Politics; South European Society and Politics;* and *Current Sociology*.

Sofia A. Pérez is an associate professor of political science at Boston University. She has written extensively on the politics of financial regulation and the relationships among other areas of economic policy, macroeconomic policy regimes, labor market regulation and wage bargaining regimes, immigration policy, welfare state change, and European integration. Her current work focuses on the consequences of monetary union for growth, inequality, and labor market outcomes. Her recent work has appeared in *Comparative Political Studies, New Political Economy, West European Politics*, and other journals.

Marino Regini is a professor emeritus of economic sociology at the University of Milan. He has been president of the Society for the Advancement of Socio-Economics (SASE) and a member of the editorial boards of several journals. His work has focused on the fields of comparative political economy; employment relations; and, more recently, higher education. Among his books are: *Uncertain Boundaries. The Social and Political Construction of European Economies* (Cambridge University Press 1995); *From Tellers to Sellers* (MIT Press 1999, with M. Baethge and J. Kitay); *Why Deregulate Labour Markets?* (Oxford University Press 2000, with G. Esping-Andersen); and *European Universities and the Challenge of the Market* (Elgar 2011).

Gemma Scalise is an assistant professor of economic sociology at the University of Bergamo and a former Visiting Max Weber Fellow at the European University Institute. Her research activities include labor market and welfare regulation, comparative political economy, and multilevel governance. She is the author of *The Political Economy of Policy Ideas: The European Strategy of Active Inclusion in Context* (Palgrave Macmillan, 2020).

Arianna Tassinari is a senior researcher at the Max Planck Institute for the Study of Societies in Cologne. Her research focuses on the comparative political economy of Southern European capitalism, labor market regulation, and industrial relations. Her work has appeared in outlets such as *Socio-Economic Review*, *Work, Employment and Society*, and the *European Journal of Political Research*.

Index

CORNELL STUDIES IN POLITICAL ECONOMY

A series edited by Peter J. Katzenstein

1987

The Political Economy of the New Asian Industrialism
by Frederic C. Deyo

The Philippine State and the Marcos Regime: The Politics of Export
by Gary Hawes

The Sovereign Entrepreneur: Oil Policies in Advanced and Less Developed Capitalist Countries
by Merrie Gilbert Klapp

State Capitalism: Public Enterprise in Canada
by Jeanne Kirk Laux and Maureen Appel Molot

The Business of the Japanese State: Energy Markets in Comparative and Historical Perspective
by Richard J. Samuels

1988

Collapse of an Industry: Nuclear Power and the Contradictions of U.S. Policy
by John L. Campbell

The Misunderstood Miracle: Industrial Development and Political Change in Japan
by David Friedman

Reasons of State: Oil Politics and the Capacities of American Government
by G. John Ikenberry

The State and American Foreign Economic Policy
edited by G. John Ikenberry, David A. Lake, and Michael Mastanduno

Power, Protection, and Free Trade: International Sources of U.S. Commercial Strategy, 1887–1939
by David A. Lake

Opening Financial Markets: Banking Politics on the Pacific Rim
by Louis W. Pauly

1989

Dislodging Multinationals: India's Strategy in Comparative Perspective
by Dennis J. Encarnation

Democracy and Markets: The Politics of Mixed Economies
by John R. Freeman

Industry and Politics in West Germany: Toward the Third Republic
edited by Peter J. Katzenstein

In the Dominions of Debt: Historical Perspectives on Dependent Development
by Herman M. Schwartz

Fair Shares: Unions, Pay, and Politics in Sweden and West Germany
by Peter Swenson